Cities of the Gods

CITIES OF THE GODS

Communist Utopias in Greek Thought

DOYNE DAWSON

New York Oxford
OXFORD UNIVERSITY PRESS
1992

Oxford University Press

Oxford New York Toronto
Delhi Bombay Calcutta Madras Karachi
Petaling Jaya Singapore Hong Kong Tokyo
Nairobi Dar es Salaam Cape Town
Melbourne Auckland

and associated companies in
Berlin Ibadan

Published by Oxford University Press, Inc.,
200 Madison Avenue, New York, New York 10016

Library of Congress Cataloging-in-Publication Data
Dawson, Doyne.
Cities of the gods:
Communist utopias in Greek thought /
by Doyne Dawson.
p. cm. Includes bibliographical references (p.) and index.
ISBN 0-19-506983-8
1. Utopias—History. 2. Utopian socialism—History.
3. Communism—History. 4. Philosophy, Ancient.
I. Title. HX806.D42 1992 335'.02—dc20 91-35643

2 4 6 8 9 7 5 3 1

Printed in the United States of America
on acid-free paper

To Bill and Peggy
and their children

And to Tom Jones
who interested me
in the ancient world

Contents

Introduction, 3

1. The Birth of Utopia, 13

The Time of Cronus, 13
The Pythagorean Life, 14
The Sexual Communism of the Barbarians, 18
The Low Utopias and Sparta, 21
The Ecclesiazusae *of Aristophanes*, 37
Household and City: The Social and Political Background of Greek Utopianism, 40

2. The Platonic Utopia: A City Without the Household, 53

The Paradox of Socrates, 53
The Paradox of Plato, 62
The Method of Plato, 71
High Utopia and Low Utopia, 77
The Academy in Politics, 92
Aristotle, 93
The Social and Political Background of Platonic-Aristotelian Utopianism, 99

3. The Cynic Way: A Life Without the Household, 111

The Problem of Cynic Political Thought: A Contradiction in Terms? 111
The Search for the Historical Diogenes, 113
A Definition of Early Cynicism: An Activist Ascetic Elite, 120
The Social Teachings of the Cynics, 130
The Republic *of Diogenes*, 146

4. The Stoic Utopia: A World Without Households, 160

Cynic and Stoic, 160
The Sources, 166
The Outlines of the Stoic Ideal World, 175
The Stoics and Society, 187
The Stoics and Politics, 195
Comments, 206

5. The End of Utopia, 223

The Decline of the Stoic Utopian Tradition, 223
The Survival of the Old Stoic and Cynic Traditions, 243

6. The Ghosts of Utopia, 258

Primitive Christianity, 258
Gnostic Christianity, 264
Patristic Christianity, 276

Bibliography, 291

Index, 301

Cities of the Gods

"Perhaps some of the gods,
or children of the gods,
dwell in such cities as this."

(Plato, *Laws* 739d)

Introduction

The main aim of this book is to provide an outline account of one of the most distinctive traditions of ancient Greek political thought: the literary depiction of imaginary ideal societies practicing communal property and communal family life. The main justification for a new survey of this material is the emphasis I place upon the Stoic utopian tradition, which has been generally neglected by historians of Greek political thought, and particularly by historians of utopianism, most of whom, so far as the ancient world is concerned, begin and end with Plato.[1]

If we are interested in utopianism with an emphasis on the "ism" (a certain type of political philosophy, whose definition we will consider shortly) then we must begin with Plato, who apparently invented it. But we ought not to end with Plato, for antiquity acknowledged an alternative utopian tradition among the Stoics and Cynics. The relatively scant attention the latter tradition has received is partly, of course, a result of the fragmentary nature of the Stoic and Cynic sources, which placed beside the *Republic* and *Laws* of Plato resemble a few insignificant and curious pieces of rubble lying in the shadow of a colossal architectural complex. But obviously the preservation of these structures depended on the prevailing ideologies and tastes of later antiquity. The reputation of Stoicism has been more hurt by the widespread opinion that its imaginary city was no real utopia at all, nor any other form of political philosophy. This interpretation, canonized over a century ago by Zeller, considered the Cynics and older Stoics indifferent to political and social life, and led to the often-repeated conclusion that the Stoic/Cynic utopia was the counterpart of modern anarchism, as the utopia of Plato resembled modern socialism.[2]

The notion that Stoic/Cynic utopian thought was purely individualistic and anarchistic implies that it belonged to what Lewis Mumford called the "utopias of escape," as opposed to the "utopias of reconstruction."[3] Escapist utopias include all the worldwide myths, legends, and folklore about gardens of Eden, golden ages, Elysian fields, lands of Cokaygne, and other more-or-less primitivistic paradises set in remote times and places; and all the sophisticated literary adaptations of this theme, from the Old Comedy of Athens to contemporary science fiction. The utopia of reconstruction, on the other hand, is a serious political theory and peculiarly Western.[4] It is a persistent tradition of speculation about the possibility of a perfect society, which defines perfection primarily as the removal of social conflict. Its vehicle is the portrayal of an imaginary and ideal society, which distinguishes it from other methods of political and ethical theorizing: the utopia does not merely state general principles but embodies them in a detailed and plausible description of the institutional structure of a perfect community, whether in the form of a proposal or a fictional narrative. The fact that its ideal society is detailed and plausible distinguishes it from the folk utopias, which to some extent provide its raw material: the serious utopia is always meant as a paradigm or goal for social and political reform. Its classic examples are Plato's *Republic*, More's *Utopia*, and the other Renaissance imitations of Plato. This tradition is also called the "social utopia," the "realistic utopia," or just "utopianism" (the "ism" implying an underlying philosophical theory). The utopian writings of the Stoics and Cynics have been generally placed among the utopias of escape on the grounds that they were private fantasies which may have had an ethical purpose of an individualistic sort but could not have had social or political goals.[5]

If we restrict genuine utopianism in the ancient world to Plato and Aristotle, we must conclude that this was an exclusively oligarchic and aristocratic tradition, permeated with a sense of ineradicable human inequalities, dedicated to rigid social hierarchy. That is a common perception,[6] and it has led us to think that ancient utopian thought has nothing to teach us. Egalitarianism is commonly assumed to be a Judeo-Christian ideal, and Thomas More is commonly given credit for introducing it into utopia.

If the main difference between serious social utopianism and the utopias of fantasy and myth is the presence of realistic goals in the former group, then we must ask where such goals are to be found in such texts as Plato's *Republic* and More's *Utopia*. Few think that Plato or More ever meant their literary proposals to be literally enacted. In fact, serious utopias have been written for different purposes, and their superficial similarity disguises the fact that there was a major break in the Western utopian tradition.

The classical utopia of Plato and his Renaissance imitators was intended as a systematic statement of principles setting up an ideal standard. It took the form of a description of a total society because that method permits a more compelling argument, a more comprehensive sociological analysis, a more powerful literary impact than the methods usually open to us in debates over current issues. It was not privatistic, or escapist, or anarchist; nor was it merely a satirical foil. It was a paradigm and a goal, meant to awaken us to a new sense of potentiality and to spur practical reforms. These reforms were to have some connection with the utopian blueprint, but the blueprint itself was not meant to be literally enacted. Cicero thought Plato meant to give us "a city to wish for rather than to hope for"; More found "very many features in the Utopian commonwealth which it is easier for me to wish for in our countries than to have any hope of seeing realized."[7]

At some point this classical tradition was transformed by the conviction that utopia is realizable. The city of desire became the city of hope. When and how this happened does not concern us here; the beginnings of the process have been traced as early as the sixteenth century, but it was not completed until the late nineteenth, when the modern type of literary utopia was fixed by the flood of utopian novels that followed Edward Bellamy's *Looking Backward* (1887). The popularity of the utopian novel has now receded along with the debate over the realizability of socialism, which was its main subject, and the dystopian novels of Huxley and Orwell are now better known than any of their utopian predecessors. But dystopianism also belongs to the modern utopian tradition. It is a product of the modern hope and fear that utopia can be realized in our countries.

Therefore we should distinguish at least three stages in the development of the so-called utopian tradition, which now appears to be a succession of loosely related traditions:

1. Folk utopias: myth, fantasy, messianic expectation.
2. Political utopianism: the "social," "realistic," "reconstruction" utopias of the philosophers. These have been of two kinds.
   a) Classical utopianism: Plato and his imitators. The ideal society as a theoretical standard.
   b) Modern utopianism: an adaptation of 2a. The ideal society as a program for political action.

The many confusions over the word "utopian" arise from the fact that this word is sometimes defined as 1, sometimes as 2a, and sometimes as 2b. Those influenced by Mannheim's *Ideology and Utopia* will think that Plato's *Republic* should not be called a utopia on the grounds that it is not tied to political realities. "Utopia" is a word they identify with category 2b; it means a revolutionary tradition that began in early-modern Western Europe and climaxed in the socialist movement.[8] On the other hand, there are at least two books on the political thought of Plato, written seventy years apart, which tell us the *Republic* should not be called a utopia on the grounds that it *is* tied to political realities. "Utopia" is a word they identify with category 1, following what is probably the commonest popular meaning of the word; it has negative and derisive connotations, implying the fanciful, useless, and wildly impractical.[9] Finally, a popular textbook on the history of political thought calls the *Republic* a utopia on the grounds that it is *indirectly* tied to political reality, being a general statement of principles. The author identifies the word "utopia" with category 2a.[10] Clearly "utopia" is a word to be used with caution. But if we avoid the semantic problem, we will notice a general agreement that Plato's *Republic* belongs to category 2a, and therefore is less realistic than the activist social programs of category 2b, but more realistic than the wonderlands of category 1.[11]

The modern socialist conception of a utopia (2b) was established by the end of the nineteenth century; and at the same time the notion spread that the Platonic tradition was the classical predecessor of socialism, and the Cynic/Stoic tradition of anarchism; for it is, or once was, just possible to believe that Plato's *Republic* advocates some kind of political program, and it has never been possible to believe that about the Cynic/Stoic utopias. Now it is easy to see that Plato's *Republic* did not belong in the same category with Marx or even Saint-Simon, but in category 2a; and if Plato's utopian principles were not really action-oriented, we must ask why those of Zeno's *Republic* were so much further removed from action as to justify their relegation to category 1 along with the golden age and the Elysian fields. I will argue that, in fact, the works about perfect societies produced by the Platonist, Aristotelian, Cynic, and Stoic schools all belonged to the same classical utopian tradition.

I think it true—to summarize briefly an argument that will be developed in later chapters—that the Cynic/Stoic utopian tradition was further removed from political action than the Platonic/Aristotelian. The *Republic* of Plato contained guidelines for the reformation of the way of life of a Greek citizen body, and, among these, guidelines by which such a citizen body might set up a mechanism of rule. The distinction corresponded roughly to our distinction between "social" and "political" reform. The evidence indicates that most, though by no means all, utopian speculation in the Cynic/Stoic tradition concentrated on the first type of proposal and avoided the second. That did not mean Stoics were anarchists concerned with individualistic and privatistic ethics. The distinction in question did not coincide with our distinction between public and private. It meant they were concerned with reforms of a public and social nature, "political" in the fullest Greek sense—they had to do with *politika*, the affairs of the polis—which did not include programs for immediate action, therefore were not "political" in one common modern sense of the word, which means "engaged in or taking sides in the struggle for governmental power."

But our definition of classical utopianism requires further refinement. We know of some classical Greek writings about imaginary and ideal societies that do not seem to fit category 2a described above. When Aristotle lectured on *politika*, he assumed that one of its central themes is the question of the *politeia ariste*, the best constitution (an expression which is as close as the Greeks came to our "utopia"), and devoted to previous discussions of this problem the material which now stands as the second book of the *Politics*. Among the theoretical writers on this subject he saw a clear distinction between Plato and the predecessors of Plato. Plato was in a class by himself because only he had proposed such radical innovations as communism in property, communism in family, and equality between the sexes. The other writers had kept closer to existing institutions. We infer that their schemes were meant as practical reform programs, and that the failure to implement them was a failure of opportunity. We know virtually nothing about these predecessors of Plato except for what Aristotle tells us, but that is sufficient to show they did not fit our definition of classical utopianism. They seem to resemble our modern utopianism (category 2b) in that they were planning a total and sometimes radical reconstruction of society. Hippodamus of Miletus may have been, in fact, closer in spirit to Edward Bellamy than to Plato; but the parallel cannot be pushed very far, because the social reconstruction proposed by Hippodamus and other Greek planners was confined to the small world of the ancient city-state and rooted in the Greek tradition of colonization, where the creation of new societies from scratch was a relatively simple and practical matter. This was a tradition which could not have existed anywhere but in classical Greece, which is why utopianism was never invented anywhere else.

One suggests with some trepidation the introduction of additional jargon into an area so amply supplied with it, but some clarification of terms seems necessary. I propose therefore the following typology for the utopian literature of the ancient Greeks.[12]

1. Utopian works of myth, fantasy, and messianism (as in the first scheme). Among the Greeks represented by legends of the golden age and the Elysian fields found in Homer, Hesiod, and other poets; and by literary adaptations of these myths, so long as these were confined to fantasy, including much fantastic history and fantastic geography.
2. Political utopianism. Of this there were two sorts.
   a. "Low" utopianism. A comprehensive program for an ideal city-state that was meant to be put into action, if possible, and in the meantime to provide a critique of existing institutions and a model for more limited reforms. It is called utopian because the reforms it envisions belong to a total, radical, long-range plan and are not the reforms of ordinary Greek politics; and it is called "low" because the program is nevertheless a real and practical program. The degree of practicality would depend on which of these two aims the writer chose to emphasize. Here belong the predecessors of Plato discussed by Aristotle in *Politics* 2; here I would also place the *Laws* of Plato, the utopian state sketched by Aristotle in *Politics* 7–8, and a number of little-known works by later philosophers, mostly Aristotelians. The tradition may be said to end with the *On the Republic* and *On the Laws* of Cicero, though these are "low" examples indeed.
   b. "High" utopianism. This is the "classical utopianism" of the earlier scheme. A plan for an ideal city-state that was not meant to be literally enacted. It was meant as a model for reform, but in a more oblique way than the low utopias. The great and original example is of course Plato's *Republic*; and I will argue that the Cynic/Stoic utopias of the third century B.C. also belong here.

The first tradition goes back to some misty Indo-European past and has analogies the world over. The second, a peculiarly Greek tradition that appeared in the late fifth century B.C., had no evident connection with the first. The third was apparently invented by Plato ca. 375 B.C. and drew on both the earlier traditions. This higher utopianism was identical with the theory of communism, a theory with very definite outlines because to Greeks it usually implied the three things mentioned by Aristotle: common property, common women, and equality between men and women. The introduction of such ideas made it clear from the start that the high-utopian proposals, unlike their low-utopian predecessors, had nothing directly to do with the goals of ordinary Greek political discussion. The fictive reconstructions of the low utopists did not differ all that much from existing institutions, since they were full expressions of ideals already present in those societies. The higher fictive reconstructions sought to establish transcendent and unattainable standards, therefore could afford and had to be utterly different from existing social realities. The high-utopian method was a thought experiment for exploring the potentialities of human nature and society, developed to discuss institutional change at a much deeper level than was possible in real political reform. Yet it never quite lost its connections to the lower type of utopia and to the world of ordinary politics, and this ambiguity imported to the high-utopian tradition a peculiar tension.

The main theme of this book is the high- or communistic utopian literature. We will be concerned with other traditions only insofar as they led the way to high utopia or led away from it; which means that in fact a great deal of the book will be concerned with them, for the communistic utopia defined above cannot be studied in isolation from a number of other traditions about ideal societies.

To us the most striking feature of these communist utopias is that communism in property is always accompanied by communism in family. They seem to take for granted the connection between "community of goods" and "community of women." To explain this connection will require some discussion of the implications of the Greek words *koinonia* (community) and *oikos* (household). This will be found in the section of the first chapter titled "Household and City." In brief, it will be argued that the Greek concept of the household embraced both property and family to such an extent that it seemed entirely natural for theoretical communism to embrace both. The patriarchal structure of the Greek household accounts for the stubborn patriarchalism of even the philosophers' terminology: even a system of complete equality between men and women is described, at least by Plato and Aristotle, as one where men share all their women. (We do not know that Stoics and Cynics used the phrase "community of women.") That is what it looked like from a male point of view, but of course from a female point of view the system could with equal accuracy be described as "community of men." Plato's patriarchal labels should not blind us to the radicalism of the content.

Some other terms have already been mentioned. Readers of this book are probably acquainted with "polis," the word for the independent city with attached territory that was the typical political unit of the classical Greeks. It is here translated as "city," "state," "city-state," or left as "polis," as seemed to best fit the context. *Politai*, the active members of the polis, can only be translated "citizens." *Politeia*, a recurrent word in such a study as this, is more troublesome. Its basic meaning is perhaps best conveyed by a phrase like "the condition of the citizen body." It often meant the arrangement of rights, duties, and offices among the citizens, and so is usually translated "constitution." Though "regime" may be a more adequate translation, I have stuck with "constitution" because of the ease with which it lends itself to adjectival forms. But we should bear in mind that *Politeia* did not have the formal legalistic connotations of "constitution." It did include the political system, but it included also the whole social system. A work like "The *Politeia* of the Lacedaemonians" attributed to Xenophon might have next to nothing to say about the organization of government, which to us is the primary business of constitutions, and much to say about marriage, and education, and daily life. The *politeia*, Aristotle said, "is in a sense the life of the polis" (*Pol.* 1295b1). "Republic" is the most misleading translation of all, but as there is no correcting it now, the *Politeia* of Plato shall remain herein *Republic* of Plato, and the titles attributed to Diogenes, Zeno, and Chrysippus shall be likewise mistranslated.

Translations are the author's, unless credited to someone else.

Notes

1. General histories of utopianism—the most comprehensive is F. E. Manuel and F. P. Manuel, *Utopian Thought in the Western World* (Cambridge, Mass. 1979)—are chiefly concerned with modern thought and with the ancient world only insofar as it provided the foundations for modern utopianism, a perspective that necessarily magnifies the position of Plato in ancient thought. The focus of Edgar Salin's *Platon und die griechische Utopie* (Munich 1921) is indicated by its title. John Ferguson's *Utopias of the Classical World* (Ithaca 1975) goes to the opposite extreme, adopting the loosest definition of "Utopia" and attempting to survey everything from mythology to millenarianism. Robert von Pöhlmann's *Geschichte des antiken Kommunismus und Sozialismus*, 2 vols. (Munich 1893–1901) was in some ways closer to the focus of the present book, but owing to misleading assumptions (obvious in its title) about the relationship between ancient utopian literature and ancient political life it was largely concerned with the history of social conflicts in the Greco-Roman world. Pöhlmann changed the title of the 1912 edition to *Geschichte der sozialen Frage und des Sozialismus in der antiken Welt*, which more adequately represented the contents; but his definition of ancient "socialism" remained unsatisfactory, and its connection to the ancient "social question" unclear (points recognized in an appendix added by Friedrich Oertel to a posthumous third edition in 1925). Other works on Greek political thought are mentioned in notes 5 and 6.

2. Eduard Zeller, *Philosophie der Griechen* 3; trans. O. J. Reichel as *The Stoics, Epicureans, and Skeptics* (New York 1879). The observation that Platonism was to socialism what Stoicism was to anarchism appeared in Adolf Dyroff's *Die Ethik der alten Stoa* (Berlin 1897), 216.

3. *The Story of Utopias* (London 1922). There have been many other attempts to classify utopias (see notes 11 and 12) but this basic distinction always reappears.

4. The closest non-Western analogies appear to be certain Taoist and Buddhist traditions of the Far East: Jean Chesneaux, "Egalitarian and Utopian Traditions in the East," *Diogenes* 62 (1968), 76–102. There have been connections there between folk utopia and political theory, but it is not clear how closely any of this corresponds to the Western tradition of utopian philosophy, and I lack the equipment to study it further.

5. On these grounds Pöhlmann's two-volume history of ancient communism dismissed the Stoics in seven pages (*Sozialismus* 2.268–74); Cynics and Stoics received equally curt treatment in Salin's work on Greek utopias (*Platon*, 181–87); and the Manuels' massive history of utopianism contains only brief mention of Cynics and Stoics, describing them as anarchists and solipsists (*Utopian Thought*, 7–8, 64–65, 415, 737). M. I. Finley has written "every significant utopia [elsewhere he calls these "social utopias"] is conceived as a goal toward which we may legitimately and hopefully strive, a goal not in some shadowy state of perfection but with specific institutional criticisms and proposals"; and did not think the Cynics and Stoics had any such proposals: "Utopianism Ancient and Modern," in *The Use and Abuse of History* (New York 1971), 178–92; first published in *The Critical Spirit: Essays in Honor of Herbert Marcuse*, ed. K. Wolff and Barrington Moore, Jr. (Boston 1967), 3–20. Similar judgments will be found in D. R. Dudley, *A History of Cynicism* (Hildesheim 1937), 36ff., 98ff.; Max Pohlenz, *Die Stoa: Geschichte einer geistige Bewegung*, 2 vols. (Göttingen 1947, 1959), 1.137ff.; M. E. Reesor, *The Political Theory of the Old and Middle Stoa* (New York 1951), 11, 59; Donald Kagan, *The Great Dialogue: A History of Greek Political Thought from Homer to Polybius* (Westport 1965), 241ff.; G. J. D. Aalders, *Political Thought in Hellenistic Times* (Amsterdam 1975), 56ff., 82ff.; I. M. Parente, "La Politica della Stoa

antica," *Sandalion* 3 (1980), 67–98. Not all have aquiesced in the general decision to banish Cynics and Stoics from the serious Western utopian tradition. They were given brief but honorable mention in M. L. Berneri's *Journey Through Utopia* (London 1950), 11. She even described Plato's *Republic* as a reaction against their egalitarianism; but that is chronologically impossible, and in fact reverses the historical relationship.

6. See Gustave Glotz, *Ancient Greece at Work*, trans M. R. Dobie (New York 1926), 154–59. For an even more emphatic statement see E. M. Wood and Neal Wood, *Class Ideology and Ancient Political Theory: Socrates, Plato, and Aristotle in Social Context* (Oxford 1978), 63–64, 79; the authors suggest that the term "communism" is inappropriate for these reactionary theories. Lewis Mumford remarks that ancient philosophers found it easier to abolish marriage and property than to do without slavery, social classes, and warfare: "Utopia: The City and the Machine," in *Utopias and Utopian Thought*, ed. F. E. Manuel (Boston 1966), 3–24; the epigram is repeated by Joseph Vogt in *Ancient Slavery and the Ideal of Man*, trans. Thomas Wiedemann (Cambridge, Mass. 1975), 35; and by Finley, "Utopianism Ancient and Modern," 180–81. Finley adds: "In antiquity it is hard to find any utopian thinking which is not hierarchical" (187).

7. Cicero, *On the Republic* 2.30.32: "requisivit civitatemque optandam magis quam sperandam." The quotation from More is from the conclusion of *Utopia* (Yale Edition of the Complete Works of St. Thomas More, New Haven 1964). I should mention that the More who speaks here is a character in the dialogue, and the extent to which he represents the position of More the author has been disputed. Whether Cicero understood adequately the intentions of Plato may also be disputed. But I think that on the point in question—the realizability of the ideal city—these quotations do represent the intentions of the authors, and in the case of Plato I will present arguments for this interpretation.

8. Karl Mannheim, *Ideology and Utopia: An Introduction to the Sociology of Knowledge*, trans. Louis Wirth and Edward Shils (New York 1936), used a definition of "Utopian mentality" much broader than what we normally mean by utopianism, and confusing to many. He included in this concept all movements to transcend the existing social order by revolutionary action, and thought it began in the sixteenth century with Thomas Müntzer and the Anabaptists. Hence nonrevolutionary political theories cannot be "utopias." See n. 11.

9. Ernest Barker, *Greek Political Theory: Plato and His Predecessors* (London 1918), 277; George Klosko, *The Development of Plato's Political Theory* (New York 1986), 173.

10. G. H. Sabine, *A History of Political Theory*, 4th ed., rev. T. L. Thorson (Hinsdale 1973), 57.

11. Discussions of the distinction between classical and modern utopianism will be found in Judith Shklar's "The Political Theory of Utopia: From Melancholy to Nostalgia," in Manuel, *Utopias and Utopian Thought*, 101–15; Elisabeth Hansot's *Perfection and Progress: Two Modes of Utopian Thought* (Cambridge, Mass. 1974); *Utopias*, ed. Peter Alexander and Roger Gill (La Salle, Il. 1984); Krishan Kumar's *Utopia and Anti-Utopia in Modern Times* (Oxford 1987), 2–32. There is an annotated bibliography of scholarly literature about utopianism by J. A. Martinez in *The Utopian Vision*, ed. E. D. S. Sullivan (San Diego 1983), 175–233; it includes little about the ancient world.

The confusion over the definition of "Utopianism" seems to have been abetted, if not created, by the nineteenth-century Marxists' designation of all earlier theories about communal property as "utopian" socialism. This usage could support any of the three definitions given in the text. It implied that the older utopists were not "scientific" socialists, therefore had no relevance to real political life. At the same time it implied that older utopists were in some sense forerunners of modern socialism, and thereby reawakened interest in them. See, e.g., Karl Kautsky et al., *Die Vorläufer des neueren Sozialisums* (Stuttgart 1895). But as this interest concentrated upon the supposed revolutionaries—producing among other results Mannheim's concept of "utopian mentality"—it tended to slight the importance of ancient Greek utopian thought. The major attempt to find parallels between Greek utopianism and modern socialism was made by Pöhlmann, who intended no compliment to either by this comparison. Marxists generally preferred More or Müntzer as a spiritual father.

12. It may be of interest to note that comparable attempts to sort out utopian, preutopian, and protoutopian genres have been made for the age of the Renaissance by J. C. Davis, *Utopia and the Ideal Society: A Study of English Utopian Writing, 1516–1700* (Cambridge 1981), 11–40, and by Miriam Eliav-Feldon, *Realistic Utopias: The Ideal Imaginary Societies of the Renaissance, 1516–1630* (Oxford 1982), 1–15. The typology of Eliav-Feldon is more comprehensive. In addition to genuine utopists like More and Campanella, she recognizes the following types of ideal-society thought in the sixteenth century: (1) models of good government implying moral rather than institutional reform; (2) idealizations of existing societies, e.g., the Republic of Venice; (3) architectural designs for model cities; (4) descriptions of a primitive golden age, whether located in classical mythology or among the native Americans; (5) programs for secret societies, real or imaginary; (6) plans for world empires; (7) prophecies concerning theocratic millennial kingdoms. The last two types were unknown to classical Greece, but we can find there parallels for all the others (if we count the Pythagoreans as a secret society, and substitute Sparta for Venice and Scythia for America). The parallels are not remarkable, as the Renaissance versions were heavily influenced by classical literature. Nor is there any mystery about the origins of the genuine Renaissance utopianism; it came mostly from the classical legacy to be examined in this book, particularly from the writings of Plato, Plutarch, and Lucian. But there was no Renaissance equivalent for what I have called the Greek "low utopia." I will suggest that it arose from an amalgam of the first three types listed above, in response to the opportunities afforded by the Greek tradition of colonization.

1

The Birth of Utopia

There are some other model constitutions, some of them produced by philosophers and politicians, some by men who were neither. All come closer to the existing constitutions under which men are now governed, for only Plato introduced community of women and children and common meals for women; the rest take as their starting point the basic necessities of life.

ARISTOTLE, *Politics* 1266a 31–36

The Time of Cronus

In this chapter we will examine several Greek traditions about ideal societies that may have contributed something to philosophical utopianism. The oldest and most general of these, the "golden age" myth, has already been mentioned, and little more need be said about it. All Greeks knew that in the time of the old god Cronus food had been abundant and toil and trouble unknown. The Homeric and Hesiodic poems had popularized a systematic version of the myth. The reign of Cronus was fitted into a scheme of world ages of Middle Eastern origin:

> In the beginning, the immortals who have their homes on Olympus created the golden generation of mortal people. They lived in Kronos' time, when he was the king in heaven. They lived as if they were gods, their hearts free from all sorrow, by themselves, and without hard work or pain; no miserable old age came their way; their hands, their feet, did not alter. They took their pleasure in festivals, and lived without troubles. When they died, it was as if they fell asleep. All goods were theirs. The fruitful grainland yielded its harvest to them of its own accord; this was great and abundant, while they at their pleasure quietly looked after their works, in the midst of good things. Hesiod, *Works and Days* 109–19, trans. Richard Lattimore: cf. 42–46, 90–92

The golden race of Cronus' time continued to exist as beneficent spirits or *daimones* (*Works and Days* 120ff.), and the happy conditions of Cronus' time continued on the plain of Elysion or the Islands of the Blessed, a paradise for departed heroes located at the ends of the earth (*Works and Days* 166–73; *Odyssey* 4.561–69), or, according to later poets, in the underworld. Cronus' time lived also in proverb. When the Attic peasantry wished to commemorate the prosperity of Pisistratus' rule they said that it had been like life under Cronus (Aristotle, *Constitution of Athens* 16.7). It lived in cult. At the harvest-time festival of the Cronia in Attica, masters and slaves exchanged places, apparently to recall the primitive equality of Cronus' time. And it lived on the comic stage. Fragments of the Old Comedy contain a number of passages about the time of Cronus, comically exaggerating its effortless plenty: rivers run with barleycakes, fish jump into pans to fry themselves, etc. The plots of some comedies seem to have turned upon a visit to this paradise, which for these purposes was located in a distant country or in the underworld.[1]

The legend of Cronus' time would provide serious utopists with a stock of metaphors, and nothing more than that. Cronus' time was an ancient myth, which the Greeks of the classical age did not confuse with reality. Common property, the major theme of the serious utopias, did not appear in Cronus' time; rather the myth envisioned a peasant paradise of spontaneous food production and total leisure; also free from sickness and aging, which removed it still further from reality. In Hellenistic times there appeared a rationalized version of the myth which made the age of Cronus a real historical period and conflated it with the communal utopias of the philosophers. But serious utopianism was already dying when that happened to it.

The Pythagorean Life

Another possible predecessor of philosophical utopianism was the Pythagorean order, a group certainly more historical than the race of gold, but almost as mysterious. Pythagoras of Samos was certainly an historical figure, a famous teacher of the late sixth century B.C. He certainly founded a school called the *Pythagoreioi*, which flourished in the Greek cities of southern Italy until the fourth century B.C. They were associated with a number of peculiar teachings: belief in reincarnation, which they shared with the equally mysterious Orphic cult; a philosophical system based on mathematical studies and number symbolism; an obscure but successful political activity, which raised Pythagoreans to positions of power in some Italian cities; a host of fantastic taboos and regulations which members of their association were bound to follow (they were forbidden to stir the fire with a knife, kill white roosters, urinate on their own nail parings, etc., etc.); and a strange form of communal organization. It is the last that interests us here. It was believed that the Pythagoreans had lived in associations sharing all property, that this communistic rule was attached to a political theory which made their communistic way of life a model for the whole of society, and that all this strongly influenced the ideal city of Plato's *Republic*, whose most striking feature is a communistic philosophical elite exercising political power.

This story would seem entirely plausible, if the outlines of ancient Pythagorean communism did not have such a tendency to blur under close inspection. Practically all the evidence for it comes from lives of Pythagoras written in the later Roman Empire, and could have been invented by "neo" Pythagoreans of Roman times, essentially mystical Platonists. The fullest account of the early Pythagorean communities is found in the *Life of Pythagoras* by the Neoplatonist

Iamblichus (ca. 300 A.D.), who probably wished to revive the Pythagorean legend as a weapon against the Christian churches; his early Pythagorean society resembles them suspiciously.

On the other hand, we know that these Neopythagorean compilations drew upon certain scholars who wrote ca. 300 B.C. and had access to fairly early Pythagorean traditions. Two Italian-Greek pupils of Aristotle, Aristoxenus of Tarentum and Dicaearchus of Messene, were authorities on Pythagoreanism. They worked at Athens, where they could have had contact with another Italian-Greek, Timaeus of Tauromenium, author of an influential history of the Greeks of the West to the year 264 B.C. It contained information about Pythagoreanism, the main Western contribution to philosophy; and a scholiast on Plato preserved from it the following passage, which he copied because he was trying to explain the origins of the saying *koina ta ton philon.*[2]

> At any rate, Timaeus says in book viii: "So when the younger men came to him [Pythagoras] wanting to associate with him, he did not immediately agree, but said that they must also hold their property in common with whoever else might be admitted to membership." Then after much intervening matter he says: "And it was because of them that it was first said in Italy: What belongs to friends is common property [*koina ta ton philon*]." (trans. Kirk)

Parallel passages in the *Lives* of Pythagoras by Diogenes Laertius (8.10) and Iamblichus (71ff.) include an account of a rigorous initiation process, the "intervening matter" omitted by the scholiast. Novices had to preserve silence for five years, during which time their property was administered by officials of the school, and they were not permitted to see Pythagoras or enter his house; at the end of this period they came up for an examination; if they decided not to join their possessions would be returned to them. All this must be based upon the histories of Timaeus, who had no known motive to invent such a thing; and it leaves little doubt that the Pythagoreans had a peculiarly disciplined organization, resembling no other pagan Greek school or sect then or later. At that period schools of philosophy were mere gatherings of like-minded individuals who were in the habit of meeting at the same place to talk with the same teacher. In the fourth century Plato created in his Academy a tighter form of organization, centered around a cult of the Muses, with buildings where his disciples could share meals and philosophical activities. It had some imitators, but none who wished to give up private property.[3]

This tradition seems credible because the early Pythagoreans were remembered as a peculiar organization in other respects. They played an important role in the politics of the Italian cities until ca. 450 B.C., when their power was broken by a massacre of Pythagoreans in their main center of Croton, and by similar persecutions in other cities. Afterwards scattered communities and individuals survived in various parts of the Greek world, including Athens; even in Plato's day Tarentum was still ruled by his friend Archytas the Pythagorean; but by ca. 300 B.C. they were gone. They might have entered politics as individuals, like Freemasons in the Enlightenment, but the tradition strongly suggests that at least in some places, probably in southern

Italy during the days of their power, they formed organized political "clubs" (*hetairiai*).[4] The common life Timaeus described was probably practiced by members of these political cliques, and intended to cement their friendship (*philia*), a word much emphasized in the Pythagorean legends. Such political activity was unique among pre-Socratic philosophers; among Socratics, the schools of Plato and Aristotle attempted at times to exercise political influence, but few of their members ever held power directly. All this suggests a highly developed organization and inclines us to accept the later descriptions of early Pythagoreanism as a semimonastic society with a hierarchical organization, a long initiation period, strict dietary rules and other ritual observances to separate its members from the larger society, and some degree of *ousia koina*, common property; though we need not believe they surrendered *all* their private possessions and private houses.[5]

Nor can we believe that this Pythagorean *koinos bios*, common life, was a significant model for the communistic utopia of Plato. Plato was much interested in Pythagorean mathematical theories, but his only comment on Pythagorean organization is that at *Republic* 600ab. Here Socrates argues that poetry is not one of the arts that make men better either in public life (*demosios*, pertaining to the people) or in private life (*idios*, pertaining to the self). Public benefactors include generals, lawgivers such as Lycurgus of Sparta and Charondas of Italy, and wise men like the Seven Sages who invented useful things. Private benefactors are those who developed a special education (*paideia*) or way of life (*bios*) for their own friends; the only example given is Pythagoras, whose followers are still distinguished by their *bios pythagorikos*.

What did Plato mean by the "Pythagorean way of life"? Not the kind of common life described many centuries later by Iamblichus, because that is presented as a political institution tied to a political theory; it is practiced only by an elite but it is intended to benefit all the citizens; it is very like the life of the "guards" in Plato's *Republic*, and if Plato had associated Pythagoras with such a plan he would not have hesitated to count Pythagoras among the lawgivers. Plato may have thought of the "Pythagorean life" primarily as an individualistic form of asceticism. That is what it seems to have meant in Plato's day on the Athenian comic stage, where Pythagoreans were frequently ridiculed for their poverty, bathlessness, and absurd taboos.[6] What made it a unique *bios* was above all the maze of proscriptions affecting diet, clothing, and every aspect of daily life. If Plato had heard that the older Pythagoreans in Italy had practiced a more communal way of life, he assumed this was for a group of private friends and not for the city.

The comments of Aristotle are even more revealing. When Aristotle discussed the predecessors of Plato's ideal city in the second book of the *Politics*, he did not mention Pythagoreans. He thought that no one but Plato had ever proposed or practiced communism, neither in women nor in goods. He thought a system where property is private in ownership but common in use would be preferable to common property; he pointed out that such common use is already practiced in some states, a good example being the common messes (*syssitia*) of Sparta and Crete. Then he adds:

> We must not forget another point that ought to be considered: simply the immense period of time during which this form of organization [Platonic communism] has remained undiscovered, as it surely would not have remained if it were really good. Pretty well all possible forms of organization have now been discovered, though no complete collection of them has been made, and many are known but are not practised. The force of our arguments would become clearer if we could see such a constitution [as Plato's] being put together in practice. . . . *Pol.* 1264alff., trans. Sinclair/Saunders

Could anything be clearer? Aristotle was particularly interested in *syssitia*, and particularly concerned to show that no form of *syssitia* had ever been practiced in which men shared anything more than food. He did not ignore Italy. He thought *syssitia* widely practiced there, thought indeed they had first been invented there by the legendary king Italus.[7] He mentions in several other contexts the somewhat less legendary Italian lawgivers Zaleucus and Charondas. He refers rather often to the constitutional history of the Italian Greek cities, and mentions Tarentum as a good example of a city where the rich maintained social stability by sharing their goods with the poor (1320b9). But in none of these connections did he mention Pythagoreans.

If Plato and Aristotle did not think of the Pythagorean associations as political groups, then how did they think of them? Probably as *thiasoi*, cult organizations. Every Greek organization that was not part of a household or a city tended to take the form of a cult whose ostensible purpose was to carry out the worship of a god. The Pythagorean societies were said to have been centered around the worship of Apollo and the Muses. Any such cult was likely to include common meals; the main function of cults was to perform sacrifices, and a sacrifice was always followed by a meal at which the worshippers shared the sacrificial meat. Any cult society might participate in politics on occasion, and then it would be indistinguishable from a political *hetairia*. Greek society was filled with groups of friends who ate together and worshipped together and sometimes engaged in political intrigue together. The special organization of the Pythagoreans was only an exaggerated form of a familiar cultural pattern. Very likely Plato and Aristotle thought of the Pythagorean society as a forerunner of their own Academy, which was also a cult of the Muses with common meals and a degree of common life; a place to be "held in common like a temple" (as Theophrastus' will said of the Lyceum); and a place intended, among other ends, to train men for political life. Plato might have thought of his Academy as a *bios*,[8] as something much more than an ordinary cult. But he would never have thought of it as a *politeia*.

Pythagorean "communism" was real enough, but it was never any sort of utopia; and if there was ever a Pythagorean political theory, there is no reason to suppose it had any connection with the Pythagorean common life. The common life probably originated because the dietary rules of the cult made exclusive common meals more than usually convenient, and to require initiates to contribute some of their property to provide these meals would be a natural expedient. The Pythagorean common life never included the one feature that would become the distinguishing mark of utopian communism: it did not try to make sex, marriage, and family life communal. They had some unusual views on sexual morality. The Pythagorean associations were said to include women as well as men, and to practice an austere code that forbade adultery for men as well as women. But that means that they retained separate households (*oikoi*); and for reasons that we will soon consider, a Greek institution unwilling to break with the household had not really broken away from the normal Greek social structure.

This is not to underestimate the uniqueness of the Pythagorean life. It more resembled a religious order than a normal Greek cult, or anything else in the Greek world. Therefore it represented a challenge to the polis, and the Greek world did not like it. After the ruthless liquidation of the Pythagorean cells in the mid-fifth century the experiment was never repeated. Much later it would seem obvious that the Pythagorean common life must have been the ancestor of the communistic political elite of Plato's *Republic*. Were not the resemblances obvious? But Timaeus or Aristoxenus or whoever introduced this notion[9] passed over obvious differences: Pythagorean communism had no constitutional role, no "community of women," probably a less than complete "community of goods." To Plato the Pythagorean life was only one of many kinds of *koinonia* (association) known to his culture in practice or in theory. There is no sign that it particularly influenced him when he set himself to design a perfect *koinonia* in the *Republic*; and it was probably the *Republic* itself that reawakened interest in the Pythagorean organization, and made people see in it a purposeful configuration that had not been noticed at the time.[10]

The Sexual Communism of the Barbarians

But the Greeks of the fifth century did know of some societies without households, all of them non-Greek. They had a peculiar curiosity about foreigners' customs, which extended most definitely to sexual customs. By the middle of the century this was satisfied by a rich collection of data gathered by Herodotus and the older geographical writers about sex, marriage, and family life among the "barbarians," which included the reversal of almost every Greek norm of behavior.

Most of these reversals concern the behavior of women. Herodotus comments on the scandalous promiscuity expected of unmarried girls among the Thracians (5.3), Lydians (1.93), Cypriots and Babylonians (1.199), and even of married women among certain Libyans (4.176). And he knows of some other barbarians with a yet more startling custom: they practiced forms of communal marriage, which he calls *mixis epikoinos*, "common intercourse." This phrase covers two different things: the first a custom of wife sharing, the second a more extreme form of promiscuity in which the nuclear family seems to disappear altogether.

Before Herodotus wrote, Greeks generally believed that the first form of "common intercourse"—wife exchange—was practiced by all the Scythian nomads of the northern steppes. Herodotus denies this, but he verifies the existence of the practice among certain relatives of the Scythians, the Massagetae of Central Asia. Among these nomads all men shared their wives freely; if a man wanted another man's wife he only needed hang a quiver on her wagon (1.216). Herodotus reports the same practice among the Nasamones of Libya, who used a pole instead of a quiver (4.172). His readers might think that this institution at least preserved the system of patriarchal marriage, albeit with an odd indifference to matters of paternity and wifely chastity. But Herodotus knows of another Libyan tribe called the Auses who had no married couples living together at all. They copulated casually like animals, and when a child grew up the men held a meeting and assigned it a father on the basis of resemblance (4.180).[11] But even here we notice men still governed, and a parent–child relationship was still discernable.

Such stories were based on accurate observation of polyandrous arrangements common among primitive societies. But Greeks tended to exaggerate everything that differed from their own institution of patriarchal monogamy and to describe it as a reversal of the norm. The same tendency to find reversals of the sexual norm among barbarians is evident in Greek mythology, most remarkably in the many legends about the Amazons, the nation of manless warrior-women who inhabited Scythia in the heroic age. To believe that barbarians reverse the norm in everything does not weaken cultural self-confidence: it demarcates and strengthens a culture by demonstrating the irredeemable otherness of all those outside it.[12] Often Herodotus shares this attitude. In most cases he probably expects his reports about barbarian sexuality to shock, titillate, and confirm his Greek readers in their conviction of cultural superiority. When he speaks of barbarians copulating in the open like cattle, he does not mean a compliment. He seems to associate the sexual promiscuity of the Massagetae and Indians with human sacrifice and cannibalism.

But sometimes other sorts of reflections can be seen in Herodotus' mirrors. The itinerant teachers of rhetoric called Sophists were already using barbarian customs as material for philosophical reflection: they showed the variability of *nomoi* (human laws and/or customs) and promoted a critical and skeptical attitude toward conventional thinking. Sometimes Herodotus can adopt this approach, as in the well-known anecdote contrasting Greek burial customs with the Indian practice of eating the corpses of their dead parents (3.38). On one occasion it leads him to look upon the sexual communism of the barbarians in a different light. He tells us that the Agathyrsi, another nomadic tribe on the borders of Scythia (that laboratory of exotic sex), have their women in common so that they can all live together like brothers, in a single family, without jealousy or hatred (4.104). It is not clear whether their *mixis epikoinos* is of the wife-swapping sort or the more total version, but it is clear that someone, either Herodotus or his informant, was contemplating this barbarian society as in some sense a model or alternative worth considering by Greeks.

There is some reason to think that Sophists were already making use of this particular barbarian example. There existed a curious tradition about the greatest of the Sophists, Protagoras of Abdera. He came to Athens about the same time as Herodotus (ca. 450 B.C.) and was associated with Herodotus in the founding of the colony of Thurii (ca. 443), about which more later. He seems to have been the real founder of the sophistic profession—the first to make political rhetoric and dialectic a high art, which he taught to the sons of the wealthy for high fees. He may have been the founder of sophistic, and therefore of classical Greek, political thought; he was the first to write a treatise *Peri politeias*, "On the Constitution," of whose contents we know nothing; his contributions to political theory, which must be reconstructed mostly from references in the dialogues of Plato, have been the subject of much discussion, which need not detain us; but it does seem clear that he was a major propagator of the rationalistic views about society and politics which were widespread in the sophistic Enlightenment and whose echoes are heard in the Attic drama. He wrote a work about the origins of society, which if accurately summarized in Plato's *Protagoras* argued that humanity had been raised from a bestial state by the creation of the polis and its "political art," which enable people to live together in peace; that all men are endowed with the capacity to learn this art, and that all should participate in political decisions; that the political art he taught was the road to concord (*homonoia*).

But he claims our attention here because a hundred years after he died Aristotle's disciple Aristoxenus of Tarentum, a biographer of earlier philosophers whom we have already encountered, made the odd remark that "nearly everything" (*schedon holen*) in Plato's *Republic* was to be found in a work by Protagoras called the *Antilogica*.[13] Aristoxenus seems to have tried to slight the originality of Plato, as witness his interest in Pythagoreanism: so many scholars have dismissed his statement about Protagoras as a malicious anti-Platonic invention. Clearly the *schedon holen* was a mad exaggeration, but possibly the responsibility for it lay not with Aristoxenus but with the doxographers who transmitted his opinion. It seems likely there was a grain of truth in this tradition. Were it a complete fabrication, would it not have been more plausible to say, "Plato's *Politeia* was based on Protagoras' Politeia"? Why the *Antilogica*?

We know nothing about the *Antilogica* but its title, which means "Contradictory Arguments," and suggests a collection of rhetorical exercises. Luckily we are better informed about the dialectical methods of Protagoras than about his political views. He claimed that two contradictory accounts (*logoi*) were possible for every question (Diog. Laert. 9.51), and that his arts could always make the weaker arguments appear the stronger. The *Antilogica* was probably a series of "twin arguments" (*dissoi logoi*), as such exercises were called, demonstrating that there are two sides to every question. Many later examples of this sort of thing have come down to us. Often they make use of the contrasting customs of various nations, especially their sexual customs, to illustrate the relativity of all beliefs and values.[14] Did Protagoras use such material also? In one of these exercises, did he introduce the example of barbarian sexual communism to suggest that some barbarians had found a better way than Greeks to achieve concord? Though Protagoras could probably have produced arguments for any form of constitution, he is portrayed by Plato as a friend of democracy, and therefore this egalitarian example may have appealed to him. If so, then Protagoras himself could have been the source of Herodotus' unexpected belief that certain barbarians on the northern steppes were advanced political philosophers. And perhaps this is why Aristoxenus could claim that Plato had plagiarized the best-known idea in his *Republic*, communism in goods and women, from Protagoras' *Antilogica*.[15]

The tradition about barbarian sexual communism is intriguing because it contains the basic idea of the later communistic utopias: the elimination of family ties to promote *homonoia*, eternal goal of Greek politics. It is possible Herodotus and his readers assumed the barbarians to share their property as well as their women, and in any case this was an easy step to take. As we will see, the Greeks found it difficult to separate the notions of property and family. In the late fifth century references to barbarian communism as an ideal of social concord could have occurred rather often in sophists' lectures, in oratory, and in the drama; Aristophanes' *Ecclesiazusae*, to which we will come at the end of this chapter, shows that some familiarity with such ideas could be assumed in an Athenian audience ca. 393 B.C.; even before that a character in Euripides' tragedy *Protesilaus* had been given the line "The female bed must be common."[16] This was not utopianism; it was rhetorical moralizing. But through such channels the notion of total community in goods and women would enter the Greek utopian vocabulary.

The Low Utopias and Sparta

Serious utopias appear rather suddenly in the late fifth century and seem to have no connection with the myths, cults, and rhetorical formulas described above. Any attempt to write the early history of this utopian tradition must consist essentially of a gloss on the second book of Aristotle's *Politics*, where Aristotle attempted to provide his pupils with a survey of previous discussions about the "best constitution," a procedure he often followed when introducing a large problem. Like all his surveys, this is a highly selective account which concentrates on certain writers and certain points in order to build up to Aristotle's proposed solution to the problem in question. Therefore it is essential to understand Aristotle's assumptions. But I will reserve comment on this problem until the end of this section. Let us begin with Aristotle's discussion of Hippodamus of Miletus (*Pol.* 1267b–1269a), the earliest writer he mentions.

Hippodamus of Miletus, Inventor of Political Utopianism

The tradition of utopian planning that Aristotle attempts to summarize in *Politics* 2 was not, for the most part, produced by "philosophers" as they were defined in Aristotle's time. It was associated with the practical planning activities that always accompanied the foundation of new colonies. Utopianism was a by-product of colonization, which made it uniquely Greek. Other ancient societies wrote about models of good government, idealized certain societies of the past or present, planned new cities in a regular fashion, and preserved legends of perfect societies like the ones we have just reviewed. When we try to break utopia down into its separate elements it is hard to find anything new—except the Greek colony.

Around 750 B.C. there began a mass migration from the overpopulated Greek homeland that in the course of the next two centuries ringed the Mediterranean and Black seas with new Greek settlements. We are accustomed to think of such a "colony" (*apoikia*, more accurately translated "emigration") as an extension of an established polis, but it is doubtful that the polis existed at the time of the first colonies, and influences doubtless ran in both directions: colonization helped to define the polis and imparted to Greek political life and thought much of their distinctive character. The self-conscious view of the state as a human invention and the experimental attitude toward politics were rooted in the colonizing experience. The colonial cult of the *oikistes*, the founder of the city, made it easy to think of a city as the product of conscious design and the work of a single individual, for everything connected with the foundation was usually credited to the "oikist." An oikist was a man of unique authority, preferably designated by the Delphic oracle; he would hold autocratic power during the period of settlement, and after his death he would receive a hero's cult in the new city. He would mark out the site, divide the land into plots for the settlers, and set aside sacred places for the gods:

> From here
> godlike Nausithoös had removed and led a migration,
> and settled in Scheria, far away from men who eat bread,
> and driven a wall about the city, and built the houses,
> and made the temples of the gods, and allotted the holdings
> *Odyssey* 6.6–10, trans. Lattimore.

The need to divide the land as equally as possible promoted regular urban design: there is archeological evidence that as early as the late eighth century colonies were being laid out in a regular pattern. Physical planning would be accompanied by social planning, for a new city required a written code of laws (*nomoi*): its settlers would often come from several different cities, leading to debate over the relative merits of different law codes; there were famous lawgivers (*nomothetai*) who specialized in this, like some of the Seven Sages; it was often the case, and perhaps the normal expectation, that the oikist would also be the lawgiver. The oikist cult was not confined to the Greek colonial world; there are signs that it also influenced the mother cities. Hero cults honoring eponymous founders existed in many older cities, and it is possible that many of these were imitations of the colonial cult of the oikist. By the seventh century a new type of lawgiver has appeared in the old cities: social reformers like Lycurgus of Sparta and Solon of Athens, invested by the citizens with autocratic powers to reconstruct the laws. This reforming lawgiver seems to be partly modeled on the oikist lawgiver. Lycurgus, probably the earliest example and certainly the archetype, had to receive his mission from Delphi like the founder of a new city, and it was said that he not only gave new laws to Sparta but carried out a new distribution of the land.[17]

The breakthrough to utopian thinking came, like many other breakthroughs, in the mid-fifth century. The great age of colonization was over by then, but there were still occasional opportunities to draft new laws for new colonies; and this legislative activity, like all other political matters, fell under the influence of the Sophists and their generalizing, classifying habits of thought. Before the middle of the century some Sophist (Protagoras, again, has been suggested) came up with the basic Greek theory of *politeiai*—that they might all be divided into monarchies, oligarchies, and democracies—and inaugurated the endless debate over which of these was the best constitution. This was never a purely academic question; it might arise every time a new polis was founded. We first hear it in Herodotus' debate among the "three Persian nobles" (3.80ff.), where it is presented as a sort of argument practical politicians are likely to have, however implausible that particular context.

The most striking opportunity of this kind in the later fifth century was the founding of Thurii ca. 443, possibly a key event in the development of utopianism. This colony on the toe of Italy was a pan-Hellenic enterprise under Athenian auspices, directed by Pericles. It is not clear who the oikist was—later there would be a serious dispute about this among colonists from different cities—but the Athenian contingent included several famous intellectuals of Ionian origin. Herodotus was one of the original settlers, and may have completed his history at Thurii. Protagoras, the most distinguished sophist of the age, wrote at least some of the laws for the colony. And the great architect Hippodamus of Miletus, who had laid out Piraeus, probably planned the town.

Hippodamus was supposed to have made some important but vaguely described contribution to the theory of city planning. Aristotle said he invented the "division of cities" (*diairesis poleon*), which apparently meant the orthogonal street plan; yet we know from archeological evidence that Greek cities were being laid out on the grid system before Hippodamus was born, including Miletus, which was rebuilt on geometric lines after the Persian Wars. We may assume Hippodamus at least wrote a treatise on town planning. He also wrote—perhaps as part of a larger work on town planning—the document summarized by Aristotle, who calls it the first "best constitution" written by someone who was not himself engaged in politics, as opposed to the real constitutions designed by practicing lawgivers (1267b22ff., 1273b27ff.).

What did Aristotle mean by that? Probably that Hippodamus was the first writer to assume the role of a fictive oikist, designing imaginary laws and an imaginary plan for an imaginary city. He combined the functions of the oikist/lawgiver and the sophist. He continued the oikist/lawgiver tradition in that his constitution was supposed to be a practical model, not a utopia in the sense that Plato's *Republic* is a utopia. Aristotle refers to Hippodamus as a "lawgiver," which is probably the persona that Hippodamus himself adopted. It would be a natural role for a citizen of Miletus, mother of many colonies. His plan was meant for a specific polis of ten thousand citizens, which would be a very large polis, though only a quarter the size of Athens. It included detailed *nomoi* regulating such things as the method of voting in lawcourts. Nothing that Aristotle reports about it seems unrealizable, given the opportunity to found a new colony; and a plan for a new colony is probably what Hippodamus' constitution purported to be. It may have been connected with the foundation of Thurii itself. But it is clear that this colony existed only in Hippodamus' imagination. He raised the oikist/lawgiver tradition to a more abstract level: his model was to be imitated by all colonies, or perhaps by all colonies of a certain type (e.g., those requiring a strong army, as his interest in military affairs would suggest). He raised political discussion to a more ideal level, for much that he proposed for his fictive city was entirely novel.

The most striking novelty was his provision for a distinct soldier class within his imaginary citizen body. The land was divided into sacred, public, and private land, which was always done at the founding of a city. But normally the public land would be restricted to marketplaces. Hippodamus' public land included one-third of the land of the polis. This public land was to be used for the support of the soldiers, though Hippodamus did not explain how they were to work it; and the soldiers would thus be free to devote themselves entirely to war. Actually Hippodamus proposed a division of the citizen body into *three* orders—soldiers, farmers, craftsmen—but as all were to have the same political rights it is hard to see what effective legal or social distinction there could be between the last two. His real innovation was the establishment of a quasi-Spartiate military class, which would effectively divide the citizen body into two groups, soldiers and civilians. The significance of this was obscured by his insistence on tripartite divisions. There were also to be three different kinds of law. (Hippodamus' affection for the number three has been attributed to Pythagorean influence or to some numerological speculation inherited from Ionian natural philosophy).

Aristotle seems slightly bemused by this man. He introduces Hippodamus with a detailed account of his personal eccentricities—we gather that anecdotes about him still circulated at Athens—as though to warn his pupils that this was not a thinker to be taken very seriously. And Hippodamus does seem an isolated figure: a Sophist architect, without predecessors or successors. When they said that he had invented the regular planning of cities, perhaps they meant that he had developed a philosophical theory about city planning. This theory would have included social and political planning; the first principle would have been the division of the territory into three parts corresponding to three orders of citizenry. If that is what Hippodamus' treatise on the city was like, it was a unique effort so far as we know. He does not appear to have left any disciples. Later constitutional planners lost interest in the physical planning of cities, except in the casual way that Plato and Aristotle treat the subject. Later architects were considered to be mere craftsmen, and Aristotle did not know quite what to do with an architect who meddled in political theory. Hippodamus may have been one of the strangest and most original products of the sophistic Enlightenment. Perhaps the most revealing feature of his fictive constitution was a law rewarding anyone whose discoveries benefitted the city, meaning political changes as well as improvements in the arts and crafts. Aristotle devoted to this proposal nearly half his critique of Hippodamus; he called it a recipe for instability, for it confused political change with technical innovation. That is probably what Hippodamus had in mind. He must have thought Protagoras' political art as open to progress as architecture, in which his own lifetime had seen tremendous advances. He wanted to create a society as open to innovation as Periclean Athens, but even readier to reward individuals like himself. Our scant information about him suggests a self-confident rationalism unprecedented in politics.

So Hippodamus appears to have been an isolated eccentric, his constitutional speculations preserved perhaps because they were attached to a more influential work on city planning, their significance never realized until the schools of Plato and Aristotle made the ideal city a central subject of philosophy long after Hippodamus was dead. But then why did Aristotle think Hippodamus was important at all? Partly, of course, because he was the first person anyone could remember who had written something that looked like a model philosophical *politeia*; but also, I suggest, because Hippodamus had introduced into the discussion of the best constitution a theme that assumed much importance in the schools of Plato and Aristotle: the imitation of Sparta.

Spartan influence on Hippodamus has been questioned on the grounds that his three orders had no exact Spartan counterparts.[18] But if Hippodamus was trying to produce a *synthesis* of the best elements found in existing constitutions—and why else would he want to plan a city that did not exist?—then he would have found it philosophically and politically appropriate to avoid exact parallels with existing constitutions. His military class could only have been modeled on the Spartiates. It was obvious to all in the late fifth century that Spartan military superiority, still unquestioned on land, was the result of cultivating a hoplite class devoted exclusively to military training; it was inevitable that Sophists interested in the best constitution should look closely at this institution, even if their sympathies lay with democracy; the supposed inventor of this system, Lycurgus, perfect model of a founder/lawgiver/hero, was unlikely to be ignored by Hippodamus. Aristotle assumes the three classes were equal in number; which gives us a military class of 3,333 warriors, about the same size as the Spartiate body in the late fifth century. It was probably assumed that the public land, from which this class was to support itself, would be worked by slaves; perhaps public slaves, perhaps public serfs like the Spartan helots, but Hippodamus chose not to go into this question, which later caused much controversy among admirers of Sparta.

Hippodamus' model differed from contemporary Sparta, and from all later attempts to imitate the Spartan constitution, in one crucial respect: his city was not to be an oligarchy. His quasi-Spartiate class was presented as the military arm of a moderate democracy, less democratic than Athens only in that offices were to be filled by election rather than lot; his magistrates were to be elected from and by all the citizens, and all the free inhabitants of the polis were to be full and equal citizens.

Aristotle thought this combination of democracy and a military elite to be totally unworkable, and if he has reported Hippodamus' plan accurately it is difficult to disagree. Aristotle pointed out that the majority of citizens who could not possess arms would be ineligible for the highest offices such as generalships, and therefore the armed one-third would be the real rulers. A full citizen who could not do military service would have been an impossible contradiction in a Greek city. Aristotle insisted on realistic definitions of citizenship; he criticized the model constitutions of Plato on the same grounds.

Despite the fundamental incoherence of his system, Hippodamus was a thinker of seminal importance: the first to write something that we can recognize as a utopia, to use a fictive literary form that all later utopists would imitate, to conceive the possibility of a written constitution as a synthesis of elements drawn from existing constitutions (the germ of the later "mixed constitution"), to think of the Spartan constitution as a universal model.

Critias of Athens and Radical Laconism

In the time of Herodotus and Hippodamus the Spartan state was admired even by democrats for its military prowess and political stability, but we can find no desire to emulate the peculiar Spartan culture, nor even much awareness that it was peculiar; no interest in the Spartan *agoge* or public education, nor even awareness that the Spartans were unique in having a system of public education. But during the late fifth century the long war with Athens made Sparta, traditional protector of Greek oligarchies, a model for oligarchic behavior in a more comprehensive sense, and the factional conflicts exacerbated by the war spread this new ideological brand of oligarchy everywhere. The victory of Sparta over the Athenian democracy in 404 seemed to prove the superiority of her institutions; and the next three or four decades, until the crushing defeats by the Thebans at Leuctra in 371 and at Mantinea in 362, saw the high point of Spartan prestige and the creative period of what has been called the "Spartan mirage."[19] An idealized image of the Spartan *politeia* fixed itself in the Greek mind as a pattern for stable oligarchy and made a lasting impression upon the nascent Greek utopian tradition.

Aristotle knew of a number of writers who had praised the Spartan constitution on the grounds that it was best suited for war and conquest, and he implies that most of these wrote before the battle of Leuctra in 371 undermined their premise (*Pol.* 1333b5–36). He mentions them in the context of a discussion about systems of education in the ideal state, for apparently it was the common theme of these writers to praise the Spartan *agoge* for its success in producing good soldiers. Aristotle also implies strongly that the kind of government favored by these writers resembled *despoteia*, the rule of a master over slaves, and not what Aristotle called "political" rule, where free men are governed by their fellow citizens in rotation. When Aristotle called a regime "despotic" he normally meant something very harsh.[20] He mentions by name only one of these writers, Thibron, the Spartan general who was sent out in the 390s to liberate the Greeks of Asia Minor from the Persians.[21] As Sparta was little given to literature, we can assume that most such writers were non-Spartan. We know there were Spartanizers or "Laconists" (*lakonistai, lakonizontes, philolakontes*) at Athens and other Greek cities in the late fifth century who emulated Spartan austerities in dress and physical culture, and who were assumed to be hostile to democracy.[22] We do not know whether this fad meant much or little, but it is clear that by this time Laconism frequently had both an institutional/political aspect and a cultural/educational aspect: it implied not only imitation of Spartan government, but imitation of the Spartan way of life.

If one considered only the first aspect, the "constitution" of Sparta in the narrower modern sense of the word, there could not have been much doubt that Sparta was an oligarchy, albeit with some peculiar features. The word *oligarchia*, "rule of the few," was vaguer than we often think. After the rise of the Athenian democracy ca. 500 B.C., it meant any city-state that was not like that: the traditional pattern, doubtless followed by most city-states at any given time, which invested leadership in a wealthy minority of landowners, and counted them the only citizens or the only active ones. In some cases these might include the entire hoplite body, all those with sufficient property to serve as heavy infantry in the phalanx; perhaps a third of the free native-born males, which was more democracy than was found in Western Europe until the late nineteenth century A.D. But many oligarchies had a ruling class far smaller and wealthier than this.[23] However the "few" were defined, their rule was typically secured in two ways: the basic political right of participation in the citizen assembly would be restricted by a property qualification; and the powers of the assembly would be curtailed by strong councils and magistracies, appointed by election and not by lot, their membership often restricted by a still higher property qualification.

The institutions of Sparta generally fit this oligarchic pattern. It was true that all the citizens or Spartiates had a voice in the assembly, and that the leading magistrates or ephors were elected from and by all the Spartiates; but the assembly was always dominated by the uniquely aristocratic and powerful Council of Elders (*gerousia*) and the even more idiosyncratic institution of the dual hereditary monarchy. It was true that there could be some question as to who the "citizens" were. Greek definitions of citizenship varied confusingly, as Aristotle found, and in Lacedaemon the situation was complicated by the size of the polis, the number of peculiar classes into which its population was divided, and the ambiguous terms used to describe these groups. The official name of the polis was "The Lacedaemonians"; but sometimes this meant the Spartiates, the only people with political rights, a small minority among even the free Lacedaemonians. The ambiguity of Lacedaemonian "citizenship" would later make it possible to claim that Sparta was a sort of democracy. But the evidence suggests that the original version of the Spartan mirage emphasized the authoritarian aspects of the system.[24] The early Laconists to whom Aristotle refers apparently did not claim Sparta to be any sort of democracy; they admired her because she was "despotic." What made Sparta an obvious model for despotic rule was the fact that she held large numbers of *Greeks* in a servile condition. Every polis had slaves, but slaves were normally expected to be non-Greek.

On the other hand, when outsiders looked at the Spartan way of life, they saw things that appeared to be the antithesis of traditional oligarchy. The Spartiates, within their own ranks, were the most ostentatiously egalitarian of all Greek citizen bodies. They called themselves "The Equals" (*homoioi*). They shared a common, formalized upbringing, the *agoge*, directed and paid for by the city, which required every Spartiate except the kings to pass through a complex series of age classes, each a rigorous test designed to produce disciplined and obedient soldiers. Each Spartiate was then assigned an estate worked by public serfs (helots) and forbidden to engage in any economic activity but landholding, or in any occupation but war. At Sparta itself even currency was said to be forbidden. Inequalities in landed property, which always existed and in the fourth century became glaring, were superficially reduced by the enforcement of a common and austere style of life. Family life was deliberately weakened by the all-male barracks society in which every Spartiate lived from early childhood. The main instrument by which the ties of property and family were weakened, and the loyalties of the citizen transferred from *oikos* to polis, was the system of common meals (*syssitia*). Every Spartiate upon entering adulthood had to be coopted by one of these messes (which corresponded in some way to the Spartan army organization, though exactly how is disputed), and continued to take his meals there even after marriage; failure to gain admission to a mess or to pay his dues meant the loss of his citizen rights.

Age classes and messing groups could be found in other Greek cities, but only at Sparta were these institutions combined into a unified and coherent system. Only at Sparta did the polis resemble a conscious work of art, in which everything had been designed to fix the thought and behavior of every individual in service to the community; and the impression of conscious design was strengthened by the insistent tradition that the system had been created *in toto* by one ancient, omniprovident lawgiver, Lycurgus. This strange society has never ceased to fascinate the world. When aristocratic circles in other Greek cities began to fall under its spell in the late fifth century, they perceived that its secret lay, not in the relatively ordinary Spartan political institutions, but in the unique collectivist features of Spartan social and economic structure.

It is doubtful that Greek oligarchs before the Spartan ascendancy had or needed anything that should be called an ideology. But when traditional aristocratic/oligarchic values were threatened by the Peloponnesian War and the democratic movements supported by Athens, some rational theory was needed, and the Spartan model provided one. Critias of Athens (d. 403) may have been a seminal figure in the creation of this Spartan myth. He wrote several works on *politeiai*, including two on the Spartan constitution, one in prose and one in verse; some fragments survive and can be supplemented by the *Constitution of the Lacedaemonians* attributed to Xenophon, the only Laconist tract to survive intact, which is probably based on Critias.[25] Both Critias and Xenophon believe the secret of Spartan success is found in the unique Spartan *nomoi*, by which they mean primarily the customs about family life and property. They praise the social and economic equality of the Spartiates, including the relative equality between men and women; but they do not value equality for its own sake, as do the democratic orators, rather because it serves the city and promotes military effectiveness. They consider the *syssitia* a valuable institution because they enforce moderation in food and drink and facilitate the indoctrination of the young, thereby producing better soldiers. The physical training of the Spartan girls in immodest costume, which shocked the rest of Greece, is praised for eugenic reasons: it produces healthy mothers who will bear better soldiers. Xenophon praises other collectivist practices: we are told the Spartiates shared one another's horses, dogs, servants, and provisions at need; that they shared wives freely for breeding purposes, and treated all children as their own; that their homogenous way of life and restrictions on money-making reduced distinctions between rich and poor and unified the citizens.[26] The opening sentences of Xenophon summarize the central theme of the Laconist school: there is a great gulf between the customs of Sparta and all others, and these unique collectivist practices are the key to Spartan political and military success.

But Critias wanted to imitate also Spartan methods of government, or at least pretended to want this when he, as leader of the "Thirty Tyrants," seized power at Athens with the support of a Spartan garrison in 404. He and his fellow conspirators gave themselves the Spartan title "ephor"; the council of thirty members may have been intended to correspond to the *gerousia*; their abortive constitutional program would have limited citizenship to the wealthiest three thousand Athenians, who may have been conceived as an elite corresponding to the Spartiates; the teaching of dialectic was banned and the metic (resident foreigner) population attacked, perhaps in imitation of Spartan hostility to sophistry and foreigners; Xenophon gives Critias a speech (*Hellenica* 2.3.34) in which he holds up to the Thirty the model of Spartan government, and the lesson he wishes them to draw is the need for rigid discipline among the rulers. In one of the fragments of his prose *Constitution of the Lacedaemonians* Critias describes the ruthless measures used at Sparta to hold the helots in subjection, the point being that in Lacedaemon one is either wholly free or wholly slave, and apparently that the one condition requires the other.[27] It is clear that Critias valued Sparta because he considered it the best model of an authoritarian and hierarchical polis and praised its egalitarian and collectivist features, to which he may have been the first to draw attention, because he saw them as means to the first end. To him Sparta was the best constitution because it represented disciplined collectivist oligarchy: the supreme *herrenvolk*. How far he meant to put any of this into practice at Athens we do not know.[28] But at least the activities of the Thirty show that this type of rhetoric was expected to appeal to aristocratic and oligarchic opinion. And there is evidence for other Laconist political experiments around that time.

Phaleas of Chalcedon and the Laconist Utopia

Aristotle remembered Hippodamus as a famous man, but he knew nothing or nothing worth relating about Phaleas of Chalcedon, not even his time or place; yet Phaleas had written a model constitution that Aristotle saw fit to discuss at some length (*Pol.* 1266a–1267b). Since his activities must have fallen chronologically between Hippodamus and Plato, the most plausible setting for them is the end of the Peloponnesian War, when the Spartans were setting up oligarchical regimes everywhere in the cities that had formed the Athenian empire, one of which was Chalcedon on the Bosporus.[29] Some of these cities must have witnessed Laconophile constitutional experiments of the sort that we know occurred at Athens between 411 and 403. Phaleas was most likely an obscure Sophist, perhaps a pupil of Thrasymachus of Chalcedon,[30] who attempted to raise these discussions to a higher theoretical plane, and perhaps to provide a cover for a real program of some kind, by circulating a paradigmatic constitution of the type invented by Hippodamus.

Phaleas' plan was designed primarily for new colonies, but he thought it would also be possible to introduce the proposed reforms into established cities in a more gradual fashion. We assume that Hippodamus had made much the same assumptions, but apparently Phaleas discussed the problem of implementing his model in more specific terms. What he proposed was a polis with a citizenry restricted to a small body of landowners, all of whom were to receive equal plots of land at the colony's foundation, and all of whom were to receive the same education. All artisans were to be public slaves.

What was novel about these proposals? The idea of equalization of landed property was what drew Aristotle's attention and preserved the name of Phaleas for posterity. But at first it is not obvious why this was thought a novelty. Distribution of land by drawing lots had always been a common practice when a new colony was founded, and we may assume the lots were usually made as equal as possible.[31] The constitution of Hippodamus—if, as I surmise, it also purported to be a plan for a new colony—probably assumed equal distribution of land. When Aristotle says that Phaleas was the first to propose equal property, he presumably means that Phaleas was the first to suggest redistribution of the land in *established* cities. He hoped to accomplish this gradually through inheritance laws, a program which Aristotle was surely right to find impractical.

Secondly, all the citizens were to receive an equal education. The implementation of this reform in established cities would not be too difficult, if the citizens had already accepted the principle of equality, and Aristotle has no comment on the matter. But Aristotle found the proposal vague. Phaleas was not very specific as to the content of this educational program, nor did he say anything about military matters. He did not, therefore, describe in detail a regimen like the Spartan *agoge* for his fictive citizens. But surely that was what he had in mind. The very idea of a common and compulsory state-controlled *paideia* could only come from Sparta. Phaleas' citizen body was to be a group like the Spartan Equals, except that they were to carry the principle of equality in property to lengths unheard of even at Sparta; and economic equality was to be supported, as it was at Sparta, by social homogeneity. Phaleas seems to have been oddly imprecise about the details, but if he was writing for an unstable, new, oligarchical regime under the Spartan hegemony he may have found precision about certain matters impolitic.

Finally, all the artisans were to be made public slaves, *demosioi*. Though Aristotle says little about it, this strikes one as perhaps a more significant innovation that the equalization of land. It was the corollary of equality: the citizen body was to be restricted to a landowning elite, which could then be consolidated by the imposition of economic equality and social/educational equality. The proposal to create a large body of state slaves was probably an attempt to duplicate the peculiar social structure of Lacedaemon. This problem came up again in all later efforts to imitate the Spartan constitution. All could see that model required a large servile work force to support a leisured citizen class. Should this work force be provided by state serfs like the Spartan helots, who were notoriously prone to rebellion? There was much discussion about this; Plato says the most vexed of all constitutional questions was that of the Spartan helotage (*Laws* 776). Phaleas was perhaps the first to raise this question; and he suggested a solution that would be followed by Aristotle and others: the place of the Lacedaemonian helots would be taken by slaves of the city. There were small groups of city slaves in many cities, like the Scythian archers who provided the Athenian police force, but so far as we know no one before Phaleas had proposed such an important role for this type of slavery. But how was *this* idea to be gradually introduced in established cities? If applied to a democratic city, it must mean that the majority of the citizens would lose not only their citizenship but their freedom. How was it that Phaleas had such specific plans for implementing the easier part of his reform program—the equalization of land within a restricted citizen body—and said nothing about how to implement the harder part, the restriction of citizenship? Perhaps Phaleas intended this only for a certain type of established city. Aristotle, in discussing the question of whether manual workers should be citizens (*Pol.* 1277b33ff.), says that in some places the working class is composed mostly of slaves or foreigners, or descended from such. Phaleas' proposals seem more practical if designed for cities where the workers had never had citizen status.

Whatever qualifications he may have added, this was still a model for "iron-fisted oligarchy."[32] Its affinities with the program of Critias seem obvious. Critias also claimed to imitate Sparta, and wanted to exclude from citizenship the greater part of the Athenian citizen body; so far as we know he did not mention installing anything like the *agoge* and the *syssitia* during his brief dictatorship, but he had written much about these institutions, and we may suppose the idea lay somewhere in the background. Critias, however, spoke of imitating Sparta directly. Phaleas had found a more indirect method: the utopian constitution, a genre invented by Hippodamus some time before. It now became, and so far as our evidence goes remained, the instrument of Laconist oligarchs, whose main purpose was to find ways to export the military elitism of Sparta to more typical Greek societies. Aristotle thought Phaleas important because he was the first who attempted to eliminate social conflict by regulating property, i.e., by proposing a more thorough regulation of property than anyone had ever proposed or practiced; by developing a certain social model, the collectivist elite, which was to attract both Plato and Aristotle. There are also hints that Phaleas understood that abstract models must be implemented at different levels of reality, suggesting the hierarchies of model cities that we find in Plato and Aristotle.

Moderate Laconism and the Mixed Constitution

After Critias was defeated and killed in 403, Laconist sentiments at Athens tended to take forms less radical and less immediately political. Two tendencies can be discerned. Some turned to a cultural and educational imitation of Sparta, an attitude best represented among surviving authors by Xenophon. His *Constitution of the Lacedaemonians* praises the *agoge*, *syssitia*, and other communistic customs but contains no hint of their basic political purpose; he does not say, as Critias said outright, that the goal of the system is to enable an elite to control a larger population; he has not a word to say about helots or other subordinate classes, for by "Lacedaemonians" he means the Spartiates only, as though nobody else lived in Lacedaemon. Except for commending their obedience to their magistrates (8.1–4), he has nothing to say about the governance of the Spartans. What he holds up for emulation is Spartan moral discipline, and he never says exactly who is to do the emulating. In Xenophon's *Memorabilia* (3.5.14ff., 4.4.15) this idealized Spartan constitution is practically identified with an idealized Athenian "ancestral constitution," meaning the state of affairs supposed to have existed before the rise of extreme democracy.

Even in Xenophon the Spartan model is not entirely defused of political impact. When he praises the Spartan ephorate and *gerousia*, he means to imply that the powers of the Athenian assembly should be reduced; oligarchy was associated with strong magistrates and councils. He tells with approval (*Hellenica* 5.3.17) how king Agesilaus organized the oligarchical exiles from Phlius into *syssitia* ca. 380. Here was a concrete example of the imitation of Spartan cultural/educational institutions by foreigners such as the *Constitution of the Lacedaemonians* tries to encourage, and here it was not apolitical at all; its purpose was to forge disciplined military/political elites capable of imposing oligarchy on Phlius. Still the Laconism of Xenophon seems theoretically compatible with a moderate democracy; the extent to which such language served as a cover for more extreme oligarchical views we do not know.

The other tendency took the form of a more serious political theory, but it did not use the same language as Critias. Before the middle of the fourth century certain Athenian schools were discussing what they called the "middle constitution" (*politeia mese*) or "mixed constitution" (*politeia mikte*). There seem to have been two main versions of this theory, though we need not try to separate them too carefully; there is little sign any Greek did.[33]

One version, apparently the original one, held that the best constitution is neither democracy nor oligarchy, but a constitution intermediate between those two extremes. This idea first appears in Thucydides: he describes the abortive Athenian constitution of 411, which gave power to those able to afford hoplite equipment, as a "moderate blending of the few and the many" (8.97.2). In *Politics* 4.8–9 Aristotle recommends a blending (*mixis*) or combination (*synthesis*) of democracy and oligarchy; he thinks it important that the blending be thorough, so that the final product might be described as either a democracy or an oligarchy with equal truth. This idea doubtless originated as an attempt to find a compromise between oligarchic and democratic factions. It was closely tied to political and social realities; it took account of only these two elements because they were the only ones that usually mattered in Greek city politics. It is difficult to believe that this version of the theory had anything to do with Sparta originally, because there was no real democracy at Sparta. The theory originated at Athens, and insofar as its supporters had any historical model in mind it was the "ancestral constitution" of Athens. Nevertheless Aristotle himself, at one point, seems to accept the view that Sparta represented an ideal mixture of democracy and oligarchy (*Pol.* 1294b18–35).

An alternative version was that held by the nameless people Aristotle mentions at *Pol.* 2.6 (1265b30ff.): the best constitution was said to be a mixture of *all* types, the more the better. This theory was specifically applied to Sparta and probably developed with Sparta in mind, because in addition to the usual oligarchic and democratic features the Spartan constitution had monarchy, and those captivated by the theory could claim that they recognized in the ephorate the principle of tyranny. This seems essentially different from the previous theory. These people were no longer speaking of a practical compromise between democratic and oligarchic socio-political forces, rather of a somewhat artificial process in which we borrow various institutions from a wide variety of constitutions, and the result was sometimes described not as a harmonious blend but as a system of checks and balances (a notion first developed in Plato's *Laws*[34]). Though the terms were used interchangeably in antiquity, it is the first version that seems more properly called the "middle" constitution, and the second version the "mixed" constitution. The second version, because it was later taken up by Polybius and applied to Rome, became the "theory of the mixed constitution" familiar to students of political philosophy. It owed its continuing popularity largely to the fact that it might mean almost anything. A "synthesis" is an arbitrary concept if the number and nature of the items to be synthesized are arbitrary, and in ancient discussions of the "mixed constitution" they often seem so. This type of "mixed constitution" did not have to have any serious connection with real democratic socio-political forces; it did not have to have any serious connection with anything.

Though the second version fitted Sparta more easily, *both* versions were being applied to Sparta in the schools of Isocrates and Plato by the 350s. The oligarchic element was always located in the *gerousia*, which was selected from certain families *de facto* and perhaps *de iure*. (This might be called the "aristocratic" element if one emphasized the fact that the Elders were supposed to be chosen for merit and enjoyed an unusual lifetime tenure.) Sometimes other typically oligarchic features were mentioned, such as the use of election rather than lot and the great authority entrusted to elected officials. The democratic element was sometimes found in the right of the assembly to elect the *gerousia* and share in the ephorate; but others saw it not so much in institutions of government as in the *agoge*, the *syssitia*, and the other habits of daily life. Since the exercise of some political powers by an assembly was not uncommon among moderate oligarchies, it was probably the second argument that constituted Sparta's strongest claim to democracy. (Besides, those who were determined to mix as many constitutions as possible used the ephors to represent tyranny; *Laws* 712, *Pol.* 1265b.) Monarchy, of course, was invariably located in the dual kingship.

Pedantic though much of this sounds, it raises a question that must be answered if we want to understand classical Laconism. How could anybody have ever thought of Sparta as a democracy of any kind? This was a system that invested absolute control over the largest polis in the Greek world, with a population that numbered perhaps in the hundreds of thousands, in a group of a few thousand men.

Sometimes the contradiction seems to have been vaguely recognized. Around 355 Isocrates called the Spartan constitution the most democratic of all because of its social egalitarianism and methods of election (*Areopagiticus* 61); ca. 340 he said the Spartan system was a democracy with aristocratic features, resembling the ancestral constitution of Athens, which Lycurgus had copied (*Panathenaicus* 153ff.); but later in the same oration he blamed the Spartiates for reducing the *demos* of Lacedaemon to slavery (so he describes the status of the *perioikoi*) and setting up a kind of democracy meant only for themselves (176ff.). The point of the final passage seems to be that a democracy that excludes the *demos* is fraudulent.

It is more surprising to find such ambiguities in Aristotle. Aristotle was aware that in ordinary language "democracy" meant a city-state where there was no property qualification for citizenship. It was taken for granted that a city-state would contain large numbers of slaves, who were usually of non-Greek extraction; and it might contain large numbers of free inhabitants of foreign extraction, Greek or non-Greek, including many of slave ancestry; and it occurred to no one that any of these people had any right to citizenship. The familiar translation "citizenship" masks for us the extent to which the *politai* thought of themselves as a sort of tribal or fictive kinship group. Only free males of the ancient native stock of a place had any claim to citizenship in it. But in the classical period it was generally assumed that in a "democracy" all such would be citizens and would exercise at least the basic citizen right of participation in the assembly. Aristotle was careful about such definitions,[35] and yet he could take seriously the theory that Sparta had significant democratic elements. In this case he was somehow willing to accept the Spartiates, a tiny minority of the native inhabitants of Lacedaemon and a minority even of the free, as the Lacedaemonian *demos*. He criticized their property qualification as undemocratic and thought that in ancient Sparta citizenship had been more open; the present situation he accepted as an anomaly (1270a34, 1271a26ff.).

We may suppose this confusion began as a rhetorical ploy by Athenian oligarchs. At Athens citizen status was defined in opposition to slavery, so that all free native inhabitants came to be considered "citizens"; at Sparta citizenship was defined in opposition to other groups of native Greeks, free and unfree, the important factor being the rule of the "citizens" over all the rest. The Spartan conception of citizenship was as quintessentially oligarchic as Athenian citizenship was democratic, and we gather that in the fifth century Laconists had not hesitated to describe Sparta in those terms. But in the fourth century some claimed that Spartan citizenship was really "democratic," indeed that Sparta was the only real "democracy."[36] This idea is best explained as an attempt by Athenian conservatives to coopt the ideals of democracy, stealing the popular slogans of "liberty" and "equality" and giving them an antidemocratic meaning. The complicated class and ethnic pattern of the southern Peloponnesus and the genuine collectivism of the Spartan Equals would have lent it plausibility; but that it gained such currency at Athens suggests that Athenian democrats were as poor in theory as they were rich in slogans. Outside their own cities, Greeks were uncertain what "citizenship" was, and more uncertain what it ought to be.

Aristotle on the History of Greek Utopianism

Aristotle divided earlier writers on the "best constitution" into two classes (*Pol.* 1260b27ff., 1266a31ff., 1273b27ff., 1274b27–28, 1288b39). The first found their models in certain established constitutions that were thought worthy of imitation, particularly those of Sparta, Crete, and Carthage; and sometimes the ancestral constitution designed for Athens by Solon, before it was ruined by extreme democracy. This canon was already well established when Aristotle wrote. Sparta, Crete, and Carthage were thought to be very similar, and different from all other states (1272b24ff.); they had long records of internal stability; they were all thought to be "mixed constitutions" of some sort, for each had a "democratic" element, usually found in *syssitia* and similar collectivist institutions, coexisting with an oligarchic/aristocratic form of government. Sparta was the basic model; Crete was simply a surrogate for Sparta, as Sparta was believed to have borrowed her peculiar institutions from the fellow Dorians of Crete; Carthage was probably admitted to this company because it was the most important barbarian oligarchy and because some of its institutions were thought to resemble the Laconian model. Solonian Athens was sometimes added because it was also thought a good example of a stable mixed constitution, and Solon and Lycurgus were sometimes paired as the two great Greek lawgivers.[37]

Aristotle's practical models for the best constitution were drawn therefore from the moderate Laconist tradition described above. Its essential premise was that the ideal form of society is that kind of "mixed constitution" best exemplified by Sparta. As we have seen, there were other versions of the "mixed constitution," and it is unlikely the Laconist type was the original one; but it was the one that most interested Aristotle. He inherited this theory from the Academy, for all its elements appear in the *Laws* of Plato. Aristotle distinguishes this moderate, mixed-constitution Laconism from the earlier, more extreme, militaristic and despotic Laconist tradition represented by Thibron (and by Critias, though Aristotle does not mention him). Aristotle was highly critical of th second group, but he belonged himself to the first, which seems to represent the mainstream of Athenian conservative thought in the fourth century. The harsh edge had been taken off the Laconist model by stressing its "democratic" features and equating it with Solonian Athens.

The second category consisted of the purely theoretical "best constitutions" that had never gotten past the stage of discussion, designed by men who had never been real lawgivers like Lycurgus and Solon, and had never taken part in politics. Aristotle does not separate the two categories all that sharply; he does not say the theoretical constitutions were *meant* only for discussion; but he does say (1288b) that they were trying to produce an absolute best kind of constitution, without regard to the practical constraints that hindered the real lawgivers.[38] He then distinguishes two types of theory: (a) theoretical constitutions that included communism and equality between the sexes (no one but Plato had ever been interested in such things); (b) theoretical constitutions that did not include communism, but stayed closer to actual states and politicians. Some of these authors were philosophers and some were *idiotai* (ordinary men, meaning those who had been neither practicing politicians like Lycurgus and Solon nor recognized philosophers like Plato and Aristotle). We cannot be sure where Aristotle would have put Hippodamus and Phaleas, but we suspect they would be among the *idiotai*; and among the more philosophical theorists he doubtless placed his own plan for a best constitution, preserved in the seventh and eighth books of the *Politics*, and perhaps some earlier efforts by some of his associates at the Academy. This group of writers I have called the "low" utopians.

Aristotle is interested in earlier writers on model constitutions, practical and theoretical, because he sees them as predecessors of his own ideal state, which is a mixed constitution based loosely on Sparta. The only practical models he thinks worth mentioning are Sparta and a series of surrogates for Sparta. Among the theoretical models the only two he thinks worthy of examination are those of Hippodamus and Phaleas: Hippodamus because his was the first, and the first to make use of the Spartan military elite; Phaleas because he was the first to propose a significant idea, a collectivist oligarchy with a more-than-Spartan regulation of property, which was imitated both by Plato in the *Laws* and Aristotle in *Politics* 7–8. It is doubtful that either claimed to be a "mixed constitution" in the formal sense meant by Aristotle, who does not apply this phrase to them; but the borrowing of elements from existing states seems implicit in the concept of a synthetic constitution, and they were doubtless among the sources of the mixed-constitution theories that proliferated in the fourth century.

From all this we infer that the utopian constitutions written between ca. 425 and ca. 370 usually took the form of plans for new colonies, but could also serve as models for reform in established cities. They were meant to be realistic programs, completely realizable only in a new colony but partially realizable anywhere. They seem essentially the theoretical branch of the Laconist tradition. Aristotle says he has reviewed everything noteworthy and does not mention any non-Laconist examples; nor is there any evidence that there ever were any. Except for its eccentric father Hippodamus, who wrote before the ideological lines had hardened, this was a conservative oligarchic tradition. Which is not surprising: Athens was the center of the Sophists, and at Athens it was the conservative faction that was interested in radical theories about alternative regimes.

The *Ecclesiazusae* of Aristophanes

No writer that we have considered so far envisioned the possibility that a Greek polis might abandon private households and other private property. Yet ca. 393 this idea appeared full-blown in Aristophanes' comedy *Ecclesiazusae*. Furthermore, the proposal that Aristophanes treated comically turned up some twenty years later as a subject for serious philosophical discussion in Plato's *Republic*.[39] The Aristophanic and Platonic versions share the following features:

1. Community of property (*koinonia ton ktematon*): Aristophanes' character "Praxagora" and Plato's character "Socrates" both think that in the best possible polis all things will be owned and used in common as far as possible.
2. Community of women (*koinonia ton gynaikon*): a male-oriented way of expressing what would be more correctly called communism in sex, marriage, and family; they propose that in such a polis there will be no separate households nor permanent marriages, and children will be raised by all. The description "community of women" is misleading because they assume that such a system will entail—
3. Sexual equality: men and women will be treated alike in every way.

There are also striking differences—the goals of "Praxagora" are democracy and hedonism, those of "Socrates" are the opposite—but still they seem variants of the same basic concept. This is, in fact, the basic Greek concept of utopian communism,[40] which was to draw the attention of various philosophers for some centuries to come. The fact that it first appears in a comedy has always been hard to explain. I will therefore summarize as much of the plot of the *Ecclesiazusae* as seems necessary to this inquiry.

The title is a coinage, and to an ancient Greek an oxymoron: "women of the assembly," women participating in politics and citizenship. As usual in the Old Comedy, the plot rests upon a fantastic premise, which is suggested by this title. The women of Athens decide to take over the polis. They disguise themselves as men, pack the assembly, and push through a resolution to turn over all affairs of government to the women, on the grounds that everything else has already been tried (456). Once in power, their leader Praxagora ("Busy in the Marketplace") realizes that to stay there she must propose some unheard-of novelty (578ff.). Therefore it is decreed that all things are to be held in common (*koinonein*), and all the citizens to have a common (*koinos*) and equal (*homoios*) way of life; all property, both land and movables, will be put into a common store; all individual *oikoi* (households) will be knocked together into a communal dwelling; all citizens will eat at *syssitia*; gold and silver will be forbidden; all slaves will be publicly owned and will do the work presently done by poor citizens, leaving the entire citizen body free to live in leisure; lawsuits will disappear and the courts of law will be turned into banquet halls. It is taken for granted that this system of communal property will entail the abolition of the family and the communal raising of children, who will regard all older people as their parents. The resulting sexual promiscuity will be curbed only by the principle of equality in pleasure, which is ensured by regulations favoring the old and ugly in sexual competition; this last is called a particularly "democratic" proposal (631, 945). The rest of the play shows this system being put into practice. The practical difficulties created by economic and especially by sexual equality are milked for laughs, but the new system remains undefeated at the end of the play. It concludes with a gigantic communal banquet, one of whose dishes has a name seventy-eight syllables long (sometimes said to be the longest word ever coined in any language, except for certain compound names used in modern chemistry), which symbolizes Praxagora's democratic, hedonistic, materialistic vision of the public good.

The general themes of this play would not have been unfamiliar to the audience. It conflates two old comic traditions.[41] One is the parody of Cronus' time, the plot of several earlier comedies, as we have seen. Some of these seem to have located the mythological paradise, or its near equivalent, in a distant land or new colony. Aristophanes had done something like this in the *Birds* (414 B.C.), where utopian expectations focus on the founding of the new city of Nephelococcygia. The other is the idea of a women's revolt. This exercised a certain fascination upon the Athenians, who even coined a word for it: *gynaikokratia*, the rule of women.[42] Aristophanes had dealt with this theme in earlier comedies (*Lysistrata*, *Thesmophoriazusae*). In the *Ecclesiazusae* he unites the two traditional comic premises by assuming that a revolt of women will restore the time of Cronus. The main point is to satirize the excesses of democratic politics, which provides the link between the two premises: extreme democracy is so addicted to reckless innovation that it can only end by giving political rights to women, and this madness leads to the even more harebrained experiment of communism. This communistic program is presented as simply a logical extension of "democratic" schemes for sharing the wealth, such as distributions of free food and clothing (411) and pay for assembly duty, which had been raised not long before this production (290ff.). It is assumed that communism must extend to sexual matters, which provides another link with gynecocracy.

Several of the motifs in Praxagora's program we have already met. Sexual communism and the communal raising of children come from the legends about the remote barbarians. Common messes, the abolition of currency, the insistence on citizen equality come from Laconist political propaganda. Even the proposal for public slavery recalls Phaleas of Chalcedon.

But here all these motifs seem to form a pattern. The fact that much the same pattern reappears in Plato's *Republic* makes it unlikely that the whole of it was Aristophanes' fantastic invention. The fact that the Aristophanic and Platonic versions of the argument are used for contrary political ends would appear to preclude the possibility of direct borrowing.[43] Therefore much ink has been spilled in the effort to identify the "common source" of Aristophanes and Plato.[44]

One obvious possibility is that Aristophanes and Plato found the idea of communism in some earlier philosophical treatise. Some scholars have assumed that such communistic proposals must have been widespread at Athens during the troubled years that followed the Peloponnesian War.[45] Against this we have Aristotle's assurance that no one but Plato had ever proposed community of women or common meals for women. That may leave open the possibility that Aristophanes knew of some thinker who dealt with such ideas but failed to work them up into a systematic treatise on constitutions, a *Peri politeias*, and therefore was not remembered as sufficiently noteworthy to come to the attention of Aristotle and his pupils when they began their researches into model constitutions half a century later. But there is nothing in the play that would lead us to associate communism with Sophists of any sort, or indeed with any particular individuals. And it is hard to believe that a thinker sufficiently obscure to escape the notice of Aristotle's school could have been known at any time to the general Athenian public, as he must have been to become the butt of a comedy.

Another possibility is that the Praxagoran program is an amalgam of various political proposals put forward by Athenian demagogues around the troubled turn of the century.[46] That seems a more plausible solution, for the play is clearly a satire on extreme democracy, and some prior acquaintance with its leading ideas on the part of the audience seems probable. But we do not know of any real program that could have suggested even vaguely the Praxagoran program. At Athens the only practical proposals for redistribution of wealth that we know about are such modest measures as those mentioned in the play.[47] An attempt to raise pay for assembly duty might well have been the *occasion* of this play, but not a source for it. And if any real proposal is being satirized here, it is difficult to understand why its author is not mentioned. Aristophanes was not usually so shy.

This perception of a common pattern may be partly an illusion, arising from a natural assumption that the target of Aristophanes' satire must have been some sort of utopian program like the one in Plato's *Republic*. But there were no such utopian programs around as early as the 390s; Aristophanes' satire could have nothing to do with what I call "low" utopias, though some of their motifs turn up unexpectedly here. We tend to forget that Aristophanes was making a joke when he pretended communism was a political theory or program.

I do find it difficult to believe that "community of goods and women" was entirely Aristophanes' invention. I think that he assumed in his audience some familiarity with the basic communistic syndrome presented in the play. They had heard that some remote barbarians were supposed to share all their goods and women; they had heard that some Greek Sophists admired them for this; they vaguely associated such things with democratic slogans and radical notions about women. If they had not learned this from Herodotus they might have picked it up from the drama, from Sophists' discourses, or from political oratory. It may have been already a rhetorical commonplace, useful to any moralist who wanted to shame the Athenians by pointing to the superior *koinonia* practiced by various foreigners.

Between Herodotus and Aristophanes two things had clearly happened to this formula. Firstly, community of women had become associated with gynecocracy. The most extreme form of "common intercourse" known to Herodotus was still male-dominated; and when he suggested that such a system might be desirable, that was because it promoted fraternity among males. Herodotus knew of some barbarians who treated women as equals in politics and war; the practitioners of sexual communism were not among these. But there was considerable discussion in late-fifth-century Athens, some of it in the theater, about the place of women in society and the justifiability of the traditional subordination of women.[48] It is unlikely that those interested in such questions failed to glance into the mirrors of the barbarians. In Aristophanes' play sexual communism is understood to imply sexual equality; the play makes better sense if we assume this association of ideas was not entirely new.

Secondly, elements from the Laconist tradition have been incorporated into the legend of barbarian sexual communism. This was a natural association; Spartans were well known to have certain communistic attitudes toward property and women. But the notion of "community of goods and women" that Aristophanes created, crystallized, or popularized was not Laconist. His play has *syssitia*, but they are not called Spartan, and they are not. At Sparta *syssitia* were not for women and not for gorging. By the time they reached the comic stage these ingredients were simmering in a monstrous democratic hash, which did not at all resemble the black broth of Sparta.

Household and City: The Social and Political Background of Greek Utopianism

Long before Plato wrote his *Republic* there existed a sophistic tradition of designing synthetic *politeiai*, dominated by the Spartan ideal of communal oligarchy; we may legitimately describe this as a variety of "utopianism." There also existed certain speculations about a more total form of communism attributed to the far barbarians; these might provoke moralism or ribaldry, but there is no evidence they as yet provoked political theory. The higher utopianism of Plato attempted to combine these two things. Before we turn to his achievement we should pause to take note of certain general features of ancient Greek society that may explain its obvious proneness to communistic notions. The evidence for the following generalizations comes mostly from Athens in the fifth and fourth centuries B.C., but they appear to be widely applicable to the Greek world outside Sparta and Crete.[49]

The first of these features presents us with an apparent paradox. The Greek economy, compared to other ancient economies, was distinguished by the fact that it was everywhere based on individual ownership. It did not normally invest any revisionary rights over landed property in the kinship group or the community, as in many primitive societies. Nor was the economy regulated by palace and temple bureaucracies, as in the Middle Eastern civilizations. Everywhere the basic social and economic unit was the *oikos*, the citizen household. This confusing word had three meanings: (1) a house, a dwelling place, which might be the home of anybody and not necessarily a citizen; (2) a *kleros* or citizen estate, the heritable property of a citizen, especially his property in land; (3) all the inhabitants of the *kleros*, including the dead, for the *kleros*, unless it had been divided, was expected to contain the tombs of one's ancestors. In the third and most abstract sense, the *oikos* was "that cluster of intangibles which constituted the family cult."[50] The first meaning we can disregard. The *oikos* as a social institution combined the second sense ("property") and the third sense ("family"). Obviously the subdivision of estates meant that in practice the two would rarely coincide, yet the *oikos* was commonly spoken of as though it were a single thing, a property/familial unit: a citizen plot, and a citizen lineage that lived on it and cultivated it in a theoretically inseparable hereditary relationship. The English word "household" in its original sense is the most adequate translation. An *oikos* in the sense of "estate" might be a single house in the town, a peasant plot of a few acres, or a vast and scattered collection of holdings. But whatever its size it was expected to be the possession of one master (*kyrios*), who was invariably a male citizen, land ownership being a jealously guarded privilege of citizenship, and for the most part the property lay at his free disposal. Not only was property holding individualistic in practice, it was fiercely competitive. It has been said that the average Greek's conception of "virtue" (*arete*) in the classical age was still Homeric.[51] A "good citizen" (*agathos polites*) was one who made every effort to maximize the wealth and power of his own household at the expense of all others in the city, and little notice seems to have been taken of the socially disruptive consequences of this value system.

But there is another side to the story. The Greek notion of ownership was by our standards, or even Roman standards, extraordinarily fluid and flexible. There was no concept of an absolute right to private property, like the Roman *dominium*. It does not seem to have occurred to any Greek in the classical period that protection of private property should be one of the major functions of the state. For one thing, property was as much familial as individual. An *oikos* was an inviolable possession, but the possession not so much of its immediate *kyrios* as of the citizen lineage whose current representative he was. An *oikos* was expected to remain within the same family, and there were strong moral and often legal sanctions against alienating or squandering it.

For another thing, property was as much communal as familial. The *oikos* was the essential building block of the polis, which may be described as a larger sort of property/familial unit. The "city" was not, as it is to us, a legal abstraction. The official name of the Attic polis was "The Athenians," a collection of some thousands of theoretically related citizen households. In many places tradition declared that the *oikoi* had been created through an original allotment of land by the polis. And where the polis was not the literal founder of the *oikoi*, it was still their lord. City and household could not exist without one another, but the city always came first. The city was always concerned to maintain the full number of households and to prevent the accumulation of households by individuals.

Therefore the sacredness of the *oikos* never led to the conclusion that private property was sacred. It seems that for practical purposes land was considered to belong in one sense to its immediate lord, in another sense to his whole kindred, and in another sense to the whole people. Apparently this ambiguity was felt to be appropriate and natural, for there seems little interest in a more precise demarcation of property rights. There was hardly even a word for them. Property ownership was normally expressed by the simple verbs "to have" (*echein*) and "to rule" (*kratein*). Marriage was spoken of in the same way: a man "had" a wife just as he "had" a house, and the word *oikos* included both possessions. Thus ordinary language made it easy to conflate marital and property relationships, and to merge the rights of the individual citizen in both areas with those of the family and the city.

This was, then, a world of competitive individual ownerships which at the same time cultivated a powerful sense of communal, even tribal, responsibility for the use of property. In particular, the obligation of the rich to share their property with the poor among their fellow citizens was an important feature of Greek life.[52] This was called *koinonia*—sharing, partnership, communion, association. It was one of a ubiquitous cluster of words that Greeks used to describe anything of a public or social nature (adjective *koinos*, common or shared, the opposite of *idios*, belonging to the private citizen; verb *koinonein*, to share or form a community). Greeks could not easily avoid using this group of words when they tried to discuss the state or society, which these terms did not distinguish. And the terms implied sharing. With respect to property, a good rich man was thought to be one who made his wealth *koinos* to all his fellow citizens. This was supposed to promote citizen concord (*homonoia*) and friendship (*philia*), virtues as prized in theory as they were uncertain in practice. This *koinonia* could take many forms. The rich were careful to establish bonds of friendship with their social equals through exchanges of good deeds; these "friends" supplied many of the services offered in more complex societies by bankers, lawyers, insurance agencies, and other occupations. The rich were also expected to benefit the whole citizen body by assuming unpaid offices, which took the place of many functions performed in more complex societies by government; and to help the poorer citizens with direct financial aid, including remissions of debts in hard times on the part of the very rich. Around 350 B.C. Isocrates claimed that in the old Athens the rich had shared their wealth so generously that its "use was common to all the citizens who needed it" (*Areopagiticus* 35). According to Aristotle, the citizens of Tarentum were said to "make property common for the use of the poor" (*Pol.* 1320b9–11). And in his critique of Plato's communism, Aristotle pointed out that the common *use* of private property was already practiced in well-run cities, mentioning specifically the peculiar collectivism of Sparta, but also with the universal Greek practice of *koinonia* in mind (*Pol.* 1263a29ff.).

The exercise of *koinonia* toward men of their own rank established alliances among the powerful; its exercise toward their poor neighbors established a network of patron–client relationships, which the powerful always found politically useful, and which philosophers were quick to see as a safeguard against the dreaded threat of *stasis* (civil strife). The ideal of sharing property was the social cement of a Greek city. It supported simultaneously the tradition of citizen solidarity and the tradition of aristocratic leadership. It had both democratic and oligarchic implications, and the philosophical theories to which it gave rise could emphasize either of these.

The ambivalent status of Greek property right made it easy, at a certain stage, for theories of philosophical communism to develop and win a hearing. These theories reflected an actual conflict, which in the late fifth century began to intensify, between the ancient communal nature of Greek landholding and the practical position of landholdings as essentially private properties. Only in an economy of private ownership could such a communistic ideal seem a radical alternative to existing society; only a society that did not hold private ownership sacrosanct could consider such a theory at all. Only in a society that had not yet reached the point of clearly separating family from property could these theories so readily embrace the notion of sexual communism. A low level of institutional development largely explains the appeal that this primitive tribal solution exercised upon the Greek mind. It seemed an obvious solution to the perennial conflict between the competitiveness of the households and the city's need for unity: merge the households into one great communal household. This was one of the criticisms that Aristotle advanced against Plato's *Republic*—that Plato had wrongly tried to merge the household and the city, seeking in the city a degree of unity possible only for the household. I suggest that Plato was indeed attempting something like that, and that some such vision had been in the minds of his predecessors when they talked admiringly of fraternal Spartans and Scythians. The total *koinonia* of the philosophers could seem merely a logical extension of the ordinary *koinonia*. It was presented as such by Plato, who introduced his proposal for *koinonia* in all goods and women by quoting the familiar maxim *koina ta ton philon*—"All things are common among friends."

Notes

1. See M. L. West, ed., *Hesiod: Works and Days* (Oxford 1978), 172ff.; H. C. Baldry, "Who Invented the Golden Age?" *Classical Quarterly* 46 n.s. 2 (1952), 83–92. The phrase "golden age" seems to have been coined by Augustan Latin poets. Greeks said *epi Kronou*, in the time of Cronus. Students of these folklore motifs often distinguish the "hard" utopia of arcadian simplicity from the "soft" type focusing on unlimited indulgence of appetites. Greek allusions to the time of Cronus might imply either. If the soft type prevailed on the comic stage it would not be surprising; but gluttony may be overrepresented in these fragments because they were preserved by Athenaeus (6.267–70), whose interests were largely culinary. One of these fragments comes from a play of Pherecrates (late fifth century B.C.) called *Miners*, the plot of which apparently included a trip to a Hesiodic eden in the underworld; another, from the *Persians*

attributed to Pherecrates, possibly had to do with Athenian expeditions or conquests in the Persian Empire; another, from the *Thurio-Persians* of Metagenes, located Cokaygne in the new Athenian colony of Thurii (ca. 443), famous for wealth and luxury.

2. Schol. in Plat. *Phaedrus* 279c. See Felix Jacoby, *Die Fragmente griechischen Historiker* (Berlin 1925–), 566F13; G. S. Kirk et al., trans., *The Presocratic Philosophers*, 2nd ed. (Cambridge 1983), 227. According to Diogenes Laertius, Timaeus attributed to Pythagoras not only the maxim *koina ta philon* but also *philia isoteta* ("friendship is equality"). The more important sources for early Pythagoreanism have been collected and translated by K. S. Guthrie et al., *The Pythagorean Sourcebook and Library* (Grand Rapids 1987): this includes the *Lives* of Pythagoras by Diogenes Laertius, Porphyry, and Iamblichus, the few fragments of early Pythagorean literature of generally accepted authenticity, and much pseudonymous literature produced in Hellenistic or Roman times.

3. The Academy was imitated by the Lyceum of the Aristotelians, the Garden of the Epicureans, and the Museum of Alexandria. See the wills of Theophrastus (Diog. Laert. 5.51ff.) and Epicurus (10.16ff.); and Werner Jaeger, *Aristotle: Fundamentals of the History of His Development* (Oxford 1948), 314ff. The doxographer Diocles of Magnesia (first century B.C.) wrote that Epicurus, when he founded the Garden ca. 300, rejected the idea of making his disciples put all their property into a common fund (*eis to koinon katatithesthai tas ousias*) like the Pythagoreans (Diog. Laert. 10.11); if the story is authentic, it shows that the Pythagorean organization was remembered by Athenian schools as a distinct alternative, which no one imitated.

4. Justin 20.4.14 speaks of a *hetairia* of young men. Such clubs were prominent everywhere in Greek political life, especially among the Greeks of Italy (Polybius 2.39.1).

5. Even Iamblichus, who calls the inner circle of Pythagoreans *koinobioi* ("cenobites," those who live in common, a term soon to be adopted by Christian monks), and describes them as holding everything in common, mentions that Pythagoras had his own house, and describes the fraternity as eating together and spending time together rather than living together in a literal sense. Diodorus Siculus, an Italian-Greek historian of the first century B.C., says the Pythagoreans had *koinonia tou biou*, but apparently what he means by this is that they retained their private property and shared it with one another as needed (8.2,10.3.5).

6. On the fragments of Middle Comedy dealing with Pythagoreans, see Walter Burkert, *Lore and Science in Ancient Pythagoreanism*, trans. E. L. Minar, Jr. (Cambridge, Mass. 1972), 198ff.

7. This passage (*Pol.* 7.10, 1329a40–b35) is generally thought to be an interpolation, but Aristotelian in substance.

8. In the perhaps spurious *Epistle* 7, Plato says he has left his disciples both a doctrine (*logos*) and a way of life (*bios*) (328a).

9. It seems most unlikely that Pythagoras could have invented the maxim "friends have all in common." This is mentioned by Plato and Aristotle as a popular saying, sometimes with reference to sharing property (*Rep.* 423e; *Pol.* 1263a29), but sometimes to friendship in general (*Phaedr.* 279c; *Nich. Eth.* 1159b31). In the *Republic* Plato had made it the motto of philosophical communism, and it was later quoted in that sense by Aristotle, the Cynics, and the Stoics. Therefore when Timaeus or his source claimed Pythagoras had been the first to say this, they probably claimed also that Pythagoras had been the real inventor of philosophical communism.

10. For this interpretation of Pythagoreanism I have relied largely on Walter Burkert, *Lore and Science*; idem, "Craft versus Sect: The Problem of Orphics and Pythagoreans," in *Jewish and Christian Self-Definition*, ed. E. P. Sanders et al. (Philadelphia 1980–1982),

3.1–22; idem, *Greek Religion*, trans. John Raffan (Cambridge, Mass. 1985). Burkert thinks that "At least for a period, in Croton and in other places, a form of communal life arose of men and women bound together by their special rules; these communities almost look like an early form of monasteries." Iamblichus is "probably following Aristoxenus" in his description of these communities (*Life of Pythagoras* 96–100), but "is writing with an eye to Christianity and may have retouched the picture" (*Greek Religion* 303, 464). For a more skeptical view see J. A. Philip, *Pythagoras and Early Pythagoreanism* (Toronto 1966), 142–46: he doubts that an early Pythagorean order or brotherhood ever existed and suggests it was invented by Hellenistic writers influenced by Plato's Academy; but as I have pointed out, the Pythagorean order was alleged to have gone far beyond the Academy in sharing property. For a less skeptical view see E. L. Minar, Jr., "Pythagorean Communism," *Transactions of the American Philological Association* 75 (1944), 34–46: he explains the silence of Plato and Aristotle on the grounds that they thought Pythagoreanism "unofficial", which I think correct; but when we consider what the distinction between "official" and "unofficial" meant to Greeks we must conclude that Plato and Aristotle failed to see anything political about Pythagorean community life at all, and therefore the picture drawn by Iamblichus must be retouched indeed.

11. Caucasians (1.203) and Indians (3.101) are also said to copulate in the open like animals, but it is not clear whether this means they practice "common intercourse."

12. The reversal motif in these stories has been studied by Simon Pembroke, "Women in Charge: The Function of Alternatives in Early Greek Tradition and the Ancient Idea of Matriarchy," *Journal of the Warburg and Courtauld Institutes* 30 (1967), 1–35; Pierre Vidal-Naquet, "Slavery and the Rule of Women in Tradition, Myth, and Utopia," in *The Black Hunter: Forms of Thought and Forms of Society in the Greek World*, trans. Andrew Szegedy-Maszak (Baltimore 1986); W. B. Tyrell, *Amazons: A Study in Athenian Mythmaking* (Baltimore 1984); Eva Keuls, *The Reign of the Phallus: Sexual Politics in Ancient Athens* (New York 1985); François Hartog, *The Mirror of Herodotus: The Representation of the Other in the Writing of History*, trans. Janet Lloyd (Berkeley 1988).

13. Diog. Laert. 3.37, 57. Diogenes Laertius found this in Favorinus, an encyclopedist of the second century A.D., who probably took it from Aristoxenus' *Life of Plato*.

14. A good example, which was once thought very early, is the little tract called the *Dissoi Logoi*: the author uses some of Herodotus' material, with such additions as the incest of the Persians and the immodest physical training of the Spartan maidens. Hermann Diels, *Die Fragmente der Vorsokratiker*, 5th ed., ed. Walther Krantz (Berlin 1934–1938) dated this ca. 400 B.C., but recently it has been argued that the tractate is a school exercise which could have been produced much later, perhaps even in Byzantine times: T. M. Conley, "Dating the So-Called 'Dissoi Logoi': A Cautionary Note," *Ancient Philosophy* 5 (1985), 59–65. It is translated in *The Older Sophists*, ed. R. K. Sprague (Columbia, S. C. 1972), 279–93. The literature of the skeptical schools of philosophy is filled with such "twin arguments"; see Diogenes Laertius' *Life of Pyrrho*, and the writings of Sextus Empiricus.

15. The suggestion that Protagoras' *Antilogica* was a source for Plato's *Republic* and also Aristophanes' *Ecclesiazusae* has been made before, and recently revived by H. D. Rankin, *Sophists, Socratics and Cynics* (London 1983), 86, 173–74, 222. Others have suggested that Plato could have been indebted to Protagoras for various other parts of the argument of the *Republic* which have nothing to do with communism: e.g., Italo Lana, *Protagora*, Pubblicazioni della facoltà di lettere e filosofia, Università di Torino, 2.4 (Turin 1950), 11–31. But the frequency with which Roman writers mention it suggests

that in antiquity, as today, communism was to the average reader the best-known feature of Plato's *Republic*; and this does much to explain the *schedon holen*.

16. A. Nauck, *Tragicorum Graecorum Fragmenta*, ed. B. Snell (Hildesheim 1964), fr. 653. Clement of Alexandria, who preserved this quotation, thought Euripides was proposing communism like Plato in his *Republic*. But wifely fidelity is a main theme of the Protesilaus legend, so this allusion to barbarian communism may not have been, in the context of the play, pro-barbarian or pro-communist.

17. A detailed history of Greek colonization is lacking; but see A. J. Graham, *Colony and Mother City in Ancient Greece* (Manchester 1964), and Irad Malkin, *Religion and Colonization in Ancient Greece* (Leiden 1987). On Hippodamus: Italo Lana, "L'utopia di Ippodamo di Miletos," *Rivista di Filosofia* 40 (1949), 125–51; J. R. McCredie, "Hippodamos of Miletos," in *Studies Presented to George M. A. Hanfmann*, ed. D. G. Mitten et al. (Cambridge, Mass. 1971), 95–100; T. D. Boyd and M. H. Jameson, "Urban and Rural Land Division in Ancient Greece," *Hesperia* 50 (1981), 327–42. The influence of colonization of Greek political thought has often been recognized, e.g., by T. A. Sinclair, *A History of Greek Political Thought*, 2nd ed. (London 1967), 6–7. The interpretation of Hippodamus which follows owes much to Lana and McCredie.

It used to be thought that Hippodamus was born ca. 500, but McCredie sees no reason to question the statement of Strabo (14.2.9) that he laid out the new town of Rhodes in 408/407. If so then he was born at Miletus ca. 475, settled in Athens and designed Piraeus ca. 450, settled in Thurii ca. 443 (that he also designed Thurii is a supposition, but a plausible one), and lived to design Rhodes ca. 408. This chronology gives him an unusually long career and means that the treatise known to Aristotle might have been written anytime during the latter half of the century.

18. E. N. Tigerstedt, *The Legend of Sparta in Classical Antiquity*, 2 vols. (Stockholm 1965–1974), 1.528 n. 117, questions Spartan influence on both Hippodamus and Phaleas on these grounds.

19. A phrase coined by François Ollier, *Le mirage Spartiate*, 2 vols. (Paris 1933–1943). The history of the Spartan legend has been treated by Elizabeth Rawson, *The Spartan Tradition in European Thought* (Oxford 1969), and by Tigerstedt's *Legend of Sparta*, to whose massive notes the reader may be referred for bibliographical information.

20. See *Pol.* 1255b16ff., 1277a33ff., 1278b30ff., 1325a16ff. By "despotic" rule Aristotle meant the rule that a master exercises over his household, particularly over his slaves. He distinguished this from "political" rule of the true and desirable sort, and considered all despotic government to be perverted by definition. Any constitution ruled in the interests of one section and not the whole could be termed "despotic" by Aristotle. Barbarian kingship was particularly despotic, owing to the slave-like nature of barbarians (1285a16). Oligarchies (meaning here the bad sort of oligarchy, not the good sort which Aristotle prefered to call "aristocracy") were by definition *syntonoteras* (most severe) and *despotikoteras* (most despotic): 1290a27. Cf. 1295b13f.

21. It may be significant that the only known Spartan writers on politics all wrote ca. 400B.C., at the time the Spartan hegemony was being established. Of these only Thibron is likely to have written for a general Greek audience. See T. A. Boring, *Literacy in Ancient Sparta* (Leiden 1979), 50ff.

22. Aristophanes, *Wasps* 463ff.; *Birds* 1281ff.; Plato, *Protagoras* 342b–c, *Gorgias* 515e. In the *Birds* Laconism is somehow associated with the Socratic circle. See my comments on this association in the next chapter.

23. We have no notion how large the ruling class of a "typical" oligarchy may have been. The only useful comment on the matter by a classical Greek writer appears to be

Pseudo-Herodes, *On the Constitution* 30–31, an oration probably delivered in 404 B.C., which suggests that an oligarchy was considered to be broad-based if one-third (presumably, one-third of the free native-born males), or all those who could bear arms (in the phalanx) had political rights. The draft oligarchical constitutions circulated at Athens during the closing years of the Peloponnesian War proposed citizen bodies of about that magnitude. But even the constitution of 411, which would have limited citizenship to about one-quarter, was thought too democratic by some Athenian oligarchs (Thucydides 8.92.11). See G. E. M. de Ste. Croix, *The Origins of the Peloponnesian War* (Ithaca 1972), 35 n. 65.

24. Many observers, including Aristotle at times, spoke of Sparta as an oligarchy without hesitation, and the fact that Sparta was the natural leader of Greek oligarchs everywhere was taken for granted (*Pol.* 1294b14ff., 1296a22ff., 1307bl9ff.). Xenophon assumed that around the year 404 all oligarchs thought Sparta the best of constitutions (*Hellenica* 2.3.34). So far as we know all attempts to imitate Spartan institutions during the years of unquestioned Spartan hegemony had the uncomplicated aim of replacing established democracies with oligarchies.

25. Ed. Diels/Krantz, 88B, 6–9, 32–37. Kathleen Freeman, trans., *Ancilla to the Pre-Socratic Philosophers* (Cambridge, Mass. 1948), 153–62; Sprague, *Older Sophists*, 241–70. The reputation of Critias is attested by the statue erected to him in some unknown city representing the triumph of Oligarchia over Democratia (Diels/Krantz 88A, 13). The attribution of *The Constitution of the Lacedaemonians* to Xenophon is generally accepted, and it is usually dated ca. 390. The fourteenth chapter contains observations about the decline of Sparta that seem out of key with the rest, leading some to consider this chapter an interpolation added after 371, and others to prefer a later date for the whole work.

26. On the *syssitia*, Critias fr. 6–9; Xen. 5. On Spartan women, Critias fr. 32; Xen. 1.3–10. On the other collectivist practices, Xen. 1.7–9, 6, 7. Spartan sharing of possessions is also mentioned by Aristotle, *Pol.* 1263a30ff. The custom of wife exchange is attested by later writers, e.g., Plutarch, *Lycurgus* 15.7, *On Lycurgus and Numa* 3.1.

27. Fr. B37, preserved by Libanius: *malista douloi te en Lakedaimoni kai eleutheroi.*

28. The Thirty in fact resembled a junta more than an oligarchy, either Spartan or conventional; and their proposed constitution was supposed to be based on the "ancestral constitution" of Athens, not Sparta. Many have thought the Spartan constitutional trappings were mere window dressing: S. Usher, "This to the Fair Critias," *Eranos* 77 (1979), 39–42; Andrew Lintott, *Violence, Civil Strife and Revolution in the Classical City, 750–330 B.C.* (Baltimore 1981), 161ff.; Paul Cartledge, *Agesilaos and the Crisis of Sparta* (Baltimore 1987), 282. For the other side see Peter Krentz, *The Thirty at Athens* (Ithaca 1982), 63ff.; and David Whitehead, "Sparta and the Thirty Tyrants," *Ancient Society* 13 (1982), 105–30. To determine just how far a politician's actions are influenced by his ideological slogans can be difficult even when the politician is alive and breathing.

29. Nothing specific is known about the constitution of Chalcedon at this time, but for the general background see Xen., *Hellenica* 1.3.2ff., 2.2.2, 3.4.7, 4.8.28, 5.1.25; H. W. Parke, "The Development of the Second Spartan Empire," *Journal of Hellenic Studies* 50 (1930), 37–79; A. Andrewes, "Two Notes on Lysander," *Phoenix* 25 (1971), 206–26. There was a Spartan harmost (governor) at Byzantium with a garrison at Chalcedon across the strait even before 408, and more or less continuously from ca. 405 till ca. 390. During the years 405–403 the Spartans planted small juntas called "dekarchies," councils of ten, in many of these cities. The Thirty at Athens was a junta of this type, and as we have seen it felt obliged to justify its rule by drafting a broader oligarchical constitution with Spartan borrowings. After 403 Sparta withdrew support from the

juntas and allowed the cities more constitutional freedom, producing great confusion. It was at this time that the Spartan general Thibron was sent to govern Asia; he may have circulated his treatise on the Spartan constitution to encourage Laconists in the Asian cities. By 389 Chalcedon was again a democracy and back in the Athenian orbit.

30. Chalcedon produced another famous intellectual, the Sophist Thrasymachus, who taught at Athens during the Peloponnesian War but went home to Chalcedon to die. In the first book of Plato's *Republic* he is made responsible for the doctrine that domination of the weak by the strong is a law of nature. It seems to be assumed that the primary application of this doctrine is to support oligarchy.

31. If a city had been founded by colonization or invasion, tradition often held that its land had originally been distributed by lot. This was true of the many Athenian colonies and cleruchies (military settlements) founded in the fifth century; true of older colonies like Cyrene (Herodotus 4.159) and Syracuse (Ath. 4.167d); and true also of cities that traced their origins to the legendary migrations of Ionians, Aeolians, and Dorians (Diodorus Siculus, 5.81, 83, 84; Plato, *Laws* 684). Since the Athenians were unusual in claiming to be the indigenous inhabitants of Attica, the normal city-foundation myth probably included division of the land by drawing lots.

32. Italo Lana, "Le teorie egualitarie di Falea di Calcedone," *Rivista critica di storia della filosofia* 5 (1950), 265–76 ("una oligarchia dal pugno di ferro," 272).

33. See G. J. D. Aalders, *Die theorie der gemischten Verfassung im Altertum* (Amsterdam 1968).

34. The third book of Plato's *Laws* (ca. 350 B.C.), the earliest extensive treatment of the mixed constitution that survives, contains both versions of the theory. The Athenian Stranger (693–702) argues that there are only two basic constitutions, which he calls "monarchy" and "democracy," but he means by this simply the opposed principles of authority and freedom, or what was usually meant by the oligarchic–democratic dichotomy; he thinks every constitution must include both of these; the most extreme form of monarchy is the Persian Empire, the most extreme form of democracy is Athens, and all other constitutions lie somewhere on the specturm in between, the best balance being achieved at Sparta and Crete. But when the Spartan system is described in detail, we do not hear of this dichotomy, but rather of checks and balances among several different elements: the Athenian says that the two kings, the *gerousia*, and the ephorate all act to restrain one another (691–92); the Spartan and Cretan speakers do not know whether to call their systems monarchies, aristocracies, democracies, or tyrannies (712).

35. At *Pol.* 1275a2ff., Aristotle attempts to define the term *polites*, citizen, noting that its meaning varied from one city to the next; a citizen was normally defined as anyone of citizen birth; slaves and foreigners were nowhere citizens, but many people who were citizens in a democracy would not be such in an oligarchy; for practical purposes Aristotle proposes to consider as citizens all who participate in political office to some extent, at least in an assembly. When he turns to the definition of democracy and oligarchy (1290a30ff.), he says that people commonly define these as the rule of the "many" and the rule of the "few," but these terms are meaningless in themselves. He points out that if we have a population of one thousand free men who are equals in every respect but property, and the poorest three hundred of them are excluded from citizenship, *no one will call this a democracy*. He clearly recognized that democracy normally meant the absence of a property qualification for citizenship, or the participation of all freeborn and native-born males in government; and in the *Politics* he normally adhered to this definition.

These distinctions would be clear enough at a place like Athens, where no distinctions of race were recognized among the native inhabitants. They may have been less clear in those parts of the Greek world where divisions persisted between original inhabitants and later conquerors, all of them Greeks; or where there existed classes of Greeks who were neither slave nor free, like the *helotai* of Lacedaemon and the *penestai* of Thessaly. The Dorians of the Peloponnesus preserved a tradition of an ancient conquest, which they felt a need to legitimate mythologically by describing it as a return of the sons of Heracles to their patrimony. Perhaps this myth seemed to support the claim of the Spartiates to be the only "people" of Lacedaemon. On the other hand, Aristotle added to his definition of democracy the caveat (1290b7ff.), "whenever the free are not numerous, but rule over a majority who are not free, we still cannot say that it is a democracy. . . ." Such a situation "existed in Apollonia on the Ionian Gulf, and on Thera; for in each of these states honours [citizen rights] were restricted to a minority—those persons of distinguished ancestry who had taken part in the original settlements" (trans. Sinclair/Saunders). These Dorian colonies seem to have had a social structure somewhat like that of Lacedaemon, but Aristotle does not tell us why he denied them the title of democracy and let it pass in the case of Lacedaemon. Was it simply because the elites at Apollonia and Thera had been overthrown?

36. Aristotle says there were "many" who described the Spartan constitution as a democracy (1294b); one of these, in some moods, was Isocrates. Aristotle also mentions "some" (1265b) who call Sparta a mixed constitution with important democratic elements, and at 1294b he seems to endorse this position himself. On the other hand, Aristotle sometimes says the Spartan constitution was an aristocracy in the time of Lycurgus, but has now turned into a democracy because of the power of the ephors (1270b, 1316a). Elsewhere he calls it a mixed constitution of aristocratic character (1265b), or an aristocracy mixed with democracy (1293b), or an aristocracy tending toward oligarchy (1307a, 1361b), or an oligarchy (see n. 24 above). Aristotle's views about Sparta clearly changed over time, probably in response to information received from his pupils' research. See R. A. de Laix, "Aristotle's Conception of the Spartan Constitution," *Journal of the History of Philosophy* 12 (1974), 21–30; we are not in a position to say what his final position was or whether he reached one. Also his use of the term "aristocracy" was confusing. In the passages cited above it probably refers not to a special type of constitution but to the equality of promoting virtue, which could be found in any constitution, especially one of "mixed" character. But his tendency to recognize some kind of democratic element at Sparta was persistent.

I find it difficult to resist the conclusions of de Ste. Croix, *Peloponnesian War*, 137, and Cartledge, *Agesilaos*, 129ff., that Spartan democracy did not mean much at any level. The arguments cited by Aristotle have the taste of special pleading. We notice that no one said the powers of the Spartan assembly constituted one of the democratic elements; yet the role of the assembly was one of the essential differences between democracy and oligarchy (cf. *Pol.* 4.14). Nothing would have enforced the hierarchical and authoritarian quality of this society like the *syssitia*, which foreign Laconophiles saw as its most "democratic" element. Some *syssitia* were better than others, and the competition to be chosen by the right ones must have created an atmosphere resembling the fraternity and eating-club societies of certain American universities in the recent past.

37. At 1273b Aristotle mentions Solon and Lycurgus as the two great examples of practical lawgivers, and describes the views of "some" who think the Solonian constitution mixed democracy, oligarchy, and aristocracy. It is not clear how Aristotle classified it. At *Pol.* 128lb32 he approves Solon's device of letting the people elect magistrates but not share in office themselves; in the *Constitution of the Athenians* 41

he calls the constitution of Solon a moderate democracy; but at 33–34 the moderate oligarchic constitution of 411 B.C. is called the "ancestral constitution."

38. The distinction between practical and theoretical models Aristotle had stated earlier in his *Protrepticus*, an exhortation to philosophy addressed to a Cypriot king. It is generally believed that this work is paraphrased in Iamblichus' *Protrepticus* 6–12. The relevant section is translated by Kurt von Fritz and Ernst Kapp in *Aristotle's Constitution of Athens and Related Texts* (New York 1950), 210–13. Here two kinds of lawgiver are distinguished. One type tries to imitate actual constitutions like those of Sparta and Crete and is compared to the kind of architect who copies other buildings directly. The other type is the philosophical lawgiver who understands the principles of justice and so forth; he is compared to the scientific architect who works with instruments like the plummet, line, amd compass. In the first category Aristotle presumably would have placed all those lawgivers and would-be lawgivers who wanted to imitate literally the Spartan, Cretan, or ancestral Athenian constitutions. The second category, the philosophical lawgivers, are those who wrote theoretical constitutions not attached to any earthly model. It has been pointed out that the author seems contemptuous of those who study historical constitutions. But by the time he wrote the *Politics* Aristotle thought practical and theoretical constitutions equally worthy of study. At *Pol.* 1288b he says that those who adopt a single city like Sparta as their model are misguided, but so are those who put forward a single theoretical city; what is needed is a wide range of models adaptable to different circumstances. The thought of both Plato and Aristotle seems to have moved in this direction, as we will see in the next chapter.

39. Aristophanes' *Ecclesiazusae* has usually been dated to 392 B.C., and sometimes as late as 389, but a recent editor favors 393: R. G. Ussher, *Aristophanes' Ecclesiazusae* (Oxford 1973), xx–xxv. Cf. Ephraim David, *Aristophanes and Athenian Society of the Early Fourth Century B.C.* (Leiden 1984), 2 n. 2.

Plato's *Republic* has been dated as early as 388, but most scholars favor a date in the 370s, and probably closer to 370 than to 380, for its completion. See the references provided by Alexander Fuks, "Plato and the Social Question: The Problem of Poverty and Riches in the *Republic*," *Ancient Society* 8 (1977), 51; reprinted in *Social Conflict in Ancient Greece* (Jerusalem 1984), 82; and Ussher, *Ecclesiazusae*, xvii.

40. The nearest thing to a general description of this system in Aristophanes is the phrase *koinonein pantas* (*Eccl.* 590): "having all in common," "sharing everything." Plato likewise calls it *panta koina* (*Rep.* 424a); he refers to the sexual aspect of it as *koinonia gynaikon kai paidon* (449d, 450c): "community of women and children." Aristotle uses such formulas as *panton koinonein* (*Pol.* 1260b39); *teknon kai gynaikon kai ktematon koinonein* (1261a4–5): "having in common children and women and goods"; *gynaikon kai teknon koinonia* (1264b30–31): "community of women and children."

41. See K. J. Dover, *Aristophanic Comedy* (London 1972), 201.

42. In Aristotle's *Politics* "gynecocracy" means any society where man are unduly influenced by their womenfolk—a condition Aristotle thought typical of several constitutions he disliked, including tyrannies, extreme democracies, and military societies (1269b23ff., 1313b32ff.). We know of two later comedies with the title *Gynaikokratia*, by Amphis and Alexis, both probably satires on Plato's *Republic*. The idea, but not the word, appears in Aristophanes.

43. The inevitable suggestion that Aristophanes took the idea of communism from Plato has been made often. The main difficulty with it is not the fact that the *Republic* was almost certainly written much later, for there could have been an earlier version, oral or written. Nor is it the absence of any reference to Plato in the play; for Plato could not have been the *real* target, Praxagora's democratic communism has nothing

to do with him. The main problem is that this hypothesis robs the play of any point: it makes Aristophanes caricature an unknown oligarchic theory to attack a nonexistent democratic theory.

The more chronologically obvious hypothesis, that Plato took the idea of communism from Aristophanes, has been made more rarely, I suppose because it is too difficult to believe that Plato borrowed his ideas from the comic stage, except to the few (to be discussed in the next chapter) who think that the *Republic* itself was meant as a comedy.

44. This literature, which is extensive and repetitious, is summarized in Ussher, *Ecclesiazusae*, xv–xx; and David, *Aristophanes*, 20–29. For the older literature see James Adam's edition of the *Republic* (1902), rev. D. A. Rees (Cambridge 1963), 1.345–55.

45. E. Pöhlmann, *Sozialismus* 1.331; J. B. Bury, *A History of Greece*, 3rd ed., ed. Russell Meiggs (London 1951), 587; Barker, *Greek Political Theory*, 87–88, 241–42, 252–53; Victor Ehrenberg, *The People of Aristophanes* (Oxford 1951), 67–68; Vidal-Naquet, *The Black Hunter*, 217–18. Ussher still favors the hypothesis of an earlier utopian philosopher.

46. Fuks concluded that "the ideas themselves [in the *Eccl.*] are not, as is commonly supposed, rooted in philosophical or folk utopianism, but in yearnings, schemes, proposals mooted in Athens in the 'nineties." See "Patterns and Types of Socio-Economic Revolution in Greece from the Fourth to the Second Century B.C.," *Ancient Society* 5 (1974), 62; reprinted in *Social Conflict*, 20. And his disciple David: "the ideas parodied by Aristophanes ... seem to be a complex mixture, an amalgam of contemporary schemes and proposals which had not yet taken the form of utopias, but provided the raw material for them" (*Aristophanes*, 22, 27).

47. Later in the fourth century proposals for land redistribution and debt cancellation became common in Greece, but we do not hear of them at Athens. There might have been such talk when the democracy was restored in 403 (see Andocides, *On the Mysteries*, 1.88; Arist., *Constitution of Athens* 40.3). Aristotle (*Pol.* 1276b) mentions a certain Diophantus who at some time had proposed increased use of public slaves at Athens, a minor element in Praxagora's scheme. David (*Aristophanes*) suggests that some demagogue might have proposed that the Athenians adopt and democratize the Spartan *syssitia*. But at Athens such Laconist ideas were associated with the oligarchic faction and especially with Critias, and one wonders if it is plausible that as soon as Critias was defeated democratic leaders began to imitate parts of his program. If any case, any of these proposals would be a long way from community of goods, and none could suggest community of women.

48. A recent survey of the problem of women at Athens is John Gould, "Law, Custom, and Myth: Aspects of the Social Position of Women in Classical Athens," *Journal of Hellenic Studies* 100 (1980), 38–59. The question of whether and in what ways women were the equals of men was being discussed in philosophical circles, especially the Socratic one, for which see the next chapter.

49. These and later remarks on Greek social and economic institutions are based primarily on the following works: Paul Vinogradoff, *Outlines of Historical Jurisprudence* 2: *The Jurisprudence of the Greek City* (Oxford 1922); Richard Schlatter, *Private Property: The History of an Idea* (New Brunswick 1951); J. W. Jones, *The Law and Legal Theory of the Greeks* (Oxford 1956); W. K. Lacey, *The Family in Classical Greece* (Ithaca 1968); A. R. Hands, *Charities and Social Aid in Greece and Rome* (Ithaca 1968); A. R. W. Harrison, *The Law of Athens: The Family and Property* (Oxford 1968); M. I. Finley, *The Ancient Economy* (Berkeley 1973); S. C. Humphreys, *Anthropology and the Greeks* (London 1978). The concept of the Greek city as fundamentally a kinship unit was the great contribution of N. D. Fustel de Coulanges, *La cité antique*. In this account

I ignore "kinship" units in between the household and the city, such as clan, phratry, and "tribe." These groupings were not universal and some might have been artificial creations of the polis. See R. L. Littman, "Kinship in Athens," *Ancient Society* 10 (1979), 5–31; and Finley, "Max Weber and the Greek City-State," in *Ancient History: Evidence and Models* (New York 1986), 88–103. If we restrict ourselves to the *oikos* and the polis we have the precedents of Plato and Aristotle: the former in the *Laws* and the latter in the *Politics* assumed that the basic social unit was the *oikos*, and the polis historically and logically an amalgamation of *oikoi*; they paid slight attention to any other grouping.

50. Harrison, *Law of Athens*, 92, 124.

51. See A. W. H. Adkins, *Moral Values and Political Behaviour in Ancient Greece from Homer to the End of the Fifth Century* (New York 1972).

52. See Fuks, "*Tois aporumenois koinonein*: The Sharing of Property by the Rich with the Poor in Greek Theory and Practice," *Scripta Classica Israelica* 5 (1979–1980), 46–63; reprinted in *Social Conflict*, 172–89.

2

The Platonic Utopia: A City Without the Household

He might have been relating a dream, or modelling a state and its citizens out of wax. ... But you must let the legislator finish describing what he really wants to do, and only then join him in considering which of his proposals for legislation are feasible, and which are too difficult. You see, even the maker of the most trivial object must make it internally consistent if he is going to get any sort of reputation.

The Athenian Stranger in Plato's *Laws* 746
(trans. T. J. Saunders)

The Paradox of Socrates[1]

The Socratic Problem

The several utopian and quasi-utopian traditions described in the first chapter furnished only raw materials for Plato's paradigm polis. The utopias of myth, comedy, and rhetoric remained in the world of fantasy; and those of the city planners and politicians, in the world of practicality. To fuse all this material together required a new philosophical inspiration, which came from Socrates. It will seem odd to call Socrates one of the founders of Western utopianism, and yet all the higher utopias of the ancient world were produced by Athenian schools that called themselves "Socratic," the first of them presented as Socrates' own teaching and the later ones stamped with his example. What was there about the teaching and example of Socrates that was so conducive to a sense of new potentialities in the city-state?

To address this question will require an approach to the "Socratic problem," but it will be an oblique approach. The reader is likely to have already some notion of the complexity of this problem and the difficulty of handling it in a few pages. Socrates left no writings but did leave a large circle of disciples who wrote about him, using a literary genre, the Socratic dialogue, which was probably invented to capture Socrates' unique method of teaching; this method, called the *elenchos* (the "refutation" or "testing" of opinions in debate) made it difficult to tell the real views of Socrates about most subjects; he was famous for professing his own ignorance, and even in his own time there seem to have been divergent interpretations of this posture; the Socratic writings of two self-proclaimed Socratics, Plato and Xenophon, have survived, but even where we can discern clear principles behind the Socratic screen it is difficult to say whether these are the views of the master or the disciple; there is an obvious apologetic quality to much of this literature, for all of it was put out after Socrates' execution and much of it for the explicit purpose of rehabilitating his reputation; and we have a few comments about Socrates from Aristotle which leave no doubt that many of the views attributed to Socrates in the dialogues could not have been his. It is not surprising that the views of Socrates, and the reasons he was executed for them, are subjects of continuing controversy. I do not propose here to solve this controversy or to determine the views of Socrates himself, but the more modest aim, which I hope will be adequate for the present purpose, of determining the general views of the Socratic *circle*.

The Socratic World View

The impact of Socrates was such that during the century after his death it seems that most philosophers at Athens, with the notable exceptions of the Epicureans and Pyrrhonists, identified themselves as "Socratics" and counted themselves among the spiritual heirs of Socrates. His influence was doubtless magnified by later doxographers, who tried to organize all the schools into orderly "successions" derived from a few prominent teachers; and some of the groups they classified as "Socratics" seem to have so little in common that a phrase like "Socratic world view" will arouse understandable skepticism. But there must be some explanation for the unique position of Socrates in the history of Greek thought. I suggest that Socrates and his immediate disciples did propagate a new and distinct outlook on life, which permeated Athenian thought in the early fourth century; and that its main characteristics were the following.

1. THE POLITICAL CRAFT

The Sophists had popularized the notion of a teachable political *techne* (art or craft). The Socratic approach may have begun as an attempt to explore the implications of the Sophists' claim to teach such a thing. In any case the Socratic movement eventually conceived its mission as that of building a firm foundation for this *techne*. Sophists had shown the practical utility of dialectic, the art of discussion and persuasion; the Socratics grasped its scientific possibilities, and hoped that logic, if applied more systematically, might bring a new order and coherence to human life. They defined, in short, a new goal for philosophy and a new role for the "philosopher," whom they soon distinguished from the "Sophist." Often they expressed this goal through the "crafts analogy," a figure of speech that occurs repeatedly in the Socratic writings of Plato and Xenophon. Nothing was thought more typical of the Socratic circle. The analogy is always introduced to make the point that moral and political excellence requires special expertise and skill, just like every other art and craft; and that all conventional approaches to morality fail because they have not tried to define the nature of the craft.[2]

2. THE CARE OF THE PSYCHE

Socratics did not hesitate to declare this ambitious goal because they thought they had found a clue to the problem, which they expressed in the somewhat enigmatic phrases "knowing the self" and "knowing virtue." They gave a new meaning to the familiar Delphic maxim, "know yourself." They identified the self with the *psyche*, a word that had many shades of meaning (spirit, ghost, soul), but to the Socratic circle came to mean the rational faculty. They assumed the main task of life was to care for this *psyche*; the word *arete* (virtue or excellence) was redefined to mean the excellence of the psyche; caring for it meant to develop the peculiar excellence of reason and to ensure that reason is dominant over all other faculties. They thought moral and political life would be placed on a sound foundation only when all citizens recognized the supremacy of reason. The youthful Plato made this the manifesto of the Socratic movement when he put the following speech into the mouth of Socrates at his trial:

> I spend all my time going about trying to persuade you, young and old, to make your first and chief concern not for your bodies or for your possessions, but for the highest welfare of your souls, proclaiming as I go, "Wealth does not bring goodness, but goodness brings wealth and every other blessing, both to the individual and to the State." *Apology* 30ab, trans. Hugh Tredennick

How does one develop the virtue of one's rational faculty? This must consist in a kind of knowledge: a Socratically virtuous person was one who possessed the knowledge of virtue, just as a medical practitioner was one who had knowledge of medicine. Therefore the first assignment for a systematic political craft was to establish precise meanings for the words normally used to express value, such as *arete*, excellence or virtue; *dikaiosyne*, virtue or righteousness; *eudaimonia*, happiness or blessedness; *sophrosyne*, moderation or temperance. In the earlier dialogues of Plato Socrates is chiefly occupied with defining such terms as these, and Aristotle (*Metaphysics* 987b) considered this his major contribution to philosophy: meaning not that he was the first to define his terms, but that he was the first to insist on careful definition of terms as an essential foundation for intellectual activity.

But it is just at this point that the Socratic mission becomes obscure to us. What did they mean by saying that moral virtues are forms of knowledge? Aristotle criticized this as an excessively intellectualistic approach to morality which ignored the importance of irrational factors in human behavior (*Nich. Eth.* 1144b). The early Socratics were ignorant of Aristotelian precisions in these matters, but surely they did not think that anyone who grasped intellectually the correct definitions of the virtues would automatically behave in a virtuous manner. When they talked about "knowing" the "soul" and the "virtues" of the soul, they must have had more than that in mind.[3]

3. THE AGENT-CENTERED CONCEPT OF MORALITY

For the above we have the testimony of Aristotle; our third characteristic is a matter of inference. There is some reason to think that ethical discussions within the Socratic circle tended to focus on the moral *agent* rather than on the moral *act*. They were not so much concerned with distinguishing good acts from bad as with the definition of a morally good *person*. Moral goodness they identified with a condition of psychic harmony, and to find the right thing to do they asked what a person possessed of such psychic harmony would do in a particular situation. This was the approach of Plato, and it was very typical of Greek ethical thought after him.[4] I suggest it may have been widespread in the early Socratic circle because this would help to explain why they were so attached to the notion that virtue is a kind of knowledge. The crafts analogy may imply an ambiguous conception of expertise, part intellectual understanding and part practiced reflex. If so, the "knowledge of virtue" they had in mind was something like a craft secret, and it offered a stunningly simple and attractive solution to all moral and political problems, for they could all be referred to this ideal moral expert or artisan, the *sophos* possessed of perfect inner harmony and a totally rational soul, based upon a somewhat mysterious "knowledge" of virtue. These terms were the more seductive because they could easily be attached to the traditional Greek ideal of the "wise man."

4. THE NATURAL-LAW CONCEPT OF THE WORLD

"Natural law" is an anachronism.[5] I use this Stoic term because it is the clearest and best-known formulation of a view that was pervasive among the Socratic schools. In brief, they had a strong tendency to think that the universe must have purpose. The Sophists tended to dwell upon the antithesis between *physis* and *nomos*, nature and convention; the Socratics, upon connections between them. The assumptions listed above seem to imply a teleological conception of morality: every human soul needs to fulfil itself in the manner described, by developing an inner harmony based upon the "knowledge" of virtue, because the soul happens to be structured in that way. And this seems to imply that the cosmos is also structured that way, governed by objective moral principles that direct everything to some purpose. But Socratics disagreed, probably from the start, over the extent to which this cosmic order was discernable by reason, about their own capacity to define it through the Socratic method, about what it was that the wise person "knew" or might hope to "know." About Socrates himself we can say nothing much except that he paid no attention to the traditional cults of the gods (one of the charges against him, tacitly admitted by Xenophon)[6] and yet was convinced of the existence of some sort of divine power which sometimes mysteriously communicated with him. Among his followers some thought the natural order and its laws could be known with certainty, producing the authoritarian interpretation of Socrates' teaching that we find—usually—in Plato and Xenophon. Others thought it could not be known except through some enhanced self-awareness or mystical intuition, producing a skeptical and individualistic interpretation of Socrates. Since they all thought of themselves as continuing Socrates' mission these disagreements took the form of divergent interpretations of what Socrates had said.

The Authoritarian Socrates

In the Socratic writings of Xenophon and (taken *in toto*) Plato, there seems a general assumption that the Socratic quest can lead to certain knowledge of moral and political truth. Aristotle also seems to assume that Socrates thought reliable definitions were obtainable. But Plato and Xenophon perceive this knowledge differently.

The Socrates portrayed in Xenophon's dialogues thinks knowledge has a definite political application, and he means politics in the usual Greek sense. He is chiefly concerned with offering advice about the management of the *oikos* and the polis (*Mem.* 4.1.2). His main goal is to train men for participation in political life (1.6.15). He is explicit as to the meaning of this: the functions of a citizen are the management of public revenue, the conduct of war and diplomacy, and the healing of factional strife (4.6.13–15). When Xenophon tries to summarize the Socratic mission, he says that Socrates was interested in every sort of knowledge useful to gentlemen (*kaloikagathoi*, the beautiful and the good, the usual term for the upperclass citizen ideal)—the nature of right and wrong, piety and impiety, government and the capacity for governing, etc. (*Mem.* 1.1.16). Knowledge of moral matters plays an important part in all this, of course. But Xenophon never separates Socrates' interest in moral terms from the traditional complex of practical interests, centered on the household and the city, which were supposed to constitute the serious existence of a Greek citizen. There is little sign in his pages that Socrates attempted to reevaluate such terms as the above, and only hints that the Socratic political craft is different from statecraft and citizenship in the ordinary sense.

But the Socrates of Plato is interested in a different kind of knowledge. The Xenophontic Socrates might think that the problems of Athens would be solved if the people would entrust themselves to aristocratic leadership; the Platonic Socrates entertains no such illusions. In the *Gorgias* he argues that Athens has *never* had a leader who understood the true art of governing, because the true art is concerned with moral improvement (515ff.). He calls himself the doctor of the polis, one who knows how to diagnose and cure the ills of the body politic in a professional manner; and refers to the Sophists as cooks of the polis, who know only how to pander to its appetites (*Gorg.* 521e.). This Socrates is interested in a political craftsmanship that has nothing to do with politics as usual. He is engaged in a search for a new elite such as is not found at all in existing states. He does not emerge full-blown until the dialogues of Plato's middle period, but even Plato's earliest dialogues present a Socrates concerned with *moral* knowledge on a level quite different from statecraft and citizenship in the ordinary sense.

On the other hand, Plato and Xenophon are not necessarily far apart. Xenophon thinks primarily of practical statecraft, but a statecraft raised to a new level by moral wisdom. There are moments when he makes Socrates' political craft seem an almost utopian goal: we are told it will stop jury courts from disagreeing about their verdicts, citizens from bringing lawsuits, and cities from fighting wars (*Mem.* 4.4.8). The last is a more utopian goal than Plato ever wanted to envision. Nor did Plato's interest in moral reformation preclude practical statecraft. The elite that Xenophon has in mind does not seem all that different from the traditional elites; the elite that Plato has in mind is different from any that has ever been, and its outlines will not become clear until the *Republic*, but it is always conceived as a *ruling* elite, differing from the old elites not in function but in effectiveness.

The political implications are authoritarian. This wing of the Socratic movement was convinced that absolute certainty in moral and political matters is possible, and that those who possess it should rule the polis. They emphasized the antidemocratic implications of the crafts analogy: every art requires special expertise; and so politics, if it is an art, should be left to the truly qualified. We know that Socrates used the crafts analogy to argue against sortition, a cherished institution of the extreme democracy, on the grounds that no one would appoint a carpenter, pilot, or musician by lot. Socrates was accused of frequently quoting the passage in the *Iliad* (2.188ff.) where Odysseus restores order to the assembly by beating the commoners: and Xenophon admits this is true (*Mem.* 1.2.58ff.), though we would not guess it from any of the dialogues. The Socrates of the dialogues does refer sometimes to the political art as an "art of kingship." He meant by this only the mythical kingship of the Homeric poems, which everyone used as a storehouse of paradigms, but unfortunately he concentrated on the one Homeric passage that has obvious antidemocratic implications.[7] The metaphors of kingship and specialized craftsmanship both suggested that in the Socratic view the masters of the political art were a small and select circle.

There was a way that the Socratic faith in experts might have been democratized: they might have hoped that the ordinary citizens would develop the necessary moral expertise. Protagoras, who had first popularized the notion of a teachable political art, seems to have held such a view. But in the Socratic literature this possibility is never mentioned, and Plato makes Socrates deny it outright in the *Apology*.[8]

There is also the fact that the members of the Socratic circle tended to be Laconists of a sort, or several sorts. Plato tells us that Socrates himself frequently praised Sparta and Crete as examples of law-abiding constitutions (*Crito* 52e). We have met Critias and Xenophon. We will meet Plato. Antisthenes too is credited with certain sayings in praise of Sparta, as when he compared the Thebans after Leuctra to schoolboys who had beaten their master (Plut., *Lycurgus* 30). An allusion in Aristophanes' *Birds* (1281ff.) suggests that in 414 B.C. Socratics and Laconists were somehow associated. The question of women's place in society, which received considerable discussion in the Socratic circle, may have been connected with their interest in the Spartan constitution, and may have been limited usually to the question of how women could best serve the ruling class. This seems to have been the case with Critias and Xenophon, and the writings of Plato and Antisthenes do not necessarily imply any broader perspective.[9]

So there would appear to be considerable evidence that the Socratic circle was surrounded by an atmosphere of authoritarian elitism, which nourished the most reactionary, aristocratic, even crypto-oligarchic views. There have been attempts to prove that the underlying charge against Socrates in 399 (a charge that had to remain unspoken because of the recent amnesty) was that he had taught the overthrow of the Athenian democracy.[10] But there is another side to the question.

The Skeptical Socrates

This interpretation of Socrates as moral and political authoritarian is difficult to reconcile with some other evidence found in the same dialogues. Frequently they portray Socrates as a skeptical thinker whose main political value seems to be a radical individualism. In the early dialogues of Plato the *elenchos* is a negative instrument which never achieves any significant conclusions; and it is hard to believe that it did achieve many unequivocal positive results in Socrates' lifetime, for otherwise there would not have been so many interpretations of his teaching. Also Socrates was famous for his habit of professing ignorance about everything. This *eironeia*, self-depreciation, is one of the best-attested parts of the Socratic legend.[11] If we assume that the historical Socrates thought absolute moral certainty was possible, there are two ways to understand his *eironeia*. We may assume it was deliberate dissimulation practiced for the purposes of the elenchus, to draw out and refute the opinions of his audience; practiced perhaps playfully at times, like the English "irony." Or we may suppose that Socrates thought firm conclusions were possible but never reached many himself, in which case his *eironeia* was sincere. But if Socrates was really the authoritarian that Xenophon and at least the later Plato took him to be, his skepticism must be explained as either a false posture or a temporary and provisional one.[12]

On the other hand, perhaps Socrates' profession of ignorance was sincere and expressed a convinced skepticism about the possibility of acquiring certain knowledge of moral and political values. Some of his own disciples seem to have believed that this was Socrates' real conclusion about the nature of knowledge, or at least the conclusion to which his elenchus led. There were several interpretations of this Socratic skepticism, all implying a highly individualistic ethic.

Some Platonic dialogues suggest that the purpose of the Socratic mission is to achieve not certain doctrine but a condition of critical self-awareness. Perhaps this is the point of the enigmatic (and possibly non-Platonic) *Alcibiades I*, in which Socrates tells the young Alcibiades that the aim of philosophy is to "know the self" in accordance with the Delphic maxim. It is not all clear what he means by "knowing the self," except that it is identified with wisdom and temperance and somehow will result in right behavior toward others and true statesmanship. But in Plato's *Apology of Socrates* Socrates clearly defends an interpretation of self-knowledge which consists in knowing what one does not know. Here Socrates is made to declare at his trial, in a context where the profession of ignorance cannot possibly be a pretense or an ironical pose, that he is wiser than all other men only in recognizing his own ignorance (*Apol.* 21b–d). This awareness of one's own ignorance is presented as the real aim of the elenchus, and as a moral ideal binding upon everyone. Life without such self-examination is said to be not worth living (38a). *This* Socrates apparently believes in the possibility of a fallible, provisional kind of knowledge gained by constantly checking one's conclusions and those of everybody else; thinks that this elenctically justifiable knowledge is the only kind of knowledge possible for humans; and when he speaks of an elite, means those wise enough to know that they know nothing for certain, wise enough to subject all their opinions to the test of the elenchus.[13]

We can distinguish a second interpretation of "self-knowledge," which we may describe as the proto-Cynic. The skepticism of the proto-Cynics also placed much importance on the moral autonomy of the individual, but with more emphasis on disciplined will than critical intellect. Xenophon at times suggests that the only possible or necessary definition of virtue was the living example of Socrates himself (*Mem.* 4.4.9: 1.2 passim) and has Socrates argue that virtue is useless without practice (3.9.1–3). The identification of virtue with ascetic self-discipline he particularly associates with Socrates' disciple Antisthenes, one of the most prolific writers among the older Socratics. In Xenophon's *Symposium*, Antisthenes is a practical moralist whose main theme is simplicity of life. Among other proto-Cynic maxims he was supposed to have said that virtue is self-sufficient for happiness, provided it is equipped with the strength of Socrates (Diog. Laert. 6.11)—perhaps the earliest use of the word *autarkeia*, self-sufficiency, to imply independence from society as a high moral ideal. The traditions about Antisthenes do not suggest he pursued this ideal with anything like the fanaticism of the Cynics who later claimed him as a spiritual father. He seems to have been skeptical about the possibility or utility of certain knowledge, but he and his disciples were much interested in dialectic and presumably thought the Socratic method valuable even if it yielded only a provisional knowledge. They may have valued ascetic autonomy partly because it left one free to pursue the elenchus. Platonic and Antisthenic skepticism may not have been far apart in the beginning. But when the latter group spoke of "knowledge" they meant not so much moral theory as a deep personal conviction about moral truth fortified by rigorous practice.

And there was a third interpretation: the school or tendency called "Cyrenaicism," founded by Socrates' disciple Aristippus of Cyrene, which endured till the end of the fourth century. Some of these Cyrenaics adopted a very thoroughgoing form of skepticism, denying that morality had any basis outside convention, and resorting to an individualistic ethic of living determined by the motives of pleasure and pain. Extreme Cyrenaics would appear to have departed altogether from the "Socratic world view" we attempted to define earlier, because the core of this world view was the search for objective grounds of morality. On the other hand, some Cyrenaics believed that dialectic was useful, that a provisional sort of knowledge could be achieved, that the "wise man" was an attainable ideal (Diog. Laert. 2.92–93). We know little about them, but enough to show that Socratic skepticism could produce hedonistic manifestations as well as the critical and ascetic versions.

Our fragmentary evidence for these minor Socratic "schools" indicates that the skeptical and individualistic interpretations of Socratic philosophy were always around, though overshadowed at first by the dogmatic interpretations familiar to us from Plato and Xenophon. Skepticism did not come into its own until the middle of the third century B.C., when it won over the Platonic Academy itself.

The existence of this skeptical tradition helps to explain certain egalitarian aspects of the Socratic movement. There is no doubt that Socrates' teaching was open to all, and that the entire Athenian population was his chosen audience. Both the method and the audience contrast strikingly with those of Plato. The apologetic writings of the disciples emphasize Socrates' habit of questioning everybody because it is the most persuasive argument they have to show that Socrates was a friend of the people, as the unsubtle Xenophon says outright (*Mem.* 1.2.60; cf. Plato, *Apol.* 29–31, 36c). There is no reason to doubt this, given the public nature of Socrates' career. At the very least, this implies that the Socratic mission was conceived as a common enterprise in which all Athenians were expected to participate in some degree. Also there seems to have been a pervasive belief in the value of persuasion and consent in the Socratic circle. In the *Crito* Plato has Socrates expound a unique doctrine of social contract which obliges the citizen to obey all the laws of his city whether he agrees with them or not. In the same dialogue Socrates affirms that he has always preferred the laws of Athens to those of any other city. (Admittedly this is a puzzle, because in the very same passage we are told that Sparta and Crete were Socrates' favorite examples of well-governed cities. Obviously Socrates' admiration for Sparta is not supposed to contradict his admiration for Athens, but Plato does not tell us how to reconcile the two.)[14] If Socrates was really a moral and political authoritarian, there is no truly satisfactory explanation for the egalitarianism of his methods, nor for the importance he seems to have placed on individual moral autonomy.[15] It is much easier to understand why a skeptical Socrates would have believed in such values.

The Socratics and Utopia

The question of which of these is closer to the real Socrates I leave to those with more space and scholarship at their disposal. There is more than one way to put all this evidence together so as to form a believable composite portrait, but unless we can establish some control on it the scissors-and-paste procedure is arbitrary. It is possible that the real Socrates, who talked for half a century, said different things at different times, and that his views changed and developed; but the intellectual development of Socrates was of no interest to any of the disciples who commemorated him so faithfully. For present purposes let us simply take these different interpretations of Socrates as self-perceptions of different parts of the Socratic movement.

However they saw themselves, Socratics were presented with a novel political problem. The Socratic circle seems to have been preoccupied with the problem of finding an elite. They were entranced by the notion that all social and political problems might be solved by developing a new kind of leadership: genuine political experts, physicians of the polis, psychically integrated human beings who could see social needs and practices in a cosmic perspective. They might conceive this elite differently. Xenophon, in most of his moods, seems to have thought about a reformed version of the traditional elite of landowning gentlemen. The mature Plato, in some moods, thought about a new elite of scientist/theologians. The young Plato in some moods thought about a new elite of skeptical critics. Antisthenes seems to have thought about a new elite of self-sufficient ascetics; and Aristippus, one of self-sufficient hedonists. But with the possible exception of the last, they all thought of this new elite as having some political role analogous to that of the old elite. Their mission was usually described in political terms. And there was no way around the fact that these practitioners of the kingly arts, once found, would be unacceptable to the city-state. The problem was not only to identify the philosophical elite, but to find a social role for it.

I suggest this was the conflict that inspired the higher utopias: the possibility of a radical transformation of society, to be brought about by the development of a new type of human being; and the inability to put this ideal into practice, which required the removal of the argument to some other level. Such Socratics as Xenophon and Aristippus might avoid this conflict, because their versions of the new elite were more easily assimilable by the old elites. But those who thought of a radically different type of Wise Man could not avoid it, and therefore were forced to think in terms of a very long-range kind of reform, which would somehow go much deeper than the usual reforms of Greek political life.

Behind this there was a second conflict. We have seen that the Socratic movement contained both egalitarian and elitist elements: the assumption that the elenchus is a universal ideal seems to have been there from the start, and so was the assumption that it can only be developed by a small and select group. I have suggested that the former view was more characteristic of the skeptical wing, and the latter of those who believed in absolute moral/political values. It was the authoritarian group that produced the higher utopias, first the Platonic version and later the Stoic. But the skeptical/egalitarian tradition was not entirely forgotten even by Plato, and by way of Cynicism it became a major influence on the Stoics.

Socrates left to his disciples an unforgettable example, a very malleable stock of ideas, and a dream that became the germ of high utopia.

The Paradox of Plato

The Modern Controversy

Egalitarian and authoritarian tendencies were at war in the Socratic tradition, and the philosophers who considered themselves Socratics tried to resolve the contradiction in different ways. Plato was obviously attracted to the authoritarian side of Socrates and pushed it to its logical conclusion in the ideal society sketched by the character called "Socrates" in Plato's *Republic*. But even in the *Republic* many have perceived a similar tension between egalitarian and authoritarian principles.

On the one hand, the way of life Plato proposes for the elite of this paradigm polis represents the most dazzling vision of human potentiality that anyone in the ancient world had ever conceived. Plato dares to offer the prospect of a total transformation of society in accordance with what seem to be rational, even utilitarian, criteria. He dares to envision a truly unified community in which individual properties and families are abolished, and in connection with this to argue for what appears to be an almost modern attitude toward the social position of woman.

But even as he offers us this vision of perfectibility, he seems to rob it of its force. For this radical transformation is limited to a ruling minority, and even there it seems to have no purpose except to enforce on the whole society a system of controls so authoritarian that many have not hesitated to label it "totalitarian." And the whole proposal is intended, among other things, as an attack on Athenian democracy, the most impressive effort to achieve a free and equal society before modern times. Plato's dream of human perfectibility is welded to an adamant conviction of human inequality, an inequality so gross that he seems to think most people incapable of sharing the dream at all.

Sinclair's *History of Greek Political Thought* sums up the paradox elegantly:

> Plato's *Republic* is the despair alike of those who hate him and those who admire him. His enemies cannot forgive his influence and prestige and so cannot ignore him; and he will not toe the line which his friends draw for him, but strays across to the enemy camp. ... Between the wisdom of the few and the docility of the rest the human race has never been so exalted or so abased. His reputation has suffered as much from adulation as from attack. Blinded by his glory and bewitched by his poetry, many see only what they wish to see and pass over the evil; others, infuriated by his inhumanity and his lordly affectation of knowledge, lose patience with the task of trying to understand him (165–66).

Is this apparent paradox the result of trying to force an ancient document into inappropriate modern categories? Would Plato and his audience have perceived any such contradiction? A brief survey of the controversy to which Sinclair refers may be a useful approach to this and other questions raised by the *Republic*. There have been two main parties to this controversy, which has overflowed the usual academic channels to an extent probably without parallel in the study of ancient texts other than the Bible. The most determined critics of Plato, generally leftist in their political views and often from outside the professional circles of classical scholarship, can see nothing in the *Republic* but a reactionary political program. The committed defenders of Plato, whose political sympathies are less obvious and who usually belong more to the mainstream of classicism, uphold a traditional idealizing interpretation of the *Republic* that effectively denies it to be a political program of any sort. In addition to these long-established camps, one can in recent years distinguish a third group, composed mostly of American followers of Leo Strauss, whose politics may perhaps be described as "neoconservative"; they also deny that the *Republic* contains a political program, but for reasons of their own.

We notice that this dispute turns largely on the question of whether the utopian proposals in the *Republic* were meant to be realizable. We notice also that to emphasize the practical and realizable aspects of the *Republic* is to bring out its authoritarian element, while to concentrate on its impractical and ideal quality is to bring out its humanitarian side. Let us consider the three approaches in turn.

The Radical Critique of Plato

Before the 1930s it was much easier to accept the traditional interpretation of the *Republic* as a remote and benign ideal of sound government. There were dissenters like Pöhlmann who saw it as a forerunner of certain modern political ideologies, but the worst thing Pöhlmann could call Plato was "socialist," and socialists themselves were sometimes willing to acknowledge Plato as a distant ancestor. The word "totalitarian" put the matter in a different light; and for the past fifty years we have seen a barrage of attacks on Plato, all emphasizing the parallels between the utopia of the *Republic* and twentieth-century totalitarian regimes.

These anti-Platonists share certain common themes. Firstly, they interpret the *Republic* as a straightforward and reactionary political program, rejecting the long academic tradition of idealizing Plato's political views. In the late 1930s R. H. S. Crossman told a large audience that the *Republic* was "not a timeless exposition of ultimate truths but a handbook for aspiring dictators."[16] Within a few years he was followed by Arnold Toynbee (*A Study of History*), A. D. Winspear (*The Genesis of Plato's Thought*), and Karl Popper (*The Open Society and Its Enemies*); the last, probably the best-known and certainly one of the most extreme statements of this point of view, characterized the *Republic* as more "topical political manifesto" than "theoretical treatise," and its author as "a totalitarian party-politician" interested in "the quest for power."[17]

Secondly, they slight the significance and originality of Plato's communistic proposals, describing these as a mere imitation of Spartan practice or a rationalization of common oligarchical ideals of the time. Winspear called Plato's communism "an idealization of actual conservative practice and institutions." Popper thought it represented Plato's conception of a primitive tribal society, with some features borrowed from contemporary Sparta. One might expect them to recognize an exception to this reactionary pattern in Plato's argument for women's emancipation, but they usually did not. Some, like Winspear, dismissed Plato's "feminism" as a sham; others, like Popper, simply avoided any reference to it.[18]

Thirdly, they see a close relationship between the *Republic* and the *Laws*. The *Laws* may be considered a practical application of the principles of the *Republic*, or a mitigated version which Plato fell back upon when he realized the plan of *Republic* was unworkable. But all find the two closely complementary.

All these writers share an obvious political and philosophical bias against Plato, which is often extended to ancient Greek philosophy in general. They tend to regard Greek philosophy, or at least its Socratic mainstream, as inherently reactionary, whether because of its aristocratic connections or its idealizing and utopian approach to social problems. The Stoic alternative to Plato's utopia they do not seriously consider.

The violently anti-Platonic diatribes of Popper's generation ceased to be taken seriously by classical scholars some time ago, but this controversy is by no means dead, nor likely to die for as long as the Greek classics retain their allure. More recent expressions of the radical critique display a less intrusive bias and understand that the relationship between the Platonic dialogues and Greek politics must be handled more subtly. But they continue to argue that the *Republic* and *Laws* constituted a sort of program that was meant to have practical and reactionary political implications, and that Plato cannot be studied without an awareness of this purpose. They still refuse to see much of a paradox about Plato's communism; it is simply dismissed as a reactionary device, and classical utopian thought in general is still dismissed as reactionary.[19]

The Traditional Defense of Plato

The usual line of defense against this radical attack is to argue that the utopian proposals of the *Republic* must be understood in an ideal or symbolic context. Criticism of specific institutional arrangements in the ideal city is considered irrelevant on the grounds that these imaginary institutions had only the most attenuated connection, or none, with the political realities of the time. Divorcing Plato's utopia from contemporary politics permits a more favorable view of its communistic institutions, which can then be seen as mythic representations of certain common social values. It follows that many of these scholars fail to see any necessary connection between the *Republic* and the *Laws*. Rather they wish to interpret Plato's utopia as a highly flexible model, a statement of principles so general that they might be applied to many different societies.

There are many variations on this idealizing interpretation, which goes back to antiquity. One version, widely held by older commentators,[20] is the individual-ethic approach: the utopian parts of the *Republic* are read as models for purely individual imitation, ethical but not political. This interpretation owed its currency to the fact that it is suggested in the dialogue itself. "Socrates" (hereinafter I use this name for the character in the dialogue, not the real Socrates unless so identified) does not introduce the question of the best constitution for its own sake; he raises it because he is engaged in a discussion of what constitutes justice in the individual, and he assumes that "justice in the citizen" can be better examined if it is "writ large," i.e., by examining "justice in the city" (*Rep.* 368e). From the beginning of the discussion it has been assumed that "justice in the citizen" and "justice in the city" are the same thing (351–52); an obvious and common-sense assumption to make in a culture that was not, in fact, accustomed to think of the individual as a moral agent isolated from his community. After the discussion of the ideal city has been completed, the only definite conclusion drawn from it has to do with individual morality: at the end of the ninth book, Socrates says that it does not even matter whether this city of words (*en logois*) can be realized on earth (*ges*), for it can still be a "model laid up in heaven" (*ourano ... paradeigma*) on which the wise man can look and "set up the government of his soul" (592ab; trans. G. M. A. Grube).

Now if this argument is to be taken literally, Socrates cannot mean that there is merely an *analogy* between justice or virtue in the citizen and justice or virtue in the city. He must mean an exact *identity* between these two things. He must mean that virtue in the *politai* differs from virtue in the polis only in that virtue is more easily observable, and its moral significance more fully apparent, in large public actions. Punctuality, for example, will seem a small virtue in everyday life but will assume terrible importance in wartime. If this is what Plato means, then the communism of the *Republic* must be interpreted as a writ-large way of saying that the individual citizen must be constantly inspired by unselfish communal solidarity. The idea certainly ceases to be shocking; or interesting.

But if so, then "justice in the city" can do nothing to *explain* "justice in the citizen," for it can tell us nothing we did not already know. Therefore it is difficult to understand why Plato bothered with all the constitutional details laid out in the *Republic*, especially the system of sexual communism and its elaborate regulations to encourage eugenic breeding and avoid incest. Communism has always been the main stumbling block for those who would see nothing in the *Republic* but an educational theory concerned with individual morality. They are forced to assume that Plato has somehow forgotten his own methodology here. The problem is compounded when we consider that Aristotle took these preposterous communistic regulations as serious proposals, worthy of long and literal-minded dissection in the *Politics*; which can only be explained by the supposition that Aristotle simply failed to understand what his teacher was doing in the *Republic*.[21]

Another problem is that Socrates' version of "justice in the city" does not seem to have much relation to "justice in the citizen" in the ordinary sense. It turns out that in the heavenly city only members of the ruling elite can *individually* possess "justice in the citizen," so only they can serve as models of just behavior. What are the other members of the heavenly city for? In the fourth book we are told they show "justice in the city" to consist in the harmony of different parts, which is somehow supposed to reflect the harmony of the just psyche. But then we are no longer speaking of the same thing but only of an analogy between two kinds of "justice," and a rather loose and obscure analogy at that.[22]

In short, attempts to read the *Republic* as a purely educational treatise concerned only with individual morality end in unsolvable puzzles. This has lent credibility to those who want to read it as a fascist party platform. A modified version of the traditional defense has therefore emerged in recent decades. Those who regard Plato as a founder of modern humanism continue to interpret the *Republic* in an ideal context, and with continuing emphasis upon its educational purpose, but now with a greater or less awareness that it must also be interpreted as a political and constitutional model.

Much of the confusion will evaporate if we reflect that when Socrates introduces these comparisons he is thinking more of moral agents than moral actions. When he says that "justice in the city" must be "justice in the citizen" writ large, he means that the highest human type can be adequately described only in its social context. And in his final comment on the connection between utopia and reality (592ab), what is it that the would-be-wise person is supposed to learn from contemplation of the city in heaven? It is not that he or she is expected to acquire an enhanced appreciation of the value of punctuality and such commonplaces. The real point is that he or she will understand the environment necessary to produce an ideal moral agent. That environment must be shown in detail because this is the only way to prove the proposition that Socrates is trying to prove: that virtue produces happiness. Only in this way can we see how justice *works*. It would make no sense to assert that justice or virtue equals happiness if it could not be shown that justice can function in a complete society. This was the essential purpose of the high-utopian method: it provided a more compelling argument about more comprehensive goals than ordinary political discourse could do. Social justice, in one sense, is just a multiplied version of individual justice; and in another sense it is something different, for it is the context without which individual justice cannot live. This context does explain something about individual justice—not about specific acts, but about the sort of individual who would ideally perform them. This is why Socrates goes into such detail about this context. This means that the utopian plan is at least conceivably a political paradigm as well as an ethical paradigm. The fact that there seem to be so few moral agents even in the ideal city remains troublesome; but we will return to this problem later.

Assuming "justice in the psyche" and "justice in the city" to be separable models, what can we conclude about their realizability? The two require one another: we are told that the virtuous person will flourish only in the virtuous city, and that the virtuous city will never exist unless virtuous people are in charge, or until philosophers are kings. This puts Socrates in a bind, as has often been observed. Yet there is a way out of it. It is explicitly said that even under present conditions it is sometimes possible, through divine intervention, for virtuous souls to appear:

> Now I think that the philosophic nature as we have defined it, provided it receive its proper instruction, will inevitably grow to reach every excellence, but if it is sown and grows in an unsuitable environment, it will develop in quite the opposite way unless some god come to its rescue ... We must realize that if any character is saved and becomes what it should, in the present state of our societies, you would not be wrong to say that it has been saved by a god's intervention. 492a–493a, trans. Grube

There is no explanation for the appearance of these virtuous characters in existing societies, just as there is no explanation for the mysterious way that prisoners get released from their chains in the allegory of the cave which follows.

But obviously Plato had to believe there were some virtuous characters or there would be no point in writing the *Republic*, whose immediate purpose is to encourage the development of more of them. These reformed individuals cannot help but try to reduce the disparity between political actuality and the ideal city. If a virtuous individual can develop through the providence of the gods (*theiou moiran*), then why not a virtuous environment? The second stage is more difficult, obviously, because it will require a good number of individuals released from their chains, and some way for them to create a *partial* copy of the perfect city. The possibility of partial and practical imitations of the ideal city is not discussed in the *Republic*, but neither is it quite ruled out. There is a studied ambiguity about the crucial passage at 592ab. Socrates says that the virtuous man will avoid political life in the actual city, "unless divine good luck (*theia tyche*) should be his"—hinting that it is in the power of the gods to create approximations of the good city just as they mysteriously create approximations of good people in an environment where none should be. It is Glaucon who expresses disbelief in the existence of the good city; Socrates merely says that it does not matter whether it exists or will ever exist.

Therefore recent defenders of Plato tend to accept the *Republic* as both an educational and a political model, and to admit that the utopian institutional structure is somehow meant to be paradigmatic in its own right. But they still insist that the ideal city is a mythic structure, a thought experiment whose political implications are indirect and by no means obvious. Many have tried to mitigate the authoritarian aspects of Plato's utopian institutions. Some have made the singularly unconvincing claim that Plato meant to abolish slavery in his ideal city, though somehow neglecting to say this explicitly.[23] Others, more plausibly, have tried to show that the role of the masses is not so passive, nor Socrates' acculturation policies so harsh, as modern readers of the *Republic* tend to think. But the more common tactic is to admit cheerfully the unpleasantness of the ideal city and then argue that we are not supposed to take its institutions as literal models. Some seem to find nothing in the *Republic* but the most general and innocuous principles. We have been told that the *Laws*, which even the most ardent modern Platonists can find somewhat unlovely, is not the only or the most faithful application of these principles; any state may be said to follow the principles of the *Republic* so long as its institutions are "so devised as to place power at the service of wisdom" and ensure "the highest degree of mutuality and harmony."[24] We have been told that Plato, though he detested the direct democracy of Athens, would have approved a representative democracy of the modern type.[25] We have been told that only certain ideological preconceptions peculiar to modern liberalism cause us to perceive Plato's utopia as authoritarian and repressive; if we can free ourselves from these chains, we will see it as a city "whose members enjoy as much real happiness, and as much real or critical freedom, as possible."[26]

The Neoconservative Defense of Plato

For the most part neither radical critics nor traditionalist defenders of Plato's utopianism see any contradiction in it, because each concentrates on one side of the theory and ignores the other. A third approach, best represented by Alan Bloom, tries to solve the contradiction in a different way. These authors see no difficulties in Plato's utopianism because they do not believe there is such a thing. In brief, they argue that the communistic plan of the *Republic* is an elaborate joke. Plato, we are told, introduces the discussion of communism only to show the dangers of pursuing the ideal of justice and other theoretical constructs to their logical conclusions. The *Republic* is therefore a satire on utopianism—"the greatest critique of political idealism ever written," Bloom calls it.[27] "Communism" was merely a fantastic invention of Aristophanes, who created the idea in the *Ecclesiazusae* to satirize democracy; the conceit was then borrowed by Plato, who made it the subject of his own fantastic comedy, the *Republic*.

Now it has generally been thought obvious that Platonic communism, whatever it was, was no sort of practical political program; and many have recognized in the *Republic* a certain element of playfulness. Touches of humor and satire are even more obvious in certain of its later imitations, especially More's *Utopia*. But it is one thing to recognize these touches, and another to say that the ideal societies depicted by Plato and More were not intended by the authors to represent valid social ideals.

A host of commentators on the *Republic* could be cited in opposition to the "Straussian" interpretation. Perhaps it will be sufficient to cite the two earliest commentators we possess. They are Plato and Aristotle. To ask what Plato himself thought is to raise a notorious problem, because Plato himself never says anything to us, unless some of the *Epistles* are genuine. Since all his other works are in dramatic form and the author never intrudes into the drama, how can we gain access to his thought, and how far can we read these dialogues as though they were treatises? But in the case of the *Republic* this problem does not seem insoluble. It is not the only dialogue where the communistic proposal is mentioned. Socrates reaffirms in the *Timaeus* and the Athenian Stranger reaffirms in the *Laws* the conviction that this plan would be the best form of society. At the very least this was a proposal that Plato wanted his audience to consider seriously.

Aristotle had much to say about Plato's communistic ideas, none of it favorable, but all of it deadly serious. He refers to this plan as a "best-constitution" proposal like those of Hippodamus and Phaleas; he usually preserves Plato's authorial distance by attributing the plan to "Socrates" (the character in the *Republic*, not the real one), but he does not seem to think this pose of authorial distance amounted to much.[28] One of the oddities of the "Straussian" interpretation is that it draws heavily on Aristotle's critique of Platonic communism (like Aristotle, they think communism unnatural because it destroys family life, permits incest, and treats men and women alike), but ignores the fact that Aristotle could accept all these as serious proposals.

Another difficulty with this interpretation is its inability to account for the key passage (*Rep.* 592ab) where Socrates says explicitly that the impracticality of his utopia would not detract in the slightest from its validity as an ideal. Another (shared with the preceding group of Platonists) is the cavalier attitude toward problems of historical context and audience. Apparently we are asked to believe that fourth-century Athenians had never heard of such a thing as a serious communistic theory, yet were receptive to satirical treatments of them.

Some Concluding Remarks

Sophisticated exponents of the first two schools are often not far apart, and it will become obvious that my own approach is indebted to both of them. The critics of Plato have reminded us that the *Republic* had a political context and purpose; his defenders, that it was nonetheless no political program. If I feel a closer affinity to the critics, in spite of the crudity and philosophical naïveté that have distinguished some of their attacks, that is because I think the *Republic* best studied in the context of Plato's total work, life, and background. Read in isolation it is a text too easy to read as you like. I think that to read it in context suggests that there was a real tension in the work of Plato between different political ideals, a tension already present in his political culture, and not merely the result of our efforts to force him into inappropriate modern categories.

One would like to apply to the texts of Plato and Aristotle the method described by Quentin Skinner in his history of Renaissance political thought:

> ...I have tried not to concentrate so exclusively on the leading theorists, and have focused instead on the more general social and intellectual matrix out of which their works arose. I begin by discussing the most relevant characteristics of the societies in and for which they originally wrote. For I take it that political life itself sets the main problems for the political theorist. ... I regard it as no less essential to consider the intellectual context in which the major texts were conceived—the context of earlier writings and inherited assumptions about political society, and of more ephemeral contemporary contributions to social and political thought. ... It has rightly become a commonplace of recent historiography that, if we wish to understand earlier societies, we need to recover their different *mentalités* in as broadly sympathetic a fashion as possible. But it is hard to see how we can hope to arrive at this kind of historical understanding if we continue, as students of political ideas, to focus our main attention on those who discussed the problems of political life at a level of abstraction and intelligence unmatched by any of their contemporaries. *The Foundations of Modern Political Thought* I, Cambridge 1978, x–xi

The difficulty of using this method on the texts of Plato and Aristotle is obvious. What we know about earlier writings and more ephemeral contemporary contributions has to be derived mostly from the same texts. Nevertheless they contain considerable comment on the relationship between their political theories and political practice. Let us now consider what Plato had to say about the problem of realizing utopia, which we have seen to be central to the interpretation of the *Republic*, and of all classical utopian thought.

The Method of Plato

Utopia and Reality in the Republic

The problem of how Socrates' program for an ideal polis can be put into action is raised several times in the fifth through the seventh books of the *Republic*. At first Socrates' audience assumes him to be describing a real constitutional program, like those of Hippodamus, Phaleas, and other constitution mongers. But when he raises the prospect of total communism in property and women, they naturally begin to wonder how such a thing could be put into practice. When this question is first asked, Socrates admits it is important but postpones consideration of it till later (450c, 457d–458b).

He returns to the question of realizability at 471–473. Now he says that his purpose is not to prove that the best city can exist, but to find appropriate *paradeigmata*, models or patterns which we ought to imitate as closely as possible. He points out that a painting of the most beautiful man possible would not be less fine if the painter could not prove that such a man existed. He says that whatever some people may think, action ("*praxis*") cannot get so close to the truth as words ("*lexis*").

This surprising statement, which was probably meant to surprise its original audience, is the first indication that Socrates is doing something different from any of his predecessors. Surely the earlier literary oikists had assumed *praxis* to be far more important than *lexis*. Hippodamus presumably thought of his fictive constitution as a *paradeigma*, but in the same way that his design for Piraeus was a *paradeigma*—a blueprint to be followed as closely as possible. Plato, on the other hand, is thinking of his political "model" not as something like an architect's draft, but as something like a work of art. We realize at this point that the discussion of political models is being raised to a more abstract level. The discussion slides effortlessly from the kinds of questions associated with technical illustration to those associated with high art, and the nature of the question changes accordingly. We started out thinking of this constitutional model as a kind of technical illustration, in which case the main question is, "Is it realizable and practical?" Now we must think of it as a kind of public statue or painting, and the question becomes, "Is it imitable?"

This was an easy transition to make because Plato's audience assumed that a work of art has a paradigmatic social purpose. It must set up a standard for men to follow. These differed from ordinary standards in that they could be so high as to be unattainable. When soldiers were exhorted to be like Achilles it was not expected that they would equal him. But it must be possible to *imitate* the model.

For this reason Socrates thinks he has dealt sufficiently with the question of practicality once he has shown that it would not be inconceivable to put the best city into practice. He proposes to find the way that a real polis can come closest to this model, and it turns out that there are only two ways of doing this: either philosophers must become rulers, or rulers philosophers. Even after that they will be unable to execute the model unless they can exile all the inhabitants over the age of ten. The utter impracticality of this scheme could not be more openly admitted, and it is not thought a cause of embarrasment to the modelmaker.

> That either or both of these things [that philosophers should become rulers or vice versa] is impossible cannot, I say, be reasonably maintained. If it were, we would rightly be ridiculed for indulging in wishful thinking. ... Whether men most gifted for philosophy have ever been forced to take charge of a city in the infinity of past time, or whether it is happening now in some foreign place far beyond our ken, or will happen in the future, let us be ready to struggle to maintain *in argument* [*logo*] that the city we have described has existed, exists now, and will exist whenever the Muse of philosophy controls a city. It is not impossible, and our *talk* [*legomen*] is not of impossible things. That it is difficult we ourselves agree. 499cd, trans. Grube (italics mine).

Our difficulties with this passage arise because we tend to think that Socrates is asking of the best city, "Is this realizable?" when in fact he is only asking, "Is this imitable?" He is interested in the question of practicality only because it is necessary to show that the model is not wishful thinking, not an escapist fantasy like the time of Cronus. He must demonstrate its validity *as a model*; but not its practicality as a program.

The recurrent allusions to works of visual or literary art remind us that this is a city of words, not action. Socrates embarks upon the description of utopia "as if we were telling a story" (*mytho*, 376d); his portrait of the just man is compared to a statue (361d), and his portrait of the just city to another one (420c). But we are halfway through the dialogue before it becomes fully apparent, in the passage quoted above, just how wide a gulf separates the city of words from action.

Still, it is always clear that the model must have *some* relation to action. Exactly how is it to be imitated? The *Republic* gives no clear answer, other than the one already mentioned: Socrates concludes at last that the best city has no immediate purpose except to serve as a model for the individual philosopher. If such a philosopher could apply this model to the characters of his fellow citizens he would make them as godlike as Achilles (501b), but this cannot happen unless he can find a clean drawing board on which to copy the divine city. These philosopher-rulers are called "magnificent statues" of men and women (540c), but we no longer hear of a beautiful image of a city, only a beautiful image of a ruler with nothing to rule.

One suspects that even the Plato who wrote the *Republic* intended this individualistic and quietistic solution only as an interim course of action, and had much more in mind for the philosopher-ruler. But not until he wrote the *Laws* a quarter of a century later did Plato offer a coherent explanation of the purposes of constitutional model building.

Utopia and Reality in the Laws

The *Laws* (ca. 350 B.C.) describes a more practical utopia purporting to be a constitution for a new colony, in the tradition of Hippodamus and Phaleas. It takes the form of a dialogue about a proposed colonial foundation in Crete. The three speakers, an Athenian, a Spartan, and a Cretan, agree that they will pretend to be oikists and lawgivers and describe the constitution in detail (702). At an early stage in this discussion, the chief speaker, an Athenian Stranger who may be Plato himself, inserts a long excursus about the relationship between real and ideal constitutions (739a). This is said to be a new "gambit" that no one has tried before in discussing new constitutions. What is new about it is the explicit recognition that political theories can be presented on several different and complementary levels. A single plan will not do because in practice we will almost always fall short of our ideal. Therefore the philosophical lawgiver must provide a series of alternatives and leave it to the real lawgivers to select the most suitable. A three-tiered model is considered adequate: it should include a design for the absolutely best constitution, one for the second best, and one for the third best.

1. The best constitution of all is that in which there is, as far as possible, total *koinonia* in all property, women, and children. Such a city can achieve perfect unity, so that all will feel pleasure and pain at the same time and praise and blame the same things. The Athenian Stranger does not know whether such a city exists anywhere in the world or will ever exist. It may be that only the gods, or the mythic golden race of Hesiod ("children of the gods") live in this way. There can be no doubt that this is a reference to the plan set forth by Socrates in the *Republic*.[29]

2. The second-best constitution is that which most nearly resembles the first but at the same time is capable of being put into practice. This is the constitution, intended for the fictional Cretan colony of Magnesia, to which the rest of the *Laws* is devoted. It is a fairly broad-based oligarchy in which citizenship is restricted to landowners (though the oligarchical nature of the constitution is disguised, as we will see). It resembles Sparta in having a public educational system, a system of common meals, and bans on commerce and currency. It resembles many new colonies in equalizing landed property among citizens. It has some resemblance to the model city of Phaleas of Chalcedon. But in other ways it resembles nothing that had ever been proposed, except in the *Republic*: it admits women to the educational program, the messing groups, and other areas of public life, and it puts severe restrictions on movable as well as landed property.

A little later the Athenian Stranger returns to the problem of implementation (745e–746c). Now it is admitted that in practice it would be difficult to enact even the second-best plan, even given the opportunity to establish a new colony (which was not a common opportunity ca. 350 B.C.). The main sticking points are said to be the proposed restrictions on property and on the size of families.

(Later it is admitted that some other parts of the plan would be very difficult to carry out: the admission of women to the *syssitia*, 781; and to the *agoge*, 804ff.; the restriction of sex to procreation for both men and women, 839.) But these difficulties are not to deter us. The plan of the *Laws* is like a wax model of a city, and the business of the lawgiver is to make the model as perfect and consistent as he can, without worrying about its practicality. Later on the politicians will decide, in consultation with the lawgiver, which elements they should implememt and which should be replaced by more practical alternatives, which presumably are to be drawn from the third-best model. The second-best city is therefore a paradigm like the first, but of a more realistic sort: we do not hear of beautiful paintings (though we return to that metaphor at 769), rather of wax models such as those an architect might use.

3. The third-best city is to be described later; but Plato, who did not live even to finish the *Laws*, never got around to this. Evidently he meant a plan for putting the recommendations of the *Laws* into practice in existing cities. The Athenian Stranger says that the oikist may found a new city or reform an old one (738). The process of reform is described at 746: politicians will consult with the lawgiver to determine what portions of the second-best model are feasible. There seems to be another allusion to this process at 709e–710d, where we are told that a lawgiver must first win over the ruling power in a city; this will be easiest in a tyranny, but it is said to be possible also in democracies and oligarchies. Even in the *Laws* the three old men seem undecided at times whether they should more resemble the philosophical reformers of the first level or the practical reformers of the third (857–59). The third level of reform is not, therefore, restricted to new colonies. It means the attempt to put the second-best model into practice even in established cities. There are passages in the *Laws* that hint at what Plato had in mind by the third level, and according to tradition his Academy had long been practicing just the kind of consulting activity that is described here. We will return to this question.

We are now in a position to see how Plato's political thought had developed. When he was in his fifties he devised in the *Republic* an entirely new method for planning political change, which I have called "high utopian." It was suggested to him by the "low-utopian" discussions that had been going on for some time among Laconophile aristocrats, but he introduced into this discussion a new element of moral and philosophical reflection. To judge from the available evidence, the older Laconism, led by his cousin Critias, had in theory aimed to produce militaristic and communistic oligarchies based closely on contemporary Sparta; and at its most theoretical and utopian level, which it apparently reached in the work of Phaleas, it was still a practical reform program. To a large extent Plato had broken with this tradition, both its values and its methods. He wanted to use the model-constitution form to develop a total conception of the good life; and to direct it, not toward ordinary political change, but toward changing the moral and institutional infrastructure of politics. He conceived the ambition of changing the climate of opinion and the social context within which the ordinary kind of political action takes place. The reform he sought was to be a long-range change in moral consciousness. He realized that in this way words might be more powerful than action, and that only through reform on this level could the mission of Socrates succeed.[30]

But at the same time Plato did not entirely abandon the older type of utopian constitution. The utopian part of the *Republic* starts out as a description of a Laconistic low utopia. The higher utopia is allowed to rise gradually out of the lower one; we are given no hint until the end of the third book, when communism is casually introduced, that Plato is doing something different from any of his predecessors; just how different does not become apparent until the long discussion of communistic institutions in the fifth book. In the *Republic* the two levels are never separated into different plans; they are different stages in the construction of utopia. The paradoxical quality in the *Republic*, which has given rise to such divergent interpretations, arises from the fact that it contains both a low utopia and a high utopia, which Socrates claims to unite into a single city, but which to many seem imperfectly joined. Those who wish to see in the *Republic* a totalitarian blueprint look at the first city; those who want a universal humanistic vision prefer the second. The two visions are finally separated in the *Laws*, where the aged Plato constructs an unequivocally low utopia of his own.

But not even the *Laws* is concerned with politics in the ordinary sense. The *Laws*, like the *Republic*, attempts to transcend the problems of conflict resolution with which ordinary politics must be concerned, and to build a society where total consensus can be assumed. The transition to the real political world is the business of the third stage. The distinction between the second stage and the third Plato might have borrowed from his predecessors. We know that Phaleas' utopia had a dual purpose: to be implemented in full should the opportunity to found a new colony appear, and to be implemented piecemeal in old cities. That is what Plato meant by his distinction between the second-best and third-best constitutions. In effect he tried to link the Phalean program of political reform to the Socratic program of moral regeneration.

The Apparent Contradictions Between the Republic *and* Laws

The neatness of this scheme arouses suspicion. It is doubtful that the coherent pattern described above was fully drawn in Plato's mind at the time he wrote the *Republic*. Some will doubt that it ever existed at all except in hindsight and will argue that the *Laws* is not a mere application of the *Republic* but a complete reconstruction of the earlier system starting from different premises.

For example, the unreal mythic quality of the ideal state is more openly admitted in Plato's later dialogues. In the *Statesman* (272) and the *Laws* (713) Plato presents his own allegorized version of the time of Cronus, when humans lived without politics or war and also, in Plato's version, without families or sexual reproduction. We are told that all this was possible because the human race was then ruled directly by divine spirits. This golden age is a sort of model for human life. We who live in the time of Zeus (i.e., in real time and real space) should try to imitate it as best we can. If we add it to the scheme developed at *Laws* 739, we may say that the *Laws* distinguishes *four* levels of political ideal:

World of Myth	1. The time of Cronus
World of Historical Reality (Time of Zeus)	2. The high utopia of the *Republic* (Kallipolis)
	3. The low utopia of the *Laws* (Magnesia)
	4. Practical reform programs in real cities

But the important distinction is that between the first level and the rest. There is no pretense that the time of Cronus is anything but a mythic fantasy. It is never identified with the *kallipolis*, the beautiful city of the *Republic* (see 519c) and Kallipolis is never quite a myth in that sense. Kallipolis may be spoken of as something *like* a myth. It is associated with the gods even in the *Republic*. In the *Statesman* (303b) we are told that a city where philosophers rule would stand out among other cities like a god among mortals. In his final comment on the possibility of realizing Kallipolis, Plato hints that it may be reserved for the gods and godlike humans of Cronus' time (*Laws* 739d). But in the same passage he holds stubbornly to the possibility that it may exist somewhere among the remote barbarians, or may come to be sometime in the future. It does not appear that Plato's views about the chances for realizing high utopia ever changed significantly. He did not lose hope of realizing it by the time he wrote the *Laws*. He never had any such hopes or intentions. Just why he brings in the time of Cronus in the later dialogues is not clear. He may be trying to relate his political utopia to the utopias of mythology, but he does not confuse the two.

It does seem that his faith in the ability of the human race to produce philosopher rulers weakened over time. In the *Republic* Socrates seems sure that this human type exists (though how it arises in such an imperfect world is left a mystery) and can be identified. In the *Statesman* there is still no question about the existence of the type, though now we are told that only one or two such may be found in a city. But in the *Laws* the Athenian Stranger seems to doubt that the true philosophical soul who knows the art of kingship can ever be found. He thinks only hints of such a character can be discovered here and there. In the world as it is, no one can be trusted with absolute power (711, 875). Even here the philosopher rulers return as the Nocturnal Council, who at the end of the *Laws* are entrusted with the interpretation and amendment of the Magnesian constitution; but this limited constitutional role is a far cry from the supreme rulership that had been enthroned in Kallipolis, and it is recognized as such. It would appear that at the end of his life Plato saw not only the philosopher's city, but the philosophers themselves, recede into myth. And as they did so he became increasingly interested in the possibility of a real constitution based on *nomoi*. In the *Republic* real constitutions are mentioned only to point out their imperfections; in the *Statesman* we are told that lawabiding constitutions might be fairly close imitations of the ideal; in the *Laws* we are allowed to hope that a second-best constitution, if realized in a new colony, might come very close to divinity (739).

In spite of this development, it seems to me that the remarkable thing about the discussions of model constitutions in the Platonic dialogues is their continuity and consistency. Even in the *Republic* Plato must have envisioned the possibility of a lower utopia of some kind. And he never thought the true "rule of the wise" could exist anywhere but in high utopia.

I propose therefore to accept the methodology described at *Laws* 739 as a primary clue to the meaning of the *Republic*. This means that we accept the *Republic* as the first and most abstract installment of a political program whose implementation was to require planning on much more concrete levels.[31] I do not imagine this to be the only valid approach to the *Republic*. Writers can be unreliable interpreters of their own work. Those who prefer to let the text of the *Republic* speak for itself are free to do so. But if we wish to discover what this text meant to fourth-century Greeks, we are on safer ground if we ask what it meant to the later Plato and to his Academy. Now let us return to the *Republic* and see how this methodology worked.

High Utopia and Low Utopia

The Founding of the City

The discussion of the best constitution in the *Republic* proceeds through several distinct stages, in each of which a different type of city is described. The earlier stages, I suggest, replicate earlier approaches to the best constitution. They are preludes to Plato's new method, which I have termed high utopia; this does not emerge until the latter half of the dialogue. The issue is developed in this dramatic way to show that high utopia is the logical conclusion of the best-constitutional question. But the dramatic form somewhat obscures the relationships among the several types of city-state.

There is a short preliminary discussion about the origins of the city (2. 369–73). This is intended as a historical description, though highly schematized and mythologized, of a universal pattern; Socrates attempts to locate the essential features of the city by examining the historical process through which all cities have developed. This passage is probably based on fifth-century sophistic discussions about the origins of human society. Protagoras had written a treatise on this subject, which Plato had imitated in his dialogue *Protagoras*. Like much Greek speculation about the distant past, the inquiry is more aetiological than historical, based upon the assumption that the essential form of a thing is revealed in its origins.[32]

This historical/aetiological discussion divides itself into two further stages, which so far as we know owed nothing to Protagoras or anyone else. At first Socrates describes the most primitive type of city, one content with bare necessities (369–72). In some ways this is presented as an ideal or at least a desirable condition; Socrates calls it the "healthy" city, implying that all other cities are diseased; many points in the description recall the time of Cronus. But the primitive city cannot be identified with the time of Cronus, for it is real and not mythological, and it is a fairly advanced society familiar with agriculture and other technologies. Commentators have always been puzzled by this primitive city. It is not clear what it is doing in the dialogue. Some have thought that the primitive city *is*, in fact, the "Republic," the true utopia, all the cities described later in the dialogue being inferior copies of it. Others have thought that at least the primitive city is supposed to provide a foundation for or a component of the utopian city developed in books 2–7, perhaps because it represents the way of life of the "producers" in the utopian city. But there is no explicit indication of this in the dialogue. The fact is that we never return at all to the primitive and healthy city. It is not revived in the later utopian city; some of its virtues may be rediscovered there, but the utopian city is devoted to warfare, the absence of which is the most conspicuous feature of the primitive city. Socrates is interested in it because it establishes the principle that social organization depends on reciprocity, upon everyone doing the task for which he is best fitted; this principle will become very important in the utopian city, but it will mean something very different there, and if this is all Socrates wanted to establish there would be no need to go into such detail about the primitive city.

The dramatic point seems to be that the primitive city, though happier than the civilized state, is a condition to which we can never return. Glaucon is contemptuous of the primitive city, calling it a "city of pigs," and at his insistence Socrates goes on to talk about the luxurious form of city that must develop out of the healthy one. Why *must* cities develop in this way? Because people like Glaucon outnumber people like Socrates in their populations.

The next stage, the luxurious city, is described so briefly (372e–373e) that it is often passed over by commentators, who see it only as a transition from the primitive city to the utopian. But it has a key role in this discussion. It is the world that we live in. In this world cities have become swollen in size and involved in constant war with their neighbors. This world is connected to the primitive world only because the principle of reciprocity still holds; but now many more specializations are needed, and the most important of these is the military. The historical city of luxury and war, so succinctly outlined in this passage, will remain the framework for everything that follows. To the end of the dialogue Socrates will assume that the vast majority of the human race must always live in the city of war; there is no possibility that they might return to the primitive city, and, more oddly, no possibility that they might adopt the utopian city that Socrates now proceeds to describe.

For as soon as Socrates begins to discuss the best form of military organization (374a) the city ceases to be historical and universal. The Protagoran method is dropped. From now on they will talk about one particular city, and this will be no historical city, but such a city as has never been. In this way the utopian part of the *Republic* commences. It will occupy the speakers from the middle of the second book till the end of the seventh.

The utopian dialogue, in turn, has two parts. The first of these extends from the middle of the second book (374) to the middle of the fifth (473). It is a model constitution of the Laconist type. Its principal feature is the "rule of the guards," a professional warrior class clearly modeled on the Spartiates of contemporary Lacedaemon. The Spartan model is not acknowledged; nor need be. To judge from our limited knowledge of earlier political literature Plato's most important predecessor here was Phaleas of Chalcedon, as the main predecessor of the preliminary discussion in book 2 was Protagoras. In discussions of excellence in the city the sophistic method, which had been restricted to cities as they are, had been superceded by the low-utopian method of planning cities that might be; and this progression is replicated in the dialogue. The transition is made so easily and naturally that it may easily be missed. As soon as they begin to discuss the best kind of army, they realize that this question raises problems that have never been solved by historical cities, especially the problem of training the best type of soldier—the limitations of the Spartan model are implicitly recognized here—and so the historical method will no longer work (375–76). Instead, Socrates embarks upon a long *mythos* describing the ideal *agoge*. His audience assumes this is a low utopia meant for literal implementation, and nothing in the dialogue, until we reach 472, suggests otherwise. Actually Socrates is undermining the premises of the low-utopian tradition, because in the middle of this section he slips in the idea of total communism, which gradually takes over the discussion. The low-utopian dialogue ends suddenly in the middle ot the fifth book, when everyone realizes that there is no way to implement communism—unless philosophers can rule. What Plato wishes to convey by means of this dramatic sequence is that any discussion about social change, once it goes beyond the immediately practical, is compelled to start thinking about changing the entire social context.

Then the discussion moves to yet another level, and from this point on will focus on the philosopher-rulers and their education. This stage, extending from the middle of the fifth book to the start of the eighth (473–544), is what I have called a *high* utopia; its main theme is the "rule of the wise"; and here, so far as we know, Plato had no predecessors at all.

All commentators have seen the difference between the "earthly city" of books 2–5 and the "heavenly city" of books 5–8. Though these utopias are united by the theme of communism, the differences are so striking that some have thought them two different utopias that Plato composed at different times and later stitched together.[33] But Socrates does not leave any doubt that the whole utopian discussion of books 2–8 is meant to be a single unit. It is admitted, for the sake of dramatic plausibility, that the difference between the rule of the wise and the rule of the guards is extreme. In the sixth book, after Socrates has defined the "philosopher," he says that philosophers can flourish only in the best constitution, and Adeimantus asks if the rule of the guards they have just discussed is the best constitution; Socrates replies that it is, except that they have yet to show the place of the philosophers in it (497c). Then when Socrates and Glaucon attempt to summarize the whole discussion at the beginning of book 8 (543), it occurs to Glaucon that they have been talking about two different cities.

> ...then, much the same as now, you were talking as if you had completed the discussion of the city [at the beginning of Book 5, where Socrates winds

> up his treatment of the rule of the guards]; you said that you would class as good the city you had described, and that the good man is he who resembled it, although it seems you had a finer city and man about which to tell us (trans. Grube)

But Socrates makes it clear to him that they have been talking about only one city, though the manner of the discussion made it seem like two. The rulers of the city must be "those who are best in the practice of philosophy and the waging of war" (543a). The rule of the guards must be united to the rule of the wise.

The argument and plot of this drama may be outlined as follows. It proceeds by asking a series of questions; the answer to each question reveals a further problem, which requires a further question.

1. The Historical Dialogue (2. 369–73). A description of how cities in general arise. Question: What does the origin of the city tell us about justice? It turns out there is no one answer to this question, for there have been two kinds of historical city.
   A. The Primitive City (369–72). Question: What is the most basic need of a city? Conclusion: Specialization of functions leading to reciprocity. It turns out this is the real meaning of justice, though we won't understand that till later. Problem: We can't stay in the primitive city.
   B. The City of War (372–73). Question: What does the city need in the developed and luxurious society we now live in? Conclusion: More specialized functions, especially for war. Problem: No city has ever developed a military specialization compatible with reciprocal harmony. At this impasse the historical discussion ends.
2. The Utopian Dialogue (2–8. 374–544). Prescriptions for the best possible city. Question: What does the potentiality of the city tell us about justice? It turns out there is no one answer to this question, for there are two kinds of potentiality.
   A. The Low Utopia (The earthly city, the rule of the guards: 374–473). Question: What is the optimal method by which a city may defend itself in the world of category 1B? Conclusion: A Laconistic constitution with a communistic military elite. Now it is revealed that this also answers the original question: justice in a world of war means a harmony of specialized functions of this particular type, which will also curb the growth of luxury that produced the problems of 1B in the first place. Problem: This method cannot be optimal without total communism, and how can that be implemented?
   B. The High Utopia (The heavenly city, the rule of the wise: 473–544). Question: What are the minimal conditions for bringing about the low utopia of 2A? Conclusion: A city ruled by philosophers. Problem: This solution is unattainable. At this impasse the utopian discussion ends.

But by the end we have seen the kind of society that would be necessary to produce the optimal type of human being, and this is taken as an adequate answer to the question, what is justice?

Each of these levels stands in a different relation to reality. We move from that which has been, to that which is, to that which might be, and finally to that which could not be. In the process we have seen every condition of society that Plato could conceive, and the optimal type of social harmony or justice that is possible in each condition.

In the *Republic* we move from the real to the ideal, and the movement is dramatic, every question arising naturally out of the preceding question, but leaving us at the end not entirely clear about the connections among the several levels. At *Laws* 739, we have the same progression through several levels of political reality, but now in the form of a summary treatise, proceeding in the reverse order from ideal to real, and now making quite explicit the connections. If we take this passage in the *Laws* as a guide to Plato's intentions in the *Republic* we will be inclined to consider more seriously than some the possibility that Plato was always interested in the practical political realization of this scheme.

The implications of this suggestion I will explore by considering in greater detail some of the key institutions of Plato's utopia.

Warfare and Slavery

Warfare is the element that ties utopia to reality. It is introduced in category 1B as the major problem of the world we live in; the whole of the utopian dialogue is inspired by the effort to solve this problem; and at its most utopian the dialogue never escapes from the harsh necessities of war.

Why does Plato assume warfare is necessary in Kallipolis? We always ask why he puts communism there, rarely why he puts war there. If the question is asked at all, we are told that Plato is being "realistic," or that he wants to make the smallest possible alterations in the structure of society, just enough to accommodate his ideal institutions. But the plea of "realism" can apply only to the earthly city, the low utopia of books 2–5. It makes no sense by the time we finish the fifth book, for by then we are engaged in a thought experiment of deliberate fantasy. Plato does not include anything in his utopia that is literally impossible—reproduction without sex is confined to the time of Cronus—but a society without war is perfectly conceivable. Socrates and his friends have no difficulty conceiving it in the primitive stage. We cannot stay there because Socrates is overpowered by Glaucon; but eventually we reach a city where Socrates is in charge and all the social evils produced by luxury can be eliminated, except for war. Why can we not go one step further and eliminate war? This would require us to imagine many unrealizable cities, instead of a single unrealizable city. It is not obvious why the one would be more difficult than the other. If we mean to construct a perfect abstract model, deliberately unconcerned with problems of realistic implementation lest these contaminate its perfection, why should the model have to include separate warring states? We will not assume this because it is "realistic." We will assume it because, for some reason, this is what we like.

I suggest that Plato liked this because he found warfare useful to justify one of the main principles of his utopia: that societies should be run by the strictest hierarchical and authoritarian methods. The necessity of war is the only reason ever given in the *Republic* for the existence of a specialized military elite; and a specialized military elite of the Spartan type, as distinct from an ordinary Greek citizen army, was important to Plato because it was associated with the most hierarchical type of Greek social structure.

I have said that the first stage of the ideal city resembles a model constitution of the Laconist type. It is assumed to be a new colony; Socrates and his hearers describe themselves as the oikists (379a). It is taken for granted that the professional soldier class which is their main interest will be modeled on the Spartiates: they are to live in a separate encampment within the city, in a sort of barracks life (415de), and it is tacitly assumed that they will constitute a smallish minority of the total population.[34] It is taken for granted that the city will have an oligarchical form of government: from the moment we hear of magistrates we understand that they will be figures of great authority like the Spartan ephors (389b–390a); everyone assumes that the soldiers will be the political rulers of the city (419e). It is not thought surprising when Socrates turns the discussion to the education of these "guards of the city" (*phylakes poleon*), for the assumption that a military elite should go through a special public *agoge* was the core of traditional Laconism (376d). It does not seem to make any difference when Socrates says that some guards are to be "rulers" and the rest "auxiliaries" (412b), for it will be a long time before he explains what he means by these "rulers," and his audience is probably thinking of some such body as the Spartan Council of Elders. Naturally the guards are assumed to function as police as well as soldiers, keeping order in "the rest of the city," which will consist of "craftsmen and farmers" (414–15). This city differs from Sparta chiefly in that the methods by which the guards keep order in the rest of the city are far less harsh, and the relationship between the two groups far less despotic; it is assumed that the artisans and farmers will also have the status of "citizens," though we are not told what this means. So far there is nothing unrealistic about this modified Laconist constitution, and the audience would expect next a discussion about how it is to be put into practice. Clearly it could be put into practice completely only in a new colonial foundation, as is suggested by the image at 415de, where the guards are visualized as marching to the site of their new city, looking for the best site to camp, and offering sacrifice to the appropriate gods.

But no real city is ever founded, Instead, Socrates just at this point leaves reality behind, when he blandly tells his companions that the guards are to have no *oikoi* or other private possessions (416d–417b). Communism is presented as a logical extension of Spartan collectivist practices, and is proposed primarily for its *military* advantages: it will eliminate discord between rich and poor, and thereby make Kallipolis invincible in war against cities of conventional social structure, which are always internally divided. The repeated military argument gives us the illusion that we are still in the world of practical constitutional programs, even while Socrates quietly severs the last ties that connect his ideal city to reality; for immediately after this "realistic" strategic analysis, he drops the first mention of sexual communism (423e–424a). The discussion has stayed in the real world just long enough to set up a military state.

One does not know how seriously Plato took these military arguments. This is supposed to be a discussion among a set of vaguely Laconophile young aristocrats ca. 411 B.C., a circle where it can be taken for granted that the type of constitution most highly regarded by "most men" is the Spartan or Cretan (544c). The assumptions about Spartan military superiority are those typical of such circles. Their wrongness was demonstrated within a few years after the *Republic* was written; the Spartan system of a hereditary soldier elite, the invincibility of which is so complacently assumed by everyone in the dialogue, turned out to be far less capable of adapting to new conditions than the more conventional Greek citizen armies. One doubts that this would have made any difference to Plato. The dramatic function of the military argument is simply to get the rule of the guards established in the beautiful city, and once that is done the military argument is largely forgotten. It is really the internal constitution that the guards are supposed to guard.

Even during this low-utopian discussion, Socrates has hinted that there is another and better method of thinking about the best constitution (435cd). The low utopia reaches an impasse at 472–73, when it is fully realized what communism entails; and then we move to the other method. From now on we will be concerned not with the rule of the guards but with the rule of the wise. We gradually understand that these "rulers" are people who have attained a very unusual psychic state, achieved by mastering the art of conceptual thought at a high level, through a rigorous lifelong program of study dominated by mathematics. They are, in the view of the mature Plato, the masters of the political art whom the real Socrates had searched for, though they are perhaps far fewer than the real Socrates had hoped for. As for the hope of realization, it has faded into irrelevance by the time we fully understand what is meant by the "rule of the wise."

Why did Plato organize the dialogue like this? We usually assume that the rule of the guards provides a necessary foundation for the rule of the wise. That seems to be what Plato wants us to assume, for the transition from one scheme to the next is artfully disguised. But in fact the two schemes start from such different premises that it is difficult to see any logically necessary connection between them. The one is a model constitution for a possible state, the other is a thought experiment about the conditions required for the optimal development of human nature. They are said to be united by the principle of specialization of function, "doing one's own thing" (*to ta autou prattein*, 433–34). But this principle means something different in every kind of city. In the primitive city all functions are equal; in the low-utopian city the only function that really matters is the military; in the high-utopian city the only function that really matters is the philosophical. Why should we have to think about the rule of the guards to imagine the rule of the wise? And once we have reached the rule of the wise, why can we not abolish the rule of the guards? Why must the rulers always combine philosophy and war?

Because the rule of the guards, I suggest, was as important to Plato as the rule of the wise. He wanted his utopia tied to the real world in certain respects, and in military affairs he did not wish to be utopian at all, because only through military arguments could he establish the authoritarian political model that remains implicit throughout the *Republic*. He was capable of proposing significant and interesting changes in the conduct of interstate relations,[35] but they are not allowed to go so far as to remove the need for the military establishment upon which Kallipolis is based. He did not want a world, or even a Hellas, entirely under the rule of the wise because the kind of ideal society he wanted to describe required *one* ideal city surrounded by a lot of extremely real ones.

Neither did Plato have any wish to abolish slavery in the ideal world. Slavery is not, like warfare, something absolutely essential to Kallipolis. (Though there is some connection between warfare and slavery. The code of war that Socrates proposes at 469–71 depends to some extent on the need to capture slaves from the barbarians.) But slavery is very convenient. It is not only the unspoken social foundation of Kallipolis but a symbol of its hierarchical pattern of social relationships. The great principle of Kallipolis is the hierarchy of reason: everyone must be ruled by reason, preferably by the reason within oneself, but if this is not possible then one must be "enslaved" by those who possess reason (590cd). This "slavery" (*douleia*) is a metaphor, but Socrates does not hesitate to apply the word to relations between free citizens, a choice of language that must have sounded to his contemporaries as startling and paradoxical as it does to us. The rule of the wise over society is precisely analogous to the rule of the mind over the body; and each of these is autocratic, a master–slave relationship. Plato idealizes slavery just as he idealizes war.[36]

This war-based and slave-based hierarchy is the key to Platonic social harmony. Only in this way, according to Socrates/Plato, can true *philia* and *homonoia* be achieved. Only when citizens are governed by reason can they be true friends; and given their unequal rational capacities, this can only be achieved by hierarchical subordination. Social harmony is defined as a condition of reciprocity, in which each does what he does best for the good of the community, and the whole community recognizes the primacy of reason (427–34); it is the social equivalent of the psychic harmony produced by the rule of reason in a virtuous person (441–43). This is the meaning of justice, and with the completion of this argument Socrates claims to have proven what he set out to prove, that justice is the happiest of conditions. It means to him the set of circumstances necessary to bring out the highest potentialities of human nature and society.

There is much emphasis on the unanimity and harmony among all three groups, philosopher rulers and guards and "producers" (*chremastikoi*). The consent of all three groups is thought essential; this is what distinguishes Kallipolis from harsh rule that the Spartiates imposed on Lacedaemon, which Socrates considers a perversion of his ideal system. One of the persistent problems in interpreting the *Republic* is the difficulty of understanding what Socrates means by this consent, and how he expects to engineer it. We often assume that acculturation is the key to the system; that the masses will be led to accept willingly the rule of their betters, and everyone will be led to accept his own place, through psychological conditioning; that this is the purpose of the educational system described in such detail in the third book. This *agoge* has a military part (*gymnastike*) reserved for the guards, but there is also an artistic/cultural part (*mousike*) in which the entire citizen body perhaps participates. But there is no sign that they do.[37] Repeatedly we are told that the educational system is for the guards. It is distinguished from the kind of training that a cobbler receives (456d), which is merely an apprenticeship in his craft—an allusion which surely implies that a cobbler in Kallipolis does not get a guard's education. Confusion about this point has arisen because Socrates does say that the censorship of art and literature, an important part of the guards' *paideia*, is to affect everybody in the city. In discussing the regulations for musical instruments he mentions that they are to apply even to shepherds in the fields (399d). Artisans are to be forbidden to make images of any improper subject, so that the young guards might grow up in a totally beautiful and healthy environment (401b). But here and elsewhere (378bc, 380b), the producers are to be censored only because of the possible effects of their activities on the psychological conditioning of the *guards*; no one seems concerned about the acculturation of the producers themselves.

The strange thing is that Socrates assumes the masses will be totally regulated and docile in Kallipolis, but says nothing about how to accomplish this. There is no question about the extent of their regimentation. Not only are their crafts, arts, and recreations to be thoroughly censored, but severe limits, of a sort unknown to any Greek society, are to be placed on their disposal of their private households: extremes of wealth and poverty are not to be allowed anywhere (421d–422a); the size of the total population is to be strictly regulated (423bc); it seems to be expected that the emancipation of women will be enforced among the producers as among the guards and rulers (455d–456a). Voluntary submission of the producers to all this is assumed throughout.

Plato's silence about the means of engineering consent indicates that he was not much concerned about this problem, which tends to occupy the minds of his modern interpreters. What he cared about was the fact of unanimity, not the means of achieving it. He wanted to portray a society where, as far as possible, "all see and hear and act in concert" (*Laws* 739, trans. Saunders). He thought it important to show how this could be achieved among the elite, for the thought no discord could arise in the rest of the city so long as the elite remained united (465b, 545cd); he assumed the consent of the rest could be managed one way or another. Repeatedly we hear that all the citizens must be brought into harmony with one another "by persuasion or compulsion," a formula suggesting that the difference between these methods does not matter much.[38]

It is not easy to fault this ideal society, once we accept its premises. If we accept the method of describing an unrealizable ideal, we will not call it "totalitarian," a word that has only created confusion. Totalitarianisms are meant to be realizable. If we reject the ideal, it will usually be because we find something repugnant about its insidious authoritarianism. But then it will be said that we are applying to Plato certain modern values, such as individual moral autonomy, which Plato certainly did not believe in, which probably no ancient Greek held as an absolute value, and which even modern liberals are not agreed upon. If we object to the assumption that absolute moral values are attainable, we will be reminded that Plato is only asking us, "What *if* they were attainable?" What, after all, is wrong with this portrait of perfect social harmony, this world where everyone has a chance to do the task he or she is best suited for and to receive the rewards that he or she is best suited for? Can there be any rational objection, based upon reasons that Plato's contemporaries might have thought valid, to the social ideal of a perfect hierarchy of specialized functions?

I suggest there can be. It has to do with the particular kinds of specialized functions that Socrates thinks important. Why must there be so many soldiers in an ideal society, and why must its educational system and everything else in it be organized so thoroughly for military purposes? Plato's apologists usually tell us that his hierarchical authoritarianism arises from his exacting intellectual standards and his desire to allow wisdom its maximal social influence. This may explain the rule of the wise, but not the rule of the guards. The useful political model in the *Republic* is not the rule of the wise, but the rule of the guards. Plato's ideal world, even in its most fantastic and thought-experimental mode, must retain warfare and slavery because it is an ideal world constructed with certain practical political ends in view.

The nature of these ends becomes much clearer in the later dialogues. At the beginning of the *Timaeus* Socrates proposes to show what the ideal city would be like if put into action. In the *Republic*, we are told, he had described a statue; now he wishes to make the statue step from its pedestal (*Tim.*19). He recapitulates the ideal city of the *Republic*, but his summary includes only the first five books; it is essentially the earthly city; there is no mention of philosopher-rulers. In the *Timaeus* Socrates never actually reaches the point of putting this city into action, but a stab at this is made in the fragmentary *Critias*. There we are told that a reasonable facsimile of Socrates' ideal city existed in the remote past—a mythical Athens that flourished nine thousand years ago, whose main feature was a communistic warrior class of both sexes. Again there is no mention of philosopher-rulers.

The *Timaeus* and *Critias* suggest that when Plato thought about practical applications of the best constitution of the *Republic*, what he thought about was the rule of the guards in books 2–5. He did not make a sustained effort to lay out these practical applications until he wrote the *Laws*; and the result leaves small comfort for those who believe the principles of the *Republic* to be compatible with modern representative democracy.

The *Laws* retraces and reworks the argument of the early books of the *Republic*, but the lowest and highest steps on the ladder of cities have practically disappeared. During the twenty years since the *Republic* Plato seems to have developed more interest in Protagoras' questions about the origins of society, for in the *Laws* there is a more serious attempt to exploit the historical/

aetiological method. The primitive and healthy city reappears briefly in a more realistic guise: now it is described as a state of society before cities arose, when people lived in separate households like the Homeric Cyclopes, without government or war (678–80). But now we are much more interested in the "city of war," the world that we live in. The *Republic* had dismissed this world briefly, finding nothing in it but evils to be corrected; but the *Laws* devotes much space (680–701) to a reconstruction of the earlier history of warring states, for the purpose of identifying the reasons why past constitutions have been successful or unsuccessful. The main lesson that Plato wishes his audience to draw from this historical investigation is that the most stable form of government is an agrarian landowning aristocracy with a "mixed" constitution, resembling Sparta, Crete, and Solonic Athens.

The speakers proceed to put this ideal into action in a draft constitution for the new Cretan colony of Magnesia. It is to have a citizen body of 5,040 equal households, whose members are to devote themselves to government and war. There will also be a population of slaves and a population (presumably quite large) of foreigners and freedmen, who will be permitted to remain in the city only for limited periods, and who will provide all the artisans, merchants, and nonslave labor. Magnesia is not a conventional oligarchy, because its citizen body has been artificially restricted from the start, as would be possible in a new colony. But it is clearly an attempt to imitate the social structure of Lacedaemon. As in the constitution of Phaleas, the citizen class must be supported by a large noncitizen population, composed not of slaves of the polis as in Phaleas, but of foreigners and freedmen, who are never even permitted to become permanent residents like the metics of most Greek cities. Magnesia is a thinly disguised Laconist oligarchy.

And there the argument of the *Laws* stops. We never return to the high theoretical level of the *Republic*, though we are told (739) that it remains the ultimate model. We hear no more about the rule of the wise. Neither here nor anywhere else did Plato find a practical role for them (unless we count the Nocturnal Council, the supreme religious and judicial committee of Magnesia). But the rule of the guards is more important than ever. A society like this, in Plato's final judgment, was the nearest possible practical expression of those principles of social harmony he had laid out in the *Republic*.

Community of Goods and Women

If the Laconist social structure of Kallipolis represent its most authoritarian and practical side, its communistic institutions represent its most egalitarian and utopian side. Communism is the main instrument through which hierarchy is supposed to result in unity and harmony. Let us now consider, again using the *Laws* as a key to Plato's intentions, what he meant by communism, and how he meant to implement it in the real world.

Before Plato wrote sexual communism was primarily associated with primitive barbarians and was thought to imply sexual freedom, even licence. There was a milder form of polyandry associated with Spartans, who were supposed to practice it for eugenic purposes. What Plato calls "community of women" is a combination of the two, barbarian in form but Spartan in spirit: an ascetic and minutely regulated system of eugenic population control, which abolishes the *oikos* only so that the individual may be totally controlled by the polis. All the guards are to remain celibate until the age of thirty (for men) and twenty (for women), and thereafter are allowed no sexual activity except at temporary "marriages," or rather couplings, which are arranged by the philosopher-rulers for the ends mentioned above. After they pass the age of childbearing, which is figured at fifty for men and forty for women, they are allowed to do what they please heterosexually. This combination of early restraint and late permissiveness may seem bizarre to modern readers. It may be less permissive than it sounds; Plato probably assumed that middle-aged guards disciplined by a lifetime of self-control and the continued pressures of their barracks society would not plunge into orgies. Still, the allowance reminds us that his asceticism is not of the Judeo-Christian type, not an aversion to certain sexual acts in themselves but a concern about their moral and social consequences. His system is more consistently repressive of homosexual behavior. The younger Plato had seen a social and moral role for *paiderastia*, but the middle-aged Plato apparently decided that to introduce that into the beautiful city was to play with fire. Erotic attachments between male guards are taken for granted, but they are not to go beyond kisses and caresses. (Whether Plato would have assumed the existence of female homosexual attachments we do not know, because at this point in the dialogue, 402d–403c, we are still thinking of male guards only.)[39] There is a fictive kinship, also modeled on unacknowledged barbarian precedents, in which all children of the same age group are assigned common "parents." This will eliminate the danger of parent–child incest, but there is no practical way to avoid all sibling incest, so Socrates, after a somewhat hasty and confused discussion, allows the latter.

One result of this system is the emancipation of women, who are to be treated exactly like men in the guard class. Often this is perceived as an anomaly, a note of individual liberation in a closed system of sexual/political control, but that is not how Plato perceived it. He simply wanted to free women (and men) from the *oikos* so as to put them at the service of the polis. He wanted to avoid the Spartan system, which weakened the *oikos* but ignored women, and thereby left them, so it was said, to indolence and license.

There has been much debate[40] over whether Plato was a "feminist." If we mean by this word someone who favors the emancipation of women so as to admit them to education and public life, then Plato was the original feminist. His female guards are to receive the same education and perform the same duties as males; Plato is probably not sure what the biological differences amount to, but he has no doubt that a rational society would minimize them. If we mean by "feminist" someone who considers women the intellectual and moral equals of men, then Plato was not one, because a number of passing remarks (*Rep.* 455; *Laws* 781, 917) leave little doubt that he assumed women to be generally inferior to men in every respect. The emancipation of women was a by-product of his system. It is difficult to revolutionize an entire society without liberating somebody.

Such was Platonic communism. Who was it for? The *Republic* makes it perfectly clear that it is to be practiced by the guard class alone (417a). But at *Laws* 739 the Athenian Stranger speaks of communism as a principle to be followed "as widely as possible" by all the citizens, as its purpose is to impose the "greatest possible unity" on the polis; and he seems to suggest (740a) that in the absolute best constitution the citizens will farm in common, a possibility which is certainly never mentioned in the *Republic*, nor could be. Then Aristotle, in his critique of Plato's *Republic*—which obviously refers to the same text called the *Republic* that we have—asserts that Socrates never decides "whether the farming class are to have communal or individual private possession, whether of property or of wives and children" (*Pol.* 1264a11–b5; trans. Sinclair/Saunders).

How to explain these contradictions? Some think that Plato, when he wrote th *Laws*, forgot what he had really said in the *Republic*; and that Aristotle, when he wrote the *Politics*, was thinking about the *Laws*, and equally forgot what Plato had really said in the *Republic*.[41] But it is a little hard to imagine Aristotle, and Plato himself, misunderstanding Plato quite so grossly. *Laws* 739 does not refer specifically to the *Republic*, but to a design for a best possible state, in which communism is to extend as far as possible. There may have been discussions at the Academy about how far it would be possible to extend communism within the framework laid down in the *Republic*. If so it is easier to understand Aristotle's mistake, given the loose Greek habits of textual citation. The form of an ancient book made it so difficult to look up exact references that authors usually relied on their excerpts, notes, and memories; and the notion of a "book" implied not so much a fixed text as an oral presentation, sometimes with commentary.

There was ample room for such commentary. As Aristotle pointed out, the role of the producers constitutes the most obvious lacuna in the *Republic*. The main purpose of the complete *koinonia* of the guards is to create a larger *koinonia*, unifying the entire citizen body, but it is never made clear how that is to be done. It is assumed that the masses will accept an extreme degree of economic, social, and sexual control, but the means of control are never explained. The Socrates of the *Republic* does not envision communism for the masses, and neither does he envision the normal Greek household society. He does not envision anything very clearly, except the desired result of total unanimity. One obvious possibility would be to extend the *koinonia* of goods and women to all the citizens in some form. The Academy may have discussed variants of this proposal; Aristotle mentions the possibility that the producers might adopt community of women without community of goods. But Plato was always clear that the absolute ideal must include the abolition of the household for at least some part of the citizens; and the second-best ideal must be one that allowed private households, while applying to these the communistic principles of the *Republic*.

Not until he wrote the *Laws* did Plato leave any clear idea of how he meant to put those principles into action. What happens to communism in the *Laws*? It becomes a model for the equalization of landed property among a citizen elite who are supported by importing slaves and foreign workers; the citizens are perhaps a larger percentage of the total population than the Kallipolitan guards, but still a minority. Every citizen household in Magnesia will have its allotment of land, but each will regard its lot as the common possession of the city (*Laws* 740a). The sexual communism of Kallipolis is translated into the austere but relatively normal code practiced by the Magnesian citizen elite, in which sex is restricted to procreation for both men and women. The sexual equality of Kallipolis is preserved, to a large extent; women are to receive the same public education as men, and some public offices and military service are to be open to them, though we hear little about this (785). Magnesian citizens, like the Kallipolitan guards, contract marriages for eugenic reasons and for the good of the city, not to accumulate property (not a temptation in Magnesia, because of its property restrictions); but the magistrates will intervene only to regulate the size of the population. In matters of property, sex, and marriage the *Republic* and the *Laws* are not so far apart as they may seem. The principles have not changed, only the degree of central planning. Even in the *Republic* Plato must have had something like this in mind as the way of life for the "rest of the city" in Kallipolis, though he may have played also with the notion of making them adopt communism in some form.

The real difference is that in the *Laws* this ideal ceases to apply, even in its most diluted form, to the mass of the people at all. In the *Republic* we are told that all the citizens, who apparently are to comprise the entire free population,

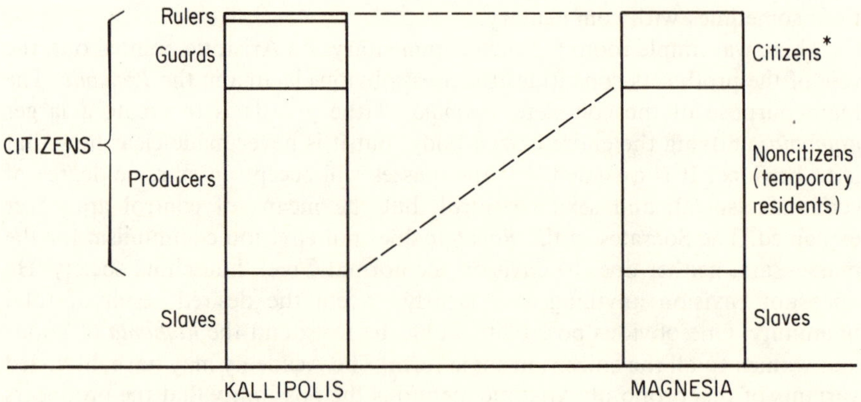

Fig. 1. *The only "statistic" we are given is that Magnesia is to have 5,040 citizen households, or a total citizen population of perhaps 20,000, implying a total population of perhaps 100,000—a gigantic polis, especially for Crete. (Aristotle pointed out the unrealism of Plato's geography, *Pol.* 1265a10–17.) My proportions are, of course, guesswork but based on the fact that hoplites were often assumed to constitute about a third of the free population.

are to achieve perfect unity and harmony. In the *Laws* we are again told that all the citizens can achieve this ideal, and the second plan is presented as a close application of the first; but the "citizens" have become a minority (*Fig. 1*).

This did not deceive Aristotle. Aristotle did not think of the five thousand citizens (actually ten thousand, for he forgets women are treated as citizens) of Magnesia as the equivalent of the "citizens" of Kallipolis; he saw them as equivalent to the "guards" of Kallipolis, a body which was probably assumed also to number several thousand:

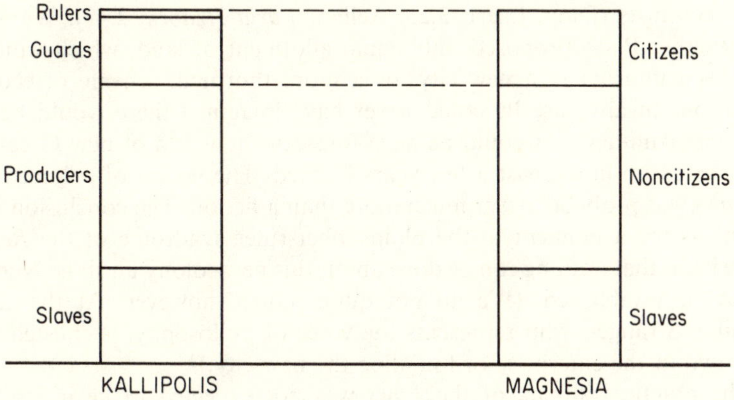

Fig. 2.

Throughout the *Politics* Aristotle tries to use the term "citizen" in a consistent way that corresponds to social realities. He calls "citizens" only those who participate in political life—assemblies, jury courts, magistracies—and he assumes that they have the right to bear arms. In his discussion of earlier utopias he criticizes both Hippodamus and Plato for obscuring this distinction. Hippodamus' constitution had "citizens" who participated in politics but did not bear arms; Plato's Kallipolis had "citizens" who apparently did neither. Aristotle did not believe in such citizens.

In the *Republic* Plato had made a serious effort to broaden and democratize the Spartan ideal, turning it into an instrument of harmony and not of repression. The effort seems to have foundered upon Plato's own conviction of unsurmountable human inequality. In the *Laws* he simply dropped it, though claiming that the traditional values of oligarchical solidarity were a satisfactory representation of his earlier ideal of citizen unity. He resorted to the ploy of redefining the citizen body: as Athenian oligarchs could claim Sparta a "democracy" by counting only the Spartiates, so Plato can claim Magnesia to represent the communal values of the *Republic* by counting only a group that in any normal Greek city would be reckoned members of the hoplite class (*Pol.* 1265a9). As soon as Plato came within sight of reality, the communistic and egalitarian aspects of his utopia faded, and its authoritarian, traditionally Laconist side came to the fore.

The Academy in Politics

According to tradition, Plato really did hope for opportunities to found new colonies. In the Seventh Epistle, generally thought authentic at least in substance, he says that in the 360s he hoped that the tyrant of Syracuse might resettle some of the Sicilian cities and give them new constitutions. It was said that the Thebans invited Plato to make laws for the new city of Megalopolis in Arcadia, which they founded ca. 362 as a bulwark against the defeated Spartans; but Plato refused to go because they would not equalize the property of the colonists (Diog. Laert. 3.23; Aelian, *Varia Historia* 2.42). We are not told whether Plato proposed only equal allotment of land, which would not have been unusual in a new city, or a more thorough scheme of economic regulation. In any case he could never have imagined there would be many such opportunities, nor could he have foreseen the world of new Greek cities that opened up in the east a few years he died. The fiction of colonization in the *Laws* was probably never much more than a fiction. The conclusion almost returns us for a moment to the philosopher-ruler syndrome of the *Republic*, for we learn that nothing can be done about this new colony until the Nocturnal Council is established. (We do not quite return, however. At the end the Athenian Stranger, who represents the voice of philosophy, is enlisted by the other two in the enterprise of founding the new city.)[42]

The practical impact of the *Laws* was not expected to lie in its largely hypothetical role as a blueprint for new colonies. Its main political function was to promote reforms in established states—the third level of political change—and to bring these under philosophical influence, a hope symbolized by the conclusion of the *Laws*. More information about this program was promised, but as it is we must make do with the comments at *Laws* 684 and 736. At the time this was written demands for land redistribution and debt cancellation were widespread in the Greek world. The Athenian Stranger speaks of these reform programs with a sympathy that must surprise those who believe Plato was merely a mouthpiece for contemporary oligarchs. But he also thinks (with good reason) that such revolutionary demands can only lead to civil strife. Therefore he proposes an alternative method of reform: the wealthy citizens should provide for the poor through voluntary distributions of their property and forgiveness of their debtors. In other words the communistic ideal of the *Republic* becomes a model for the traditional system of aristocratic patronage, made more effective though the reeducation and moral reform of the upper classes.

Only in the case of communism does Plato explicitly say how his utopias were expected to affect political practice. But clearly his audience was expected to find other practical applications. The applications of the hierarchical principle seem fairly obvious. Both the *Republic* and the *Laws* insist on the inequalities of human talent, the functionality of strict social stratification, the need to restrict citizenship to a small and cohesive group that can be freed from the degrading necessities of manual labor. We may suppose that at the third level of reform politicians were expected to draw the lesson made explicit by Aristotle: the poor should be excluded from political rights if possible, and in any case extreme democracy should be avoided. We can only guess what Plato thought to be the practical applications of the bizarre sexual code of the *Republic*. Perhaps he hoped that his ideal of sexual communism would help to reduce citizens' identification with their private *oikoi* and merge the *oikoi* more completely into the polis. He perhaps hoped that it would lead to a more austere sexual morality; and encourage, not equality for women, but a more rational attitude toward women's roles that would make them more serviceable to the city.

There is some reason to think that the discussions at Plato's Academy were much concerned with practical applications of the utopian models. According to various traditions, about ten Greek cities asked Plato or other members of the Academy to advise them on constitutional matters; and the Academy also established a connection with the Macedonian court.[43] Some of these stories may be apocryphal, but there is no reason to doubt the general pattern. These overtures were presumably the result of the circulation of the *Republic* and the reputation it won for the school; the precise classification of political models and their uses that we find in the *Laws*, and the still more precise classifications we find in Aristotle, represent the results of years of political study and consulting.

We conclude that the *Republic* was always rooted in Greek politics. It was always meant to provide a new ideological basis for an aristocratic and oligarchic society. Its most practical political lesson, and the lesson probably of greatest interest to contemporaries, was its defense of hierarchy—the Laconistic or low-utopian side of the *Republic*. What has fascinated the centuries is the high-utopian side: the vision of perfect harmony achieved through communism. But Plato could not show how to put this into practice and left it in utopia. In the end, it appears that the only practical result he could hope to achieve was something surprisingly ordinary: a revitalized aristocracy devoted to community service; the ancient ideal of *koinonia* uniting rich and poor, requiring now an exacting discipline on the part of the rich, but still dependent upon the willingness of the rich to submit to it. Perhaps Plato found this a disappointing solution also.

Aristotle

The Method of Aristotle

The program laid out in the *Laws* was continued by Aristotle, especially after he set up his own school at Athens ca. 335. At the conclusion of the *Nichomachean Ethics* he proposes to establish an empirical basis for the study of politics by assembling a collection of constitutions. According to tradition, he and his pupils wrote constitutional histories of one hundred and fifty-eight cities and tribes, mostly Greek; only fragments of these survived until a papyrus containing the *Constitution of Athens* turned up in 1890, but the results were embodied in the *Politics*.

At the beginning of the fourth book of the *Politics* Aristotle sets forth a program for political studies which may be described as an elaboration of the three-stage program of *Laws* 739 (1288b21ff.).

1. The first task of political science is to identify the absolutely best constitution, without regard to the actual circumstances of individuals and states; the city that we would live in if we could, within the bounds of possibility, live exactly as we like (cf. 1260b27, 1325b33ff.). He means the sort of literary effort that assumed an oikist/lawgiver with absolute powers. This is the most careful definition anyone had ever attempted of what we call "utopianism." Earlier efforts of this kind Aristotle discussed in the second book, and as we have seen he recognized a difference between a lower utopianism that stayed close to the necessities (*anankaion*) of political life, and a higher form that so far transcended these as to abolish the patriarchal household. The first type of utopia Aristotle thought useful, and in the seventh and eighth books he contributes one of his own.

2. The second level contains a more practical constitution, but Aristotle defines this defferently from Plato. To Plato the most preferable constitution after the absolute best was that of the *Laws*. Aristotle considers Magnesia a utopia of the first class: it requires a fictive oikist, and in Aristotle's view it would be virtually as unrealizable as Kallipolis.[44] Aristotle prefers to define the second-best constitution as the most common (*koinos*) type, meaning one that would be within the reach of almost any state or at least available to the largest number of states in existing circumstances. Elsewhere he identifies this all-purpose constitution with the "middle constitution," also called simply "the constitution" (*politeia*, implying it is the only true constitution). We have seen that more than one version of the "middle" or "mixed" constitutional ideal was around, and more than one appears in Aristotle; but his preferred version is a constitution based on the "middle people" (*mesoi*), with a property qualification that excludes from citizenship those below the hoplite census. This "middle constitution" is one of the more troublesome problems in the *Politics*.[45] As we will see, it is far from clear whether we ought to describe it as a utopia of any sort. It seems likely that Aristotle never made up his mind about it.

3. The third level is again the level of practical reforms in real cities. But Aristotle makes a further distinction here.

A. There is the best constitution that is available to a city under the circumstances. The key word here is "circumstances," which the first ideal ignores entirely, and the middle-constitutional ideal, it would seem, ignores to a large extent. He means by this essentially the socio-economic pattern found in a particular city as a particular time, which makes some cities suitable for democracy and others suitable for oligarchy, and within those categories predisposes a city for a certain type of democracy or oligarchy. In Aristotle's view the political philosopher will not advise a city to adopt oligarchy if the circumstances of the city make it better suited for democracy.

B. Finally there is the sort of constitution that is based upon a mere assumption (*hypothesis*). Apparently what Aristotle means by this is that sometimes a city will want a certain type of constitution, whether or not this constitution is the "best" for it in any of the definitions of "best" given above. In that case it is the task of the political philosopher to advise them on how to establish and maintain the sort of constitution they want, even when the philosopher knows it is not the best thing for them in any sense.

The great defect of earlier political philosophy, in Aristotle's view, was that it tended to concentrate on some single model, whether a utopian city or some real city like Sparta. He thought it the responsibility of the true philosophical statesman to give good advice to *any* state under *any* circumstances (1288b39ff.), based upon empirical research into all the existing types of constitutions and the factors that tend to preserve and destroy each of these. This dazzling program is carried out in the fourth, fifth, and sixth books of the *Politics*. But we are concerned here with a rather less original Aristotle—Aristotle the commentator on, and continuator of, the Greek utopian tradition.

Aristotle's Critique of Utopian Communism

Aristotle's basic assumptions about ethics made him extremely critical of all efforts at high-utopian social engineering. He thought the total moral regeneration of society neither possible nor necessary, thought virtue and happiness could be achieved quite adequately in existing societies, and saw no need for utopian speculation on the high levels pioneered by Plato. He returned to the traditional notion of citizen virtue as a balanced outlook requiring a variety of skills and a certain amount of property and good birth. Naturally he rejected the idea of communism *per se*. But he saw fit to discuss the idea at length, and his comments have rarely received high marks from modern scholars, who find them ungenerous, nitpicking, and excessively concerned with institutional details rather than with the total mythic vision of the *Republic*. I suggest that this critique, though disorganized and elliptical like much else in the *Politics*, is rather more acute than usually thought. Aristotle understood that the utopia of the *Republic* was supposed to be a total mythic vision; he never criticizes it for being unrealizable; when calls it unworkable he means unworkable as a model; and he correctly thought Plato's institutional details relevant to this question.

Perhaps Aristotle's most telling objection was that Plato had failed to make clear the relationship among the different classes in the model city, and especially the position of the "producers," whom Aristotle assumed to be the vast majority of the citizens. He found Plato unclear as to their place in the educational system, their role in government, and their participation in the communistic economy. He pointed out that if the masses were to practice the same communistic life as the guards, there would be no difference between them, and the masses would not accept their subordinate position in the state. On the other hand, if the masses were to live like ordinary Greek citizens, then they would be subject to all the discords of property and family which Plato's plan was supposed to eliminate; and the guards would then resemble an army of occupation, except that the masses would be more difficult to control than the helots of Lacedaemon. Nor was it clear how the ruling class could be open to talent; Plato had said that gifted producer children could be promoted to guard rank but failed to explain how, in such a highly stratified system, it would be possible to transfer children from one track to another. Aristotle saw that the great fallacy of the *Republic* was its promise to synthesize the values of democracy and oligarchy, unity and hierarchy, equality and inequality. We understand clearly enough how the oligarchical part will work. We never understand the other.

Aristotle's argument against community of women is also worthy of note here because of its possible affect on later communistic speculations. Essentially he claims that eliminating the family would be offensive to piety. In such a system as Plato's there must occur instances of violence, slander, and above all incest among close relatives, without allowing any opportunity for ritual purification because they will never know who their relatives are. In fact Plato had gone to great lengths to prevent incest, introducing complicated regulations to avoid sexual contacts between parent and child. But he could not eliminate the possibility of sibling incest, so Socrates is made to admit that brother–sister unions might be allowable in Kallipolis, contingent upon approval by the Delphic oracle (*Rep.* 461).[46] Presumably Plato threw in the oracle to protect himself from charges of impiety, but this did not assuage Aristotle:

> It is equally curious that Plato, while making sons shared by all, wishes to prohibit sexual intercourse between lovers, but not love itself, nor its most unseemly manifestations, as between brothers or between father and son, where the mere unindulged passion is itself unseemly. And why prohibit sexual intercourse that is otherwise unobjectionable, merely on the grounds of the excessively powerful pleasure it gives, and yet believe that it makes no difference if intercourse takes place between brothers, or father and son? 1262a32–39, trans. Sinclair/Saunders

Aristotle exaggerates. A Kallipolitan youth could not be a fictive "son" to *all* the older guards. Still, should the rulers decide to increase the population and maximize matings, something like the situation described by Aristotle would be conceivable. But in any case one doubts that Plato ever intended to allow sexual attractions between fictive "fathers" and "sons." This would be easy to prevent, as sexual attractions between fictive "fathers" and "daughters" are prevented. Possibly Aristotle was misled by Socrates' remark at 403b that male lovers in Kallipolis will limit their physical contacts to touching one another as fathers touch their sons. This is said before communism is introduced, so nobody in the dialogue notices that many of these men must *be* fathers and sons in the fictive sense, and some in the biological sense as well. One suspects that Plato would have barred father/son incest, fictive as well as biological and emotional as well as physical, had he been confronted with the question. Nevertheless Aristotle is right to point out that there could be no way to avoid incestuous homosexual attachments between brothers, who would have no means of ascertaining their relationship. (It seems surprising that Aristotle says nothing about heterosexual incest, but perhaps he sees no need to run this point into the ground.)

These criticisms are open to the charge of excessive literal-mindedness, for Plato was not advocating incest of any kind, merely making the point that in a perfectly rational society the family would not be necessary. But a serious point lurked behind this apparently absurd controversy. The Aristotelian critique, with its unexpected obeisance to the power of taboo and ritual, implies that certain matters, especially family/household relationships, are sacrosanct. When he says that the ideal states of Plato ignored necessity, he seems to have in mind the necessities of the patriarchal household. In refusing to question this institution Aristotle was setting limits to speculation about the ideal state, and later philosophers who wished to break through those limits and revive Plato's ideas about communism and sexual equality would have to deal with Aristotle's objections.

The Low Utopia of Aristotle

But Aristotle still thought it useful to speculate about the city of unconditional excellence, provided one did not question the household, and designed such a lower utopia himself in the seventh and eighth books of the *Politics*. He dropped the fiction—perhaps little more than a fiction even in the earlier utopists—that this was a plan for a new colony, but he retained the literary convention of describing a complete imaginary society. It is, even in its incomplete form, a very detailed constitution.

This city may be described as a more realistic version of Plato's Magnesia.[47] Once more the basic principle is the limitation of citizenship to a landowning class, whose members are forbidden to engage in manual labor or low occupations and are to devote themselves entirely to war, government, and religion. There are collectivist elements: all citizens must eat at *syssitia*, for which public land is set aside; there is a system of public education. There is no suggestion of equality for women, but there is considerable regulation of marriage and family life: the size of the population is controlled by compulsory abortion, the age of marriage is fixed by law, extramarital intercourse is punished both in husband and wife. How much further Aristotle would have gone in regulating his imaginary citizens we do not know, as the surviving part of his educational plan is concerned mostly with the early childhood years and with music. The work will be done either by slaves or by serfs; in either case it is important that they be of barbarian stock; in either case a large force of slaves or serfs belonging to the city will be needed to work the public land and provide the common meals of the citizens. The idea of using public slaves recalls a suggestion made by Phaleas and various other proposals. The idea of using barbarian serfs was probably suggested to Aristotle by the example of the Mariandynoi, an Asiatic tribe held in a servile condition by the Greek city of Heraclea Pontica. Both are intended as surrogates for the Lacedaemonian helots, and either would be a more reliable work force because the helots were Greeks and notoriously rebellious.[48]

The model differs from existing Greek cities chiefly in that it attempts to copy the Spartan institutions of a separate soldier class and common meals. Aristotle, like Plato, believed these institutions were of remote antiquity—the first he traced to ancient Egypt—and tested by time. Like Plato, he thought the ideal city would be a broad-based oligarchy, as collectivistic as the Spartan and more sexually puritanical.

The narrowness of this ideal should not blind us to the flexibility of Aristotle's thought. He knew that the question, "What is the best constitution?" was meaningless unless one asked, "Best for whom, and where, and when, and under what conditions?" He did not think extreme democracy one of the preferred constitutions, but he thought it suitable for the circumstances of Athens in his day, and it is doubtful that he would have advised the Athenians to adopt a less democratic system. Nevertheless, he thought it important to keep in mind an absolute ideal of what a society should be, and his ideal was the one described. What did it mean in practice?

The Peripatetics in Politics

Here we encounter the problem of Aristotle's "middle constitution." Repeatedly this is described as the most universal constitution, the one possible for the largest number of states. But we are also told that it occurs rarely (1296a22–b1), because it can only succeed where the *mesoi*, the middle people who are neither rich nor poor, are the strongest element in the state; since most states are polarized between rich and poor, most tend to be either democracies or oligarchies. Throughout this discussion of the middle constitution (4.11–13) it seems to be assumed that the distribution of wealth in a state determines the constitution, and that the distribution of wealth cannot be altered. Though the *mesoi* are never defined, Aristotle seems to have in mind usually the hoplites, the substantial peasantry; he thinks that to bring about a mixed constitution this class must be sufficiently large and prosperous, a situation now found rarely. But if this type of city is rare, how can it at the same time be "common" (*koinos*)?

The contradiction is never resolved. It seems to arise from Aristotle's indecision as to whether the middle constitution is a utopia or simply a description of a type of constitution. He often speakes of it as a lower utopia that cities should try to imitate. He mentions that Plato's Magnesia resembles such a middle constitution (1265b26), and so does his own utopia in books 7–8. But if existing cities are to imitate it they will have to equalize wealth among their citizens, and Aristotle stops short of proposing reforms that would be adequate to this end. He says there has been only one leader who "was prevailed upon to allow a system of this kind" (trans. Sinclair/Saunders)—a baffling allusion, but whoever Aristotle has in mind he clearly means that the level of reform needed to establish a middle constitution is possible, and that it has almost never been tried.[49]

If Aristotle wished to recommend such reforms we ought to find his recommendations at the third level of his political program, where he discusses the means of establishing and maintaining the several kinds of democracy and oligarchy. He thought the best of all democracies was the moderate democracy with a low property qualification, and the best of all oligarchies the moderate oligarchy with a somewhat higher property qualification; the only real difference between them would seem to be that the one includes an actual majority of the people and the other a large minority; in either the hoplites will exercise a dominant influence; both are so close to Aristotle's ideal middle constitution that often it is hard to tell the difference. And he does mention ways to develop such constitutions. He praises Solon for establishing a moderate democracy at Athens (2.12). He commends various ancient laws found in many cities that make ancestral estates inalienable, forbid the accumulation of landed property, or limit indebtedness (6.4). He thinks it advisable for any democracy to increase prosperity through private and public benefactions to the poor (6.5). Even in oligarchies he recommends lavish displays of private generosity on the part of magistrates, but for a narrower and more cynical purpose—the citizens are to be bribed to accept the rule of the oligarchs with sacrificial banquets, public buildings, and votive offerings (6.7). But none of this could bring about the middle constitution, and it is nowhere suggested that such a degree of change would be possible by any peaceful means. There is an underlying assumption that existing constitutions are not to be tampered with. The middle constitution is *koinos* only in potentiality. We have a sense that in Aristotle, as in Plato, utopian impulses were in conflict with a fundamental social and political conservatism. However radical their premises, the practical effect of their utopian goals was to buttress traditional aristocratic and oligarchic values.

In the next generation the school of Aristotle became even more closely tied to oligarchical politics. We know of no one, neither in the Lyceum nor in the Academy, who tried to continue the high utopianism of Plato. The Lyceum became allied with the rising Macedonian monarchies. Several Peripatetics wrote treatises *On Kingship*, including one by Aristotle himself to Alexander the Great, and one by his successor Theophrastus to Cassander, the Macedonian general and later king who then ruled Greece. A few years after Aristotle died his school finally took power in the person of his disciple Demetrius of Phalerum, a prolific writer on politics. In 317 Cassander made Demetrius dictator of Athens, and for the next ten years he ruled the city of Socrates with the aid of a Macedonian garrison. He established a new constitution under which the poorer citizens were excluded from the assembly, the powers of the assembly sharply curtailed, sortition abolished, and a large police force set up to censor morals. Such was the ultimate expression of utopia on what Plato had called the third-best level, and such was its nearest equivalent to the philosopher king.

The Social and Political Background of Platonic-Aristotelian Utopianism

After the Spartan hegemony was broken at Leuctra in 371, social conflict in the Greek cities acquired a new intensity. The first manifestation of this was seen at Argos in 370, when the people tried, executed, and confiscated the property of one thousand two hundred wealthy citizens who were accused of conspiring to overthrow the democracy. During the 360s serious outbreaks of *stasis* (civil strife) are known to have occurred in several other cities. In 357 there was a particularly violent revolution at Syracuse, second or third-largest city in the Greek world: the tyranny was overthrown, and the next year the democratic faction passed a resolution calling for the redistribution of all *oikoi*. Their orators justified this unprecedented measure with a new slogan—"Equaliy is the beginning of freedom." Though the Syracusan land reform was quickly halted and a new tyranny imposed, this movement is the clearest evidence that a new kind of *stasis* was appearing.

The traditional kind of *stasis* was political, a conflict for power between democratic and oligarchic factions. The new *stasis* was economic, a struggle for land between rich and poor; its central demand was "redistribution of the land" (*ges anadasmos*), often accompanied by demands for the cancellation of debts. In the late 350s Plato wrote as though propertied citizens everywhere lived in fear of these demands (*Laws* 684); somewhat later Aristotle described most cities as bitterly polarized between rich and poor (*Pol.* 1296a22–b1).

The Macedonian hegemony that finally replaced the Spartan in 338 tried to restore social stability by supporting the wealthy everywhere. Under the leadership of Philip II, the Greek cities were united in the League of Corinth, which attempted to establish a sort of Concert of Hellas for the suppression of revolution. All the member cities swore an oath not to permit land redistribution, debt cancellation, unlawful confiscations, or manumission of slaves for revolutionary purposes; and the League was prepared to use force against cities that violated the status quo. The League was not overtly antidemocratic under Philip and Alexander, but in the long run the Macedonian hegemony, which differed from any previous hegemonic effort in that it was to have a long run, would work to weaken political democracy as well as movements for social and economic reform.

It is clear that in the fourth century B.C. the Greek cities were experiencing a fairly general social crisis of a more violent sort than they were used to, but it is not easy to say just what was new about this situation. Some find the basic cause of the crisis in a growing concentration of wealth which eventually destroyed the homogeneity of the polis.[50] Others doubt that the structure of the polis society and the nature of its dissensions had changed that much and suspect that even in the fourth century *stasis* was more political than economic.

Models of social crisis and revolution derived from the experience of modern Western nations are certainly of questionable applicability. The social coherence and tribal unity of a Greek polis always worked to prevent conflict along strictly economic lines. The political "parties" that we find everywhere in ancient city-state politics were not like modern parties. It has been suggested that the best term for them is "factions."[51] They were informal, nameless groups of citizens held together by "friendship," that all-important word again; by individual, one-on-one, patron–client relationships that united a powerful citizen to a circle of his less powerful neighbors. Therefore every political movement among the poor had to have leaders among the *dynatoi*, the rich and powerful;

and every case of *stasis* involved some powerful households fighting other powerful households. Originally *stasis* meant rivalry among the *dynatoi*, but the constant competition for clients involved more and more citizens in these rivalries, and required up-and-coming *dynatoi* to make larger promises to the poor. These conflicts remained limited so long as the cities remained truly autonomous, but this was no longer the case by the late fifth century. By then *stasis* had become an instrument of international diplomacy and war, with Athens everywhere supporting the factions of the people and Sparta those of the few. This situation received a classical analysis from Thucydides in his account of the *stasis* at Corcyra; he thought the economic/ideological slogans a mere facade masking a plain struggle for political power, whose main cause was foreign intervention. In the passage already cited, Aristotle attributed the extreme polarity between rich and poor which characterized fourth-century Greece largely to the policies of the hegemonic powers, clearly meaning the Athenians and the Spartans.

This factional model of ancient Greek social contrast implies that the "rich" and "poor" whose struggles fill the pages of ancient historians were not distinct economic classes, like the rich and poor of the industrial age.[52] They are better described as different ranks or statuses within the same citizen order. The most important barriers of citizen solidarity were hardly ever broken; the most revolutionary program known was an attempt to equalize shares of land among members of this order; no program ever attempted to appeal to those outside the citizen body; none ever considered manumission of slaves except as a war measure. Nor was there much sign of a social division between "peasants" and "city," such as we find in other ancient societies.

Therefore it may be possible to interpret the *stasis* of the fourth century according to the Thucydidean model: as a basically political conflict, in which economic motives were incidental and class interests in the modern sense nonexistent. The usual program of the poor in the fourth century was political democracy, as before. If there was more *stasis* in the fourth century, the cause perhaps was not so much economic change as the extreme political instability and constant warfare that filled the decades between the ascendancy of Sparta and that of Macedon.[53]

Still, all agree that something changed in the fourth century. Perhaps the Thucydidean model remained the most useful explanation of Greek social conflict, but even that model does not strictly separate political and economic factors, nor can these be separated. It is obvious that political democracy could have an economic impact, and it is probable that the poorer citizens desired it chiefly because it was a means of protecting their economic interests. Important though the juridical status of citizenship was, it was always recognized that the citizen order was everywhere divided by these economic interests; and the patron–client ties that pervaded classical city politics did not prevent economic conflicts, they merely prevented economic interests from coinciding absolutely with certain factions.

There is no doubt that after ca. 370 B.C. the struggle for political advantage was increasingly bound up with economic interests, popular movements, and a sort of class consciousness, or at least a sense that the *penetes*, the poor, were a distinct group of citizens with a special program. It is not hard to see how this program defined itself. In earlier times all confiscations of property were usually followed by redistributions of land, this being the way that a victorious faction rewarded itself and its opponents after the liquidation of its opponents. This was what happened at Argos in 370. But it happened there on a perhaps unprecedented scale, which suggested the possibility of carrying out land reform without the pretext of trials and confiscations, on the grounds that equal distribution of land is a good thing in itself. Such a program required some ideological justification, and we find the germ of one in the Syracusan declaration of 356: (political) freedom requires (economic) equality. This point would have been reached rarely, but a single instance of it would have been unsettling enough to the propertied.

The utopian writings of Plato and Aristotle were meant to reassure them. They provided a new ideology to reform and revitalize traditional aristocratic values; their practical goal was the creation of a unified and disciplined upper class, generous with patronage and immune to the temptations of faction. In time the practical goal became increasingly evident. It ended in tyranny.

But even while Demetrius of Phalerum ruled, other visions of utopia were taking shape at Athens.

Notes

1. I borrow this phrase from Gregory Vlastos' essay, "The Paradox of Socrates," in *The Philosophy of Socrates*, ed. Gregory Vlastos (Garden City 1971), 1–21. It refers to the apparent contradiction between Socrates' egalitarian methods and his authoritarian claims to knowledge. Vlastos has since revised his views on Socrates, but I think the paradox remains.

2. Socrates was said to be talking always of craftsmen: Plato, *Symp.* 221e; *Gorg.* 491a; Xen., *Mem.* 1.2.32ff., 4.4.5. It has been said that there are some five hundred references to the crafts analogy in the dialogues of Plato.

3. M. J. O'Brien, *The Socratic Paradoxes and the Greek Mind* (Chapel Hill 1967), argued that Socratic assertions like "Virtue is knowledge" and "No one does wrong voluntarily" were rooted in ordinary Greek ways of thinking that had nothing to do with intellectualism: words for "know" and the like did not clearly distinguish the factors of intellect, will, emotion, and character, any more than does ordinary English usage in phrases like "I have a mind to ..."

4. The distinction between "agent-centered" and "act-centered" ethics I take from Julia Annas, *An Introduction to Plato's Republic* (Oxford 1981), 157ff.; the phrase "psychic harmony" from Vlastos' "Justice and Happiness in the *Republic*," in *Platonic Studies* (Princeton 1973), 111–39.

5. I use the phrase "natural law" loosely. Some would distinguish natural *laws* (implying a set of fixed rules) from natural *justice*, which is what I mean here. See Gisela Striker, "Origins of the Concept of Natural Law," *Proceedings of the Boston Area Colloquium in Ancient Philosophy*, ed. J. J. Cleary (Lanham 1987), 2.79–94; and Brad Inwood, "Commentary on Striker," 95–101.

6. Socrates was accused of not recognizing the gods of the city and introducing

other new deities. Xenophon (*Mem.* 1.1.1–9) tries to refute this charge by pointing out that Socrates participated in sacrifices and received messages from a private *daimonion.* Apparently this was all that could be said in his favor. His *daimonion* was not associated with any god and created suspicion that he practiced a secret cult. Similar things had been said of the Pythagoreans. See Burkert, *Greek Religion*, 179–81.

7. These accusations were made by the Sophist Polycrates, who wrote a speech or pamphlet attacking Socrates a few years after his execution. The preamble to Xenophon's *Memorabilia* (1.1–2) is an attempt to refute them.

8. At *Apol.* 31e, Socrates tells the court that *no* just man like himself can ever enter politics in a democracy like Athens and escape with his life. The possibility of educating the masses could not be more definitely written off.

9. Five of Socrates' disciples are known to have written about the "woman question." In addition to those mentioned above, the obscure Aeschines of Sphettos wrote a dialogue called *Aspasia* about the deeds of famous women. Antisthenes is supposed to have said "Virtue is the same for men and women" (Diog. Laert. 6.12), but this may mean that their virtues are identical in kind, not equal in quantity. Xenophon attributes such a view to Socrates: in *Symposium* 2.9, "Socrates" declares that women have the same abilities as men, but adds the damning qualification, "except in intelligence and strength." Plato seems to have had the same attitude, as we will see.

10. The elitist aspect of the Socratic circle have been heavily emphasized in several recent works that portray Socrates as a "saint of counter-revolution"—a phrase coined by E. M. Wood and Neal Wood, *Class Ideology*, and an interpretation popularized by I. F. Stone's *The Trial of Socrates* (Boston 1988). There is no question about the existence of the political charge, but we cannot be sure how important it was in Socrates' own time. Half a century after his trial the orator Aeschines told an Athenian court that Socrates had been executed because he was the teacher of Critias (*Against Timarchus* 1.173). This is the only reference to the trial by someone outside the Socratic circle, and it must reflect common opinion. But it is possible the pamphleteer Polycrates was responsible for the idea; we know from Xenophon that the charge of guilt by association played a great part in his attack on Socrates; we do not know how common it was at the time of the trial. And I am more skeptical than some of the extent to which Plato's *Apology of Socrates* can be read as an authentic record of what went on at Socrates' trial.

Some of the evidence for the conservatism of the Socratic circle has been exaggerated. Too much has been made of the upper-class origins of Socrates' disciples. Where else would he have found disciples? Two members of the circle, Critias and Charmides (both kinsmen of Plato), were leaders of the Thirty, and only one, Chaerophon (a well-known follower of Socrates), fought for the people in that year; but if this was really a training ground for oligarchs, is it not surprising to find even one such? Too much has been made of a passage (Xen., *Mem.* 3.7) where Socrates advises the same Charmides to enter politics, telling him he need not be afraid of the "silliest" and "weakest" of the citizens. It does not matter whether the choice of terms is Socrates' or Xenophon's; in either case the remark does not express opposition to democracy, merely a form of snobbery that was as common in ancient democracies as it is in ours; and the purpose of the speech, after all, is to persuade Charmides to enter democratic politics.

Antisthenes, who also wrote much on politics, has been described as a crypto-oligarch like Xenophon and Plato, but there is no serious evidence for this. We need not conclude that he was opposed to democracy in principle because he criticized demagogues in a work called *The Statesman* (Ath. 5.220d; perhaps identical with the *On the Republic* or *On Law* mentioned by Diog. Laert. 6.16), or because he mocked Athenian generals (Diog. Laert. 6.8); the latter were not considered one of the democratic elements in the constitution. He shared the vague Laconism of the Socratic circle, but his may have been ethical rather than political, as was the case later among the Cynics. According to a fairly early anecdote—from the biographer Hermippus of Smyrna, late third century B.C.—Antisthenes meant to speak at the Isthmian Games on the relative merits and demerits of the Athenians, Spartans, and Thebans, but excused himself when he saw large crowds from all those cities in attendance (Diog. Laert. 6.2), expecting none of them to be pleased by his comments on their systems. For the even more obscure Laconism of Socrates, see n. 14.

I doubt that the formal charge of impiety (which seems to be taken seriously by Socrates' apologists) was a cover for a political accusation; rather it expressed a suspicion of subversion in which political and religious elements were difficult to separate. Polycrates, who identified Socrates as the teacher of Critias, also said that Socrates taught the youth to despise parents, kinsmen, and friends, and told them that only the "wise" deserved respect and trust. This charge seems to reflect a confused sense that the Socratics were trying to set up some new source of authority outside the household and the city; this suspicion had produced the caricature of the Socratic circle in Aristophanes' *Clouds* a quarter of a century earlier; one suspects it was much more damaging than the subsidiary suspicion of oligarchical/tyrannical conspiracy.

11. Various people accuse Socrates of *eironeia* in the dialogues of Plato (*Symp.* 216e; *Rep.* 337a) and Xenophon (*Mem.* 1.2.36, 4.4.9); and Aristotle mentions it as a characteristic of Socrates (*Nich. Eth.* 1127b).

12. Among recent studies, the view that the profession of ignorance was a pretense is defended by Norman Gulley, *The Philosophy of Socrates* (New York 1968); and the view that it was a provisional expedient masking a hypothetical authoritarianism, by Richard Kraus, *Socrates and the State* (Princeton 1984).

13. See Gregory Vlastos, "Socrates' Disavowal of Knowledge," *Philosophical Quarterly* 35 (1985), 1–31. A rather similar view is held by T. H. Irwin, *Plato's Moral Theory* (Oxford 1977), 39ff.: Socrates claimed a kind of "true belief" that he tried to turn into knowledge.

14. Did he mean Sparta was well governed but Athens still better governed? Or that Athens was worse governed than Sparta and yet more acceptable to him because its democracy allowed more freedom for philosophy? The first view is defended in Kraus' *Socrates and the State*, the second by Clifford Orwin in his exchange with Kraus in *Platonic Writings, Platonic Readings*, ed. C. L. Griswold, Jr. (New York 1988).

15. The contradiction is often recognized. Gulley, who thought the profession of ignorance a pretense, wrote, "It is very unlikely that Socrates was aware of this apparent incompatibility between his individualistic views and the authoritarianism implicit in his conviction that certainty was possible in ethics and that those who had attained it should be rulers" (*Philosophy of Socrates*, 178–79). Kraus, who thought Socrates' authoritarianism hypothetical, concluded that "the seeds of antidemocratic authoritarianism lay dormant in Socratic conversation" but "were held in check by his strong sense of human limits" (*Socrates and the State*, 309).

16. Crossman's *Plato Today*, originally a series of BBC lectures, was first published in 1937; the quotation, taken from his introduction to the second edition of 1959 (7), represents his characterization of his earlier approach, not his final judgment on the question.

17. Popper, 4th ed. (London 1962), 1.153, 155, 169.

18. Winspear, 2nd ed. (New York 1956), 242–43, 267–68; Popper, 1.46ff. Cf. Toynbee, *Study of History* (Oxford 1939), 6.24ff. An anthology of the literature of this

controversy has been edited by Renford Bambrough, *Plato, Popper, and Politics: Some Contributions to a Modern Controversy* (Cambridge 1967).

19. See the works of the Woods and I. F. Stone, cited in n. 10, and de Ste. Croix, *The Class Strugle in the Ancient Greek World* (Ithaca 1981), 70–71, 411–12, 557–58.

20. R. L. Nettleship, *Lectures on the Republic of Plato*, 2nd ed. (London 1901), 4–5, 67–69; A. E. Taylor, *Plato: The Man and His Work*, 6th ed. (Oxford 1952), 273 (offering the example of punctuality); Barker, *Political Theory*, 187–88, 206; C. H. McIlwain, *The Growth of Political Theory Thought in the West* (New York 1932), 32–33.

21. Barker felt that the "tyranny of principles" led Plato to go too far in legislating for his ideal state, producing "a certain oscillation between a practical attempt at construction, and the theoretical exhibition of a state based on ideal principles": *Political Thought of Plato and Aristotle* (London 1906), 161. Cf. N. R. Murphy, *The Interpretation of Plato's Republic* (Oxford 1951), 76; McIlwain, *Political Thought*, 39.

22. I touch lightly here on one of the most-discussed problems in the *Republic*, the question of what Plato means by the comparison between the two kinds of justice. For an introduction to this problem with references to earlier literature, see Annas, *Plato's Republic*, 153ff.

23. The nonexistence of slavery in the *Republic* has been argued by Adams (commentary on *Rep.* 465c, 469c); R. B. Levinson, *In Defence of Plato* (Cambridge, Mass. 1953), 139ff.; John Wild, *Plato's Modern Enemies and the Theory of Natural Law* (Chicago 1953), 50; R. W. Hall, *Plato* (London 1981), 77–78; Brian Calvert, "Slavery in Plato's *Republic*," "*Classical Quarterly* n.s. 37 (1987), 367–72. Their arguments have been refuted, I think decisively, by Gregory Vlastos, "Does Slavery Exist in Plato's *Republic*?" *Platonic Studies*, 1140–46. The key passages are *Rep.* 433d, 469b–471c. Calvert points out that slaves are not mentioned among the basic necessities of the city at 371e; but what Socrates is describing there is the primitive city, which has no need of slaves, soldiers, and many other luxuries needed by the developed city. C. D. C. Reeves *Philosopher Kings: The Argument of Plato's Republic* (Princeton 1988), 216–17, thinks slaves might exist there but could not be very important because they have to be captured from the barbarians: "There is no question, therefore, of the Kallipolis being based on slavery, as Athens was, or of slaves being essential to its functioning." This ignores the extent to which Greeks assumed slaves would normally be of "barbarian" origin and used this as a facile justification for slavery. Aristotle thought slaves had to be non-Greek and this did not hinder him at all from assuming that society must be based on slavery; nor need it have. Reeves also ignores the implications of *Rep.* 469c, where slave raids against non-Greeks are assumed to be essential.

24. Levinson, *Defense of Plato*, 383. Cf. Wild, *Plato's Modern Enemies*, 33: the *Republic* merely sets forth a "clear and rationally defensible conception of the human good," "based on the natural needs of man," which must be present in "any moral inspiration for a better state."

25. Robin Barrow, *Plato, Utilitarianism, and Education* (London 1975), seems to think the principles of the *Republic* amount to little more than the recognition that some degree of social regulation is necessary, and calls them "compatible with a representative democracy such as our own" (174–75).

26. Reeves, *Philosopher Kings*, 234: "Even if we retain our liberal suspicion about the possibility of a science of values, we might still, by coming to see merit in the idea of critical freedom, also come to see the *Republic* in a new light—not as a totalitarian hymn to the benefits of repression and unfreedom, but as an attempt to design a polis whose members enjoy as much real happiness, and as much real or critical freedom, as possible."

27. Alan Bloom, *The Republic of Plato* (New York 1968), 410. Bloom's interpretive essay, attached to this translation of the *Republic*, is perhaps the clearest statement of this point of view; see especially 380–88, 409–11. Bloom has defended it in an exchange in *Political Theory* 5(1977): Dale Hall, "The 'Republic' and the 'Limits of Politics'," 294–313; Bloom, "Response to Hall," 315–30. Bloom also alludes *in passim* to this interpretation of the *Republic* in his *The Closing of the American Mind* (New York 1987). Other versions of it: Leo Strauss, who inspired but cannot be held fully responsible for all this, *The City and Man* (Chicago 1964); J. H. Randall, *Plato: Dramatist of the Life of Reason* (New York 1970); J. F. Wilson, *The Politics of Moderation: An Interpretation of Plato's Republic* (Lanham 1984); M. P. Nichols, *Socrates and the Political Community: An Ancient Debate* (Albany 1987).

28. He is certainly careless about Plato's personae. The plan of the *Republic* is attributed to "Socrates," but at 1265al the plan of the *Laws* seems to be attributed to him also, though he never appears in that dialogue; and at 1266b5 both plans seem to be attributed to Plato (cf. the possibly interpolated 2.12).

29. Though some have doubted it, including George Grote. The ambiguity arises from the fact that the Athenian Stranger seems to mean by the first state one where communism is practiced by all, which is not found in the *Republic* we have. Therefore it has been suggested that the first state is one practicing universal communism, not mentioned elsewhere in Plato's writings; the second is the one described in the *Republic*; and the third is the one described in the *Laws*. But this interpretation renders the passage unintelligible. See the discussion of this problem by Fuks, "Plato and the Social Question: The Problem of Poverty and Riches in the *Laws*," *Ancient Society* 10 (1979), 33–78 (reprinted in *Social Conflict*, 126–71), 73 n. 180; and the solution suggested below.

30. The following essays are particularly relevant to the distinction I attempt here: P. H. Partridge, "Politics, Philosophy, Ideology," *Political Studies* 9 (Oxford 1961), 217–35; reprinted in *Political Philosophy*, ed. Anthony Quinton (Oxford 1967), 32–52; H. J. N. Horsburgh, "The Relevance of the Utopian," *Ethics* 67 (1957), 127–38; W. A. R. Leys, "Was Plato Non-Political?," *Ethics* 75 (1965), 272–76; reprinted in Vlastos, *Plato*: *A Collection of Critical Essays* (New York 1971), 2.166–73; F. E. Sparshott, "Plato as Anti-Political Thinker," *Ethics* 77 (1967), 214–19; reprinted in Vlastos, 2.174–83; Leys, "Afterthought," in Vlastos, 2.184–86.

31. It is worth noting (though hardly a compelling point in its favor) that Middle Platonist commentators adopted this interpretation. A handbook of Platonism written by Albinus in the second century A.D. distinguished three levels of political teaching in Plato's works: the ideal state of the *Republic*, the real state of the *Laws*, and the practical reforms of the *Epistles*. See František Novotný, *The Posthumous Life of Plato* (The Hague 1977), 106–11.

32. We know that there was in the fifth century a considerable literature dealing with the origins of culture, besides Protagoras' work *On the Original State*. It seems that a certain rationalistic and progressive view of the remote past had won a wide currency. It rejected mythological primitivism altogether and assumed civilization to be the result of a series of human inventions. The basic idea behind Plato's *Protagoras* speech was probably widespread: aetiology is useful because if we understand the original nature of anything we learn something about the way it functions in contemporary society. See Thomas Cole, *Democritus and the Sources of Greek Anthropology* (Cleveland 1967).

33. John Burnet thought that the "earthly city" of books 2–5 was the contribution of Socrates (the real one), and that Plato, at the time he wrote the *Republic*, inserted into this Socratic program the "heavenly city" of books 5–8, which was a product of

studies pursued at the Academy. See *Greek Philosophy, Part One,* (London 1914), 339. The notion that Socrates could have been the inventor of communism was explicitly refuted by Aristotle and has been generally abandoned; but it does seem possible that someone in the Socratic circle wrote a low utopia resembling that of Phaleas which became a source for *Rep.* 2–5.

34. Socrates says at one point that the guards might number as few as a thousand (Rep. 423a), and Aristotle at one point takes that to be their absolute number (1265a9). Aristotle also assumes that the producers would constitute almost the whole of the population (1264a12). Various scholars have estimated the guard class to constitute between 5 and 15 percent of the citizens (see Fuks, "Plato's *Republic*," 71 n. 70), but these guesses are useless because we are given no hint as to the size of the total population. The figure of one thousand is probably meant to be minimal, and Socrates probably uses it because that is about as small as a polis army could get and still function as an independent military force. But Aristotle confirms our general impression that the guards are supposed to be a small minority.

35. The Kallipolitans will regard all wars between Greeks as civil strife and will never destroy, dishonor, or enslave defeated Greek enemies; and somehow they will compel or persuade all their neighbors to adopt the same rules. Total warfare and enslavement will be visited only upon non-Greek peoples. It is implied that these opportunities, especially the need to acquire slaves, will promote pan-Hellenic unity (373de, 469b–471c).

36. It has been suggested that slavery is a basic metaphor even in Plato's metaphysics, where the divine mind rules matter like the human mind the body, and the master the slave, and the philosopher-king the ideal city. See Gregory Vlastos, "Slavery in Plato's Thought," *Platonic Studies*, 147–63; and A. W. Gouldner, *Enter Plato: Classical Greece and the Origins of Social Theory* (New York 1965), who describes Plato's metaphysics as "a projection of the slave relationship onto the universe" (350–59).

37. Whether the educational program of Kallipolis includes the producers has been much argued. A recent summation of the question by Reeves, *Philosopher Kings*, 186–91, who decides it in the negative, seems to me convincing.

38. At *Rep.* 414b compulsion is for use against external ememies, persuasion for citizens, but immediately afterward (415e) it is admitted both methods will be needed to keep the citizens in line. All classes must be brought into harmony by persuasion or compulsion (421b, 518–19). In the *Statesman* Socrates will be made to argue that it makes no difference to the true ruler whether his subjects are willing, any more than the consent of a patient matters to a doctor (293). The formula "by persuasion or compulsion" is recurrent in the *Laws*.

39. The restrictions on homosexual behavior occur in the discussion of the guards' "musical" education. Prostitution is also forbidden, but at a later point, during the discussion of "gymnastic" education (404d). Prostitution was a pleasure like food and drink; *paiderastia* was a more elevated temptation. Kenneth Dover's by now classic study *Greek Homosexuality* (Cambridge, Mass., 1978) suggests that the sort of *paiderastia* that was acceptable between citizen males at Athens was expected to avoid all public references to physical intercourse, as this would lead to the imputation of effeminacy and prostitution to one of the two, with possible damage to his citizen rights. What Plato proposes in the *Republic* and more explicitly in the *Laws* (835–42) may be described as an internalization of this public norm. The puritanism of it remains novel: Socrates means that the guards are to *really* avoid homosexual intercourse even with prostitutes and slaves, proscriptions unheard of at Athens. We notice that it is also possible under Socrates' system for a guard to be denied all heterosexual intercourse until the age of

fifty. But even in the ideal states Plato does not "prohibit homosexuality," as we are always being told. He did not imagine that possible. He assumes that in the most ideal state homosexual love will be common and open; he thinks it possible (in the ideal state only) to sublimate it completely. The practical ethic this implies is probably the more-or-less sublimated homosexuality of the *Phaedrus*.

40. Many modern feminists seem to notice only Plato's misogyny and to ignore the fact that his misogynistic and coldly utilitarian brand of feminism lends a powerful support, though somewhat unexpected and backhanded, to their cause. The point is recognized and the modern literature on this question summarized in Natalie Bluestone's *Women in the Ideal Society: Plato's Republic and Modern Myths of Gender* (Amherst 1987).

41. Barker (*Greek Political Theory* 370–71) suggested that in the *Laws* Plato came to realize "that the communistic ideal is for gods or the sons of gods" and simply "colours it more in retrospect." I cannot believe that Plato ever hoped to see communism realized. Barker suggested also that the reference to common farming at 740a has to do with the time of Cronus. But the time of Cronus was not supposed to have farming of any kind.

42. On the problem of the conclusion of the *Laws:* Leonardo Tarán, *Academica: Plato, Philip of Opus, and the Pseudo-Platonic Epinomis* (Philadelphia 1975), 19–24.

43. In addition to Plato's well-known visits to the Syracusan court in the 360s, there were later Academic meddlings in Sicilian politics. It was said that Plato was asked to make laws for Cyrene but again refused. Several of his disciples advised the tyrant of Atarneus, and Aristotle was not the only one found at the court of Macedon. Others were said to have advised various cities. Several prominent Athenian politicians, including Lycurgus, Phocion, and possibly Demosthenes, were pupils of Plato, and we hear of some other Platonists who rose to power in their native cities. Most of this information comes from a passage in Plutarch's *Against Colotes* (1126cd) which lists twelve Platonist politicians in order to show that their practical activities were more commendable than the useless schemes of Plato's *Republic* and *Laws*. This is an anti-utopian rhetorical topic contrasting men of words and men of deeds, which we will meet again in writers of Roman times. But there is no reason to doubt there really were Platonists in politics. Cf. Diog. Laert. 3.46–47; Aelian, *Var. Hist.* 12.30; Plut., *Mor.* 779d. A more anti-Platonic rhetorical tradition is preserved by Athenaeus (1106e, 508d–509c), who lists five Platonists who aimed at tyranny, none of them found in Plutarch's list. This anti-Platonic tradition seems to be based upon Demochares' "Oration Against the Philosophers," which we will consider in the fourth chapter; its fragments have been collected by Ingemar Düring, *Herodicus the Cratetean: A Study in the Anti-Platonic Tradition* (Stockholm 1941), 149–51. See also F. L. Vatai, *Intellectuals in Politics in the Greek World from Early Times to the Hellenistic Age* (London 1984).

44. Aristotle seems to think the *Laws* ought to have portrayed an ideal that is within the reach of most states, like his own "middle constitution," but fails to do this because its ideal is too utopian. "For, apart from the sharing of wives and property, he constructs the two constitutions on very much the same pattern: the same kind of education, the same life of freedom from essential tasks, and the same arrangements for common meals—except that in the *Laws* women also are to have common meals, and the number of those bearing arms is 5,000, not 1,000" (*Pol.* 1265a1–9, trans. Sinclair/Saunders). Aristotle takes the number 1,000 too literally (see n. 34) and is mistaken about the presence of women at *syssitia*: in the *Republic* we are told repeatedly that female guards will do everything the males do, and there is a reference to their eating together at 458c.

Some other of Aristotle's mistakes about the *Laws* are more difficult to understand. He says it pays no attention to foreign affairs or to population control, when it discusses both. It has been suggested that he used an earlier and shorter version of the *Laws* than the text we possess: G. R. Morrow, "Aristotle's Comments on Plato's Laws," in *Aristotle and Plato in the Mid-Fourth Century*, ed. I. Düring and G. E. L. Owen (Göteburg 1960), 145–62.

45. When Aristotle introduces this ideal at *Pol.* 3.7 he calls it the *politeia*, "the constitution," though noting that this is also the word for constitutions in general. We receive the impression that this definition of *politeia* was already established, probably at the Academy, for we find something close to it in Plato's *Laws* (712). Aristotle clearly means by it a constitution based on the hoplites.

At 4.8–9 the *politeia* is described as "mixed" constitution blending oligarchy and democracy; it does this by establishing a property qualification that excludes from citizenship all those poorer than the hoplites. (At this point Aristotle mentions some other theories of the "mixed constitution" which do not exclude the poor—1294a35–b13. But the one that he favors seems to be the hoplite *politeia*.)

At 4.11–12 this hoplite *politeia* is described as a "middle constitution" because it is based on the "middle citizens" who are neither rich nor poor; and this is clearly identified with the second-best or "common" constitution of 4.1. It is only possible where the middle group is large, and rarely found now because the middle group is usually small. At first it is difficult to understand how the middle group, if it means the hoplites, can be small. But what Aristotle says is that the middle group must be *kreitton*, stronger, than either the rich or the poor. He cannot mean by this that they must be simply more numerous than either, for surely it would always be the case that a group called "middle" would be more numerous than a group identified as "rich." He must mean that wealth has to be distributed evenly enough so that the hoplite smallholders become numerous and influential enough to dominate the community; the point at which they reach critical mass he leaves undefined, but he could see that this was not happening in the Greek world of his day.

Another confusing passage appears in 4.13 (1297b1): Aristotle recommends that a *politeia* set a property qualification low enough to include the majority [of possible citizens]. That sounds like a moderate democracy, whereas the kind of hoplite *politeia* he discussed earlier seemed more oligarchical. But perhaps he is speaking here of "constitutions" in the more usual sense. The differences between the ideal middle constitution, the moderate democracy, and the moderate oligarchy do not seem that significant anyway. A recent useful discussion of this problem: John Creed, "Aristotle's Middle Constitution," *Polis: Newsletter of the Society for the Study of Greek Political Thought* 8.2 (1989), 2–27.

46. All guards who participate in one of the periodic mating festivals are to regard as their offspring all children born after that festival, and there are to be no sexual relations with any of them (*pace* Aristotle). All children of the same age class are to regard one another as fictive siblings; but the language of 461d leaves it unclear whether they are to be allowed to form sexual unions. Probably this will be allowed, since none of them could be biological siblings. Then Socrates adds "But the law will allow brothers and sisters to live together if the lot so falls and the Pythian approves" (trans. Grube). We do not know whether this appeal to the Delphic oracle refers to a general approval for the entire system or a separate approval for each case of incest, but in either case there would be no need to bring in Delphi were Socrates not speaking of something very extraordinary; therefore he means to allow full biological siblings to mate, and after their childbearing years to form voluntary unions. Greeks accepted marriages

between half-brother and half-sister, but what they thought about full sibling incest is obvious from Plato's nervousness and Aristotle's horror, not to mention other evidence. Presumably Socrates is compelled to allow this because the only way to prevent it would be to introduce still more complicated regulations, restricting marriages between people of different age classes. This might result in an entire generation containing few individuals who would be allowed to reproduce, and might also plunge this whole discussion over the edge of preposterousness, on which it already trembles.

47. Ephraim David, "Aristotle and Sparta," *Ancient Society* 13 (1982), 67–103, points out how closely Aristotle's utopia follows the Laconist model.

48. Besides Phaleas' constitution there had been other, less ambitious, proposals for increased use of public slaves. Aristotle mentions one of these without giving any details (1267b13). The author of the tract *On Revenues* attributed to Xenophon recommended using public slaves in the Attic mines.

On the barbarian serfs: *Pol.* 1327a40–b17, 1329a26, 1330a25–33. The Mariandynoi had been mentioned by Plato (*Laws* 776) as a work force superior to the Spartan helots. Aristotle in the *Politics* refers often to the constitution of Heraclea Pontica. The barbarian serfs of Heraclea attracted attention because they seem to have been the best example of a barbarian nation held in a helotlike condition by a Greek city, therefore provided a solution to a problem that vexed all Laconists—how to reproduce the servile work force upon which Spartan power rested without incurring the undesirable political (and by now moral) consequences of enslaving fellow Greeks. See de Ste. Croix, *Class Struggle*, 160.

49. There have been many attempts to identify this nameless reformer. Paul Andrews, "Aristotle, *Politics* 4.11.1296a38–40," *Classical Review* 66 n.s. 2 (1952), 141–44, counted sixteen different conjectures. I share his view that Aristotle was probably alluding not to some figure as well known as Solon or Lycurgus but to some personal patron of his, Atarnean or Macedonian, and to some point in Aristotle's life when he had entertained stronger hopes of putting the middle constitution into practice.

50. The economic interpretation of the fourth-century crisis has been emphasized by Fuks in several of the essays collected in *Social Crisis*, especially "Redistribution of Land and Houses in Syracuse in 356 B.C. and Its Ideological Aspects," 213–29; reprinted from *Classical Quarterly* 18 (1968), 207–23.

51. Barry Strauss, *Athens after the Peloponnesian War* (Ithaca 1986), 1–44, presents a "factional" model for the study of ancient Greek politics.

52. The appropriateness of Marxist, Weberian, and other modern terminologies for ancient social divisions has been the subject of much dispute; e.g., Finley's *Ancient Economy*, 45ff., the rejoinder to it in de Ste. Croix's *Class Struggle*, 81ff., and the edition of *Arethusa* (8, 1975) devoted to Marxist interpretations of the classical world. It is clear that the Greeks conceived society very largely in terms of formal juridical hierarchies, the most important such distinction in the classical age being that between the *politai* and everyone else; we usually refer to these groupings as "orders" or "estates." And it is equally obvious that they knew these orders were always divided into more informal groupings based on wealth, usually described as the "rich" and "poor" or similar terms, which have at least a strong resemblance to our economic "classes." The vagueness of the economic terms seems significant. De Ste. Croix has suggested that the real "rich" were those with sufficient property in land and slaves that they could live in leisure and cultivate the life-style of a "gentleman," a *kalos kagathos*. We have seen that Aristotle seems to think of the "middle" as essentially a class of kulaks, which implies that the "poor," assumed to be the majority everywhere, are very marginal peasantry or completely landless. Still, these are loose and flexible divisions.

53. This interpretation has been suggested by Lintott, *Violence, Civil Strife*.

3

The Cynic Way: A Life Without the Household

Menippus in his *Sale of Diogenes* says that when Diogenes was captured and sold he was asked what he knew how to do, and he replied "Rule men."

DIOG. LAERT. 6.29

The Problem of Cynic Political Thought: A Contradiction in Terms?

Toward the end of the fourth century the Platonic-Aristotelian tradition was challenged by a rival vision of utopia, which was attributed to both the Cynics and the Stoics. Whether the new utopian theory was of Cynic or Stoic origin is an important question, which will require a discussion at some length of the relationship between these closely affiliated schools.

There was a work called the *Republic* (*Politeia*) which antiquity generally attributed to the most famous of the Cynics, Diogenes of Sinope (ca. 405–ca. 323 B.C.). This Cynic *Republic*, to judge from the meager surviving references, was very similar to the later utopian works produced by Stoics. All the Cynic/Stoic utopias resembled Plato's Kallipolis in their absence of property and family ties but differed from Kallipolis in their egalitarianism, universality, and sexual freedom. Furthermore, the central text of Stoic utopianism, the *Republic* of Zeno, was said to have been written when Zeno was still a pupil of the Cynic Crates, Diogenes' leading disciple, and was considered the most Cynic of the Stoic classics. All this has led most modern scholars to assume what was generally assumed in antiquity, that the egalitarian type of utopia was a Cynic teaching appropriated by the early Stoics.

As we observed in the introduction, the assumption that this was originally a Cynic teaching has led many of these scholars to dismiss all Cynic/Stoic utopianism as a political theory. We are told that Cynics taught complete indifference to the state and to social convention (an opinion so common that the hippies of the 1960s were routinely compared to Cynics in academic circles), and therefore their conception of an ideal society could have had no relevance to the problems of political and social life. We are told that this Cynic/Stoic utopia could not have been a "genuine," "realistic," "social" utopia like Plato's

Republic. It could not have been a political theory at all. It must have been some sort of anarchist or escapist fantasy.

But anarchists do not usually write utopias. If the Cynics really taught an ethic of individual freedom that had no use for the state or political life, then a Cynic political theory seems oxymoronic. And if it was only an escapist fantasy, then an escape to what?

Two logically satisfying solutions to this problem have been proposed. The older solution, put forward by German scholars of the late nineteenth and early twentieth centuries, accepted the Diogenic *Republic* as a genuine utopia, and tried to reconcile Cynic utopianism with Cynic anarchism. These scholars were willing to believe that the Diogenic *Republic* must have been the kind of work that ancient authors said it was, and they correctly saw that the problem is to find the relationship between this utopian theory and the Cynicism that we read about in the same ancient sources. They generally accepted the ancient doxographical tradition that portrayed Cynicism as a Socratic school founded by Antisthenes, to whom several political works were attributed, and so saw nothing inherently implausible in the notion that Cynicism might have had a political philosophy of a utopian sort. They assumed therefore that the individualistic and apparently anarchistic ethic practiced by the Cynics must have been conceived as in some way a preparation for utopia. Zeller thought the Cynics hoped to set an example for the rest of society. Did not Diogenes compare himself to a chorus trainer, who pitches a note too high so that the chorus can strike the right tone (Diogenes Laertius 6.35)?[1] But the implications of this musical metaphor are not clear. Does the right tone (*prosekon tonos*) mean the utopian state? If so, after the chorus gets there what is to become of the trainer? Some thought the individualistic Cynic life was a transitional stage: in the utopian society Cynics were to become a ruling elite like the guards of Plato.[2] But nothing in the Cynic tradition known to us suggests that any Cynics thought their teaching would end in any such result. The tradition suggests consistently that all Cynics assumed the Cynic life to be a perfectly adequate end in itself, not temporary, and not a transition to anything.

Therefore some scholars have held that the Diogenic *Republic* was not a utopia at all. It was merely a description of the Cynic way of life as it actually existed, mockingly called a *politeia* to hint that this way of life offered an alternative to the society of the polis. This *Republic* could have contained no description of an ideal state of society, and could have had no real connection with the later utopian philosophy of Stoicism, though Stoics clearly made some use of the Diogenic *Republic*.[3] This is on first consideration an attractive solution, for we know from the poems of Crates that the early Cynics did in fact portray their fraternity as a kind of mock polis. It is easy to think that the work by Diogenes called the *Republic* merely extended this metaphor. This interpretation also permits a more serious view of Stoic political thought, which it detaches from its Cynic origins.

But the ancient testimony, scanty though it is, will not easily permit such an interpretation. The sources say that the Diogenic *Republic* proposed not only sexual communism but the raising of children in common; not only the rejection of private property but the use of dice for currency; not only withdrawal from politics but the abolition of war. These are not private goals. They could belong only to what we commonly call a utopia, a complete imaginary society like the one described in Plato's *Republic*. Also there is the fact that antiquity generally believed this Diogenic *Republic* had been the model of the *Republic* of Zeno. Plutarch referred to the *Politeiai* of Plato, Diogenes, and Zeno as the three leading examples of ideal states, and said they were all based ultimately on the Spartan constitution (*Lycurgus* 31). The comment is difficult to interpret,[4] but at least it implies that the Diogenic *Republic* took the form of a political treatise and had obvious similarities to the other two examples.

Neither solution fits the evidence. The Diogenic *Republic* seems to have no discernable relationship to anything else in the Cynic tradition. Most scholars still accept Diogenes' authorship of a *Republic*, but often they are driven to admit that the notion of a Cynic political theory seems an inexplicable contradiction.[5] Thus the study of Cynic political thought reached an impasse long ago, out of inability to decide whether its subject ever existed. Clearly the problem must be approched on a broader level, by inquiry into the nature and purposes of Cynic philosophy as a whole.

The Search for the Historical Diogenes

But to turn to the history of Cynicism is to encounter the same problem on a larger scale. Scholars are not agreed that Cynicism was a philosophy at all; few think it was a philosophical school with a consistent body of doctrine like Stoicism or Epicureanism. Yet it is obvious there was a well-defined Cynic tradition that endured for several hundred and perhaps a thousand years in the Mediterranean world. It is difficult to see what defined it so clearly and made it persist so stubbornly. It is also difficult to reconstruct the teachings of the early Cynics, not only because the sources are late and fragmentary, but because the peculiar relationship between Cynicism and its great successor the Stoa has obscured the original Cynic vision as thoroughly as Plato has obscured the original Socrates. This situation will excuse what will appear to be a lengthy digression on modern interpretations of Cynicism.

Who Were the Original Cynics?

During the first half of the twentieth century the study of Cynicism was dominated by the theory that the Cynic movement always contained two traditions or sects, the one called "rigorist" or "ascetic" and the other described as "mild," "lax," "hedonistic," or "eudaemonistic." Scholars tried to find the oldest layer of material in our sources through the methods of New Testament criticism, identifying one of these traditions with the original Cynicism and using it as a test of authenticity.

One view, developed by German scholars early in this century, held that the "rigorist" (*streng*) element in the sources represents the original Cynicism.[6] In support of this view we are told that the development from rigor to laxity is a natural one (sometimes with reference to the history of medieval religious orders); and that the most rigorist anecdotes are attached to Diogenes, whom no one would have portrayed as an extreme ascetic had he not been one. There is some disagreement over the definition of this rigorist Cynicism, but its main features are harshly ascetic standards in diet and other bodily needs, resembling Hindu or medieval Christian asceticism more than anything else in the pagan Greek world, and a self-reliant individualism carried to the point of antisocial misanthropy. The introduction of *der Laxe* is attributed to Crates, Diogenes' principal disciple, and even more to Bion in the following generation, because the stories about them indicate a less extravagant asceticism and more interest in reaching a broad audience. We are told that later Cynics tried to turn Cynicism into a more popular teaching, putting themselves on the same level as their audience and developing a practical, realistic morality that would be suitable for all people and not just for Cynics. This tradition has been called "hedonistic" to suggest that it was influenced by the doctrines of the Cyrenaics, with whom Bion was supposed to have studied; and "eudaemonistic" to suggest that these Cynics shared the traditional aims of Greek moral philosophy.

The "rigorist" interpretation implies that Diogenes was the real founder of Cynicism: the notion that Cynicism was a Socratic philosophical school traceable to Antisthenes is dismissed as an invention of late doxographers. It implies also that what Diogenes founded was not a philosophy or a school at all: he started a tradition, but it consisted of little more than a way of life, an attitude, a pose, a handful of slogans; it had no theoretical base and no ethical teaching, being by definition antiintellectual, antisocial, and amoral.

This interpretation of Cynicism, well known in the English-speaking world through Dudley's *History of Cynicism* (1937), held the field for a long time, and is principally responsible for the inability of scholars to make much sense of "Cynic political thought." The image of Diogenes as an extreme "rigorist" is impossible to reconcile with the Diogenes whom Plutarch describes as a utopian social philosopher and the equal of Plato. As we have seen, the contradiction is widely recognized.[7]

But there is an alternative interpretation of the history of Cynicism, developed mainly in Sweden, which starts from the opposite assumption: that the original Cynicism was "mild" and that "rigorism" was introduced later. The major exponent of this theory, Ragnar Höistad, accepted without difficulty the ancient doxographical tradition that Cynicism was a Socratic school and saw Cynic asceticism as simply an exaggerated form of the asceticism of Socrates. Höistad's Cynics did not practice asceticism for its own sake but as an instrument to achieve traditional Greek ethical goals; Höistad's Cynics were concerned with social and educational aims from the start; and there is no reason why Höistad's Diogenes could not have been a utopian political thinker.[8] In support of this view Höistad relied heavily on the portrait of Diogenes found in late Stoic writers, especially Dio Chrysostom; but he also argued convincingly that the serious educational purpose, large literary production, and consistent body of doctrine, which all antiquity attributed to the early Cynics, are not compatible with the extreme rigorist conception of that movement. The extremely ascetic and anarchistic traditions about Diogenes Höistad assigned to a late and degenerate type of Cynicism that had succumbed to Oriental influences.

The modern discussion of Cynicism has been largely dominated by this alleged conflict between rigorist and mild Cynic sects, but by the 1940s this discussion had reached an impasse. The two schools of thought never really engaged one another, and it is not easy to see how they could have done so, since they started from totally contrary and equally untestable premisses. For the next several decades there were, so far as I know, no significant monographs on Cynicism in any language.

The two tendencies they described certainly existed. The ancient traditions about Diogenes and the other early Cynics fall into two groups. On the one hand we have a large mass of unconnected anecdotes and sayings, scattered through many ancient authors but best represented by the confused body of anecdotal material which forms the central section of the *Life of Diogenes* by Diogenes Laertius. The Diogenes presented in these stories is primarily the rigorist Diogenes. This is the Diogenes who has lived through the centuries: the burlesque theatrical sage who carries a lantern in daylight and performs indecent acts in the agora; the defiant old derelict who sprawls on the stairs at the center of Raphael's *School of Athens*, untroubled by the disputations of the wordy philosophers who swirl around him. On the other hand, Diogenes Laertius has also preserved several Cynic doxographies, or summaries of Cynic doctrine, which would lead us to think that Cynicism always had a core of systematic ethical and political teaching exactly like the other schools. The rigorist interpretation of Cynicism concentrates upon the anecdotes; the mild interpretation, upon the doxographies.

But neither can make sense of this tradition as a whole. Höistad's interpretation makes it easy to accept Diogenes as a philosopher and utopist: Höistad thought Diogenes' *Republic* might have resembled that of Plato rather closely, though doubtless more radical in details. But Höistad did this at the cost of eliminating the harshly ascetic side of the Diogenes legend, which compels us to ask where this tradition came from. Those who think rigorism a late development offer no explanation for it except for vague allusions to "Oriental" influences. This is the more puzzling because the alleged conquest of Cynicism by rigorist ascetics must have happened during the later Hellenistic age, when the Cynic tradition seems almost moribund and very few Cynics are known to us even by name. (The most famous of these, the erotic poet Meleager of Gadara, seems an improbable candidate for this role.) One is inclined to agree with those who think the rigorist image came from the founders, if only because it could have come from nobody else. But how to reconcile the Gerhard/Dudley Diogenes with the doxographies? As we have seen, those who think this tend to conclude either that Diogenes never wrote a *Republic*, or that he wrote a *Republic* that was somehow quite different from the one ancient sources describe; and both solutions seem to contradict too much of the ancient testimony.

Also, none of the efforts to define this distinction seem altogether satisfactory. From both sides we have been told that the rigorist Cynics practiced asceticism for its own sake, but it is not clear what "asceticism for its own sake" could mean. (Have there been any ascetics, even in India, who did this literally?) Nor is it clear what is meant by "laxity": the term sometimes refers to a decline in the observance of the original ideal, and sometimes to its replacement by a different ideal and a new observance. The failure of ancient writers to distinguish these two rival Cynic sects, which appear so distinct to some modern eyes, is another troublesome point.

Over all this there hangs the problem of the sources, which rivals that of the New Testament. The ancient texts that deal with Diogenes and his disciples at any length were written down between three hundred and eight hundred years later. Some of these fragments can be traced back to earlier (i.e., Hellenistic) writers, but the haul is disappointing, and the number of fragments that can be traced to writings by the early Cynics themselves is miniscule. Recent scholars therefore have largely abandoned the attempt to break this material apart into earlier and later Cynic doctrines. We seem to have here a biographical/doxographical tradition about early Cynicism which exhibits a surprising degree of consistency, and at the same time a number of puzzling inconsistencies. Where did this tradition come from, and what purpose did it serve? Several recent textual studies, and the long-awaited appearance of a critical edition of the Cynic texts, have reopened the problem of Cynicism and suggested new approaches.[9]

The Origin of the Cynic Doxographies

We know hardly more for certain about Diogenes the Dog than was known to Dio Chrysostom in the second century A.D.: which was simply that many of his sayings were remembered, some of them authentic and some not (Dio 72.11). There was extant at that time an enormous mass of written material about the sayings and doings of Diogenes and his followers, and a good part of this has survived, especially in the collection of "Lives and Opinions of Eminent Philosophers" written by Diogenes Laertius in the late second or early third century A.D. This contains the long *Life of Diogenes* and short biographies of nine other Cynics who lived in the late fourth and early third centuries B.C. It is our most valuable source because the author, who was uncritical but diligent and honest, tried to put together the best portrait of Cynicism he could by compiling material from earlier biographers and doxographers, relying heavily upon Hellenistic sources.[10]

There is another collection that purports to be based on the traditions of the Cynics: the spurious *Epistles* attributed to Diogenes and other early Cynics, which are believed to have been composed at various times and by various hands under the Roman Empire. But their provenance, date, and purpose are so obscure that they are best used as sources for late Cynicism, and not for primitive Cynicism unless they are confirmed by other sources.

Other writers of Roman times have preserved much Cynic material, but in questionable forms. Dio, Epictetus, and other Stoics have transmitted a Stoicized or Neostoicized version of the Diogenes legend; the emperor Julian, a Neoplatonic version of it; Lucian, a satirical image of it; and Philodemus of Gadara, an Epicurean attack upon it in the papyrus fragments of his *On the Stoics*, a source of particular interest not only for its early date (first century B.C.) but for its information about the Diogenic *Republic*.[11]

Diogenes Laertius is not only the main source for early Cynicism, but the only source that provides a systematic account of Cynic teaching. The sixth book of the *Lives*, which is devoted to Cynicism, includes three doxographies: one inserted in the *Life of Antisthenes* (6.10–13), one in the *Life of Diogenes* (6.70–73), and one at the end of the book (6.103–105). As we have seen, these passages are the main support of those who believe Cynicism was from the start a serious philosophy modeled on other philosophical schools.

Now the major advance in Cynic studies in recent years has been the realization that these doxographies, in the form we have them, are in all probability of *Stoic* origin.[12] They come from some Stoic epitome which stressed the continuity between Cynicism and Stoicism and portrayed the two as complementary approaches to philosophy. Stoics did not generally share this view of Cynicism after the middle of the second century B.C. (at latest); one influential Stoic writer who did share it was Apollodorus of Seleucia (late second century B.C.), author of a series of *Eisagogai* (Handbooks) on Stoicism, including one on *Ethics*, which are frequently cited by Diogenes Laertius in his lives of the Stoics; we know that Apollodorus held a favorable view of Cynicism (7.121), so it is probable that his *Ethics* was the source of Diogenes Laertius' Cynic doxographies. There are also sufficient parallels between the Cynic doxographies in the sixth book and the Stoic doxographies in the seventh book to suggest that the *Ethics* of Apollodorus was an important source for both. In both doxographies the main theme is the *koinonia* that unites Cynicism and Stoicism; Cynicism is described as the short road to virtue, Stoicism as the long road (6.104, 7.121); the Cynic doxographies point out resemblances between Cynic and Stoic teachings, describe Cynic teachings in Stoic terms, and place much importance on Antisthenes, who was supposed to be the link between Cynicism and Socrates. The idea that Cynicism and Stoicism were closely related Socratic schools, based upon the canonized succession of teachers Socrates–Antisthenes–Diogenes–Crates–Zeno, came from the Stoic tradition represented by Apollodorus. As we shall see, this was not the only version of the history of Cynicism and Stoicism known to antiquity; it probably owed its wide currency to the fact that it was adopted by the influential scholar Sotion of Alexandria, whose *Successions of the Philosophers* (early second century B.C.) provided a basic scheme explaining the relationships among the schools that was followed by many later doxographers, including Diogenes Laertius.

If we accept this hypothesis, than we must recognize that the intellectual framework behind Diogenes Laertius' sixth book ("Lives of the Cynics") and seventh book ("Lives of the Stoics") represents a particular Stoic tradition that was bent on establishing the *koinonia* between the two schools. This is a great breakthrough in the study of Cynicism, but it also means that this study has once again reached a sort of impasse, much like the impasse reached by New Testament scholars when they generally realized that the Gospel tradition is a finished literary product and there is no obvious way to take it apart and use the fragments to reassemble more primitive Christian traditions. Our "Cynic doxography" is a late-Hellenistic Stoic manual. It is clear that parts of it must represent an authentic early Cynicism, and we can still try to determine which parts those are; but it is no longer possible to believe that this doxography *in toto* represents primitive Cynic teaching, and if we wish to analyze it we must first find some kind of touchstone, some conclusion about the nature of primitive Cynicism that can serve as a test of authenticity.

The Origins of the Cynic Anecdotes

If the doxographies have become impenetrable, we must try to find such a touchstone in the Cynic anecdotes. At first this material seems far less promising than the doxographies. It is a chaotic mass of stories accumulated through many centuries, and there is rarely any way to determine their provenance or date. And yet everyone who has studied this material has been struck by the general similarity of its themes. There was definitely a Cynic tradition, which persisted with astonishing tenacity. But if the doxographies have been contaminated with Stoicism, so may the anecdotes. The problem is to isolate from this material the elements that seem to be certainly pre-Stoic.

What were the ultimate sources of this material? The founders of Cynicism left a copious literature—dialogues, letters, poetry, diatribes—but virtually all of this has vanished except for the titles preserved in the catalogs of Diogenes Laertius, and some scraps of Crates' poems, which are the only primitive Cynic writings preserved in their original form. We have more information about the Diogenic *Republic* than about any other work attributed to an early Cynic; but the *Republic* is the knottiest problem of all. We are on safer ground if we try to generalize about the *forms* of early Cynic literature.

Two tendencies are evident from the start. One is a desire to popularize moral philosophy. The genre most closely identified with Cynicism was the *diatribe*, the popular lecture or sermon. In pre-Cynic days this word could mean simply "pastime." We do not know just when it came to mean "sermon," nor do we know that Cynics were exclusively responsible for its development. But Bion of Borysthenes (early third century B.C.) is usually thought to have perfected the form, for he left many "diatribes" in written form (Diog. Laert. 2.77, 4.47), from which numerous fragments survive; these are filled with the popular moralizings and witty sayings that are characteristic of the later Cynic/Stoic literary tradition, characteristic also of the sayings attributed to Diogenes.

The second tendency does not take the form of a genre. It is a pervasive technique of making serious points in a humorous fashion, especially through the parody of serious literature and mythology. The Greeks had a word for this: *spoudaiogeloios*, "seriocomic." The term was particularly applied to Menippus of Gadara, the famous Cynic satirist of the early third century B.C., but the mode, if not the word for it, was much earlier. It had flourished in the Old Comedy and the satyr play; and when the stage turned to tamer subjects in the fourth century, *to spoudaiogeloion* become a trademark of the Cynics. There were scandalous "tragedies" attributed to Diogenes or some other early Cynic, probably obscene burlesques of classical Attic tragedy, meant to be read and not acted, which turned the legends of traditional mythology upside down to make serious points. Crates also wrote "tragedies," and the surviving fragments of his poetry include *paignia* (light verse) and parodies of Homer and Solon. The obscure Monimus of Syracuse, disciple of both Diogenes and Crates, wrote *paignia* that were "mixed with hidden seriousness" (Diog. Laert. 6.83). In the next generation Menippus wrote mythological burlesques in a mixture of prose and verse which provided models for Lucian.[13] Both the diatribe form and the comic mode are evidence that the Cynic movement was trying to reach a wide audience from an early date; and in this respect it seems unique among philosophical schools of the time.

To assist this effort to popularize philosophy, Cynics soon began to produce collections of *chreiai*. A *chreia* (literally "something useful") was an anecdote about a famous person, usually containing a pointed saying. It is probable that this use of word *chreia* was popularized by Cynics.[14] The typical Cynic diatribe would have been built around *chreiai*, as are the extant fragments of the diatribes of Bion and Teles, and most *chreiai* will have originated in diatribes. As early as ca. 300 B.C. Cynics were circulating collections of *chreiai*, presumably to be used for other Cynic diatribes, in the same way that medieval preachers drew on published collections of *exempla*. These collections of *chreiai* may be the principal sources of the anecdotes about Diogenes and his disciples preserved by Diogenes Laertius and others; though *chreiai* could also be preserved by biographers or any other genre.

In dealing with a tradition such as this, questions of authorship and date are usually hopeless. *Chreiai* were made to be recycled, and their original sources were soon forgotten. Often the same anecdote is attributed to more than one philosopher, not all of them Cynics. Only a small number of anecdotes can be traced back to collections of the third century B.C., and even these, of course, are post-Stoic. One of the earliest collections of *chreiai* was in fact compiled by Zeno, founder of Stoicism.

But one group of anecdotes is of particular interest. Scattered through the anthology of Stobaeus (fifth century A.D.) there is a collection of excerpts from the diatribes of Teles of Megara, an otherwise unknown teacher of Cynic sympathies, who quotes many anecdotes about Diogenes, Crates, and Bion; and these diatribes can be dated from internal evidence ca. 240 B.C. A complete or near-complete diatribe, whose provenance and date are known, is incomparably more useful for the reconstruction of early Cynic thought than any number of anecdotes and sayings isolated from their original context. What makes the diatribes of Teles even more useful for our purposes is the fact that they show not the slightest sign of Stoic influence. And he wrote at the end of the great century of Cynicism. I propose therefore to use Teles as our touchstone. First we will try to define the main features of Cynicism as Teles conceived it; then ask whether the very few anecdotes attributable to sources earlier than Teles are compatible with this conception; then ask the same of the very large group of anecdotes to which no date can be assigned.

A Definition of Early Cynicism: An Activist Ascetic Elite

The Cynicism of Teles: The Two Levels of Philosophy

In the diatribes of Teles, the Cynic message is quite clear. The constant theme is adaptation to circumstances (*peristaseis*), the easy acceptance of every possible condition of life, including poverty, sickness, exile, age, and death. This state of mind is called *apatheia*, freedom from passion. It allows one to enjoy an easy (*rhaidios*) life, filled with contentment, cheerfulness, and equanimity. This goal is sometimes described as *eudaimonia*, a common term in the Greek moral vocabulary, but here used with a special connotation: it is identified with a state of psychic contentment, a wholly inner quality; it has acquired much the same meaning as the English word "happiness."

> For thus the happy man [*eudaimon*] will also be the one beyond passion and disturbance. For whoever is in distress and pain and fear, how could he be satisfied with life, or if he is not satisfied how could he be happy? Teles, fr. 7, "On Freedom from Passion" (*Peri Apatheias*), Hense 56, trans. O'Neill

The independence that guarantees this imperturbable peace of mind is called *autarkeia*, self-sufficiency. This *autarkeia* does not necessarily mean the peculiar style of mendicant life called "Cynic" in later times. Rather it means a state of mind adaptable to *any* way of life, including that of a rich man. There is a quotation from Bion comparing life to a play: as a good actor performs well any part he is given, a good man is ready to play well any part he is given by fortune, whether king or vagabond, ruler or subject, rich man or poor. In the same diatribe Teles goes so far as to say that bearing poverty with contentment is not necessarily more commendable than bearing wealth with contentment; the ideal is simply to make no distinction between the two (fr. 2, *Peri Autarkeias*, Hense 5ff.)

Teles thinks that the *apatheia/autarkeia* ideal was the teaching of Diogenes, Crates, and Metrocles, who are his main heroes. He sees no differences among them. All taught that anyone can attain *autarkeia*, all were concerned with teaching ordinary people to cope with ordinary problems. Teles quotes a saying of Crates which shows that even a rich man could be called a philosopher, provided he had the right *attitude* to wealth. This quotation seems to come from a diatribe, the response to an imaginary interlocutor being a feature of that genre.

> And therefore Crates replied to the man who asked, "What will be in it for me after I become a philosopher?" "You will be able," he said, "to open your wallet

> easily [*rhaidios*] and with your hand scoop out and dispense lavishly instead of, as you do now, squirming and hesitating and trembling like those with paralyzed hands. Rather, if the wallet is full, that is how you will view it; and if you see that it is empty, you will not be distressed. And once you have elected to use the money, you will easily [*rhaidios*] be able to do so; and if you have none, you will not yearn for it, but you will live satisfied with what you have, not desiring what you do not have nor displeased with whatever comes your way." fr. 4a, "Comparison of Poverty and Wealth," Hense 38, trans. O'Neill

Teles' Diogenes teaches the same lesson. Upon hearing a man complain that Athens is an expensive place, Diogenes takes him to the marketplace and shows him how cheap lupineseeds and figs are (fr. 2, Hense 12–13). The point of this story is not that the man should imitate Diogenes' peculiar mode of life, but rather that he should adapt himself to his means cheerfully. This is what modern scholars have called "mild" or "eudaemonistic" Cynicism.

On the other hand, the philosophers most admired by Teles *do* have a most peculiar way of life. Teles describes Diogenes and Crates as poor (*penetes*) and as beggars (*epaitai*) (fr. 2, Hense 14). They lived in public buildings such as temples and baths, ate only the simplest foods, and wore nothing but the rough cloak (*tribon*) which also served as their only bedding. This way of life sets them apart from other schools. We are told that Metrocles, so long as he was a pupil of Theophrastus the Aristotelian and Xenocrates the Platonist, was accustomed to luxury and always dissatisfied; but when he left them for Crates he began to live in the fashion described above and so discovered contentment (fr. 4a, Hense 40–41).[15]

Teles does not use the term *kynikoi* (the doglike) for these men. We know they had long been called that, but in 240 B.C. it may still have been a term of abuse. Teles uses the traditional terms "philosopher" and "wise man." But he knows a distinct tradition of philosophy, which is distinguished by voluntary poverty, begging, and absence of a fixed abode. It is a Diogenic tradition. To judge from the extant fragments Teles may have thought Crates more important than Diogenes, but still Diogenes is the earliest representative of this tradition he mentions. (He mentions Socrates with admiration, but without any suggestion that Socrates led this way of life. Antisthenes, significantly, is not mentioned at all.) This is what modern scholars have called "rigorist" or "ascetic" Cynicism. What is the connection between these two levels? How did Teles conceive the relationship between the vagrant mendicant life and the general audience?

At one point he seems to suggest that the vagrant life is useful only as a refuge in hardship (fr. 6, Hense 53–54). But more often he describes Diogenes, Crates, and Metrocles as voluntarily embracing the life of destitution because they found it desirable in itself. We are told that it is easier for a philosopher to be poor than rich, as only poverty brings complete peace of mind and freedom from worry.

In short, Teles everywhere assumes the existence of two distinct audiences, and two kinds of philosopher. A philosopher may be a "Cynic" (to use the word later adopted universally for the Diogenic tradition) in the strict sense, emulating the vagrant life of Diogenes and Crates. Or a philosopher may be an ordinary citizen who merely emulates their detachment from wealth and all other circumstances that depend upon fortune. On the first level *autarkeia* means an independence both psychological and economic; on the second level, only a psychological independence; but psychological independence is always the goal for both.

Teles assumes the two levels are entirely complementary and require one another. The function of the higher level, the true Cynicism, is not to induce everyone to become beggars, but to set an example for everyone through a dramatic demonstration that it is possible for a philosopher to adapt easily to any circumstance. The higher philosophy is valuable in itself, for the philosopher to whom it brings freedom; but we gather Teles would not be much interested in it if he did not think it contained also a message for the general audience to which his diatribes are addressed.

Is the Evidence for Primitive Cynicism (ca. 350–ca. 250 B.C.) *Compatible with Teles?*

The foregoing analysis has hardly settled the question. No one has ever doubted that Teles understood Cynicism as a popular ethical teaching; but believers in an original rigorist Cynicism thought him one ot the "mild" Cynics who softened the original Cynic message to reach a wide audience. So let us consider the evidence, such as it is, for the teachings of the Cynics during the century before Teles.

The mendicant life described by Teles was sufficiently well known at Athens by the end of the fourth century to be ridiculed on the comic stage, and its professors were called the "dog-like men." A fragment of Menander describes Monimus as a *sophos* (wise man) who was also a dirty begger (*prosaiton kai rhypon*) and carried his possessions in a wallet (*pera*, Diog. Laert. 6.83). In another fragment Menander called Crates a *kynikos* who went about in a cloak (*tribon*) and kept a bizarre household: his wife Hipparchia accompanied him in public in the same attire, and he gave his daughter to a suitor for a month's trial (Diog. Laert. 6.93). Crates was again ridiculed for his ascetic dress in a comedy by Philemon (6.87). So the popular image of the Cynic lifestyle was fixed by this time, and the Cynic had replaced the Pythagorean as the stereotypical philosophical eccentric.[16] We notice that the stereotype included not only poverty, but something else unmentioned by Teles: Cynics, it is clear, were already famous for *anaideia*, "shamelessness," the deliberate flauting of all social and especially sexual conventions. (We should remember, however, that our selection from Teles has been twice edited: Stobaeus' collection of excerpts was itself taken from some earlier anthology. If there was *anaideia* in the original Teles it may well have been weeded out.) About the same time Epicurus wrote his *Bioi* (On Ways of Living) on the now-fashionable topic of how a philosopher should support himself: in the first book he argued that a philosopher will not enter political life or become a tyrant, in the second that he will not become a Cynic (*kyniein*) or beg (Diog. Laert. 10.119). The Cynic life was seen as a serious alternative for a philosopher.

Our most authentic evidence for their teaching, the poems of Crates, are ambiguous about their audience. Crates sometimes uses the term "philosopher" for begging Cynics; the city of the wallet in his best-known poem (Diog. Laert. 6.85) is clearly a place reserved for these. Another poem, a mock complaint about the low pay of philosophers compared to prostitutes and some other occupations, must mean "philosopher" as a distinct profession (Diog. Laert. 6.86). But other poems teach a message of moderation, frugality, and justice that could apply to anybody. One disclaims any desire for illustrious wealth (*chremata klyta*), which is not a particularly austere standard. One implies that the Cynic life teaches a useful political message: dissensions can be cured by a diet of lentils.[17] On the whole the verses suggest that Crates, like Teles, had in mind two sorts of philosophical life and two levels of *autarkeia*, the one higher than the other but both valid and complementary; that the purpose of those who lived the life of the wallet on the higher level was to set an example for their fellows; and that this philosophy had, on both levels, clear public goals.

Was Diogenes any different? There are three allusions to him by his contemporaries, and none suggests that he was. The earliest allusion to him, by Aristotle (*Rhetoric* 1411a24), shows that in his own lifetime he was already nicknamed "The Dog" and that people were already quoting his sayings; and it gives us the one indisputably authentic Diogenic saying, "Taverns are the mess halls [*syssitia*] of Attica." This reveals an ascetic attitude toward food and drink, but not the individualistic asceticism of the rigorist image. It suggests rather that Diogenes shared the admiration for Spartan communal discipline common among Athenian philosophers.

Then there is the famous anecdote about Diogenes and the mouse, attributed to Aristotle's disciple Theophrastus.[18] In one of his dialogues Theophrastus told how Diogenes (whom it would appear was already a semilegendary figure, though Theophrastus must have seen him with his own eyes) had discovered the secret of the Cynic life by watching a mouse run about. The secret he thus discovered is called the "way of circumstances" (*poros tes peristaseos*), and it means a life of vagrancy like that of an animal. Theophrastus assumed that Diogenes' claim to fame lay in his being the first to adopt a certain style of life: living in public places, sleeping in his *tribon*, and carrying his food in a *pera*. The mouse story is often taken as evidence that Diogenes was more ascetic than later Cynics. But does the story necessarily imply that everyone should live like Diogenes? More likely the "way of circumstances" meant to Diogenes exactly what it meant to Bion and Teles: one must be prepared to adapt to *any* circumstances. What strikes Diogenes about the mouse is that it needs no luxuries. But presumably it would take luxuries were they available. We see even in Teles that the Cynic way might also be described as a "way of hardships," *poros ton ponon*, and a writer who used those terms would have the begging Cynics in mind; but one who calls it a "way of circumstances" probably has both levels of Cynicism in mind.

Our third witness is reported indirectly, like Theophrastus, but in this case we deal with a disciple of Diogenes. Onesicritus of Astypalea, after his association with Diogenes at Athens, became a pilot on the eastern expedition of Alexander the Great, and wrote a history of the expedition. Strabo (15.1.65) has preserved a passage from this work in which Onesicritus described his encounter with certain Indian wise men who were accustomed to sit nude on hot rocks to test their endurance. One of these gymnosophists, named Mandanis, explained their doctrine thus:

> Mandanis' remarks, Onesicritus said, tended to show that the best doctrine was that which freed the soul from pleasure and pain. Pain and hardship [*ponos*] are different, the one being hostile, the other friendly to man. Bodies are exercised by hardship so that the understanding may be strengthened. Civil strife [*stasis*] may then be ended, and good counsel prevail both in public matters and in private affairs. Mandanis said he had advised Taxiles [an Indian king] to submit to Alexander, for if Alexander were the better man he ought to obey him, and if he were not he might improve him. trans. Brown, *Onesicritus*

It has often been pointed out that this is Cynic doctrine, very close to the doxography in Diogenes Laertius 6.70ff. Onesicritus may have honestly convinced himself, perhaps with the assistance of incompetent translators, that he had found the teachings of his master Diogenes confirmed by the legendary gymnosophists of India. In any case he is in all probability using the Indian sage as a mouthpiece to expound his own interpretation of Diogenes' teaching. And for us the most interesting thing about that interpretation is its explicit avowal of a political purpose. The Indians' asceticism, which is pointedly described as more extreme than anything ever attributed to any Cynic, is not practiced for its own sake, and is not primarily intended to achieve internal self-sufficiency. Its main purpose is to strengthen the understanding so that the ascetic can give good counsel to his fellows in private and public affairs. If we can accept Onesicritus' Indians as more-or-less Cynics, then this is the earliest statement of the goals of Cynicism we possess.

None of the early references to Diogenes suggest an interpretation different from that of Teles. Cynicism was from the beginning concerned with a practical morality addressed to the needs of ordinary people. This was not a mitigation of an original individualistic asceticism. The individualistic asceticism and the popular message were always different aspects of the same thing. It was always "rigorist" because the novel thing about it was the striking Cynic lifestyle. But this lifestyle was always intended to serve a philanthropic purpose, and the passages we have discussed suggest several ways it could have this effect. Firstly, it provided an example for ordinary citizens, encouraging them to imitate the wise man's *autarkeia* in at least an inward sense, and thereby making them more contented. Secondly, imitating the wise man will make the ordinary citizens better citizens: it will eliminate *stasis* in the city by eliminating the temptations of luxury (a theme mentioned several times in Crates' poems); and somehow it will also make the citizens more generous to one another (according to Crates or Teles). Thirdly, the Cynic discipline trains the wise man so that he can give good counsel to his fellow citizens (according to Onesicritus). To us it is far from obvious how Cynicism was supposed to produce all these effects. We will return to this problem. But it is clear that Diogenes the misanthropic urban anchorite (why *urban*, after all?) and Diogenes the popular urban preacher were one and the same. There were always two levels of Cynicism, and the purpose of the higher Cynicism, which was identified with the mendicant life, was to influence the mass of the citizens through both example and precept. And on both levels Cynicism was always "hedonistic" or "eudaemonistic," because on both levels the aim was to produce a psychic state of contentment, ease, and freedom from care.

Is the Evidence for Later Cynicism Compatible with Teles?

Nor, on the whole, does the later Diogenes legend contradict Teles. The legend does seem to be divided into "rigorist" and "mild" strains, but there are several reasons for this illusion.

For one thing, the people who were identified as "Cynics" in the late fourth and third centuries B.C. embraced an extraordinary variety of lifestyles.[19] Diogenes was "heard" by many *andres politikoi*, men active in politics (Diog. Laert. 6.76), who probably did not try to live like Diogenes. Onesicritus was remembered by Diogenes Laertius as one of Diogenes' major disciples but it is obvious he could have led the "Cynic life" only in a partial or temporary fashion, as he was chiefly famous as Alexander's officer and historian. Even Crates, who was remembered as a beggar, is said in some traditions to have retained some of his property and to have given his children a conventional upbringing. The "Cynics" of the following century included a politician and general, Cercidas of Megalopolis; Bion, court philosopher to the Antigonids; and the famous literary man Menippus. Many scholars have found it difficult to determine who was a Cynic and who was not, because if "Cynic" means one who followed the example of Diogenes literally there seem to be practically none. This situation is best explained if we assume there were always two levels of Cynicism, just as we find in Teles: there were "philosophers" in the strict sense, a small elite of disciples who copied the dramatic lifestyle of Diogenes; and "philosophers" in the looser sense, meaning those who admired and patronized the first group and adopted some part of their teaching, but who sought *autarkeia* in the spiritual rather than the literal sense.

Furthermore, what was this "example of Diogenes"? Those who still believe in an original Cynic rigorism may point out that the most ascetic anecdotes are practically restricted to Diogenes. But this does not prove that the ideal ever changed. The ideal pattern was an ideal pattern, perhaps never followed entirely by anybody. Most disciples of Diogenes, even those who tried to be "Cynics" in the strict sense, probably followed it very partially. Stories illustrating the ideal pattern naturally tended to attach themselves to Diogenes because he was the founder. (Just what it was he founded we will consider in a moment.) Naturally the idealization of Diogenes increased over the centuries, until he came to stand somewhat apart from all the rest of the Cynic tradition. We have seen that he did not seem to stand apart to Teles and other early commentators.

Secondly, there was an inherent ambiguity in the relationship between the two levels, such as is found in other types of asceticism. In any ethic like this the extremely ascetic life will be considered, at one and the same time, a rejection of the ordinary life and a model for it. The anecdotes consistently portray Diogenes as a popular preacher and giver of sound advice to the public. Even more so Crates, who was remembered as a sort of father confessor to the Athenians, nicknamed *Thurepanoiktes* (Dooropener) for his habit of entering households to dispense moral advice. It seems consistent with this image of Cynicism when we read that Diogenes was accompanied by many disciples, heard by prominent men of Athens, and sought out by famous visitors to the city like Alexander the Great. But there is another Diogenes in the legends: an isolated misanthrope, who spends his time reviling the citizens and receives many insults and physical assaults in return; a prophet without honor, without friends, without disciples, and without even a boy to wait on him.[20]

This is not necessarily a contradiction. The legend must emphasize the hardships endured by Diogenes, endurance of hardships being the essence of the Cynic way; so it was necessary to believe Diogenes had been rejected and scorned in his own lifetime. When Diogenes expressed his contempt for human folly and wickedness, he was excoriating vice as a preacher is expected to do. When he demonstrated unprecedented ascetic behavior, he was claiming to be an unprecedented wise man who was worth listening to. Theatricality was the novel element in Cynic asceticism. Socrates goes barefoot in snow to accustom himself to hardship; but when Diogenes goes about embracing icy statues in winter—a highly visible activity, as statues were usually erected in public places—he is trying to draw attention to himself (Diog. Laert. 6.23). And why should he do that if not to attract an audience? An early *chreia*, from the collection of Metrocles, throws some light on the question of Diogenes' popularity in his own lifetime: we are told Diogenes mocked some young revelers, was beaten by them, and afterwards publicly shamed them by carrying around his neck a tablet with their names (Diog. Laert. 6.33). The story suggests that Diogenes' criticisms could be roughly received, but also that he was not without public support. The Cynic isolated himself to draw crowds.

And thirdly, there was an inherent ambiguity in the goals of Cynicism, which has helped to foster the illusion that there were two Cynic sects. As Teles saw it, the objective of Cynicism was to endure hardship (*ponos*) for the sake of ease (*rhaidion*) and pleasure (*hedone*). The doxography (a section which Goulet-Cazé considers to be authentically Cynic) defines the end of Cynicism as "pleasure from the despising of pleasure" (6.71). An ethic like that will appear rigorist it one stresses the means, and hedonistic if one stresses the end. I will argue later that many apparent contradictions in the anecdotes, such as those about Diogenes' mendicancy, are best explained as attempts by different authors to emphasize different aspects of the Cynic message; some anecdotes show us the rigorist means and others its hedonistic end. But the difference between means and end does not correspond to the two social levels of Cynicism: the higher level of *autarkeia* required far more *ponoi* than the popular level, but on both levels the ultimate aim was always pleasure and ease. Nor does the difference between means and end correspond to the difference between the two social roles of the higher Cynicism: the Cynic as isolated misanthrope and the Cynic as popular preacher both pursue the ultimate aim of pleasure and ease.

The Original Cynic Experience

The original Cynicism was not a school in the ordinary sense, but it was a very distinct movement. It was recognized by the group of catchwords we found in Teles: self-sufficiency, passionlessness, ease as a moral criterion, *eudaimonia* in the sense of inner happiness. It specialized in the development of new literary forms designed to bring this message to a large audience. (Given the simplicity of ancient bookmaking techniques, there seems no reason to think this literary production incompatible with ascetic poverty.) Why was it not a school? In part because Cynics never had a formal organization, a recognized succession of leaders, or a canonical body of texts like the schools of Plato and Aristotle. But in these respects Cynics were typical of the smaller Socratic schools of the fourth century, like their rivals the Cyrenaics. There was a more important difference. Cynicism did not seem like a school primarily because it was unconcerned with doctrine and dialectic.

This was what set the Cynics apart from all other philosophers. They abandoned the pervasive intellectualism of Greek philosophy and identified the wise man with a certain discipline or way of life. This conclusion is supported by several considerations. One is the absence of anything that could be called a theoretical base in the fragments of Teles and other early sources. Cynics had certain basic ideas in common, but these hardly constituted a body of theory.

Secondly, there existed a doxographical tradition which held, in opposition to the tradition received by Diogenes Laertius, that Cynicism was not a philosophical school. Diogenes Laertius mentions that some classified Cynicism not as a school but as an *enstasis biou*—"plan for living," "life management" (6.103). The source of this view was probably Hippobotus, whose *Peri Haireseon* (On the Sects) was written sometime between the late third and late first centuries B.C. Hippobotus distinguished nine schools or sects of philosophy and refused to include the Cynics, the Eleans, and the Dialecticians (Diog. Laert. 1.19). We are not told his reason for this opinion, but most likely he was one of the *tines* (some people) mentioned at 6.103 who called Cynicism an *enstasis biou*. He probably defined a *hairesis* as a group with a systematic and uniform body of doctrine.[21] In the first century B.C. the *On Philosophy* of M. Varro presented another classification of the schools in which Cynicism was defined not as a school but as a mode or fashion that might be adopted by *any* school (Augustine, *City of God* 19.1). Four centuries later the emperor Julian tried to defend Cynicism as the universal and natural philosophy, in opposition to those who considered it a degraded form of philosophy (*Or.* 6.187). Both Julian and his opponents seemed to feel that Cynicism, whatever it was, was not a philosophy in the usual sense.

Thirdly, there are good reasons to think that the early Cynics described the Cynic life as a "short road to virtue" (*syntomon ep' areten hodon*), a formula that could only mean that Cynics rejected systematic philosophy. This phrase was found in Apollodorus' *Ethics* (Diog. Laert. 6.104, 7.121), where it was a way of defining the complementary relationship between Cynicism and Stoicism, in accordance with the doxographer's purpose of emphasizing the *koinonia* between the two: as I will argue later, the formula is best interpreted to mean that the "long road" consisted of theory. The phrase "short road" was frequently applied to Cynicism by later writers, both Cynic and non-Cynic.[22] It seems very unlikely this formula was introduced into Stoicism in Apollodorus' time, when the Stoa was turning against Cynicism. It must go back to the founders of Stoicism; and it probably goes back before them to the Cynics, because the formula seems to express a Cynic point of view and to suggest that Cynicism is the *superior* road to virtue. If so, this phrase is an important clue to the self-image and self-definition of primitive Cynicism. When the concept of a philosophical school as a dogmatic system was being formulated in the Hellenistic age, Cynics were sometimes not counted as such a school because they did not consider themselves to be that.

What made Cynicism something other than a philosophy was its novel, conspicuous, dramatic lifestyle. It was the belief that doctrine and life were the same thing that gave Cynicism its peculiar cultic flavor, and makes the Cynics seem to our eyes more like a religious sect or order than a Greek philosophical school. The point of the Cynic life was always quite clear. Cynicism, far from being antisocial, was a new social role, not unlike the role assigned to holy ascetics in some other societies. The Cynics thought of themselves as an ascetic elite who withdrew from all property and family ties so that they could act as independent social critics and mediators.

Asceticism is often a histrionic ritual of disassociation, in which an individual demonstrates that he or she stands outside all familial and economic interests so as to confront society from an objective position. We should not identify asceticism with anarchism or think it incompatible with philanthropy. The ritual may take many forms, but it always includes a physical and/or psychological discipline demonstrating that the ascetic is a person set apart. It promotes an ethic that recognizes two radically different norms of human life: one of these is higher than the other and requires a complete rejection of the other, yet each norm is accepted in its own sphere and the lower norm remains the general cultural pattern.[23] This sharp distinction between ordinary and extraordinary norms was characteristic of the civilization of India from an early date, and this is why modern scholars have so often perceived something "Oriental" about Cynicism. But it is neither plausible nor necessary to think Cynics borrowed anything directly from India. Their ascetic solution with its two-level ethic was something that many different societies have stumbled upon, and the Cynic version of it was entirely Greek.

There were obvious Greek models for it. Plato speaks as though the wandering beggar priests of Orpheus were a familiar sight in fourth-century Athens (*Rep.* 364b–365a); they hung about the doors of the rich and promised rewards in the afterlife through their magic incantations and sacred books. There had already been a philosophical version of the Orphic cult in the Pythagoreans of south Italy, who taught much the same doctrines of after-life and reincarnation but linked these to mathematical studies and number symbolism. Pythagoreans were still around in the fourth century and were known at Athens, for they are ridiculed in fragments of the Middle Comedy for their ragged and unwashed appearance in terms similar to those later used of Cynics on the comic stage. What was unique about the Orphics and Pythagoreans was that each represented a *bios*, a strict and distinctive way of life marked off by dietary taboos and, in the case of the Pythagoreans, also sexual abstinence and a host of fantastic regulations covering all aspects of daily life. Both were associations that in some sense tried to replace the household and the city. There was ample room for such societies to arise because Greek cults, unlike other ancient religions, never developed any sort of priestly class, in the sense of a group with a special discipline, way of life, and fixed traditions; nor did Greek cults practice asceticism except for the occasional dietary prohibitions before sacrifice.[24]

There can be little doubt that the Pythagorean order was the immediate model for the Cynic *bios*, though they were a very marginal group at Athens. When the Indian gymnosophists asked Diogenes' disciple Onesicritus what Greek wise men resembled them, he mentioned Diogenes, Pythagoras, and Socrates—but not Antisthenes (Strabo 15.1.65). Some later doxographers said that Antisthenes had been the first to adopt the Cynic habit of cloak, staff, and wallet; but Sosicrates in the second century B.C. thought that Diogenes had borrowed it from the Pythagorean Diodorus of Aspendus (Diog. Laert. 6.13).[25] Still, what the Cynics borrowed from the Orphic/Pythagorean tradition was only its economic regimen. They were interested in none of its ideas. Cynics were untouched by Pythagorean philosophy or Pythagorean sexual abstinence, and they carried on an active polemic against all magic, initiations, and dietary taboos. Cynic asceticism was determinedly innerworldly, and therefore different from every other significant type of ancient asceticism—the Hindu or Jain type that Onesicritus met and misunderstood in India, the Orphic/Pythagorean type that the Cynics replaced, the Christian type that would one day replace the Cynic. Like all ascetics the Cynic claimed a unique knowledge, but it had nothing to do with another world. Like the Socratic wise men, and most other Greek wise men, Cynics based their claim to authority upon a superior knowledge of the nature of this world.

For Cynicism, if not a Socratic school, was definitely influenced by the Socratic tradition, and represented another attempt to solve the Socratic problem. Socratics generally felt the solution to all political problems must lie in the development of extraordinary human beings. Plato decided this elite must be a group of highly trained intellectuals. Antisthenes, as we have seen, had a different vision. He was skeptical of the possibility of certain knowledge, but he felt that the example of a perfect and self-sufficient wise man might somehow be enough. He made much use of the myth of Heracles (the subject of several of his writings, Diogenes Laertius 6.2, 104–105) because Heracles was the supreme example of virtue attained through strenuous hardship (*ponos*). This approach to ethics, this identification of virtue with *ponos*, this reinterpretation of Heracles as suffering hero formed the intellectual core of Cynicism. Antisthenes' saying that virtue was self-sufficient (*autarke*) if it had the strength (*ischys*) of a Socrates (Diog. Laert. 6.11) was perhaps the most proto-Cynic thing attributed to him, for it implied that virtue required physical as well as mental training. But Antisthenes was not a Cynic in the later sense. He did not give up intellectual training. His interests were polymathic, and his disciples, called by Aristotle the *Antistheneioi*, were concerned with logical questions (Arist., *Met.* 1043b); but Diogenes Aristotle called simply the Dog and thought of as a coiner of popular moralisms. Antisthenes' political writings seem to have envisioned a more conventional social role for the wise man than the Cynics did.[26]

Cynicism began when someone united the Socratic/Antisthenic moral ideal to the Orphic/Pythagorean ascetic *bios*. The moral ideal could thus be put into practice through a discipline or method of training just as in any other art or skill—was not this already suggested by the constant crafts analogies of the Socratics—and the wise man thereby brought to earth and made immediately recognizable to everybody. A highly distinctive *bios* could be achieved by the simple expedient of giving up *oikoi*, living without visible property or family. At the same point it was decided to abandon conventional studies; and there would have followed quickly the Cynic style of popular lecturing, the peculiar Cynic vocabulary, and the peculiar social position of the Cynic sage as a spiritual leader who abjured political power. (The Pythagoreans had acquired a bad reputation because they had failed to do the last.) If it was not Diogenes the Dog who was responsible for all this, one can think of no one else, nor can one account otherwise for the unique position of Diogenes in the Cynic tradition.[27]

The Social Teachings of the Cynics

The Cynic View of Property

I have said that the lengthy doxographical passage at Diogenes Laertius 6.70–73 seems to be based on Apollodorus' *Ethics*, and designed to make Cynicism seem a more systematic school, and closer to Stoicism, than it probably was. But the passage must rest on a base of authentic Cynic teaching, which Goulet-Cazé has tried to unearth. The doxography can be broken down into the following sections:

1. Description of the *askesis* or system of training of the Cynics (6.70–71).
2. Statement of what appears to be a theory of property (72).
3. Statement of a theory of law (72).

4. A theory of sexual communism, inserted among some common Cynic maxims (72).
5. An argument against religious taboos, including the prohibition of cannibalism, taken from the Diogenic "tragedy" *Thyestes* (73).

The painstaking analysis of Goulet-Cazé has shown that the first part of the *askesis* passage is Stoic, but the core of the passage is taken from an authentic Cynic work, perhaps the *Techne ethike* (Art of Ethics) attributed to Diogenes (6.80). The essentially Cynic part of the passage states that virtue is the result of a *gymnasia*, or physical training: just as artisans, musicians, and athletes develop extraordinary skills by constant practice, so the *psyche* can be trained to the effortless performance of virtue; to choose such hardships (*ponoi*) is according to nature (*kata physin*), and produces *eudaimonia* and pleasure. As we have already seen, this message was the heart of Cynicism. This is what Diogenes began to preach and practice at Athens ca. 350. This is the message of Teles a hundred years later. The intellectual content of their teaching seems to be practically limited to this.

This passage on law (6.72) has also been the subject of an analysis by Goulet-Cazé, who concluded that it is entirely Stoic: it echoes passages from Cleanthes (SVF 3.328, 613), and the favorable view of law and government that it expresses is not typically Cynic. The statement on communism (6.72) can only come from the Diogenic *Republic*, and I will reserve comment on it until the end of this chapter. The summary of the *Thyestes*, an early Cynic mock tragedy (6.73), is useful for its information about Cynic views of religion and will also deserve further comment. But our first concern is the theory of property presented in 6.72:

> Diogenes, using the sorts of arguments I have mentioned above [in the *askesis* passage], said that all things belong to the wise: for all things belong to the gods and the gods are friends to the wise, and all things are common among friends; so all things belong to the wise.

This saying, with slight variations, was attributed to Socrates, Antisthenes, and Crates as well as Diogenes.[28] It may be inserted in this doxography because the school of Apollodorus thought it very similar to the Stoic doctrine of property. But as we shall see the Stoic doctrine of property was more elaborate and legalistic than this. Nothing quite like this formula was ever attributed to anyone but a Cynic, and there are several reasons to think it an authentic teaching of early Cynicism.

For one thing, the "theory" is expressed in a typically Cynic form. It is so cryptic and riddling that it has often been dismissed as a joke (e.g., Gomperz, *Greek Thinkers*, 2.164–165). In fact it *is* a joke. It belongs to the Cynic tradition of parody. In this case what is being parodied is the passage from Hesiod quoted above (p. 13), describing the "golden race" of Cronus' time; a race of men who were "friends of the gods" (*philoi theoisin*) and possessed "all goods" (*panta esthla*), living from the bounty of nature without toil, care, or conflict.

This passage was known to practically everyone in the Cynics' audience and they would have understood immediately that the Cynics were claiming to live in Cronus' time. We notice also that a little later Hesiod describes the road to virtue as long and rugged (290), a line that probably suggested the characterization of the Cynic road as short and rugged.[29]

What was meant by this? Cynic jokes were *spoudaiogeloia*, humor with a hidden seriousness. The serious meaning is that the Cynic is a "friend of the gods" because he imitates the self-sufficiency and ease of the gods. The idea that self-sufficiency, wanting nothing, is one of the properties of divinity was well known before Cynicism appeared.[30] Perhaps even more familiar was the notion that the gods live at their ease, for the Cynic watchword "easily" occurs repeatedly in Homeric descriptions of the gods' activities. The concept of the "gods' friendship" is a common motif in the Cynic sources,[31] and it always means that the Cynic becomes godlike through voluntary restriction of his wants to a minimum; the purpose of his *askesis* is to achieve such control of his appetites that he will want nothing that cannot be easily supplied, and therefore will possess everything that he wants. The object is freedom from desire, the aim of all asceticism; but the Cynic version is not to be confused with the Buddhist, for the Cynic object is never to eliminate *all* desire, rather to control desire for the purpose of achieving the most pleasant and tranquil life possible.

The slogan has a secondary meaning, which is distinctively Cynic: it is intended to serve as a justification for mendicancy. To say "All things belong to the gods" might refer to the self-sufficiency of the gods, or might refer to the notion that all wealth belongs to the gods and humans have only the loan of it. This was another familiar moralism (e.g., Eur., *Phoenissae* 555–57), and it recurs frequently in the fragments of Bion and Teles. To them it means that only the wise man knows how to use wealth rightly. The selfish rich, they say, do not really own anything: they are always needy because they always want more, and they do not know how to use rightly the wealth that they have.[32] "All things are common among friends"—a maxim already used in philosophical discussions of *koinonia* by Plato and Aristotle—means that friends must share their wealth. Cynics were fond of these wordplays about ownership, usually turning on the paradoxes that no one really "owns" property, and that the best way to possess property is to behave as though it is everyone's. The formula at Diogenes Laertius 6.72 is in the same vein.

Who are these "friends" who are to share their wealth? Doubtless the wise men leading the Cynic life, for there are several sayings to the effect that wise men are friends of other wise men,[33] and we may easily suppose that the true Cynics were expected to share what they had with one another. But we hear little about this, nor would we expect to hear much: self-sufficiency, not fraternity, is the dominant motif throughout the Cynic tradition. There are indications that the "friends" of the Cynics could include a much wider circle. The Cynic might describe his entire audience as his "friends." It was possible for a Cynic to share his wealth with his fellow citizens. Upon his conversion to the Cynic life by Diogenes, Crates paid no further attention to his large estate, and according to one tradition he distributed it all among the Thebans. But another tradition said that on Diogenes' advice he let the land revert to goat pasture and threw the money into the sea; and yet another held that he kept part of his inheritance and bequeathed it to his heirs.[34] The act of distributing one's wealth to one's fellow citizens, which would become *de rigeur* in the conversion stories of the Christians, is a rare thing in those of the Cynics. A Cynic conversion means primarily renunciation of wealth, not generosity with it. We suspect it was the wider circle, the "hearers" of the Cynics, who were mostly supposed to set an example of generosity. They were supposed to be generous to all, or to all the people Greek popular morality considered deserving; the many Cynic maxims about the proper use of wealth seem to assume this. But there are clear hints they were expected to be especially generous toward the true Cynics; that the wise were expected to live off the unwise; and that the real point of the riddle in Diogenes Laertius 6.72 is to justify the philosophical mendicant life.

Bion was explicitly charged with this. The obviously hostile source that lies behind the *Life of Bion* in Diogenes Laertius says it was a proof of his selfishness that he often quoted the maxim "All things are common to friends" (4.53), which can only mean that he used it as an excuse for avarice in begging, and that Cynics were expected to put the saying to such uses. The evidence of the comedy shows that mendicancy was part of the popular image of the Cynic from the beginning. It was said that Diogenes began this practice out of necessity (Diog. Laert. 6.49) but continued it from choice. In some anecdotes he accepts alms as though taking what belongs to him and expects his benefactors to be grateful (6.34, 46, 62). His benefactors are called his "friends" (46). When he urges his hearers to stretch out their hands to their friends (29), we suspect that "friend" means any potential benefactor. He says he does not beg (*aitein*) from these friends but merely reclaims (*apaitein*) what belongs to him (46); which is clearly an allusion to the saying that the wise man owns all things. In the Cynic Epistles, this justification for mendicancy is even more explicit: there we are told that the Cynic asks for what is in accordance with nature, which belongs to him anyway, and pays for it with his teaching (*Ep. of Diogenes* 10, 38; *Ep. of Crates* 2, 26).

These begging anecdotes fall into two groups: the one emphasizes Diogenes' restraint in begging, and the other his shamelessness. In the first group we find a Diogenes who accepts only what he needs, refuses dainties, and spurns gifts from bad people (Diog. Laert. 6.26, 55, 57). Crates follows both criteria when he refuses a gift of wine from the tyrant Demetrius of Phalerum (6.90). In the *Epistle of Diogenes* 38, it is said that Cynics take alms *only* from those who will benefit from their teaching. But most anecdotes bring out the impudence and importunacy of Diogenes' begging (Diog. Laert. 6.49, 56, 59, 60, 67). It is one of the many reasons why he was called the Dog. This Diogenes takes anything from anybody (6.35, 54, 56, 64, 66). The contradiction is sometimes blatant: Diogenes refuses cakes in Diogenes Laertius 6.55, and accepts them in Diogenes Laertius 6.56. This apparent contradiction has lent support to the theory of a division between "mild" and "rigorist" Cynics. I have already argued that it is better explained as a contradiction inherent in the Cynic ethic, which required the wise man to accept nothing and accept everything, depending on his circumstances. In the collection of *chreiai* that provided Diogenes Laertius with his source, the two cake-eating anecdotes might have been paired deliberately to bring out the two aspects of the Cynic ethic.

There is another kind of hedonistic anecdote that is clearly intended to be derogatory: Cynics are accused of parasitism and greed. Bion (Diog. Laert. 4.53) and Menippus (6.99) are accused of this even in the generally pro-Cynic tradition followed by Diogenes Laertius. The accusation is made against Diogenes himself, and Cynics in general, in the anti-Cynic tradition represented by Lucian. But these "hedonists" are accused of being bad Cynics, not of being a sect of Cynics.

In short, the formula about property at Diogenes Laertius 6.72 does not express any sort of philosophical theory, as does the Stoic formula which it superficially resembles. It is a mythological parody which compares the Cynic life to the time of Cronus. It seems related to several different themes in the Cynic literary tradition, but these cannot be put together to form a coherent argument. This is best described as a metaphor for the Cynic life which Cynics found useful in a variety of contexts. The main point, and the most unmistakably Cynic point, about the formula seems to be its implicit justification for mendicancy: the Cynic lives in Cronus' time because he supports himself from the bounty of nature and society, owing everything and owning nothing at the same time, and thereby setting everyone an example of the right use of property. Both the form and the content of the passage suggest that it is an authentic early Cynic tradition.

The Cynic View of the Oikos

Ancient testimony is unanimous that Cynics rejected the *oikos*. The more authentic evidence for early Cynicism suggests that rejection of the *oikos* in favor of a vagrant mendicant life was practically a definition of Cynicism. Therefore we may accept without hesitation the equally unanimous ancient testimony that Cynics always rejected marriage on principle. In this they were peculiar among the philosophical schools.

Yet no clear justification for the refusal to marry is ever offered. We possess several Cynic witticisms attacking marriage, but these reflect conventional Greek misogyny; they could have been, and were, attributed to many different philosophers.[35] The only specific complaint against marriage by Cynics is that its exclusiveness breeds adultery and jealousy; and this is simply a variant of the common Cynic objection to property in general, namely that it is a source of dissension.[36] The refusal to marry goes unexplained because the explanation seemed obvious. Marriage was inseparably tied to the acquisition and protection of property. The word *oikos* implied both family and property. Those who wished to set an example of life unencumbered by excess property must not acquire households and must not marry. This deliberate attempt to fashion a way of life outside the household raises two questions about primitive Cynicism which have occasioned much controversy. Firstly, to what extent did this attitude imply a conscious social egalitarianism, particularly toward women and slaves? Secondly, to what extent did Cynics propagate unconventional notions about sexual morality? Both questions are extremely relevant to the problem of Cynic "utopianism."

There seems little doubt that in *practice* the Cynic order admitted men and women to its ranks on a basis of unprecedented equality. The principle that virtue is the same in men and women is attributed to Antisthenes in our Cynic doxography (Diog. Laert. 6.12); this is one of the common features uniting Cynicism and Stoicism that the compiler wished to emphasize, but the legend of Hipparchia is sufficient evidence that it reflects an early Cynic tradition. To say that the virtue of men and women is identical in kind does not necessarily imply that they are equal in quantity; yet the same legend of Hipparchia suggests that early Cynics could go very far toward practical social equality. We know of earlier women who dabbled in philosophy. In the early fourth century Athens had Arete, daughter of Aristippus of Cyrene, who was counted a full-fledged philosopher in her own right, with disciples of her own. But Hipparchia seems rather different, and was remembered as such. She was not only a Cynic philosopher herself, but a member of the only husband-and-wife team known to ancient philosophy. This was also the only Cynic marriage known to antiquity, but it was thought a confirmation of rather than an exception to Cynic antimarital principles; for it was a *kynogamia* ("dog marriage," a term used by Crates himself, according to the *Suda*), one of the most spectacular examples of Cynic effrontery. She was a woman of respectable citizen family who rejected wealthy suitors to go about in public with Crates wearing Cynic dress, at a time when women of her class did not choose their husbands, read philosophy, or go about in public at all. We are told there were countless stories about her, which makes us cautious (Diog. Laert. 6.98); but that she went about in public wearing the *tribon* is verified by a passage in Menander (Diog. Laert. 6.93).

The ancient writers were struck by the fact that Hipparchia attended dinner parties with her husband. We are more struck by the fact that they were invited to them. These stories do not suggest a Diogenic life of destitution and social rejection. They suggest that this Cynic couple had found a certain degree of acceptance in parts of Athenian society in the late fourth century. They suggest what we might call bohemianism. Nowhere is it said that Crates and Hipparchia begged, and the more reliable traditions about them do not indicate that their children were raised as Cynics in the strict sense.[37] Hipparchia was remembered because she was the wife of the famous Crates, and perhaps the only woman of good family who ever lived as a Cynic. But she could not have been the only female "Cynic." If noncitizen females sometimes chose to live with Cynics we doubt that much notice would have been taken; and no one would have spoken of a "marriage," which is why the union of Crates and Hipparchia remained the only *kynogamia*. The later Cynics were sometimes accompanied by women, who were thought to participate in the Cynic life to some extent, and were said to seduce women and boys under the pretext of introducing them to the Cynic life.[38]

It is obvious the true Cynic rejected ownership of slaves, just as he rejected all excess property. We would assume that even without the evidence of an early anecdote—one in which Diogenes refuses to look for his runaway slave Manes on the grounds that it would be absurd if Manes could live without Diogenes but not vice versa (Teles, fr. IVa, Hense 41 = Diog. Laert. 6.55). But the example of slavery points out the limitations of the Cynic social critique. For it was only the small band of true Cynics who were expected to reject the household and its subordination of women and slaves. The larger circle of Cynic hearers were no more expected to abandon families, slaves, and social distinctions than they were expected to abandon property. They were merely expected to acquire the right attitude toward these things. The Cynic maxims are filled with practical advice about the ordering of households, of a most conventional sort: adultery is condemned, women are exhorted to modesty and sons to obedience. Diogenes was supposed to have attacked those who were envious of the rich (Diog. Laert. 6.28), for the Cynic ideal was simple indifference to wealth. I doubt that these maxims represent a softening of an original radicalism. The Cynics' ascetic solution with its two-level morality contained an obvious and built-in conservative element, as do all such ethics. If one accepts the existence of an extraordinary norm, everything done on that level is defused of social impact, because those who do it are extraordinary by definition. The story that Diogenes himself was sold as a slave, source of numerous *chreiai*, was so popular because it furnished the most dramatic demonstration possible of Cynic indifference to fortune; but also perhaps because it implicitly assured everyone there was nothing socially subversive about Cynicism. This implicit message explains why the apparent radicalism of the Cynic ethic was accepted so easily by Greek society.

Not only was Cynic egalitarianism confined to the Cynic elite, but also it may not have been an "ism" of any kind. Was there any *theory* behind the Cynic attitude toward women and slaves? Aristotle devoted a lengthy refutation (*Politics* 1254–55) to the view that slavery was "against nature," and because we know of no other pre-Stoic philosophers who might have held such a theory it is often assumed that Aristotle had the Cynics in mind. But it is not necessary to assume this. We know that the question of whether slavery was "natural" had been bandied about long before Cynicism appeared. The Sophist Alcidamas asserted that "no man is a slave by nature" in an oration supporting the liberation of the Spartan helots in 370.[39] That is all we know about his oration, but it is significant that this theory could be used in political speeches to defend the general principle of *eleutheria*. The *example* of the Cynics may have lent support to this theory, and in that sense Aristotle may well have the Cynics in mind in *Pol.* 1254–55. But we do not know that the early Cynics had any theory about "nature" at all. "Nature," and the opposition between "nature" and "convention," are among the most common catchwords in Cynic literature; but they had been that to Greek thinkers for a hundred years before Cynicism appeared, and we do not know exactly what significance the Cynics attached to these terms. Doxographical explanations are very likely to reflect later Stoic interpretations, for Stoics had their own definite ideas about "following nature," and this phrase was one of the common Cynic/Stoic features emphasized by those who wanted to show the unity of the tradition. In a moment we will consider further the question of what Cynics might have meant by "nature."

Let us turn to the problem of Cynic sexual ethics. The traditions contain much material about early Cynic sexual behavior, which in later times was widely considered scandalous. But in fact the anecdotes generally reveal principles that were thought conventional in the fourth and third centuries B.C. The later Cynics may have acquired a reputation for libertinism largely because they preserved the values of an earlier time into the more repressive climate of the Roman Empire.

Suspicion of sexual passion is a pervasive element in these anecdotes. Cynics were expected to abuse prostitutes and those who pursued them. It was said that Crates, or Diogenes, had frequented brothels to exchange invective with the staff, habituating himself to their insults as part of the Cynic *askesis*.[40] Effeminate males are another favorite target. Sometimes this is difficult to distinguish from the abuse of prostitutes, male effeminacy being closely associated with male prostitution in the Greek mind. But signs of effeminacy/prostitution in a young male of the citizen class threatened his status as a citizen.[41] Ordinary prostitution (involving the services of noncitizens) was not usually condemned by moralists unless it led to excessive indulgence; imputation of the same to citizens was a grave matter. Both these attitudes were rooted in popular morality, which placed strong emphasis on the value of self-control and thought ability to resist sexual desire a proof of manliness. Cynics claimed to be the most "manly" of philosophers,[42] so it would seem natural for their preaching to harp on the conventional code of manly virtue and to attack the prostitute and the effeminate—both seen as threats to manliness, the one an external enemy and the other a sort of fifth column.

On the other hand, Cynics were not supposed to object to prostitutes if the prostitutes are hired in a proper frame of mind. Evidence for Cynic opposition to prostitution is found in the poems of Crates, but there is also fairly early evidence for the other attitude. The great Eratosthenes, head of the Alexandrian library (and said to have been Zeno's pupil), reported that Crates took his son Pasicles to a brothel and told him "that was the marriage of your father" (Diog. Laert. 6.88). We do not know why Eratosthenes cited this *chreia*, but Diogenes Laertius clearly thought the point was to illustrate the attitude toward sexual morals most commonly associated with Cynics: sexual urges are to be satisfied in the quickest and easiest way possible. Crates means to condemn the conventional *gamos* based on property, and uses this language to make it clear to Pasicles that the *gamos* of Crates and Hipparchia was not like that. But he could not mean to approve prostitution *per se*; Crates' own poems reveal a deep suspicion of prostitutes, and Diogenes Laertius follows this with another saying attributed to Crates (whether this one is also from Eratosthenes is not clear) condemning both conventional marriages and unions with *hetairai*, the former being compared to tragedy and the latter to comedy. The point is that the ideal Cynic sexual life, like the partnership of Crates and Hipparchia, is unlike either. Marriage is disliked only because it is connected with property; prostitution is disliked only because it leaves one open to the danger of infatuation, the exaggeration of desires beyond the point of easy satisfaction that was so important to Cynics. *Paiderastia* is disliked only because it entails the danger of infatuation for the active partner, and for the passive the much worse danger of effeminization.[43]

This view of sexuality was by no means limited to Cynics. Xenophon attributed the same attitude to Socrates and Antisthenes: the wise man gives no thought to sex unless moved by physical desire, which he then proceeds to satisfy as easily as possible, preferably with ugly women because of their availability (*Mem.* 1.3.14; *Symp.* 4.38). Similar views were attributed to several Athenian philosophers of the fourth century. Stilpo, leader of the little-known "Megarian" school, had both a wife and an *hetaira*; far more remarkably, he had an unchaste daughter whose behavior he refused to condemn on the grounds that it matched his own (Diog. Laert. 2.114). He was said to be one of the "hearers" of Diogenes, meaning he was a Cynic in at least the broader sense of the word. Another minor Socratic, Aristippus, was remembered for many sayings in defense of prostitution. (Asked why he lived with Lais of Corinth: "I have Lais, not she me." Diog. Laert. 2.67, 69, 74, 75, 81.) It has often been noticed that he taught a doctrine of moral self-sufficiency and adaptation to circumstances that seems practically undistinguishable from Cynicism, and that many *chreiai* were attributed indiscriminately to Aristippus and Diogenes. His follower Theodorus the Atheist, remembered as friend and perhaps lover of Hipparchia (6.97), argued explicitly for the propriety of sex with both boys and women (2.99). Menedemus, pupil of Stilpo and head of the obscure "Eretrian" school, was sometimes called a Cynic (2.140): it was said that he kept a bizarre household, living with a younger philosopher who was his lover and sharing the same wife with him. In the next century Arcesilaus, head of the Academy, was said to be the lover of an older Platonist, Crantor, with whom he lived; also he never married, lived with *hetairai*, pursued boys assiduously, and quoted the maxims of Aristippus in defense of his conduct. Most of these teachers belonged to the skeptical wing of the Socratic tradition, and most had some connection with or resemblance to the Cynics, who were probably seen as the most extreme examples of Socratic skepticism. These traditions about their private lives (the accuracy of which is not really important) are sufficient to show that philosophers belonging to these schools were expected to display a certain deliberate permissiveness in sexual morality, which contrasted sharply with the sexual puritanism of Plato and Aristotle. Some were said to flaunt convention by keeping homosexual households or tolerating unchaste wives, but the common attitude is simply that sexual pleasures are harmless if kept under control. This was a conventional Greek view. These philosophers represented the permissive side of the traditional morality, as Plato and Aristotle represented its austere side, and one may suspect the former were closer to popular morality. Naturally the Cynics continued that tradition. Their views on sexuality seem identical to their views on food and drink: nothing matters except adaptation to circumstances. There was no division between "rigorist" and "mild" Cynicisms. There was a good deal of ambivalence, but there was also much ambivalence in the popular sexual morality in which

Cynicism was rooted. A Cynic might be able to stretch the "hedonistic" aspect of this ethic very far without obviously violating any Cynic principles.[44]

Cynic sexual morality did not contain anything very new or shocking. What was unconventional about Cynicism was not its principles but the freedom with which Cynics talked about them. Nothing was more characteristic of Cynicism than the tradition of *parrhesia* ("speaking everything"), which Diogenes called the finest thing in the world (Diog. Laert. 6.69). The purpose of the philosopher's hard-own independence was to enable him or her to express views freely, bringing into the streets the frankness that had once been heard on the comic stage. Just how far they took this freedom it is now impossible to say. The most notorious of all anecdotes about Diogenes represents him masturbating in the agora, and remarking that he wished it were as easy to satisfy hunger by rubbing the belly. (Or, in another version, that if all men did likewise Troy would never have fallen. We notice that again adultery is condemned chiefly as a source of dissension.)[45] Later generations also cherished the belief that Crates and Hipparchia had intercourse in public. Generally these demonstrations were attributed only to the first generation of Cynics; though Lucian seems to imply that even in his day Cynics practiced comparable, if unspecified, public lubricities.[46] What was so easy to accept in Lucian's time became incredible two centuries later. St. Augustine could not believe that even the early Cynics had so violated the natural laws of modesty; he preferred to think that they had only pretended intercourse under the cover of their cloaks; and he was certain that the later Cynics, shameless lot though they were, had done nothing of the sort (*City of God* 14.20). Augustine may have been closer to the truth than the pagans, if for the wrong reasons. These are not the only Cynic anecdotes that sound like excessively literal readings of a preacher's exempla. We shall never know whether Diogenes really went about the agora with a lantern in daylight, nor whether he really masturbated there. Histrionic demonstration, it is true, was the essence of Cynicism. But it is possible these were merely proposals found in some Cynic diatribe.

The Cynic View of the Polis

In the first century B.C. Philodemus wrote that no Cynic recognized any city or any law (*On the Stoics* 7, ed. Dorandi). The later tradition supports him. Cynics are invariably portrayed as cityless, for the same reason that they are homeless. The following passage seems to be a summary of a diatribe above five activities inconsistent with *autarkeia*:

> He [Diogenes] would praise those who were about to marry and yet never married; and those who were about to sail and yet never sailed; and those who were about to enter politics and yet never entered politics; and those who were about to have children and yet never had children; and those who were prepared to live with rulers and yet never approached them. Diog. Laert. 6.29

The refusal to marry comes first in the list, but lack of an *oikos* would effectively bar one from political participation. Therefore Diogenes was called *aoikos* and *apolis*, a man without a household and without a city (Diog. Laert. 6.38); and the Cynic life was always defined as a condition where one cared nothing for marriage, children, or country (Lucian, *Philosophies for Sale* 9). In the ancient world it was difficult to abandon one of these things without the others. This helped to spread the impression, widespread among both ancient and modern writers, that Cynics were indifferent to the welfare of the community.

There is no need to rehearse our arguments against this view. Withdrawal from the polis was expected only of the Cynic elite. There could have been no suggestion that their general audience avoid political life any more than property. Even the Cynic elite may have had nothing to withdraw from in most cases. Diogenes was an exile who never became a citizen at Athens or Corinth, and the same may have been true of most of his serious followers. Crates and Hipparchia were remembered as unusual people because they were members of privileged citizen families who voluntarily abandoned their estates, in the face of opposition from their kindred. They probably had few imitators. But this does not mean that Cynics could not have political views. Onesicritus, at least, thought that one of the purposes of the Cynic life was to exercise an influence on public affairs. Is there any sign they tried to exercise influence of a political nature?

The commonest impression left by the anecdotes is that Cynics were antimonarchic. There is a very early and authentic piece of evidence for this. Zeno's collection of *chreiai* about his master Crates contained an anecdote which drew a contrast between Crates and Aristotle (Teles, fr. IVb, Hense 46). Crates is reading from Aristotle's *Protrepticus*, dedicated to a Cypriot king, and decides to devote his own attention to a shoemaker, whom he thinks a likelier candidate for philosophy than a king.[47] This shows that early Cynics made much of their avoidance of courts, and thought this distinguished them from other philosophers, particularly the schools of Aristotle and Plato. There are many anecdotes in which Diogenes mocks Plato (whom it is unlikely he ever met in real life) for attending the court of Dionysius, tyrant of Syracuse (Diog. Laert. 6.26, 50, 58, 67); in others he ridicules Aristippus for this, calling him "the king's dog" to imply that the true Cynic cannot be owned by any king (2.66, 68). Most such anecdotes are anti-Macedonian. Diogenes reproaches Philip for his greed (Diog. Laert. 6.43); stories about his confrontations with Alexander the Great are legion, and usually turn on his refusal to pay court to Alexander;[48] Callisthenes, Aristotle's nephew, is mocked by Diogenes for his attendance on Alexander (6.45); Diogenes accepts a cloak from the Macedonian regent Antipater only to show that a Cynic will take anything from anybody, this being one of the "shameless" begging stories (6.66); he refuses to go to the court of Alexander's successor Perdiccas (6.44), and treats Perdiccas' rival Craterus the same (6.57). As Diogenes appears in the tradition as Alexander's opposite, so Crates is made the critic and counterpart of Demetrius of Phalerum, the most successful exponent of the Peripatetic policy of cultivating kings (Diog. Laert. 6.90; Ath. 10.422cd; Plut. 69cd). The great exception to this antimonarchic and anti-Macedonian tradition is Bion, a courtier of Antigonus Gonatas; but Bion was remembered as an untypical Cynic in more ways than one.

On the other hand, the purpose of these anecdotes is to show the independence of the Cynic, not the undesirability of monarchy as a system of government. Democratic leaders receive the same treatment. In several anecdotes Diogenes mocks Demosthenes and other popular leaders at Athens, calling them "servants of the mob" (Diog. Laert. 6.24, 28, 34). We know of one quasi-Cynic who was a democratic leader. Menedemus of Eretria, who was probably called a "Cynic" for his *parrhesia*, was elected to high office by the Eretrians and defended the democracy against the Macedonians (Diog. Laert. 2.130, 140, 143); but it is said that the Eretrians elected him in spite of his Cynic tendencies, not because of them; and that Crates ridiculed him for taking part in politics (2.126, 131).

As for Sparta, we know from Aristotle that Diogenes admired the Spartan *syssitia*, and there are some other anecdotes that express a sense of affinity between the Cynic and Spartan disciplines. But none of these imply approval of Spartan political institutions, and some are critical. The remark that there were good men nowhere in Greece, but good boys at Sparta (Diog. Laert. 6.27), expressly distinguishes Spartan educational from Spartan political values. In the *Epistle of Diogenes* 27, Diogenes says he was not permitted to enter Sparta, though he alone had realized the Spartan ideal of virtue. The distinction between ethical and political Laconism, always implicit among Spartan sympathizers, is overt in these Cynic anecdotes.

All this suggests that Cynics avoided association with political leaders of any stripe. The only contemporary statesmen for whom Diogenes has a good word are the generally admired Epaminondas of Thebes and Agesilaus of Sparta (Diog. Laert. 6.39). Lucian and many others thought this meant they cared nothing for city or country. More likely is the explanation given by Onesicritus: they sought a kind of influence that required the renunciation of power; and they were trying to develop a new kind of authority and so did not want to be captured by any of the old ones. They appear to be antimonarchic more than anything else because in their day the greatest threat by far to the independence of the philosopher came from the rising Macedonian monarchies. The list of five things a true Cynic must not do in Diogenes Laertius 6.29 includes two political precepts: there is the general injunction not to participate in politics (*politeuesthai*), meaning primarily the politics of the city-state; this is what Crates attacked Menedemus for doing at Eretria, and this had been the major temptation to philosophers in earlier generations; but by Crates' time the big temptation was that covered in the second precept, that philosophers should not live with potentates (*dynastai*), meaning the many Greek courts that sprang up in the wake of Alexander.

Cynics therefore avoided association with political programs in the usual sense. The political message in Cynic teaching is usually that political problems will fade away if people will try to achieve *autarkeia*. There is much praise of justice, but it is usually defined in a negative way: *dikaiosyne* is the absence of those discords that arise from the pursuit of property, pleasure, and reputation.[49]

Still, it may be possible to discern in this material certain political implications of a more positive sort. The antimonarchic traditions are primarily intended to secure the independence of the philosopher, but they imply also a deeper sort of antimonarchism. Zeno's anecdote about Crates and the shoemaker conveys not only that the true Cynic avoids courts, but that the chosen audience of the true Cynic are the common people. One of the stereotyped roles of the Cynic is censor of kings and scourge of tyrants, defender of the values of the classical polis against all forms of authoritarian rule. When an unnamed tyrant improbably asks Diogenes what bronze is best for statues, Diogenes replies "That from which Harmodius and Aristogeiton were forged" (Diog. Laert. 6.50). The anecdotes in which the tyrants have names may be no more historical than this, but they testify to an implicit alliance between Cynicism and the polis against the princely courts. Cynicism was a way of life not imaginable except in the independent polis. Its birthplace was the Athenian democracy, and its social values were associated with Greek democratic traditions: the Cynic brand of egalitarianism was a democratic ideal; the Cynic watchwords, *parrhesia* and *eleutheria*, were democratic slogans.

Nor are the Cynic Laconist traditions entirely without political implications. Strabo has preserved a passage from Onesicritus describing the land of Musicanus, which Onesicritus claimed to have visited when he was with Alexander's army in India (Strabo 15.1.34). In fancifulness this far outdoes Onesicritus' impressions of Indian philosophy. It is in fact a description of a utopian society, of the sort that became fashionable in Greek geographical literature in the years after Alexander's march. The Indians of Onesicritus are a happy and just society who know neither crime nor warfare, have meals in common like the Spartans, and own no slaves,[50] using instead the services of young men. This picture seems to be based on an extremely idealized conception of the Spartan constitution, with elements drawn from Cynic teaching, such as the absence of slavery and warfare. It would be hazardous to build much on such a fragment as this, but it does seem likely that to some extent this represents Onesicritus' notion of what an ideal Cynicized society would be like. If so, then it was always possible to translate Diogenes' egalitarianism into socio-political terms. And there are other signs that Cynics admired the egalitarianism of the Spartan constitution but disapproved of its exclusiveness. One of the diatribes of Teles (fr. III, "On Exile," Hense 28) describes the Spartan *agoge* in terms even more idealized than those of Onesicritus: we are told that the system is completely open to talent, and that anyone, even foreigners and helots, can be admitted to it. This passage is intelligible only because it can be dated very close to 240 B.C. It belongs to the period of the Spartan revolution, when the Spartan citizenship was being opened to noncitizens. But it is significant that a Cynic could welcome this development. There are some other Cynic traditions of uncertain date that express dislike for the Spartan political system, particularly its treatment of helots.[51] The poems of Cercidas of Megalopolis (late third century) take us deeper into the period of the Spartan revolution, which changed many things. But it is worth mentioning that Cercidas, a general of the conservative faction during a period of bitter class struggle in the Peloponnesus, produced in his Second Meliamb one of the most passionate appeals to the rich to share their goods with the poor that can be found in all pagan literature. It confirms one's impression that connections between Cynic egalitarianism and socio-political egalitarianism, though not necessary, were easy to make.

In an ascetic system like Cynicism, the extraordinary norm followed by the elite never represents any immediate threat to the social order. But it always represents a critique of the social order, and it always has some potential for long-range social impact. I suggest therefore that the Cynic indifference to current political issues, so often misconstrued as anarchism, was part of a half-conscious strategy to influence society in a much slower and deeper way; and that Cynics retreated from the public life of democracy in part to preserve the social values of democracy. The radicalism of their ideal did lie so much in any specific prescription as in the dramatic model of the Cynic life itself: a way of life that constituted a visible rejection of the whole household society and its patriarchal relationships of property and power, and a claim to offer an alternative, not as a refuge for the weak but as a bastion of moral leadership.

The Cynic View of Nature

The way of life just described, which entailed the rejection of all excess property and consequently withdrawal from the *oikos* and the polis, was often described as "following nature." To follow nature was to achieve that state of mind which was the purpose of the Cynic *askesis*, and which was also described as self-sufficiency, apathy, freedom, and happiness. It is time to ask what Cynics meant by this "nature."

Often we are told that Cynics identified the state of nature with the conditions of primitive societies and animal life; that they were the originators of that theory about the origins of society, common among the later Stoics, which explained the development of civilization as a decline from a happy primitive state.

The evidence for this interpretation seems at first formidable. We have seen already that the Cynic life was described in Hesiodic terms that implied Cynics had returned to the golden age.[52] The most extended treatment of the Hesiodic myth is found in the Sixth Oration of Dio Chrysostom, where the parallel between the golden age and the Cynic life is expanded into what appears to be an elaborate historical and anthropological theory. There Diogenes says beasts and primitive humans lived according to nature, happily and healthily, but Prometheus ruined humanity by introducing the arts of civilization, which are the source of all evils; then Diogenes discovered how to return to the blessed primitive state by ridding himself of luxury, property, and public affairs. This so-called anthropological theory, we are told,[53] lay at the heart of all Cynic teaching. But was it really a theory of any sort?

When Greek intellectuals at that period tried to apply rationalism to the stories of traditional mythology, they did one of two things. One way was to reduce myth to history, leaving the gods out of it. This is what we call "euhemerism" after one of the later practitioners of the method. The other was to reduce myth to physical or moral allegory, leaving history out of it.[54] In the fifth and fourth centuries B.C. the latter seems the method usually applied to the myths about the origins of man. Greek writers who speculated about the origins of civilization did not consider the golden age to have been a real historical period, and when they used mythology they thoroughly allegorized it. Protagoras' work on the origins of culture (if its content is accurately reported by Plato) used the story of Prometheus to symbolize the rise from savagery to civilization, but clearly did not think Prometheus an historical person. Plato bestowed a similar literary embellishment upon the Hesiodic myth, which became a symbol of the perfect society in the *Statesman* and the *Laws*, without believing that the time of Cronus ever had any existence outside his imagination. Certainly there were later scholars who attempted a euhemeristic approach to the Hesiodic myth, interpreting the golden age as a real historical period when all property and women were common, and this primitivistic historical theory eventually found its way into philosophy. We know a euhemeristic interpretation of Hesiod was around by the end of the fourth century B.C., so it would have been possible for early Cynics to adopt it. But would they have been interested?

More likely they were attracted to allegorized mythology, because it was useful to moralists. The Sophists had already developed this method. Xenophon (*Mem.* 2.1.21–39) reports a speech of the Sophist Prodicus in which the Heracles myth is imaginatively reworked in dialogue form to furnish a moral allegory about the choice between vice and virtue. This is the sort of thing we imagine Antisthenes to have done in his writings on Heracles, turning the myth into an allegory to illustrate the new ethic of virtue won through physical *askesis.* Sometimes these allegories were comical. Xenophon (*Mem.* 1.3.7) represents Socrates retelling the story of Circe, who turned the men of Odysseus into pigs, so as to make it an allegory about the dangers of greed; and we are told that he meant this to be both humorous and serious.

Cynics specialized in such *spoudaiogeloios* treatments of myth. One of the seven mock "tragedies" attributed to Diogenes, the *Thyestes*, contained a long attack on religious taboos which is summarized in the doxographical section in Diogenes Laertius (6.73). It was argued by some character in this dialogue that there is nothing improper in stealing from a temple, or in eating the flesh of any animal, or even in eating human flesh; the last point was supported by reference to the corpse-eating Indians of Herodotus.[55] The tragedy called *Oedipus* had a similar theme, if it is the source of a speech put into Diogenes' mouth by Dio (10.29–30): Diogenes argues that Oedipus should either have concealed his incest or made it legal, since chickens, dogs, asses, and Persians do not object to incest with their mothers. Presumably the point of the first tragedy was that Thyestes incurred no religious defilement because he was unintentionally tricked into eating his own children; and of the second, that Oedipus could not have been defiled by unintentional incest.

These parodies belonged to the Cynic attack on *deisidaimonia*, a word usually translated "superstition." This seems to have been a major theme in early Cynic preaching. Many anecdotes show Diogenes ridiculing temples, divinations, prayers, ritual purification, salvation through mysteries, and the belief that the gods punish evil; and stigmatizing these practice as *deisidaimonia.*[56] This word, which once meant simply "fear of the gods," had by the late fourth century acquired a pejorative connotation—unreasonable scrupulosity about cultic practices—which first appears in the portrait of the "superstitious man" in Theophrastus' *Characters* (ca. 319 B.C.). The word did not usually imply rejection of the traditional cults; more often it distinguished proper worship from improper. But the Cynic view of the cults seems wholly negative. Since they were uninterested in cosmology on principle, the early Cynics probably had no particular opinions about the gods. In the anecdotes they usually turn aside questions about the gods with humorous professions of ignorance . What aroused their consistent opposition was the fear of divine intervention in human affairs, because they saw this popular belief as a barrier to *autarkeia.* Their mythological parodies concentrated on those myths most likely to encourage "superstition."

The Cynics, then, made much use of mythology of all sorts, but in an irreverent burlesque manner peculiar to them, sometimes standing traditional stories on their heads. They do not seem a likely source for a literal interpretation of the Hesiodic myth. When they turned the Promethean myth on its head, making Prometheus a villain, they did not take him to be an historical figure any more than Protagoras had done. Naturally they hit upon the Hesiodic myth of the golden age and used it as a foil to the Promethean story. The golden age and the Heracles legend became the favorite mythic representations of the Cynic life. But the golden age was not an historical or anthropological theory to them. Cynics could use examples drawn from barbarian custom and animal behavior to show the relativity of various *nomoi,* for that was an ancient line of argument; certain types of animal behavior, like that of mice and dogs, provided them with especially relevant illustrations; but they did not think the life according to nature *was* the life of a mouse. They thought nature had something to do with justice among men, and not with mice.

The term "nature" appealed to the Stoics; we do not know that it was so commonly used among the early Cynics. It was one of several descriptions of the spiritual state the Cynic *askesis* was expected to achieve; they also called it happiness, freedom, virtue, reason, god, *autarkeia,* apathy, *atyphia* (freedom from illusion). Their most fundamental postulate seems to be *autarkeia*; but *autarkeia* often seems to imply something much less negative than we convey by the usual translation "self-sufficiency." It seems to carry also the connotation of "spontaneity". *Autarkeia* freed the Cynic from all motives for exploiting others; and left him or her free to help others, which only the free are qualified to do. It was only necessary to achieve freedom through the *askesis,* and then to follow one's impulses. Freedom would automatically result in the exercise of *parrhesia* to help others. Indifference to property would automatically result in an urge to share it. Cynicism was based on the theory, or rather the intuitive assumption, that human life reduced to absolute simplicity is absolutely altruistic. One who had learned that the easy and pleasant way of life was to live for the present could not help but spread this message to those around, by example and by precept. All philosophical activity that was not devoted to this individual psychic reformation was considered useless, because it could deal only with the world of the ordinary norm. Cynics believed nothing was possible in that world except insubstantial opinions, which they compared to a great fog (*typhos*); and the Cynic life, to a safe island rising out of the mist.[57]

This optimistic concept of virtue Cynics inherited from the Socratic tradition. Socratics generally assumed that all moral problems will be solved if we can find the right moral agent, the person possessed of psychic harmony. It is taken for granted that such a person will want to help others. In Plato's *Republic* it is assumed that the intellectual powers of the rulers will automatically confer moral superiority, and without much more by way of rational justification than Cynics gave for the perfection of the wise. The Cynics were different mostly because they would not intellectualize the wise one. They were more in accord with Greek tradition than they are usually taken to be, but at the same time they had developed Greek philosophy along lines that seem more closely parallel to the great religions of the East.

The *Republic* of Diogenes

We can now return to the question with which we started. Would a Cynic utopia have been a contradiction in terms? Not, I think, for the reasons usually given. If the interpretation advanced here is correct, Cynicism was at any time in its history compatible with social and political interests. Cynicism was an offshoot of the Socratic tradition that carried to extremes its individualistic, ascetic, mystical, skeptical strain; but Cynics always assumed that philosophers so trained would wish to benefit society because few Socratics and few Greeks held any other concept of virtue; and because their "short cut" to virtue was meant to produce ascetic leaders who would be walking repositories of virtue, and in a good position to benefit society. They differed from most older schools in insisting that the wise one could confer these benefits only in an indirect fashion, as the wise one necessarily abjures power. It was a solution to the problem of the relationship between philosopher and society. The success and persistence of the Cynic tradition is evidence that the solution was found saitsfactory.

But we must still ask whether Cynicism was compatible with the particular *kind* of social and political interest expressed in the Stoic utopian works. Let us briefly summarize what we know about the *Republic* that Diogenes was supposed to have written. Most of our information concerns its scandalous sexual ethics. It proposed "community of women" with free choice of partners, unlike the regimented eugenic system of Plato; and the raising of children in common.[58] We are told that choice was left free indeed: the ideal city permitted every kind of incest, the boldest promiscuity on the part of both genders, a homosexuality so unrestricted that the system could also be called "community of boys," and even rape if necessary, though one can hardly see why it should be. Women dressed and behaved exactly like men, even exercising with them in the nude. We have a few nonsexual items: weapons of war would be useless, dice (knucklebones) would be used in place of currency, and in some fashion cannibalism was advocated.[59] We will consider later what may have been meant by all this. For the moment, let us note merely that all these proposals were identical or very similar to proposals in the utopian writings of Zeno and Chrysippus.

As for the history of the text, we know that it was accepted as a genuine work of Diogenes, and commented upon in some detail, by Cleanthes, who was head of the Athenian Stoics after Zeno (ca. 262–ca. 232); and that his successor Chrysippus, head of the school from ca. 232 till ca. 207, mentioned it with approval in not less than eight of his works. Antipater of Tarsus, head of the school in the late second century, recorded his amazement at the *apatheia* expressed in the *Republics* of Diogenes and Zeno. We do not know the context of this remark, but *apatheia* in the mouth of a Stoic did not usually connote disapproval. All this we know solely from the chance survival of some papyrus fragments of an anti-Stoic tract by an Epicurean philosopher of the first century B.C. After Antipater we know of no Stoic references to Diogenes' *Republic* at all, for the utopian tradition then dropped out of Stoicism. But it is clear that by the late third century B.C. Stoics were familiar with this work and accepted it as Diogenes'.

But some others did not accept it. In the late third century the Peripatetic Satyrus of Alexandria, who wrote many biographies of famous men including what was probably the earliest life of Diogenes, denied that Diogenes had ever written anything. The seven tragical parodies Satyrus ascribed to Diogenes' disciple Philiscus (Diog. Laert. 6.80). Satyrus may have been influenced by the doxographical tradition that denied Cynicism constituted a philosophical system, for these people probably doubted that it had a literary canon either. But there were some scholars who accepted Cynicism as a philosophical school and still denied that Diogenes had written a *Republic*. In the early second century Sotion of Alexandria produced his influential *Successions of the Philosophers*, which canonized the notion that Cynicism was a Socratic school fathered by Antisthenes and credited Diogenes with fourteen works; but the *Republic* and the *Tragedies* were not among them (Diog. Laert. 6.80).

We know from Philodemus that in the first century B.C. many Stoics denied Diogenes had written this *Republic*, because they thought it a scandalous work and wished to disassociate it from Diogenes, whom they continued to revere. But Philodemus argued that the earlier Stoics had accepted it as genuinely Diogenic, that it was written in the manner or style (*tropos*) of Diogenes, and that libraries and catalogs attributed it to him. One of these catalogs has been preserved by Diogenes Laertius (6.80) from an unknown source: it is longer than Sotion's catalog and has little in common with it, and it includes both the *Republic* and the *Tragedies*.

Von Fritz thought that the doubts about Diogenes' authorship of the *Republic* arose from the efforts of the later Stoics to discredit it, and this view has won wide acceptance.[60] But the third century B.C. seems too early a date for such a reaction. What Stoics would have rejected utopianism in general, or the Diogenic version of it in particular, at a time when the all-influential Chrysippus was defending both, and when the political and social views of the Stoa, from all evidence, were in their most radical phase? And if there was already an anti-Cynic party within the Stoa, why should Alexandrian Peripatetics have been involved in their campaign?

In fact, the evidence is totally inconclusive. There were traditions that Diogenes left writings (Diog. Laert. 2.112, 6.31, 6.48), but his earliest biographer disbelieved all these, and we know of no axe he had to grind. Aristotle knew of no such work as this when he wrote *Politics* 2, for he says there had been no communistic theories except Plato's; but that leaves open the possibility that Diogenes wrote it toward the end of his long life, or wrote it earlier and did not widely circulate it, so that Aristotle never knew of it. Philodemus assumes that Diogenes' *Republic* was the model for Zeno's *Republic*, but we notice that Philodemus quotes no allusion to it by Zeno himself, though he seems to have ransacked early Stoic literature for such references. (If Philodemus had known of any such reference in the writings of Zeno, surely he would have mentioned this at the beginning of his sixth chapter, where he collects all references to the Diogenic *Republic* in writings of Cleanthes, Chrysippus, and their successors.)

What had happened? By the late third century there existed a large Cynic literature which included all sorts of works attributed to Diogenes, the authenticity of which was already a matter of much dispute. At about that time the "succession" of Cynic teachers rather mysteriously died out, perhaps because Cynicism had been largely absorbed by the Stoa. Whatever the reason, the decline of an independent Cynic tradition would have reduced the chances of getting at the truth about the Diogenic corpus.[61]

We can distinguish two groups who were interested in the history of Cynicism at that time. The Athenian Stoic tradition, eventually embodied in Diogenes Laertius, tried to make Cynicism look like a regular school with a systematic teaching, a recognized succession of leaders, and an authentic canon of writings; and emphasized the *koinonia* between Cynic and Stoic. The Diogenic *Republic* was an important document to these Stoics because communistic utopianism of a certain type was an important point of resemblance between the two schools. This motive is especially clear in Diogenes Laertius 7.131:

> They [the Stoics] think it right that women should be common among the wise, so that a man may use whatever woman he falls in with; so say Zeno in his *Republic* and Chrysippus in his *On the Republic*, and also Diogenes the Cynic and Plato.

This probably comes from the Stoic handbooks of Apollodorus (late second century B.C.). It tries to mitigate the radicalism of the Cynic/Stoic utopianism by (falsely) identifying it with the utopianism of Plato, but nevertheless it makes no attempt to conceal the fact that Cynic/Stoic utopianism meant free choice of partners. This must represent the tradition of the third-century Attic Stoa. Down to the time of Apollodorus we have no evidence that any Stoics thought anything different.

Then there was the Hellenistic scholarly tradition centered at Alexandria. Some of these scholars, especially Hippobotus, doubted that Cynicism had ever been a school or a succession; others, especially Sotion, accepted the Stoic view described above. Some, including Sotion, rejected the Diogenic *Republic*; others, according to Philodemus, accepted it. There is no obvious explanation for this difference.

I have already suggested that Hippobotus was probably closer to the truth. Cynicism was a flexible way of life that recognized no authority. It did have a certain skeptical and mystical content, but its external aspects, such as *parrhesia* and ascetic dress, could be imitated by any philosopher. It seems significant that a hundred years after Diogenes died there was no agreement on the authenticity of a single one of the many works ascribed to him. But we can conclude nothing from this about the authorship of the *Republic*. Given the methods of textual criticism then available the different catalogs could represent little more than different strands in the constantly growing legend of Diogenes, and we need not assume they represent ideological bias. Diogenes Laertius has also preserved two different catalogs of the works of Aristippus (2.84–85), and here again we find a short catalog from Sotion and a much longer catalog from some unnamed source, with little overlap. The explanation seems obvious: Diogenes and Aristippus were eminently quotable philosophers and obvious subjects for the literary forger's art, especially after the successions of their disciples died out in the third century. We can do nothing now with Philodemus' claim that the *Republic* was in the style of Diogenes. Many Greeks had extraordinary sensitivity to stylistic differences, but clearly this did not help them reach agreement about the Diogenic corpus. It is an instrument that can serve the forger as well as the critic; it cannot help the critic in dealing with a corpus that contains not a single work of unquestioned authenticity; and anyway it is probable that much Cynic literature was written in much the same popular diatribe style. If the Diogenic *Republic* was a forgery that appeared in the late third century B.C., there is nothing remarkable in the supposition that the leaders of the Stoic school were taken in by it.[62] It required a shorter time for Christians to accept the Pastoral Epistles as genuinely Pauline.

Instead we should ask whether the work so described is at all likely to have been a product of early Cynicism. The real question is the one put by Zeller a hundred years ago: what was the relationship between this alleged utopian ideal and the actual Cynic life? It is not easy to find one. Crates' poetry shows that Cynics conceived the Cynic fellowship as a sort of alternative to the polis, and they described this conceit in language that sounds utopian but is not utopian at all. It is typical Cynic burlesque mythology. The most famous example is the parody of the *Odyssey* in which Crates praises the polis of *Pera*, the city of the wallet: a city where no one owns anything, and war and conflict do not exist, because no one cares for money, glory, or lust.[63] In the same vein Crates called himself a fellow citizen (*polites*) with Diogenes in the land of *Penia* (poverty) and *Adoxia* (disrepute). (Diog. Laert. 6.93). They could speak also of a city of the unwise that stood in opposition to the city of poverty: Diogenes, or perhaps Bion, called love of money the *metropolis* of all evils.[64] The Cynic antipolis was worldwide. When Diogenes was asked the name of his city he said, in one version, "Everywhere"; and in another, that he was a *kosmopolites*, citizen of the world. In another poem Crates declared that his country was as wide as the world.[65] They meant, of course, something negative, that they belonged to no existing polis; but Cynic negation was usually double-edged, and there is also the implication of membership in something larger. The city of the wallet is a metaphor for the Cynic life, suggesting the fellowship that united all wise people; but also a metaphor for what the larger community might be like were it to imitate the wise. When we read that there is no war in the city of the wallet, we are no longer sure whether the image refers to the Cynic life or to a real city. I suggest it means both. The image sums up the whole Cynic message: a sage demonstrating that peace of mind can be attained by elimination of selfish desire, and leavening the whole of society by example.

But this is no utopia. What Crates is describing is the world he lived in. The Cynic fellowship was rooted firmly in the polis and could not have existed without it. The city of the wallet and utopia are contradictory images. There is no evidence that Cynics wanted a world in which everyone imitated literally the radical Cynic *askesis*; their assumption seems to be that the existing organization of society would work well enough if everyone absorbed something of the sage's equanimity.

If Diogenes really wrote a *Republic* envisioning a world in which everyone lived the Cynic life, the vision was oddly forgotten by his immediate disciples. Crates preferred the more practical ideal of the city of the wallet. Onesicritus could think in a more utopian vein, but the ideal Hindu society he depicted in his history contained no mention of communism, just the traditional Spartan practice of *syssitia*. Onesicritus could contemplate abolishing slavery and war, but there is no sign he had heard about abolishing the household. Even among the later Cynics it is difficult to find traces of genuine utopianism.[66]

One is inclined to think that the sorts of social and political interests that occupied Cynics were not such as produce utopias. Asceticism and utopianism are rather similar solutions in that both set up an ideal radically removed from ordinary life, but for that reason they are perhaps contradictory. Cynicism did not have any need for a utopian theory, because it was always more religious order than philosophical school and the salvation that it offered was too complete and instantaneous.

I suggest that the Diogenic *Republic* was one of two things. It is possible that Diogenes, or some other early Cynic, really wrote a *Republic*, but if so this was a playful utopia like those of the Old Comedy; and a parody of the *Republic* of Plato, in the Cynic burlesque tradition. Aristotle did not include it among the serious utopias because it was not one. Nevertheless it was *spoudaiogeloios*: it was intended as a serious critique of the Platonic utopia, particularly its authoritarianism and military organization. It would have suggested to the Stoics the possibility of a serious utopia based on Cynic values. Thereafter it was always associated with the Stoic utopian writings, and it had the *form* of a utopia, which is why some ancient authors describe it as one. We could not tell from most references to them that the Diogenic *Tragedies* were not real tragedies.

The other solution—perhaps a simpler one, perhaps easier to square with our evidence for the content and history of the text—is that the Diogenic *Republic* was a third-century Stoic forgery based on the *Republic* of Zeno and intended to support the theory of a close *koinonia* between the Cynic and Stoic traditions. In either case, there was no real Cynic utopia. It was Zeno who first tried to create a serious utopian vision inspired by the Cynic life.

Notes

1. Zeller, *Socrates and the Socratic Schools*, trans. O. J. Reichel (New York 1985), 333–34.

2. Theodor Gomperz, *Greek Thinkers: A History of Ancient Philosophy*, trans. G. G. Berry (London 1905), 2.160ff.: the mere existence of Diogenes' *Republic* "proves that the vagrancy and the mendicancy of the Cynic, as also his withdrawal from public affairs, were regarded by the founders of the school as temporary makeshifts. . . ." R. Helm, "Kynismus," in Paully–Wissowa 12, col. 12 (1925) accepted this view. Gomperz's suggestion that in the Cynic ideal society Cynics were to become a ruling elite has been tentatively revived by Ferguson, *Utopias*, 89–97. In support of this view Ferguson points to a passage in Dio Chrysostom (8.14) in which Diogenes proposes that gluttons be banished from the city, or boiled down for their fat like pigs. Ferguson suggests that this passage came from the *Republic* (though Dio nowhere mentions that work) and that it explains why the *Republic* was said to advocate cannibalism. This is indeed almost the only Cynic tradition that seems to propose a political action; but surely it is nothing but a humorous anecdote, as Dio took it to be. If it contained any allusion perhaps it was to the fairly widespread Greek scapegoat rituals in which an unpopular individual was first feasted and then stoned out of the city in order to purify it; in some places, the purification may at one time have entailed human sacrifice. See Burkert, *Greek Religion*, 82–84.

3. Salin, *Platon*, 182: Diogenes' *Republic* contained no *Staatsordnung*, only a collection of precepts and examples for a dirty and disorderly "life according to nature," called a *Politeia* only because after Plato anyone claiming to be a philosopher had to write a work with this title. H. C. Baldry, *The Unity of Mankind in Greek Thought* (Cambridge 1965), 110: "We may guess that if Diogenes did write a *Politeia*, its subject was life within this [Cynic] fellowship of the wise, not an ideal state in the ordinary sense." Likewise Sinclair, *Greek Political Thought*, 244–46, 264; and Andrew Erskine, *The Hellenistic Stoa: Political Thought and Action* (Princeton 1990), 27–29. Erskine argues that the *Republic* of Diogenes was less radical than the *Republic* of Zeno because it was concerned with the life of the sage in existing society; e.g., we are told that the city described by Diogenes contained gymnasia, while the city described by Zeno abolished them. But we are also told that women exercised in the nude in these gymnasia of Diogenes, and how could that happen in existing society? And how were wise men in existing societies to practice that communism in women and children which is the best-attested feature of the *Republic* of Diogenes?

4. The detailed comment on these sources will be reserved for the next chapter, where I will argue that this passage is a rhetorical topic focused on a comparison between men of words and men of deeds, or between utopian and practical statesmen; sometimes the former are said to imitate the latter, sometimes vice versa, but in neither case are statements about imitation to be taken literally; they are required by the rhetoric. And all utopian writers are lumped together for these purposes. But at least this shows Diogenes was regarded as a member of that company.

5. Zeller accepted that the Cynics had utopian goals, but he could not reconcile this with what he knew about Cynic moral teaching. "Allowing a conditional necessity for states and laws, the Cynics refused in their homelessness to take any part in civil life. They wished to be citizens of the world, not of any one state; their ideal state, so far as they do sketch it, is a destruction of all civil life" (*Socrates*, 326).

Several later writers have expressed the same sense of anomaly about the Diogenic *Republic*. Dudley, *History of Cynicism*, 37: "It is the extreme of individualism. To call it a political system at all is doubtless a contradiction, unless we are prepared to admit with Blake the possibility of a benevolent anarchy."

T. S. Brown, *Onesicritus: A Study in Hellenistic Historiography* (Berkeley1949), 31: "The loss of the *Republic* is especially to be deplored, both because of the interest inherent in a treatise on government by a man who fundamentally did not believe in government and because of its undoubted influence on Zeno's lost work on the same subject." Four pages later Brown remarks that Diogenes' sexual communism was "anarchical," not "constructive" like Plato's version, and suggests Diogenes was merely trying to shock. This desperate solution, which scholars have occasionally called upon to explain away the apparently antisocial aspects of Cynicism, is particularly unsatisfactory in this case, because we know the early Stoics held the same shocking views on sexual communism.

W. W. Tarn, *Alexander the Great* 2: *Sources and Studies* (Cambridge 1948), 404–5: "It [Cynicism] was not a *philosophy* like those of the four schools, with a body of doctrine; it was a way of life, a mode of thought, and was entirely *negative*... it never *constructed* anything, anything which affected men otherwise than as individuals; Cynicism and universalism are a contradiction in terms." Tarn was willing to solve the contradiction by methods worthy of his subject: he cut the Gordian knot and denied that Diogenes ever wrote a *Republic*. That is the only way the problem can be solved, if Tarn's premises are correct.

6. G. A. Gerhard, *Phoinix von Kolophon: Texte und Untersuchungen* (Leipzig 1909), passim; and idem, "Zur Legende vom Kyniker Diogenes," *Archiv für Religionswissenschaft* 15 (1912), 388–408; Kurt von Fritz, *Quellenuntersuchungen zu Leben und Philosophie des Diogenes von Sinope* (Leipzig 1926); and idem, "Cynicism," in the *Oxford Classical Dictionary*, 2nd ed. (Oxford 1970); André Oltamare, *Les origines de la diatribe romaine* (Geneva 1926); Dudley, *History of Cynicism*, 48–49, 52–53, 66–69, 104; Brown, *Onesicritus*, 25–31; A. J. Malherbe, "Cynics," in *The Interpreter's Dictionary of the Bible: Supplement* (Nashville, 1976).

7. The views of Ferrand Sayre, *Diogenes of Sinope: A Study of Greek Cynicism* (Baltimore 1938), revised under the title *The Greek Cynics* (Baltimore 1948), may be described as an extreme statement of the rigorist position, but with some peculiar features. Sayre regarded Diogenes as an isolated megalomaniac who had no real connection with Cynicism; he thought the Cynic sect, a fraternity practicing ascetic mendicancy, did not originate until the second century B.C., probably under Indian influence. One notices that extreme rigorists like Sayre and Tarn (see n. 5) will conclude that Diogenes could never have written a *Republic*.

8. Ragner Höistad, *Cynic Hero and Cynic King*, (Uppsala 1949); and idem, "Cynicism," in *The Dictionary of the History of Ideas* (New York 1968). "The historical Diogenes represented a perhaps extreme, Socratic type of asceticism which is consistent with corporate and social ideals of an idyllic and eudaemonistic character, with the emphasis largely on educational ends" (*Cynic Hero*, 138). His interpretation is largely followed in Kindstrand's edition of Bion (see n. 9).

9. The most useful recent studies known to me are Marie–Odile Goulet–Cazé, "Un

syllogisme stoïcien sur la loi dans le doxographie de Diogène le Cynique. A propos de Diogène Laërce VI 72," *Rheinisches Museum für Philologie* 125 (1982), 214–40; above all, her *L'ascèse cynique: un commentaire sur Diogène Laërce VI 70–71*, Histoire des doctrines de l'antiquité classique 10 (Paris 1986); and Jaap Mansfeld, "Diogenes Laertius on Stoic Philosophy," in *Elenchos: Rivista di studi sul pensiero antico* 7 (1986), 295–382.

The fragments of the older Cynics (those of the fourth century B.C.) have now been edited with an extensive commentary by Gabriele Giannantoni, *Socraticorum Reliquiae*, 4 vols. (Naples 1983). The second volume contains the Cynic fragments, with the Cynic Epistles and the relevant passages from Dio Chrysostom and Lucian in the appendices; notes are in the third volume, indices in the fourth. There is a French translation of Cynic material by Léonce Pacquet, *Les cyniques grecs: fragments et témoignages* (Ottawa 1975) but this includes no Greek or Latin texts. Still useful, though replaced by Giannantoni, is the edition of Antisthenes by F. D. Caizzi, *Antisthenis fragmenta* (Milan 1966). The papyri about Diogenes were collected by Italo Gallo, *Frammenti biografici da papiri* 2: *La biografia dei filosofi* (Rome 1980), 237–390. There is an English translation of Crates' poetry in the Loeb Classical Library, J. M. Edmonds, *Elegy and Iambus* 2 (London 1931); and one of the Cynic Epistles by A. J. Malherbe, *The Cynic Epistles*, (Missoula 1977).

Cynic writers of the third century B.C. are not included in Giannantoni. Bion has been edited by J. F. Kindstrand, *Bion of Borysthenes: A Collection of the Fragments with Introduction and Commentary* (Uppsala 1976). The fragments of Teles were edited by O. Hense, *Teletis reliquiae* (Tübingen 1909), and translated into English by E. N. O'Neill: *Teles (The Cynic Teacher)* (Missoula 1977). The poems of Cercidas are available in several editions, including one with translation in the LCL: A. D. Knox, *Herodes, Cercidas, and the Greek Choliambic Poets* (London 1929).

10. Diogenes Laertius has received a modern edition by H. S. Long (Oxford 1964) and a slightly bowdlerized English translation in the LCL by H. D. Hicks (London 1925). Major studies include Richard Hope, *The Book of Diogenes Laertius* (New York 1930); Jorgen Mejer, *Diogenes Laertius and his Hellenistic Background* (Wiesbaden 1978); and the proceedings of the international conference on Diogenes Laertius at Amalfi in 1985, published in *Elenchos* 7 (1986). The basic work on the *Life of Diogenes* was von Fritz's *Quellenuntersuchungen* (see n. 6); there is also Gallo, *Frammenti biografici* 2.239ff.; Giannantoni, *Socr. rel.* 3, n. 41, pp. 371–76; and Mansfeld's article in *Elenchos* 7. There is little that can be said about the author except that he had no obvious philosophical position and compiled this work for a noble patron; he might have worked at Nicaea in Bithynia, no center of learning, which would explain why his material is so out of date; but to concentrate on classical and early Hellenistic writers at the expense of later times was then a common fashion.

The *Life of Diogenes* consists of the following. Book 6.20–23 is a connected biographical account, probably from some earlier *Life*. Book 6.24–30, 32–69, 75–76 contain a chatoic mass of anecdotes (*chreiai*), often reported indirectly and summarily. Interspersed among these anecdotes are two versions of the *Sale of Diogenes*, one from the satirist Menippus (third cent. B.C.) and one by an unknown Eubulus (6.30–32, 74–75); and a doxographical summary (6.70–73). There follows an account of Diogenes' death (6.76–79); then Diogenes Laertius attaches his usual appendices on Diogenes' writings and on other men with the same name (6.80–81).

11. The fragments of Philodemus have recently been reedited with an Italian translation by Tiziano Dorandi, "Filodemo. Gli Stoici (PHERC 155 E339)," *Cronache Ercolanesi* 12 (1982), 91–133. See also R. G. Andria, "Diogene Cinico nel papiri Ercolanesi," *Cronache Ercolanesi* 10 (1980), 129–51.

12. I will not recapitulate in detail the arguments for the primacy of Apollodorus' *Ethics* as a source for Diogenes Laertius. 6–7; these will be found in the writings of Goulet–Cazé and Mansfeld (n. 9).

13. See Lawrence Giangrande, *The Use of Spoudaiogeloion in Green and Roman Literature* (The Hague 1972).

14. On the origins of *chreiai, gnomai, apophthegmata, and apomnemoneumata*, see Arnaldo Momigliano, *The Development of Greek Biography* (Harvard 1972), 72; J. F. Kindstrand, "Diogenes Laertius and the *Chreia* Tradition," *Elenchos* 7 (1986), 217–43; Gallo, *Frammenti* 2.239ff. The earliest known *Chreiai* collections were non-Cynic: one was attributed to the Peripatetic Demetrius of Phalerum (Diog. Laert. 5.81). Metrocles produced ca. 300 B.C. the earliest known Cynic collection of *chreiai*, at least some of which were about Diogenes (Diog. Laert. 6.33). Crates' more famous disciple, Zeno the Stoic, wrote *chreiai* or *apomnemoneumata* (memoirs) about Crates (6.91, 7.4). One of the works attributed to Diogenes in the catalog of Sotion was a collection of *Chreiai* (6.80); this was more likely a collection *about* Diogenes, and must have been a Cynic production of the third cent. B.C. Theophrastus wrote some kind of collection about a Diogenes (5.43), and if this was our Diogenes, as seems likely (cf. 6.22), it shows non-Cynics were also collecting stories about him by ca. 300 B.C.

15. Teles (fr. 4a, Hense 40–41) describes Diogenes as sleeping in public buildings; as does the section of Diogenes Laertius which seems to be based on an earlier *Life* (6.22). Teles does not mention the famous "tub" (actually a *pithos*, wine vat). It is mentioned in one of the *Epistles* of Diogenes (6.23), which if not authentic were at least early; but there it seems to be a temporary expedient, not his normal home as in the later legend.

16. Plutarch, who wrote a lost biography of his fellow Boeotian Crates, and therefore was familiar with biographical traditions about the early Cynics, describes both Diogenes and Crates as propertyless beggars and sees no differences between them (*Mor.* 87a, 466e, 499d, 831f).

17. The poem on wealth is a parody of Solon (Julian 7.213b, 9.199d–200a; Edmonds, no. 1). The poem on the lentils (Plut. 125f; Ath. 4.158b; Edmonds, no. 10) meant, according to the gloss by Plutarch, that luxury is the cause of *stasis* and tyranny.

18. Theophrastus was certainly the source of the mouse story (Diog. Laert. 6.22), and von Fritz argued that he was also the source of all of 6.22–23. If so, his dialog included a discussion of the precise details of Diogenes' life and regimen, suggesting that soon after Diogenes died the origins of the Cynic life became a subject of considerable interest.

19. On the disciples of Diogenes see Giannantoni, fr. 137–42; and the appendix to Goulet-Cazé's *L'ascèse cynique*, which includes a catalog of all individuals identified as Cynics in the ancient world. She lists thirty people who were called Cynics in the fourth–third centuries B.C., most of them alleged disciples of Diogenes himself.

20. Diogenes is a dog whom no one hunts with (Diog. Laert. 6.33, 55). No one listens to him (6.27). He has not even a boy attendant to bury him (6.52). He suffers abuse from the citizens (6.41–43, 46, 61, 66). Other portraits of Diogenes as isolated misanthrope: Dio 4.12–14; 8.7–11, 26; 9.4, 6–7; Julian 6.190d. For the tradition that Diogenes was friendless, see n. 33.

21. On Hippobotus see G. B. Donzelli, "Il *Peri Haireseon* di Ippoboto e il Kynismos," *Rivista di Filologia e di Istruzione Classica* n.s. 37 (1959), 24–39; John Glucker, *Antiochus and the Late Academy* (Göttingen 1978), 176–80; Mansfield, "Diogenes Laertius on Stoic Philosophy"; Goulet-Cazé, *L'ascèse cynique*, 28–31. Arnim thought

Hippobotus wrote in the late third century; Glucker argues for the late first. Other references to Hippobotus suggest that he was skeptical of the orderly succession of Cynic masters that we find in the Stoicized doxography of Diogenes Laertius. He thought Crates not a pupil of Diogenes the Dog but of the mysterious Bryson (Diog. Laert. 6.85). He seems to have made Mendemus the pupil of an Epicurean (6.102). And he may have tried to slight Zeno's connections with Cynicism, making him the pupil of the logician Diodorus (7.16, 7.25).

22. See V. Emeljanow," A Note on the Cynic 'Short Cut to Happiness,'" *Mnemosyne* 18 (1965), 182–84; and Goulet-Cazé, *L'ascèse cynique*, 22–28. Other references to the phrase: *Epistles of Diogenes* 12, 30, 37, 44; *Ep. of Crates* 13, 16, Plut. 759d; Julian 7.225c.

23. I know of no very useful comparative treatment of asceticism. Some of the comments in W. O. Kaelber, "Asceticism," in *The Encyclopedia of Religion* ed. Mercia Eliade (New York 1987) are relevant here. For the distinction between ordinary and extraordinary norms see Franklin Edgerton, "Dominant Ideas in the Formation of Indian Culture," *Journal of the American Oriental Society* 62 (1942), 151–56. The distinction between otherwordly and innerwordly, or active and comtemplative, religious orientations, which I mention below, comes of course from Max Weber's 1915 essay "Religious Rejections of the World and Their Directions," trans. in *From Max Weber: Essays in Sociology*, ed. H. H. Gerth and C. W. Mills (New York 1958), 323–59.

24. On the uniqueness of the Orphic/Pythagorean *bios* see Burkert, *Greek Religion*, 301ff.

25. See Burkert, *Lore and Science*, 198–205.

26. The political fragments of Antisthenes are collected in Caizzi, frs. 43, 100–105; and Giannantoni, 2. frs. 68–78, with commentary at 3. n. 40.

27. I make no attempt here to solve the complicated chronological problems surrounding Diogenes' arrival in Athens and his relationship with Antisthenes. See Giannantoni, 3. n. 42. The only data that seem reasonably secure are that Antisthenes was still alive, but about ninety years old, in 366 B.C.; that Diogenes was exiled from Sinope and came to Athens sometime around the middle of the century; that Diogenes lived into his eighties and died about the same time as Alexander the Great (323). The chronological gap between Antisthenes and Diogenes, and the poverty of the tradition about their relationship, seem to rule out a close connection, nor is that necessary to account for an obvious spiritual influence. Like Zeno on Cyprus, Diogenes might have started reading "Socratic books" while still on the Black Sea. Antisthenes left many such Socratic books, and also left disciples at Athens. The exile of Diogenes has been dated as late as ca. 340. I incline toward an earlier date, not because I think it necessary to believe that Diogenes knew Antisthenes personally, but because I find it difficult to imagine anyone inaugurating a regimen like the Cynic life in late middle age.

28. Attributed to Diogenes again in the anecdotal section of Diogenes Laertius (6.37), and by Plutarch (1102f); attributed to Crates in *Epistles of Crates* 26, 27; attributed to Antisthenes at Diogenes Laertius 6.11; attributed to Socrates in *Epistle of Diogenes* 10.

29. Perhaps the immediate source was a famous speech by Prodicus (Xen., *Mem.* 2.1) in which Heracles has to choose between the long and rugged road to virtue and the short and easy road to vice.

30. See W. K. C. Guthrie, *History of Greek Philosophy* (Cambridge 1969), 3. 230–31. A fragment of Euripides, pertinently enough from his tragedy *Heracles*, says god is all-sufficient and has need of nothing.

31. Diogenes Laertius gives us another summary of Cynic teaching at the end of the book, containing the following: "Diogenes said 'it is characteristic of gods to want

nothing, and of godlike men to need little' (6.104)." Cf. Diog. Laert. 6.44; Dio 6.31; Pseudo-Lucian, *Cynic* 12. Socrates too is supposed to have said that he was nearest to the gods because he had fewest wants (Diog. Laert. 2.27).

32. There are saying of Bion to the effect that fortune does not give wealth to the rich, but only loans it (Kindstrand, fr. 39a–d). Teles quotes Bion as saying that the illiberal do not own anything, any more than bankers own the wealth deposited with them (Teles, fr. IVa, Hense 36 = Kindstrand fr. 41). Other sayings of Bion: fortune owns wealth (Kindstrand, fr. 38a–c); the miser does not own his wealth, but is owned by it (Kindstrand, fr. 36–37 = Diog. Laert. 4.50). Bion's saying, "wealth is the sinew of deeds" (Kindstrand, fr. 46 = Diog. Laert. 4.48) reveals a still more positive attitude toward wealth; the skepticism of Oltramare (*Origines de la diatribe romaine*, 11–12) about this passage seems unjustified, in view of the evidence cited here. We have already discussed Teles' "Comparison of Poverty and Wealth" (fr. IVa, Hense 33–44): it compares the illiberal (*aneleutherios*) man who is always in want to Crates, who was always in plenty. Metrocles was supposed to have said money was harmful unless used worthily (Diog. Laert. 6.95).

33. Sayings about the friendship of the wise are found both in the doxographical (6.12, 105) and anecdotal (6.25, 29, 68) section of Diogenes Laertius. The notion that Cynics were friendless on principle is restricted to late anti-Cynic writers like Philodemus and Lucian.

34. The three accounts of Crates' conversion are found in Diogenes Laertius 6.87–88, where each is attributed to a different Hellenistic doxographer.

35. Bion (Diog. Laert. 4.48) or Antisthenes (6.3) said an ugly wife is a *poine* (punishment) and a beautiful one *koine* (common property); in this case we can assume they did not have in mind any philosophical doctrine of sexual communism. Diogenes said marriage is too soon for the young and too late for the old (6.54); similar sayings were attributed to Thales (1.26) and Socrates (2.33).

36. Crates was supposed to have said that the marriages of adulterers—apparently there is no other kind of conventional marriage—are like the plots of tragedy, always ending in murder and exile (Diog. Laert. 6.88). When Antisthenes sees an adulterer fleeing (i.e., from outraged male relatives, who were empowered by law to kill anyone caught in the act of corrupting a woman of their *oikos*), he remarks that the man could have escaped this danger for an obol, the price of a cheap prostitute (Diog. Laert. 6.4). The version of this anecdote attributed to Diogenes in Stobaeus 3.295.1–2 has a more moralistic flavor.

37. The fragment of Menander mentioned above says that Crates gave his daughter for a month on trial; but this implies that he envisioned a conventional marriage for her eventually. An early anecdote (from the polymath Eratosthenes, who wrote in the third century B.C.) describes the son of Crates and Hipparchia as an ephebe at Athens (Diog. Laert. 6.88), which implies citizenship and a fairly conventional upbringing. According to Demetrius of Magnesia, a doxographer of the first century B.C., Crates left money in trust for his sons to inherit should they turn out to be *idiotai* (ordinary people), but for distribution among the Athenians should they become philosophers (6.88). Only one late source has Crates raise his son as a Cynic: in *Epistle of Crates* 33 he gives such instructions to Hipparchia.

38. Lucian, *Runaways* 18; *Passing of Peregrinus* 43. In Athenaeus the term *cynamuia* (dogfly) is applied to a Cynic (3.126a) and to a courtesan (4.157a), perhaps implying that the latter is the sort of woman who accompanies Cynics. In *Ep. of Crates* 28, Crates uses the example of the Amazons to assure Hipparchia that women are the equals of men—meaning here, equal in all respects. Cf. *Ep. of Diogenes* 32.

39. See Robert Schlaiffer, "Greek Theories of Slavery from Homer to Aristotle," *Harvard Studies in Classical Philology* 47 (1936), 165–204; reprinted in *Slavery in Classical Antiquity*, ed. M. I. Finley (Cambridge 1960), 93–132.

40. A poem of Crates describes hunger, time, and suicide as appropriate remedies for *eros* (Diog. Laert. 6.86); and prostitutes are a frequent target of Crates' satires (6.85–86). On Cynics visiting brothels, see Diogenes Laertius 6.90 and Gregory Nazianzen, *Carmina moralia* 537, 494–96; on Diogenes' warnings against *eros* and against prostitutes of both genders, see Diogenes Laertius 6.61, 62, 66, 67.

41. Epictetus (*Disc.* 3.22.10) speaks as though the popular image of a Cynic is someone mainly occupied with reviling effeminates, i.e., men who take excessive care of their skin and hair. For examples of Cynic antieffeminacy it is only necessary to turn the pages of Diogenes Laertius at random. One of these anecdotes will convey the general flavor: Diogenes tells an effete youth, "Nature made you a man, but you force yourself to be a woman" (Diog. Laert. 6.65; Ath. 13.565c).

42. The Cynicizing wing of Stoicism was called the manly (*andreios*) branch (Diog. Laert. 6.14). The Fourth Oration of Dio draws an extended comparison between the manly Cynic and the eunuch Sophist.

43. Cynics did not attack the conventional "manly" form of *paiderastia*. Bion's remark that you can't catch a soft cheese with a hook (meaning that a certain youth was effeminate and unsuited for philosophy) implies acceptance of the traditional educational and philosophical uses of pederasty. Another saying implies an untraditional sexual frankness about the matter: "He even abused Socrates, declaring that if he [Socrates] felt a need for Alcibiades and kept away from him, he was silly; and if he had no need for him, he was doing nothing out of the ordinary" (Diog. Laert. 4.49). Kindstrand (*Bion*, 271) thinks this did not indicate "approval of pederasty," but was meant as a "shocking paradox." Cynic shocking paradoxes were supposed to contain serious points, and the point here seems precisely the same as that of the more famous anecdote about Diogenes' public masturbation. Nor was it necessarily a contradiction for Bion to censure Alcibiades for his flirtatiousness with men and women (4.49). He was just expressing the common double standard more candidly than most: it was considered effeminate for a wellborn youth to offer his favors to a man, but the man did nothing wrong in accepting them. For a similar frankness about homosexual matters even in Roman times, see the *Epistle of Diogenes* 35. It was commonly believed that Cynics saw nothing wrong in having sexual relations with boys, and in later times, when the more puritanical Platonic-Aristotelian tradition dominated philosophy, this was a common charge against them. That much is clear from the fragments of Philodemus (first century B.C.), which are discussed below. See also Sextus Empiricus, *Outlines of Pyrrhonism* 3.200.

44. Diogenes was supposed to have enjoyed the favors of the famous courtesan Lais of Corinth for free (Ath. 13.588ef). This is another anecdote originally told about Aristippus, and is certainly a malicious anti-Cynic invention, like the similar stories told by Lucian and the Christians about Diogenes' licentiousness, and probably also the tradition that Bion was a shameless boy chaser (Diog. Laert. 4.53). But the Cynic pose of *autarkeia* would have been an easy disguise for such pursuits.

45. Diogenes Laertius 6.46, 69; Dio 6.16–20; Lucian, *Philosophies for Sale* 10; Ath. 4.158f. Some versions, such as the *On Education* attributed to Plutarch (5c) and the *Ep. of Diogenes* 44, imply that masturbation was Diogenes' preferred or sole form of sexual outlet, since activities requiring partners took up too much time and money; but Dio says he passed up no easy satisfactions (6.12,30).

46. Lucian, *Philosophies for Sale* 10; Apuleius, *Florida* 14; Sextus, *Outlines* 1.153,

3.200; Clement, *Miscellanies* 4.19.121; Tatian 3. An equal candor about digestive processes was attributed to Diogenes and Crates: Diogenes Laertius 6.46, 69, 94; Dio 8.36.

47. See R. F. Hock, "Simon the Shoemaker as an Ideal Cynic," *Greek, Roman and Byzantine Studies* 17 (1976), 41–53.

48. Collected in Giannantoni, fr. 31–49; the other political anecdotes in 25–30, 50–54.

49. E. g., Stobaeus 3.360.5ff: Diogenes calls justice the most useful and pleasant of all things, because it brings peace of mind and freedom from trouble.

50. Greeks did not generally recognize anything in India that corresponded to their own institution of chattel slavery. Somewhat later Megasthenes, Seleucid ambassador to the Mauryan court, reported that there were no slaves in India (Strabo 15.1.54).

51. Tigerstedt, *Legend of Sparta*, 2.16ff., 217, 224, 315 n. 228, 369 n. 404.

52. The Cynics in Lucian's *Runaways* (17) live in "the freedom of Cronus' time" (*eleutheria he epi Kronou*); cf. *Ep. of Diogenes* 32.3; Dio 6.21–34, 8.33, 10.16; Maximus of Tyre 36. A collection of passages on this theme is translated in A. O. Lovejoy and George Boas, *Primitivism and Related Ideas in Antiquity* (Baltimore 1935).

53. Vidal-Naquet, *The Black Hunter*, 290: the Cynics "in absolute seriousness decided in favor of a return to savagery. . . . The lifestyle that the Cynics were supposed to adopt was based on deliberate transgression of all interdictions, especially those of a dietary or sexual nature, upon which society is founded. . . ." Cynics demanded a return to the golden age "here and now." I think the author takes too seriously the charges that Cynics practiced cannibalism and incest. He is probably thinking of the tradition that Diogenes ate raw meat (Diog. Laert. 6.34, 76), an extreme manifestation of asceticism certainly, but not necessarily implying any primitivistic theory. I have suggested already that Cynic *anaideia*, insofar as it was not confined to literature, was a publicity stunt. For another skeptical view of Cynic "primitivism," see J. F. Kindstrand, *Anacharsis: The Legend and the Apophthegmata* (Uppsala 1981).

54. See J. Pepin, *Mythe et allégorie* (Paris 1958); Paul Veyne, *Did the Greeks Believe in Their Myths?*, trans. Paula Wissing (Chicago 1988).

55. On the seven tragedies see Giannantoni, fr. 128–34, and notes. Satyrus of Alexandria, in the late third century B.C., assigned them all to Philiscus of Aegina, Diogenes' disciple. Favorinus of Arles, in the second century A.D., thought they were by someone named Pasiphon, possibly of the Eretrian school. In antiquity most seem to have accepted Diogenes' authorship, and some of those who questioned it, like the emperor Julian, were obviously motivated by the fact that the tragedies were notorious examples of Cynic impropriety. It seems safe to take them as products of an early Cynic milieu. The other titles were *Heracles, Helen, Achilles, Chrysippus, and Medea.* Stobaeus (3.655.11–17) may have left us a summary of the *Medea*, and if so it was more respectable than the others, for it turns Medea into a Cynic who subjects disciples to the *askesis*.

56. Diogenes Laertius 6.24,37,39, 42, 43, 45, 48, 59; Cic., *On the Nature of the Gods* 3.34.83, 3.36.88; Tertullian, *To the Nations*. 2.2; the fragments of Bion in Kindstrand, *Bion*, 224–41, with commentary. See H. A. Moellering, *Plutarch on Superstition* (Boston 1963).

57. According to a line from Menander, Monimus said "All opinion is *typhos* [mist or illusion]" (Diog. Laert. 6.83). In Crates' poem, the city of the wallet lies in the middle of *typhos* (6.85). *Atyphia* was one description of the Cynic end: Clement, *Misc.* 2.21.130; Julian 6.190b. Another poem of Crates applies the term *typhos* to the useless disputations of intellectualist philosophers like Stilpo (Diog. Laert. 2.118). Likewise Zeno (Diog. Laert. 7.22).

58. "He [Diogenes] said women should be common, and recognized no marriage

except where a man who persuades lies with a woman who consents; and for this reason he thought sons should also be common" (Diog. Laert. 6.72). Cf. Diogenes Laertius 7.131.

59. The information about weapons, currency, and cannibalism comes from the sixth chapter of Philodemus' *On the Stoics* (ed. Dorandi). The dice currency is mentioned also by Athenaeus, 4.159c. Philodemus' seventh chapter purports to summarize the views of Diogenes' *Republic*, and Zeno's *Republic*, but in fact much of it seems to be a hostile description of Cynic and Stoic practices in general. The Stoics in question are clearly the Cynicizing wing of the school. He says they all live like dogs, exercise uninhibited *parrhesia*, wear doubled cloaks, indulge freely in homosexual practices, including the rape of boys, masturbate in public, acknowledge no city and no law, and regard all other people as children, lunatics, invalids, and false friends. But the following passage must describe the Cynic/Stoic utopia. I omit some repetitions and lacunae. "Boys are common to all [for sexual purposes]. They have sexual relations with their own sisters, mothers, cousins, brothers, and sons. There is nothing, not even the use of violence, that they refrain from in order to copulate. Women make advances to men and induce them to copulate in any way they can, and if unsuccessful they offer themselves in the marketplace to anyone available. All copulate with all they meet. Husbands do it with their maidservants, and the wives, abandoning their husbands, with anyone they want. Women wear the same clothing and participate in the same activities as men, differing from men in no respect. They exercise nude together in race courses and gymnasia." There follows a fragmentary sentence which Dorandi and other editors interpret as an allusion to cannibalism and parricide.

60. Von Fritz, *Quellenuntersuchungen*, 55ff. His arguments were not accepted by Tarn (*Alexander* 2.404–9), whose case for the inconclusiveness of this evidence seems to me compelling.

61. Diogenes Laertius 6.95 gives the "orthodox" succession of teachers. Crates taught Menippus, Theombrotus, and Cleomenes; Cleomenes taught Timarchus and Echecles; Theombrotus taught Demetrius and Menedemus. None of these people is likely to have remained active much past the middle of the third century. The same is true of the maverick Bion (ca. 335–ca. 245), who stood outside this succession. This is probably a Stoic version of the history of Cynicism which makes the succession seem more orderly than it was, but still it seems that no one could find any important Cynics after ca. 250 B.C.

62. Not really remarkable even if we credit the tradition (found only in the Byzantine lexicon known as the *Suda*, s.v. Cleanthes) that Cleanthes was himself a pupil of Crates. Someone may have confused him with Zeno.

63. Edited by Giannantoni but more readily available in Diogenes Laertius 6.85.

64. Diogenes Laertius 6.50; Bion, fr. 35a–c, with Kindstrand's commentary.

65. Diogenes Laertius 6.63, 72, 98; Lucian, *Philosophies for Sale* 8. Also ascribed to Theodorus the Atheist (Diog. Laert. 2.99), a Cyrenaic with Cynic connections. Quoted in Apollodorus' doxography as another parallel with Stoic teaching, but the poems of Crates show it was an authentic early Cynic maxim.

66. The author of the *Ep. of Diogenes* 47, written sometime during the early Roman Empire, confronts the objection that if everyone became Cynics there would be no more marriages or children. He replies that then the human race would become extinct, which would be as lamentable as the extinction of flies or wasps. If he has ever heard of a theory that the whole world might be converted to Cynicism, he has no interest in it. And this was written long after the *Republic* of "Diogenes" was generally accepted as an authentic early Cynic text.

4

The Stoic Utopia: A World Without Households

Because of the eminence of its power and beauty, what we say seems like a fiction, and not a doctrine that accords with man and man's nature.
CHRYSIPPUS, *On Justice* (Plut., *Mor.* 1041f)

Cynic and Stoic

At the Tail of the Dog

Two traditions about the origins of Stoicism are represented in our sources: one that emphasized the Cynic connection, and one that tried to ignore it. We have seen that the Cynicizing tradition dominates the Cynic and Stoic doxographies of Diogenes Laertius. In this tradition Zeno was originally a Cynic, a principal disciple of Crates; Cynicism and Stoicism are complementary roads to philosophy; Cynicism is a Socratic school founded by Antisthenes. This interpretation can be traced back at least to the handbooks of Apollodorus in the late second century B.C., and I would argue that it can be traced back to Zeno. The objections to this view[1] arise chiefly from the assumption that there must be some contradiction between the dignified ethics of the doxographies in Diogenes Laertius 6–7 and the bizarre moral teachings attributed to early Cynics in general and to early Cynic/Stoic utopians in particular. I have argued that early Cynicism was compatible with such a dignified ethic, and here I will try to show that the same can be said of the early utopian doctrines.

In his doxographies Diogenes Laertius follows the old, Apollodoran, Cynicizing tradition; the anti-Cynic tradition crops up in the biographical sections of his *Life of Zeno*. Among the sources he quotes two seem to be informed by this interpretation: the *Chreiai* of Panaetius' disciple Hecaton, and a work called *On Zeno* by Apollonius of Tyre; both written in the early first century B.C., both reflecting the "Neostoic" position of Panaetius' circle, which as we know from Cicero and Philodemus was then trying to sever the connection between Cynicism and Stoicism. Hecaton and Apollonius gave an account of Zeno's conversion to philosophy in which the credit goes not to Crates but to Zeno's study of "the ancients" (Diog. Laert. 7.2). Apollonius made Stilpo of

Megara, not Crates, the main influence on the young Zeno: when Crates tries to drag Zeno away from Stilpo's lectures by his cloak, Zeno tells him a philosopher must be seized by the ears (7.24). There existed a doxographical tradition which cast the Stoa as an offshoot, not of Cynicism as in Diogenes Laertius, but of the little-know Dialectical school, associated with the Megarians of Stilpo.[2] The statements that Zeno studied with Megarians and Academics for ten or twenty years after leaving Crates (7.2, 4) were intended to show how slight was the Cynic influence. Other stories have Zeno resisting Cynic shamelessness even when he was still Crates' pupil: he rebukes a Cynic who tries to beg from him, he throws his cloak over Crates and Hipparchia when they engage in their customary public coition.[3] He is generally portrayed as an ascetic of the Socratic type, not a Cynic; he lives abstemiously but attends symposia and according to Hecaton could indulge himself at them.[4]

Diogenes Laertius was surely right to prefer the first tradition. Several considerations leave no doubt about the importance of the Cynic connection to the early Stoa. The fact that Crates was Zeno's teacher and an important influence on him is sufficiently confirmed by the appearance of *Memoirs of Crates* in the catalog of Zeno's writings (7.4). The anti-Cynic tradition does not attempt to deny this, merely to minimize it. Oddly enough, the claim that the *Republic* was written when Zeno was Crates' pupil (7.4) confirms it as clearly as anything: Greeks rarely noticed the dates of a philosopher's works, no one would have noticed this except those who wanted to minimize the Cynic connection by pushing it back into Zeno's youth, and they would not have made such an admission had there been any way to deny the fact that Zeno had once been a Cynic.[5] All sources agree that Zeno had more than one teacher, but it was a rare philosopher in that age who did not. The persistent tradition about a *koinonia* between Cynic and Stoic is difficult to explain unless there really was one from the start. We have seen that the metaphor "two roads to virtue," often used to describe this *koinonia*, was probably of Cynic origin, which supports the tradition that the Stoa was originally an offshoot of Cynicism.

It may also be relevant to consider what we know about the organization of Zeno's school. When he came to Athens ca. 312 B.C., he found two types of philosophical school there. The Academy and the Lyceum were cults of the Muses, with buildings and endowments bequeathed by the founder to his disciples, who had meals in common there; this model would soon be imitated by the Garden of Epicurus and the Museum at Alexandria. The other schools were loose gatherings of like-minded individuals, which accounts for the difficulty later doxographers had in classifying them. Among these, there were degrees of informality: some lectured to pupils sitting on benches arranged in a circle, others simply frequented public places and talked with whomever would listen; if they were Cynics, harangues of the crowd and exchanges with hecklers might be expected.[6] The group that gathered around Zeno ca. 300, at first called "Zenonians," was a school of the most informal type: they assembled in the Painted Stoa on the Agora, the most obvious public meeting place in Athens, where Zeno kept a certain spot free of idlers by walking up and down

(7.5). In one anecdote Zeno lectures somewhere to an audience seated on benches, but even beggars are admitted to the class (7.22). We receive the impression that Zeno led a sort of modified Cynic life. His teaching methods were informal, but he talked to two or three at a time. According to Cleanthes, he would beg from bystanders, but asked only for copper coins—small change—and did this only to keep crowds away (7.14). Contemporary comedies celebrated his frugality in food and dress (7.27), and in the next generation the satirist Timon ridiculed his followers as a crowd of ragged beggars (7.16).

A powerful Cynic imprint on the early Stoa is undeniable, and no one has seriously tried to deny it. But it has never been clear what this Cynic influence meant. As we have seen, Cynics were probably much closer to the general tradition of classical Greek moral thought than we usually think, but there is no question that they had broken sharply with the intellectualism of that tradition. They reduced "knowledge" to an intuitive understanding acquired through ascetic discipline. They would not speculate about nature, for that would distract attention from the sage, avatar of spontaneous natural virtue; they would not dwell upon precepts for ordinary life, for that would give the impression morality could be reduced to rules. Zeno of Citium seems to have been a Cynic who returned to the assumptions of traditional philosophy. At some point he became dissatisfied with the Cynics' dogmatic assertions, felt no more need for their histrionic demonstrations, and adopted the more general view of the philosopher's task, which required a systematic cosmology and a systematic code of ethics. By doing this he would seem to have repudiated Cynicism altogether. But somehow he did not.

The Long Road to Virtue

One problem is the difficulty of determining how much of the later Stoic system was owed to Zeno.[7] He was certainly responsible for the Stoic division of philosophy into logic, physics, and ethics (Diog. Laert. 7.39), and as soon as he became interested in the first two he was not a Cynic any longer. He certainly began, though his followers completed, the construction of an elaborate cosmological synthesis based upon ideas drawn from many earlier thinkers. In the completed form of this system, "nature" is conceived as an intelligent force (also called reason, fate, god, Zeus, the designing fire) pervading all matter, a vast rational order directing everything in the universe to a predetermined end. Human reason is a spark of this cosmic reason, and human virtue means being in tune with it. The new system, which was to become perhaps the most influential cosmology ever produced by Greek paganism, combined two attractive ideas that had only been adumbrated by earlier philosophy: the notion of the cosmos itself as a unified, orderly, living thing; and the notion of human reason as a direct participant in and manifestation of the cosmic reason. Stoic ethics was absolutely dependent on this concept of nature, and this nature could only be apprehended through logical and physical studies. The parts of the system were so interlocked that it is impossible to say which came first, but it is clear that Zeno could not have proceeded very far in this direction without making a complete break with the Cynics.

Zeno's contribution to systematic Stoic ethics is more certain, for we know he was responsible for the Stoic definition of the *telos*, the end of action, and for at least some of the key terms in the peculiar Stoic moral vocabulary. This is sufficient to show he was responsible for the central Stoic doctrine, the self-sufficiency of virtue. All Stoics held that virtue was the only good and sufficient for *eudaimonia*; and they would apply the term "good" to nothing else, considering all conventional values to be morally indifferent (*adiaphora*). But it was admitted that some of these indifferent things had a certain objective value; they were not virtue, but if used in the right way they were conducive to virtue. These things were called "preferables" (*proegmena*) or "things in accordance with nature" (*ta kata physin*). To deal with these preferred things in accordance with the promptings of nature was to perform "proper functions" (*kathekonta*). The natural preferences included life, health, pleasure, beauty, strength, wealth, reputation, birth, ability, skill, and all other values of ordinary life. This was an effort to create a systematic technical language for the discussion of ethics, capable of distinguishing purely moral value from every other kind of value; the most radical conclusion ever offered to the Socratic search for firm definitions of the excellences of the soul. When Zeno coined such terms he had already abandoned the Cynic belief that a purely moral approach, a spontaneous following of one's impulses, would be sufficient; he felt the need for a wider frame of reference, a philosophy of nature capable of distinguishing good impulses from bad. Therefore the later Stoic synthesis, compounded inseparably of logic, physics, and ethics, was already present in outline in Zeno's teaching.[8]

This synthesis has obvious affinities with the older schools of systematic philosophy, particularly the Academy,[9] but it is not obvious that it owes anything whatever to Cynicism. Therefore it has always been difficult to determine exactly what the later Stoics meant when they said—pro-Cynic and anti-Cynic alike—that Zeno wrote his *Republic* at the tail of the Dog.

A solution has been offered by Goulet-Cazé: Stoic doctrine may have owed little to Cynicism, but Stoic practice may have owed much.[10] She has argued persuasively that the Cynic doxography laid out in Diogenes Laertius 6.70ff. was compiled by a Stoic, and that it conflates two different notions of *askesis* (exercise), the one Cynic and the other Stoic. Cynic *askesis* meant the cultivation of bodily endurance; Stoics, on the other hand, always spoke of a *ditte askesis* (double exercise) both physical and spiritual. On this basis Goulet-Cazé has identified as Stoic the opening passage in the Cynic doxography (6.70):

> He [Diogenes the Dog] said exercise is of two sorts, one of the soul and the other of the body; the latter kind is that by which constant training gives rise to those perceptions that leave us free to perform deeds of virtue. The one is imperfect without the other, for soundness and strength are as important to the soul as they are to the body.

The spiritual *askesis* is the more valuable, but the soul will not acquire the necessary force unless the body also is trained in endurance. This principle is found in later Stoic writers; that it went back to Zeno's circle is supported by the fact that two of his disciples wrote treatises *On Exercise* (Diog. Laert. 7.166, 167). This throws a new light on the Cynic/Stoic *koinonia*. What united Cynics and Stoics and distinguished them from other schoools was the importance they placed on physical discipline; what separated Stoics from Cynics was that Stoics thought spiritual exercises were more important, and therefore retained the Cynic *askesis* only in a modified form.

Perhaps we are now in a position to understand more clearly what Stoics meant by the "two roads to virtue." The Cynic interpretation of this phrase we have already considered. The "short road" certainly meant the Cynic life, the "long road" meant theoretical philosophy, and the superiority of the short road is clearly implied: those who undertook the Cynic yoga were to pay no attention to logical and physical studies; their *askesis* must have involved something very dramatic and immediately recognizable; for all practical purposes it was probably identified with mendicancy and rejection of the *oikos*.

But what was the Stoic interpretation of the two roads? It is widely assumed they identified Stoicism with the long road, and by the short road meant Cynicism as defined above. If so, they meant to point out the availability of both alternatives, and the formulation seems to imply inescapably that the shorter is at least equally valid. Sometimes we find the short (*syntomos*) road described also as a rugged (*syntonos*) road, suggesting that it is reserved for the hardy few, but even that seems to imply it is for an elite. It is difficult to see how any Stoic could have held that a sage could dispense altogether with theoretical studies. Since the *ditte askesis* teaching is presented in Diogenes Laertius 6.70 as a *Cynic* teaching—attributed to Diogenes himself—it seems possible that the short road of the Stoics was not the real Cynicism but rather a Cynicized Stoicism: the double exercise of mind and body, requiring only a modified form of physical asceticism, and compatible with logical and physical studies.[11]

We notice also that the biographical tradition about Zeno shows him approaching Cynicism within a *Socratic* framework. He is supposed to have been attracted to philosophy by reading Xenophon's *Memorabilia* or other "Socratic books" (dialogues by Plato, Antisthenes, or others?) after he came to Athens, or even when still on Cyprus; and to have joined Crates because he saw the Cynic life as an attempt to put the teachings of Socrates into practice.[12] Whether or not these stories are true they indicate a certain view of Cynicism that was very influential in the early Stoa; it stressed far more than the early Cynics ever did (to judge from the evidence considered in the preceding chapter) the credentials of Cynicism as a philosophical school traceable to Socrates through Antisthenes; it may be described as a deliberate attempt by Stoics to coopt the Cynic tradition. The two-roads doctrine fits this context well if we suppose that what Stoics usually meant by it was the distinction between Stoic practice (a modified form of Cynic asceticism) and Stoic theory.

We need not assume they *always* meant that, for we know there was more than one opinion in Zeno's circle about these matters. His maverick disciple Aristo of Chios returned to something like the original Cynic viewpoint, though he expressed it in Stoic terms; he was remembered as no true Stoic, but the Cynicizing Stoics also explained him as just another example of the *koinonia* between Cynicism and Stoicism (Diog. Laert. 6.103, 105). The appearance of a figure like Aristo suggests there was quite a spectrum of opinion in the early Stoa about the definition of the Cynic life, the proper balance between asceticism and theory, the proper relationship between Cynic and Stoic.[13]

It may be instructive to compare the development of the Cynic movement to that of the Christian asceticism which replaced it in the fourth century A.D. The original form of the Christian monastic life was that of the anchorites or hermits, out of which there later arose the communal or cenobitic type of monasticism. As cenobitism became dominant it brought the hermits under its control; by the early Middle Ages the hermit life was considered a perfected form of the cenobitical life; even the history of monasticism was rewritten to conform to this pattern, for in the Latin legends about the first monks the cenobitical communities were made to come first and the hermit life was made a later offshoot. *Mutatis mutandis*, something like that seems to have happened to the individualistic *askesis* of the Cynics: it was to a large extent taken over by the Stoic school, which conceived it essentially as a perfected Stoicism, a short cut normally open only to those who were already well advanced on the long road. Clearly many Cynics never accepted the subordinate role to which the Stoics tried to confine them, and there are some hints of controversy;[14] but the very meager evidence for the survival of an independent Cynic tradition after the time of Chrysippus may mean that it had been largely absorbed by Stoicism.

The Stoics and Utopia

There was another important difference between Cynic and Stoic ethics. All true Cynics seem to have believed that the ideal of the wise person was attainable. If there were no wise people then Cynicism made no sense, for it consisted of very little except the cult of these charismatic saints, made easily recognizable by their dramatic way of life. But Stoics never thought the wise person really existed. They insisted there were no degrees in virtue: either one was perfectly wise and good, or one was not. The wise person had achieved a total harmony between individual will and cosmic reason, such as would ensure that *all* actions and motives would be virtuous. He was a perfect rational being, who understood the principles of nature so well, and had so thoroughly disciplined his mind and body through the double *askesis*, that he acted spontaneously in accordance with those principles, out of an unalterable disposition that did not permit him to do anything else. Since everyone who fell in the smallest degree short of this ideal was counted unwise or inferior (*phaulos*), the human race was divided into two classes, the wise and the unwise, with no overlap. And Stoics admitted, apparently without embarrasment, that the wise were so rare as to be nonexistent for all practical purposes.[15]

It is not clear why their ideal had to be unattainable, except that such perfectionism seems to have been, to certain people, a logical consequence of the Socratic search for an ideal moral agent. Plato, by the end of his life, also reached the conclusion that the wise were so thin upon the ground that they did not count except as an ideal. What Plato did to the practical statesmanlike ideal of Xenophon, Zeno did to the practical ascetic ideal of Crates. Zeno ceased to be a Cynic when he decided it would not be possible to attain enlightenment by the Cynic way; and when he and his followers asked what a truly enlightened mental state would be like, they faced the conclusion that it would probably not be possible to attain it at all.

So the longer road led back to utopia. Having adopted a moral perfectionism more systematic than Plato's—for their ideal combined the two traditions of Socratic perfectionism, the intellectualist and the disciplinary—Zeno was naturally drawn to Plato's method, oddly neglected by Plato's own disciples, of depicting an ideal society in order to analyze ethical principles. The right condition of the soul demanded by nature would have to be seen in its full social context, which could never be found in ordinary life. Many of the assumptions behind the Platonic and Zenonian ideal societies were identical; the final products were to look very different because they were based on different social models. The primary flesh-and-blood model behind Plato's Kallipolis was Sparta; the model behind Zeno's city was primarily the Cynic fellowship of disciplined ascetics. To understand what this difference meant we must first try to reconstruct as much as we can of the Stoic utopian literature.

The Sources

We have more information about the contents of Zeno's *Republic* than about any of his other works—a remarkable amount of information, when one considers how vague ancient authors usually were about textual citation—and there have been two attempts to reconstruct it.[16] Here I will provide a translation of and commentary on the more significant passages, not only from Zeno's *Republic* but from Stoic works that were associated with it.

Diogenes Laertius

Our knowledge of Stoic ethics depends mostly on three late epitomes: the third book of Cicero's *On Ends*: the anthology of Stobaeus, whose Stoic material comes from the epitome of Arius Didymus, court philosopher of Augustus; and the seventh book of Diogenes Laertius, containing lives of the early Stoics. The first two sources are significant for their silence about the utopian theory, which tells us that by the first century B.C. Stoic handbooks did not generally include it. Diogenes Laertius, though at least two centuries later, is our most valuable source because his biographical sections on Zeno and Chrysippus include material about their utopias from hostile sources; and even his doxographical sections, which are drawn from a wide range of doxographers and sometimes identify them by name, preserve a few utopian items from Stoic sources. The fact that his seventh book, which seems originally to have included Stoics who lived as late as the first century A.D., breaks off in the middle of the *Life of Chrysippus* is a major loss for historians of Stoicism.

REFERENCES IN THE STOIC BIOGRAPHIES OF DIOGENES LAERTIUS

A. For a time he [Zeno] was a pupil of Crates; and when he wrote his *Republic*, some said jokingly that he had written it at the tail of the dog. *Life of Zeno* 7.4

B. Yet some, including the followers of Cassius the Skeptic, attack Zeno for many things: first, they say that he declares the general education useless at the beginning of his *Republic*; second, he says that all who are not virtuous are foes, enemies, slaves, and strangers to one another, including their own children, their own brothers, and members of their own households. Again, in the *Republic* he describes the virtuous alone as citizens and friends and sharers of the same household and free men, so that to the Stoics parents and children are enemies: for they are not wise. Likewise in the *Republic* he decrees women to be common, and takes 200 lines to forbid the building of temples, law courts, and gymnasia in cities.[17] Concerning currency he writes thus: "We do not think it necessary to provide a currency either for exchange or for foreign travel." And he commands men and women to wear the same dress and to conceal none of their parts. Chrysippus, in his *On the Republic*, says that the *Republic* is the work of Zeno. He [Zeno] discusses matters of love at the beginning of the work entitled *The Art of Love*; but also he writes much the same thing in his *Diatribes*. These sorts of things are found in Cassius, but also in the rhetorician Isidore of Pergamum; the latter says that those passages in bad repute among the Stoics were deleted from the books of Zeno by Athenodorus the Stoic, director of the Pergamene library; but then the same passages were replaced, after Athenodorus was detected in this fraud and placed in a dangerous position. And so much for the rejected writings of Zeno. *Life of Zeno* 7.32–34

C. Some run Chrysippus down because he wrote much in disgraceful and improper language. [There follows a long passage objecting to the terms used by Chrysipus in one of his interpretations of mythology.[18]] And in *On the Republic* he says that we may have intercourse with our mothers and daughters and sons. He says the same thing in his *On Things not to Be Chosen for Their Own Sake*, right at the beginning. In the third book of *On Justice*, he takes up 1,000 lines to command the eating of dead bodies. [There follows a long quotation from his *On Ways of Living* dealing with the question of how the wise man should support himself.] And he is blamed for these things. *Life of Chrysippus* 7.187–89

REFERENCES IN THE STOIC DOXOGRAPHIES OF DIOGENES LAERTIUS

D. And [the wise man] will marry, as Zeno says in his *Republic*, and will produce children. *Life of Zeno* 7.121

E. The wise man will love boys whose forms reveal a capacity for virtue, as Zeno says in his *Republic*, and Chrysippus in the first book of *On Ways of Living*, and Apollodorus in his *Ethics*. *Life of Zeno* 7.129

F. It seems fit to them that women be common among the wise, so that a man may use whatever woman he falls in with, as say Zeno in his *Republic* and Chrysippus in *On the Republic*; but also Diogenes the Cynic and Plato. We will be fond of all children equally in the manner of parents, and the jealously associated with adultery will disappear. *Life of Zeno* 7.131

Sextus Empiricus

From Diogenes Laertius it is convenient to turn next to Sextus Empiricus, another doxographer of the second or early third century A.D. His handbooks of Skeptical philosophy preserve another version of the Skeptical critique: the attacks on Stoicism are found mainly in *Outlines of Pyrrhonism* 3.199–209, 245–49, and in *Against the Professors* 11.189–96. The arguments are taken from a series of excerpts similar in content to Diogenes Laertius B and C. Again the more shocking opinions of the principal early Stoics are cited to prove that Stoic ethical teaching is opposed to ordinary human custom; therefore the Stoic claim to teach an art of living based on certain principles is false, and the only sane moral position is that of the Skeptic, who accepts the conventions of the general society. The arguments of Sextus concentrate more on sexual morality than did the arguments of the "school of Cassius" and consist mostly of vague assertions: we are told that Cynics and Stoics approve of homosexuality, that some philosophers approve of adultery (community of women?), that Stoics approve of prostitution. But the following passages seem to be connected with the Stoic utopian theories.

G. The followers of Chrysippus say intercourse with mothers and sisters is indifferent. *Outlines of Pyrrhonism* 1.160

H. And Chrysippus in his *Republic* declares that a father may have children by his daughter, a mother by her son, a brother by his sister. And Plato, in more general terms, held that women should be common. [Sextus mentions the Persian and Egyptian practice of incest as further evidence of the relativity of moral opinions.] *Outlines of Pyrrhonism* 3.205

I. He [Chrysippus] says in his *Republic*: "It seems to me right to do these things, which are customary among many peoples, and correctly so: a mother may have children by her son, a father by his daughter, a brother by his full sister." And in the same work he introduces cannibalism among us; at least he says "And if any part of a living creature be cut off, and is useful for food, we should not bury it or throw it away, but consume it, so that from our own parts a new part will grow." And in his *On Proper Functions* he says explicitly of the burial of parents: "When our parents die we should bury them in the simplest way, as through the body, like nails or teeth or hair, were nothing to us, and we need give it no care or attention of that kind. And so the meat, if useful, should be used for food, just as we should use one of our own parts like a foot when it is cut off: but if it is useless for food we should bury it and leave it, or burn it and scatter the ashes, or treat it as refuse and pay no more care to it than we do to nails and hair." *Outlines of Pyrrhonism* 3.246–48; *Against the Professors* 11.192–94

Philodemus of Gadara

The fragments of *On the Stoics*, written at Rome by the Epicurean Philodemus about the middle of the first century B.C., have a unique importance because they are comments upon a living issue, not the residue of a long-dead controversy. Though rendered far more accessible by the recent edition of Dorandi, the text is still filled with breaks and difficult readings; and as it is also lengthy, I will here quote or summarize only the most relevant passages.

J. . . . the *Republic* of Zeno. This work contains certain errors, but as Zeno wrote it when he was young and thoughtless they may in part be excused. [This is an opinion Philodemus attributes to certain contemporary Stoics who were embarrased by Zeno's *Republic*.]

Zeno did not stay forever young and thoughtless. And he gave evidence that he always kept very much the same judgments about everything. So the ancients, of whom he was a great admirer. . . . [Thus Philodemus refutes the Stoic argument quoted above. The allusion to the "ancients," Dorandi suggests, meant that Zeno was a follower of the older Cynics.]

. . . They overlook the fact that at the beginning of the work he explains that it sets forth what is suitable for the time and place in which he lived. But if he had done such things he would be blameworthy; and insofar as they are impossible principles, he has legislated for men who do not exist, neglecting those who do exist. . . . [Evidently this is said to refute certain Stoics who claimed, as part of the young-and-thoughtless line of defense, that the *Republic* could have no relation to the real world and was therefore harmless.] *On the Stoics*, c. 2, cols. 9–12, ed. Dorandi

K. Stoics have the audacity to say that they accept Zeno only insofar as he was the founder of their doctrine of the end [*telos*]. But in fact they admire all the rest of his doctrines. For it is foolish to accept the doctrine of the end and not the other doctrines which harmonize with it. And if we accept the doctrine of the end it follows that we must accept the things laid out in the *Republic*. *On the Stoics*, c. 4, col. 14

L. Then they try to restrict their defense only to that section that has to do with sexual intercourse [*diamerizein*]. Yet there are so many evils collected in that section that they are really telling us that they speak in defense of the whole *Republic*, not just one part of it. *On the Stoics*, c. 5, col. 15

M. But since there are some in our time who question also the *Republic* of Diogenes, which the older Stoics did not, it must be said that this is indeed the work of Diogenes; it has his style, and it is so listed in catalogs and libraries. [This chapter has already been discussed, but its information about early Stoic writings may be summarized here.

Cleanthes commented in detail on the Diogenic *Republic* in his *On Clothing*. Chrysippus mentioned it in eight of his works. Its dice currency was mentioned in *On Things not to Be Chosen for Their Own Sake* and in the first book of *Against Those Who Differently Explain Wisdom*. Its cannibalism was mentioned in the third book of *On Justice* and the seventh book of *On Proper Functions*. Chrysippus mentioned Diogenes' teaching on the uselessness of weapons when he discussed that subject in his own *On the Republic*. It was also mentioned in Chrysippus' *On the City and the Law*; and praised in his *On the Life According to Nature* and *On Beauty and Pleasure*. Antipater, leader of the school in the mid-second century B.C., mentioned the *Republics* of Zeno and Diogenes, apparently with admiration, in his *Against the Schools*. *On the Stoics*, c. 6, cols. 15–17

N. Philodemus' seventh chapter, describing the sexual promiscuity found in the *Republics* of Zeno and Diogenes, has already been translated in part (ch. 3, n. 59). This is what was called "community of women." This is that section about *diamerizein* which in the eyes of Philodemus' Stoic opponents constituted the most embarrasing thing about Zeno's *Republic*. *On the Stoics*, c. 7, cols. 18–20

Plutarch of Chaeronea

Plutarch, a Middle Platonist of the early second century A.D., approached Stoicism from a definite and antagonistic philosophical viewpoint, as did the Skeptical and Epicurean writers we have just considered. He and Philodemus are the only writers we have whom we may assume, with some probability, to have actually read the Stoic works they criticize. But the comments of Plutarch are of special interest because of the philosophical sophistication they sometimes reveal; and because he is of all these authors the best known to us, leaving us in an unusually good position to evaluate his knowledge, purposes, and habits of quotation. His comments on Stoic utopianism fall into two groups: his biographical works contain two illuminating passages about Zeno's *Republic*, toward which he affects a favorable attitude for rhetorical purposes; and his polemical works contain several openly hostile references to Zeno and Chrysippus.

REFERENCES IN THE BIOGRAPHICAL WORKS OF PLUTARCH

O. The amazing *Republic* of Zeno, founder of the Stoic school, is directed by one principle: that we should not live in cities and demes separated by different laws, but should regard all men as our demesmen and fellow citizens, and there should be one way of life and one world order, like a herd feeding together under the care of a common law. Zeno wrote this to create a model based on a dream or vision of an orderly philosopher's constitution. But out of these words Alexander produced deeds. *On the Fortune of Alexander* 329ab

P. The principle followed by Lycurgus, then, was not to leave behind him a city that rules a large number of other cities; rather he thought that in a whole city, as in the life of a single man, happiness consists in virtue and internal harmony, and so he arranged and constructed everything to this end, that his citizens might become free and self-sufficient and temperate and stay that way for as long as possible. Plato took this as the foundation of his *Republic*, and also Diogenes and Zeno, and all others who are praised for writing about such matters; but they left nothing but writings and words. Lycurgus brought forth not mere words, but a city of deeds, beyond imitation. ... *Life of Lycurgus* 3.1–2

REFERENCES IN THE POLEMICAL WORKS OF PLUTARCH

Q. [Zeno] wrote against the *Republic* of Plato. ... *On Stoic Self-Contradictions* 1034f

R. Also it is the teaching of Zeno of Citium that temples of the gods ought not to be built. For a temple that is not worth much is not holy, and the works of builders and craftsmen are not worth much. *On Stoic Self-Contradictions* 1034b

S. [In *On the Republic*, Chrysippus] says that the citizens will not do or contrive anything for the purpose of pleasure; and he praises Euripides, quoting these verses of his:

For what need mortals save two things alone,
Demeter's grain and draughts of water clear?

Then a little further on he praises Diogenes for saying to the bystanders as he masturbated in public, "Would that I could thus rub the hunger too out of my belly." Now, what sense does it make to praise in the same work at once the man who repudiates pleasure and the man who for the sake of pleasure does things like this and engages in such obscenity? Furthermore, after he had written in the books concerning Nature that beauty is the purpose for which many of the animals have been produced by nature, since she loves the beautiful and delights in diversity, and had appended a most irrational argument, namely that the peacock's tail on account of its beauty is the purpose for which the peacock has come to be, in his work [*On the Republic*] again he has vehemently censored people who keep peacocks and nightingales. It is as if he were legislating in competition with the lawgiver of the universe and deriding nature for bestowing her love of the beautiful upon animals of a kind to which the sage denies room in his city. ... [In *On the Republic*] he says that we are almost on the point of painting pictures on the privies too and a little later that some people embellish their farmlands with tree-climbing vines and myrtles "and they keep peacocks and doves and partridges for their cackling and nightingales." *On Stoic Self-Contradictions* 1044b–e, trans. Cherniss

T. In one of his books of *Exhortations*, he [Chrysippus] says that sexual intercourse with mothers or daughters or sisters, eating certain food, and proceeding straight from childbed or deathbed to a temple have been discredited without reason. He also says that we should look to the beasts and infer from their behavior that nothing of this kind is out of place or unnatural. *On Stoic Self-Contradictions* 1044f–1045a, trans. Long/Sedley

U. I could wish that Zeno had placed those couplings (*diasmerismoi*) in a symposium and treated them in a playful manner, rather than in a serious work like his *Republic*. *Convivial Questions* 653e

Athenaeus of Naucratis

Athenaeus compiled his enormous dialogue the *Deipnosophistai* (Sophists at Dinner) early in the third century A.D. Of all our sources he may be the latest in time, and of all he is the most magpie-like in his methods and the most devoid of serious interest in philosophy. But he has given us (in addition to a reference to the dice currency of Diogenes, mentioned in the preceding chapter) the following passage, which is one of the most intriguing of all references to Zeno's *Republic*.

> V. Pontianus said that Zeno of Citium regarded Eros as god of friendship and freedom, and the provider in addition of concord, but of nothing else. Hence in the *Republic* Zeno said: "Eros is a god which contributes to the city's security." Athenaeus 13.561c, trans. Long/Sedley

Iambulus

Our final item is not really a "source." An otherwise unknown Iambulus wrote, sometime in the third or second century B.C., a novel about a voyage to an island in the Indian Ocean inhabited by an ideal society called Heliopolitans (People of the Sun). Its plot is summarized by Diodorus Siculus (2.55–60), who appears to take it as factual geography, and indeed it sounds hardly more fantastic than much that passed for such. Most works about Greek utopianism have devoted to this passage much attention, to which I have nothing to add. It seems to have been a sort of science-fiction novel, a strange mixture of traditional geography, authentic information picked up from recent travellers' accounts of the southern seas, and, in some degree, utopian philosophy. There are unmistakable parallels with Stoic utopian thought. The Sun People live in complete harmony and equality and practice community of women and children. It has been described as a "distorted and exaggerated version" of Stoic utopia.[19] It may provide us with a few additional details about the Stoic utopian literature, which will be mentioned later; but none of these can be certain, as we know nothing about the author's sources, nor anything about his purposes, which may have been limited to entertainment. It is sometimes said that Thomas More did something important to the utopian mode by presenting a perfect society in a fully realized narrative form, not an outline proposal like that of Plato (and probably Zeno); but the Hellenistic Greeks knew how to write utopian novels too, and it is not obvious that it made any difference. It is significant that utopian themes were well enough known to educated Greeks to furnish the plot of a novel. Iambulus was read widely enough to last a few centuries and be parodied by Lucian in the *True Story*.

Another example of the genre, of less interest here, was the novel of Euhemerus, which Diodorus also summarized (5.41–46, 6.1). It described an island inhabited by three classes: priests who owned most of the property, soldiers who were given salaries by the priests, and farmers who were allowed nothing but their houses and gardens. It has been supposed to reflect the influence of Plato's utopias. If the alleged Stoic influence on Iambulus was as distorted as this, one's caution increases.

Conclusion: The Rejected Works

Zeno certainly wrote a *Republic*. It was probably only one book long: Clement of Alexandria calls it a "book," and most of the works of Zeno, who was famous for conciseness, were no longer than that (Diog. Laert. 7.4). Platonists thought of it as an attack on the *Republic* of Plato (Q),[20] but we need not assume that was Zeno's primary purpose; perhaps what invited the comparison is the fact that he was exploiting Plato's utopian method. Like Plato's *Republic*, his book described an ideal constitution based on philosophical principles (O); and it was said that it started from the same assumption as Plato, that "justice in the city" and "justice in the citizen" require one another, implying that it attempted to portray both an ideal psychic harmony and an ideal social harmony (P). Like Plato's *Republic*, it contained a series of prescriptions stating how things would be done in the best possible constitution and contrasting these arrangements with the existing ones (B, O, R).[21] The sexual aspects of this. theory were also treated in Zeno's *Art of Love* and *Diatribes*.

Late in the third century Chrysippus, the great systematizer of Stoicism, produced a *Republic* or *On the Republic*. It was similar in form to Zeno's work: the author posed as a fictive lawgiver, and the direct quotations show he advanced a series of criticisms of existing society accomanied by prescriptions setting forth how things would be done in an imaginary society (I, S). This *Republic* was perhaps the most systematic statement of Chrysippus' political theory; aspects of it were developed in his other ethical works.

The third famous work of this type was the mysterious *Republic* attributed to Diogenes the Dog, which by ca. 250 B.C. had been accepted into the Stoic canon by Cleanthes and thereafter was much used by Chrysippus. I have argued that this work must have been either a Cynic parody or a Stoic forgery, and that the importance Stoics assigned to it suggests the latter.

The three *Republics* were often linked, and in fact the evidence does suggest that the Cynic/Stoic utopias were similar in general principle, the main common theme being a version of sexual communism that was obviously freer than Plato's. We are informed of some differences in emphasis, and doubtless there was much difference in detail; but given the paucity of the evidence, it seems justifiable to treat them together, on the assumption that at least the works of Zeno and Chrysippus were variants of the same basic theory.

The three works by Zeno are called the "rejected works" by Diogenes Laertius because after the time of Panaetius the Stoics generally disapproved of them. An attempt to deny the authenticity of the *Republic* failed, but they may have succeeded in getting rid of the *Diatribes* and the *Art of Love*. (The catalog of Zeno's works in Diogenes Laertius 7.4 does not include the *Diatribes*; it does include a *Techne*, which may have been the *Art of Love*, but could as easily have been an *Art of Rhetoric*.) They disputed with some success the authenticity of the *Republic* of Diogenes. They could do nothing about the *Republic* of Chrysippus. But in fact all these works were "rejected" by the common school Stoicism of the Roman Empire, in that they ceased to play any part in ordinary Stoic teaching.

Three groups can be distinguished in this controversy. Firstly, there are the Neostoics, a term I will use for both "Middle" and "Late" Stoicism, or for the mainstream of Stoicism after Panaetius (d. ca. 129 B.C.). They are well known to us from the Stoic literature of the Empire. They rejected the Cynic tradition or admitted it in a very adulterated form, and they had no use for theories about an ideal state. Their views are represented in A–C and J–M. It is clear from those fragments that their main objection, and in some cases their only one, was to the sexual morality of the utopian writings.

Secondly, there is the Cynicizing Stoic tradition represented for us by Diogenes Laertius (D–F), and probably by Plutarch (O) and Athenaeus (V). This seems to be based largely on the handbooks of Apollodorus, written just before the revisionism of Panaetius triumphed. This tradition is not to be identified with Neostoicism: it glorifies the Cynic background of the Stoa, accepts the *Republic* of Diogenes, emphasizes the links between the *Republics* of Diogenes and Zeno, describes forthrightly the kind of sexual communism found in these works. To these Stoics the "rejected works" were not rejected. (Though there are signs of unconvincing attempts to mitigate the rejected teaching. F says that Cynic/Stoic sexual communism was the same as Plato's; V implies that its homosexuality was purely nonphysical.) They emphasize dignified ethical aspects, not the lurid matters described by Philodemus. But why should we assume Philodemus' emphasis is the correct one?

The third group, which has left us practically all our useful information about the contents of the rejected works, consists of philosophical critics of the Stoa. We have a Skeptical version, an Epicurean version, and a Middle Platonic version of this critique. All make much use of the rejected works because they were seen as a vulnerable point in Stoicism. The tradition probably goes back to the attack on Stoicism launched by the New Academy in the third century B.C., in which case some of the arguments rehashed by Sextus Empiricus may have been five hundred years old.

There is a close resemblance between the Epicurean version (J–N) and the Skeptical version (B, C, G–I). Both schools believed a philosopher must accept conventional morality. They treat the prescriptions of the *Republics* as though they were to be literally implemented, and present them in the most shocking light, concentrating heavily on their sexual morality. They declare, in similar language, that these proposals are so impractical they could be implemented only in the most primitive societies.[22] They emphasize the internal divisions of the Stoa on these matters, to puncture the Stoic pretense of dogmatic certainty.

But Plutarch's critique is more sophisticated. He has only two slight allusions (S, U) to the sexual "immorality" of the Stoic utopias, and does not mention sexual communism at all. He has no interest in reviving long-dead controversies within the Stoa; he presumably knew that these theories about ideal states were no longer accepted by contemporary Stoics, any more than such a Platonist as himself accepted the utopias of Plato. He has no interest in explaining that these theories are impractical; he knew that they belonged to a type of philosophical inquiry that did not much interest him or his contemporaries, but an inquiry to which questions of practicality were of little relevance. The general impressions about Stoic utopianism that we receive from Plutarch are not incompatible with the general impressions we receive from the Cynicizing Stoic excerpts. This leads us to hope that the Stoic utopian theory is not totally irrecoverable. First let us try to establish some essential facts about it.

The Outlines of the Stoic Ideal World

Was the Stoic Utopia a Universal Society?

It is clear that the "best constitution" portrayed in Zeno's *Republic* was not confined to a single city; clear not only from O, where the casual and incidental way Plutarch introduces this contrast between the Platonic and Zenonian utopias confirms his testimony, but also from B, where we learn that Zeno's *Republic* had to do with "cities" and that no money would be needed there even for travel. And we know that warfare did not exist in the utopia of Zeno (O), nor in those of Chrysippus and Diogenes (M). To do away with commerce and war Zeno and his imitators clearly had to deal with more than one city, so the ideal society they discussed was always a "*cosmos*," a whole world of ideal cities. Its precise geographical extent did not trouble them—the excerpt used in O emphasizes not extent but absence of juridical boundaries—but obviously it had to be large enough to preclude war, and Plutarch's interpretation of O seems to imply that the half-Phoenician Zeno made no distinction between Greek and barbarian. Since the philosophical city-states that made up this cosmos would all be identical, the Stoics probably confined themselves in practice to describing a single city; this would explain why our sources sometimes put polis in the singular (P, S, V).[23]

The most obvious effect of this universalism would be the prevention of warfare. The promise that imitation of the Cynic life would eliminate war had been a feature of the mock-utopian poetry of Zeno's teacher, Crates. This must have been the most obvious reason why Zeno's *Republic* was considered a reply to Plato's. Furthermore, a universal society that eliminated war would leave open the possibility of a more egalitarian social structure, since the necessity of warfare is the only reason for the existence of a class of guards in Plato's city. But were the Stoics interested in that possibility? We can assume they wanted peace; did they also want equality?

Why Was Education Declared Useless?

It is much more difficult to determine the internal organization of these "cities." We know from Cassius the Skeptic (B) that Zeno stated at the beginning of the *Republic* that the *enkyklia paideia*, the general education, was useless. This statement was thought shocking by the opponents of Stoicism, and at Diogenes Laertius 7.129 we find a hint that some Stoics were embarrased by it: "Chrysippus says the general subjects of instruction are useful." This excerpt, like the ones at D–F, sounds like an attempt to mitigate the more radical utopian teachings.

It is difficult to determine exactly what Zeno meant by this because the meaning of *enkyklia paideia* was changing in his own lifetime. In the Hellenistic world the phrase took on an almost religious significance, as the possession of a standard Greek education based on the classics and the gymnasium became the essential symbol of Greek culture, the thing that distinguished the Greek-speaking classes in the new cities from the rural barbarians surrounding them. The new importance of "education" was recognized by the popularity of treatises on the subject, and one of these writers was Zeno himself, who wrote *On Greek Education, On Listening to Poetry*, and *Homeric Problems* in five books (Diog. Laert, 7.4). If Zeno actually used the phrase "general education" in the *Republic*, we cannot be sure what its exact connotations were, and it is possible that the suggestion it be abolished did not seem quite as shocking then as it did to later generations.

There are several possible interpretations. If we take Zeno's statement literally, and understand *enkyklia paideia* in the broadest sense, then he was expressing the Cynic view that *all* the ordinary subjects at *all* levels were worthless, and that the only worthwhile *paideia* was the Cynic discipline.[24] If that is what Zeno meant then he was still a Cynic when he wrote the *Republic*. I have suggested that is hardly likely. Real Cynics had no need of utopias; the fact that Zeno did shows he no longer believed the wise person dwells among us, and was interested in a much more systematic ethical and political philosophy. (And note the comments of Philodemus in J, K.)

Another possibility is that Zeno was referring to what we call secondary education, which was a possible meaning of *enkyklia paideia* in later times.[25] It is unlikely that he was speaking of the primary schools taught by *grammatistai*, as these were concerned only with basic reading, writing, and counting. And it is unlikely he meant the higher education associated with the ephebate and the gymnasium, for that was always flexible and allowed many variants, including a Stoic philosophical education. But he may have meant the intermediate stage, concerned mostly with classical literature, music, and athletics, with a smattering of math—the core *enkyklia paideia*, the essential key to Greek culture. If so, perhaps what he proposed in the *Republic*, and developed in greater detail in his educational works, was an alternative curriculum based on allegorical interpretation of Homer; another version of the reformed *paideia* that Plato proposed for the guards in his *Republic*. As we will see, there is evidence that Zeno made some sort of provision for the education of the young in his ideal cities. The purpose of such a curriculum will have been to prepare them for advanced studies in Stoic philosophy.[26] The main difficulty with this interpretation is that it is not clear why Cassius the Skeptic or anybody else would have found such an idea so objectionable. Surely an educational program based so heavily on Homer would not have been described as a complete rejection of the *enkyklia paideia*.

I incline therefore to a third interpretation, which was suggested by Festa and by Baldry: Zeno was referring to Plato's *Republic*, and he meant to deny the validity of the elaborate educational plan which Plato proposed for his ruling classes. If the summary at B reproduces accurately the organization of Cassius' polemic, then Cassius made the following points about Zeno's *Republic*. Firstly, Zeno declared the general education useless at the very beginning. Secondly, he separated the wise from the unwise, and thereby declared worthless all our relationships of household, city, and other institutions. In the first point, Zeno was probably criticizing the basic principle of Plato's *Republic*, which is that the just individual and the just city can be produced by *paideia*. If so, then Zeno did not really mean to abolish the ordinary educational curriculum, to the reform of which he seems to have devoted a large proportion of his writing. He only meant that no conceivable pattern of education could do what education is supposed to do in Plato's *Republic*—produce a wise man. If so, then perhaps it was only later, when the *enkyklia paideia* had become a sacred cow, that Zeno's statement about its essential moral uselessness came to seem offensive.

But perhaps all that we can conclude with reasonable certainty is that Zeno opened with an attack on conventional education which opened the way to a more sweeping critique of Greek institutions; and in opposition to all this, set forth his ideal of the wise man, declaring that in the best possible constitution only such wise men as these would be citizens. The last principle also raises difficulties.

Was the Stoic Utopia an Egalitarian Society?

According to Cassius the Skeptic (B) Zeno declared the virtuous (*spoudaioi*) to be the only citizens, the only *oikeioi* (members of the same household), the only friends, and the only free men—the exclusive possessors of every title of social value. But Plutarch (O) says that all men would be citizens in that ideal world. How to reconcile the two statements?

Some think that the ideal city must have included both the wise and the unwise, with the unwise subordinate to the wise. Then Zeno's ideal city would have resembled Plato's, an oligarchy of virtue organized on the principle of strict hierarchy.[27] Plutarch would not have thought such a hierarchy incompatible with social harmony; neither, perhaps, did the Stoics. Stoics repeatedly described the distinction between wise and unwise in the language of rulership: only the wise man knew how to command, only he was fit to be a king, a general, an admiral, a lawmaker, a holder of public office, a judge, an orator, a head of a household, an estate manager. Much of this talk went back to the founders of Stoicism.[28] Would early Stoic principles have permitted social hierarchies in a world governed by reason? This depends largely on our interpretation of the following passage, a summary of Stoic theory about social subordination. We cannot be sure that it all came from Chrysippus:

> Only he [the wise man] is free, but the inferior are slaves. For freedom is the power of autonomous action, but slavery is the lack of autonomous action. There is also a different slavery which consists in subordination, and a third consisting in possession as well as subordination; this last is contrasted with despotism, which is also a morally inferior state. Besides being free the wise are also kings, since kingship is rule that is answerable to no one; and this can occur only among the wise, as Chrysippus says in his work "On Zeno's Proper Use of Terminology." For he says that a ruler must have knowledge of what is good and bad, and that no inferior man has this. Likewise only the wise are holders of public office, judges and orators, where no inferior man is. Diog. Laert. 7.121–22, trans. Long/Sedley

It is clear that the third type, chattel slavery, and its correlative, despotic mastery (*despoteia*), are by definition contrary to nature, therefore they could not exist in a world where everyone followed nature. But is the second type, called simply "subordination" (*hypotaxis*), also contrary to nature? One possible interpretation is that *hypotaxis* means a nondespotic submission to legitimate authority. Then the excerpt implies that such legitimate subordination is in accordance with nature; and if this comes from Chrysippus, it means that there might have been a place for such legitimate subordination in the early Stoic utopia.[29] How could the wise rule, when they could neither use force nor succumb to force (Stobaeus 2.29.3 = SVF 1.216)? We would have to suppose the masses in the ideal world to be a thoroughly regulated crowd like the producers of Plato. This would be necessary to account not only for their voluntary submission but for the absence of punitive laws, traditional religion, and commerce in all classes.

But we cannot recognize this docile population in Cassius' savage description of the inferior. In Plato's city the masses are subordinate to their rulers, but they are all citizens and friends. In Zeno's cities the masses are noncitizens and *enemies* to everyone (B). That a Greek city should contain noncitizens was taken for granted; that it should contain slaves was taken for granted; that it should contain enemies was inconceivable. We cannot reconcile Cassius' picture of unbridgeable social division (B) with Plutarch's Stoic excerpt describing a perfectly harmonious society where all share the same laws and the same way of life, grazing together like a common herd (O). B and O are not talking about the same group of people.[30]

Therefore the alternative interpretation is more plausible. The excerpt must mean that *all* "slavery" is contrary to nature. It seems clear that the wise have nothing to do with any kind of "slavery," and that all the inferior are "slaves" by one definition or another. *Hypotaxis* means all compulsory relationships. All the hierarchies of superior and inferior that make up ordinary society are considered forms of "slavery"; only the form that includes outright possession bears that name in ordinary language, but in Stoic terms every other form of compulsory subordination is a disguised slavery. This can only be an early Stoic doctrine, for it is impossible to imagine Stoics after the time of Panaetius using such terms. Also we are told it was a general Stoic teaching that only the wise man can rule, and that *only he can obey*;[31] therefore if there was subordination in the ideal world it could only be the subordination of wise to wise, not unwise to wise. The slaves and inferior described in the passage quoted above are identical to those described as slaves and inferior in B. They could not have had any place in the ideal world. When O says the ideal world embraced all men, it means "all *wise* men." Zeller was correct when he described the Stoic utopia as a "polity of the wise."[32] Zeno, and doubtless Chrysippus after him, were assuming a world in which all people would be completely rational followers of nature in the Stoic sense. All existing cities, by contrast, they described as based on slavery of some kind; and Plato's attempt to reform such a slave system by educating the rulers they dismissed as useless.

Why No Temples, Law Courts, Gymnasia, Currency?

Zeno said no temples, law courts, or gymnasia were to be built in the cities (B). Dyroff pointed out long ago that this proscription seems to be a comment on Plato's *Laws*, for these are the three main types of public building that surround the agora of Plato's Magnesia.[33] A comparison of this passage from the *Laws* with another fragment of Zeno supports this suggestion. At *Laws* 778d, the Athenian Stranger, immediately after he speaks of the temples and law courts to be built at the center of the city, decides that the city shall imitate Sparta in putting up no walls; and mentions the old saying that city walls should be made of bronze or iron (weapons), not of stone. Several famous Spartans were supposed to have said that a city should rely on weapons and men rather than on walls.[34] And we find the following saying attributed to Zeno: "We ought to adorn cities with the virtues of their inhabitants, not with monuments"; by *anathemata*, monuments, he meant the statues and other votive offerings that crowded the temple precincts of Greek cities (Stob. 4.27.12–14 = SVF 1.266). This sentence is very likely to come from Zeno's *Republic*, as Festa thought. Perhaps Zeno picked up on Plato's comment about the uselessness of walls, and criticized Plato for not going far enough; he said that not only walls, but also temples, law courts, and gymnasia were unnecessary, and he changed the wording of the old Spartan maxim to make this point. Statues commonly appeared in all three types of structure. If this is what he meant, then Zeno's prohibition on public buildings of these types was a prohibition on all ornate and expensive architecture, on the grounds that such luxuries were not in accordance with the simplicity of the Stoic city. We recall that Chrysippus' *Republic* seems to have prohibited public paintings, along with every other luxury.

But there would also have been special reasons for prohibiting those specific types of building. The reason for the prohibition on temples we are told: in the Stoic cities the cults of the gods were to be replaced by the worship of the universal Reason.[35] The argument is clearer in the following fragment of Zeno, which may well be from the *Republic* as Festa thought, and in any case clarifies this point: "We ought not to build temples to the gods, but to possess divinity in the mind alone; or rather to consider the mind as god, for it is immortal" (Epiphanius, *Against Heresies* 3.2.9 = SVF 1.146). It is obvious why a city without crime or litigation would need no law courts.

The prohibition on gymnasia seems to be contradicted by Philodemus (N), which contains a reference to gymnasia in the ideal cities of "Diogenes" and Zeno. It may be that the two texts differed on this detail, and that Philodemus is here referring only to the Diogenic *Republic*. Or perhaps Zeno's prohibition on gymnasia was connected with his attack on Platonic notions of education and intended to abolish only large and costly public gymnasia such as those Plato put at the center of Magnesia. The gymnasia of the *Laws* are associated with Plato's state-controlled educational system, and with military training.

Zeno was opposed to both these institutions, and we may assume he shared the Cynic dislike for professional athletics;[36] but one can think of no reason why Stoic wise people should reject physical training altogether. In fact they insisted on the importance of a dual *askesis* combining mind and body, and as we shall see there would have to be an educational system of some kind in the ideal city; but it would not require elaborate gymnasia.

Zeno seems to have spent some two hundred lines, a great part of the *Republic*, it was only one roll in length, in commenting on *Laws* 778ff., to make the point that a city of the wise would have no need of conventional civic architecture, nor of the conventional civic institutions—religious, legal, educational, military, athletic—that it housed. Plato retained all these things in some form, Zeno wished to propose something more radical. Plato assumed, both in the *Republic* and the *Laws*, that the growth of luxury is irreversible, while Zeno and Chrysippus were capable of assuming that a city of the wise would do nothing whatever for pleasure (cf. S).

Apparently there were to be no public buildings at all around the Stoic ideal agora; but there may not even have been an agora, since all currency was fobidden. On this point the several versions of Stoic utopia may have differed, for *astragaloi*, knucklebones or dice, were used as currency in the *Republic* of "Diogenes," and apparently in that of Chrysippus also. But this is not necessarily a contradiction. In Plato's *Laws* (741e–744a) the common Greek currency is permitted only for foreign travel, and the Magnesians use among themselves some valueless medium of exchange like the iron bars used at Sparta, which Plato does not specify. On this point we have Zeno's exact words: "We do not think it necessary to provide a currency either for exchange or for foreign travel" (B). Once again the language suggests strongly that Zeno was criticizing the *Laws* of Plato as well as the *Republic*. (The implications of this suggestion we will consider later.) Zeno meant that in *his* ideal city the ordinary currency would not be needed for either domestic or foreign exchange, as all citizens would be alike everywhere in that cosmos. This would still permit a valueless medium of exchange, but it is probable that Zeno followed Plato's example and did not bother to specify it. "Diogenes" filled in this detail.

Why did the author of the Diogenic *Republic* pick knucklebone dice for the medium? Perhaps an allusion to the familiar story that Diogenes was told by an oracle to alter the coinage of the city (Diog. Laert. 6.20–21), meaning that he should change all conventional values. Also the use of dice as a symbol of wealth was a rhetorical topic. A fifth-century comedy by Cratinus described the men of Cronus' time playing dice with loaves of bread to illustrate the superabundance of food in the golden age (Ath. 6.267e). The thirtieth oration of Dio Chrysostom (30.35), expanding upon the ancient simile comparing life to a banquet, says that men who play with coins are like revelers who play with dice at the banquet table. Dio makes so much use of the anecdotes about Diogenes the Dog that it seems possible this notion came ultimately from the Diogenic *Republic*; the banquet simile was recurrent in Cynic and Stoic literature, as we shall see. In any case Dio suggests the probable context of the knucklebone-dice currency: even in this world currency is really as worthless as dice to those who see clearly, and in a rational world we would act on this principle and use dice for currency. Such inversions of conventional values would be a perennial motif in the utopian repertory.[37]

The absence of coinage and general economic austerity confirms what we would assume anyway, that there would be complete communism in property in the Stoic ideal world. Community of goods is nowhere explicitly mentioned in our sources, but that is because it is assumed to accompany community of women, and the scandalized attention of the doxographers is entirely riveted by the Stoic notions about the second of these.

In a world without private property or armies or state education or state religion or law codes or law courts, would there be any need for government at all? It is possible that the constitution of the Sun People in the novel of Iambulus was borrowed from the Stoics: they are divided into "associations" (*systemata*) or "kinship groups" (*syngeneia*) including up to four hundred people, in each of which the eldest member acts as a magistrate with kinglike powers. This egalitarian rotating monarchy would have been compatible with Stoic principles and with the institutions of Stoic utopia. Stoics defined a city as a *systema anthropon*, an association of humans (Dio 36.29). When Zeno said there would be no *poleis* or *demoi* (O) he meant that all would follow the same laws and customs and would have no local attachments or loyalties, not necessarily that there would be no form of organization whatever. There were certainly units called "cities," meaning simply agglomerations of population. It is possible Zeno or Chrysippus mentioned that there would have to be local units to replace "demes." The egalitarian Land of Musicanus which Onesicritus the Cynic had discovered in India had a similar rotating arrangement, in which young men took the place of slaves. To Greeks the notion of citizen equality always implied rotation in office (cf. Aristotle, *Pol.* 1261b). Those who wanted to imagine a completely egalitarian society might naturally think of functional rotation as the obvious alternative to Plato's functional hierarchy. In any case we may assume that government in the Stoic ideal world was minimal, noncompulsory, and concerned only with certain administrative functions.

Did the Stoics Teach Incest?

We turn now to the most fully documented aspect of Stoic utopianism: its sexual morality. Most commentators have followed the general interpretation laid out by Zeller over a century ago. Zeller thought the Stoic ideal state was not a state at all; that the early Stoics were incapable of "hearty sympathy" with the state or the family; that their ethical teachings contained much that was "repulsive" and "revolting" and their ideal "state" was designed to give free rein to these anarchical tendencies. The real problem, Zeller thought, was the ethical "onesidedness" Stoics inherited from Cynicism, which led them to neglect the "moral importance of actions"; the Cynic/Stoic ideal of virtue completely disassociated the private sphere from the public and ignored the rules that constitute social life. In the 1890s he was followed by Dyroff, who concluded that the Stoic utopia was the ancient counterpart of anarchism, as the Platonic utopia resembled socialism; and by many others, as we have seen.

Zeller did think that some of the most "repulsive" aspects of Stoic utopian thought were actually less repulsive than they seemed. He was particularly concerned to explain away the ancient charges that Stoics advocated cannibalism and incest. According to Diogenes Laertius (7.121) the Stoics believed the wise would practice cannibalism "in some circumstances" (*kata peristasin*); according to Origen (*Against Celsus* 4.45 = SVF 3.743), Stoics thought incest morally indifferent because it would be right were a wise man and his daughter the only humans left on earth. Zeller concluded from these passages that Stoics discussed cannibalism and incest only as theoretical possibilities in very exceptional circumstances. The "circumstance" to which Diogenes Laertius alludes was probably the danger of starvation. The charge that Stoics freely advocated incest and cannibalism, made by several ancient pagan and Christian writers, was dismissed by Zeller as pure slander.

Here again Zeller has been widely followed, and the effect of this interpretation, though it was intended to exculpate the Stoa, has been to strengthen the impression that there must have been something wildly impractical and unreal about their social and political thought. It is hard to take seriously a political theory seriously concerned with such issues as these, beside which the quibbles of late-medieval scholasticism seem hardheaded realism. This could only be attributed to "einem Hang zu dialektischem Spiel und zu einem lebensfernen Fanatismus der Folgerichtigkeit" (Pohlenz, *Die Stoa* 1.138). Nor did this explanation suffice to explain away all the evidence of anarchism. Zeller could not deny that the early Stoics taught community of women, meaning by this something much more sexually permissive than Plato meant, and there was no way to explain this as a theoretical possibility for certain rare and extreme cases.

Zeller's interpretation has led to two widely shared views about Stoic political thought: firstly, that it was full of antisocial, anarchistic, "Cynic" (in the worst sense) tendencies, and its utopianism little more than a travesty of Plato's; secondly, that it was purely abstract and theoretical and given to the discussion of questions of extraordinary impracticality. As we noted in the introduction, many have concluded that Stoic utopianism could not have been a political theory at all, its worldwide community of sages being only a metaphor for the bond that unites wise and good people in every country. This has strengthened also the impression that Hellenistic political thought in general was remarkably divorced from real political life. I will argue this view is mistaken.

First let us reconsider the provisions affecting sex, marriage, and family in the Stoic utopias. It is clear that in the ideal world the fellowship of the wise was to replace the bonds of kinship entirely. This new kinship was to be established through sexual communism, which was to eliminate jealously. Philodemus (N) makes the system sound like a brothel, and Athenaeus (V) like a monastery. Each can serve as a corrective to the other. Just how much to believe of Philodemus' lurid seventh chapter we do not know, but it induces us to take literally the doxographers' statements about the permissiveness of this system: sexual relations were to be unrestricted as to person, gender, place, and time, and women were to exercise the same sexual freedom as men. (Iambulus may have preserved an additional detail for us: among his Sun People all the women suckle all the infants in rotation to ensure equality of affection.) But this was a philosophical *eros* whose real aim was to cement the friendship of the wise and establish harmony. Philodemus is not to be believed when he says rape was permitted, for this would contradict both Stoic principle and the words of the doxographers, who emphasize that sexual relations would be based on consent.[38] Athenaeus is not to be believed when he implies that pederastic relations were nonphysical; there was no point in repeating the anecdote about Diogenes' public masturbation if it did not mean that sexual pleasures are harmless when done for rational motives.[39]

The purpose of this sexual communism was not pleasure, but what Zeno called Eros. Eros was a real god with ancient cults in some places, but since the time of Hesiod he had figured also in poetry and philosophy as a personified abstraction representing cosmological and psychological forces. The immediate background of Zeno's doctrine was doubtless the philosophical exploitation of Eros in Plato's dialogues, and Zeno doubtless meant by this a philosophical love similar to the concept of love developed in Plato's *Phaedrus* and *Symposium*. In those dialogues Eros, without losing its primary connotation of sexual desire, becomes a term for every form of passionate desire, an element found in all worthy activities; in its higher forms, a love of moral and intellectual excellence. But even in those dialogues Plato believed the physical consummation of love between individuals was an impediment to the higher forms of love, and in his designs for ideal states he allows only the most grudging room for it. There he is chiefly concerned with the dangers of physical sexuality, which he thought strengthened the appetitive part of the soul at the expense of the higher functions. Zeno clearly allowed a much larger place for Eros, and emphasized his public and civic role. The statement that Eros is a god who contributes to the *soteria*, preservation, of the city (V) may mean that Zeno called him Eros Soter—Saviour of the City, like Zeus Soter and Athena Soteira at Athens. Zeno could not have thought the physical Eros a necessary impediment to the moral/intellectual Eros. Doubtless he was influenced by the Cynic tradition of frankness about bodily matters, and perhaps also by the fact that Stoic psychology assumed the soul to be unitary; since they did not believe there was a separate appetitive function to which sexual desire could be assigned, they would not have shared Plato's conviction that the physical aspect of Eros had to be totally sublimated if it was to lead to the philosophical quest for truth.

Several references to the matter (E, L, N, U, V) suggest that the Eros Zeno had in mind was largely homosexual, but we may assume that in the ideal city this Eros would be directed toward and by both genders. We have a quotation from Zeno's *Diatribes*—another "rejected work," which was said to teach the same erotic doctrine as his *Republic* (B)—in which he tells his audience to have intercourse (*diamerizein*) equally with males and females, equally with one's *paidika* (boyfriend) and with those who are not *paidika*. This injunction appeared in a passage about the education of the young. It was the frank sexuality that shocked Sextus (*Outlines* 3.245; *Against Prof.* 11.190) and his sources, but the original point was probably equal treatment of the genders. Zeno was probably arguing that the educational value of *paiderastia* should be bestowed on both girls and boys, not confined to the latter as in Greek custom. Even Plato had assumed that in a society where males and females were educated together, *paiderastia* (a gender-free term which literally means "love of youth," though in practice "love of boys") would be felt toward girls as well as boys (*Laws* 836a).

In Zeno's *Republic* both homosexual and heterosexual relations were intended to promote friendship, concord, and freedom. Eros meant the affection that the wise feel for other wise people, particularly the bond between the adult wise and those who were learning to be wise. The emphasis on the educational value of the bisexual Eros (E) shows that Zeno's ideal society did have some kind of educational system.

But why all the incest? Philodemus (N) thought this one of the most shocking things about the Diogenic and Zenonian utopias, and Chrysippus was even more identified with the issue. The quotation from Chrysippus' *Republic* given by Sextus (I) is sufficient to show that Zeller's explanation will not do. Whatever Chrysippus was thinking of, he was not thinking of a hypothetical situation in which a wise man and his daughter would be the only people left on earth. That must be an interpretation put forward by later Stoics to explain a teaching of Chrysippus that they had come to think embarrasing. There was some more important reason for Chrysippus' interest in the ethics of incest. And I suggest this reason is not hard to find. Most modern commentators seem to have missed the connection betweem "incest" and "community of women." To Greeks the most objectionable thing about the notion of sexual communism was that it made the possibility of accidental incest unavoidable. Plato could not succeed in avoiding it entirely, which drew Aristotle's condemnation. Aristotle would have objected even more strenuously to the Stoic system of communal marriage, in which no blood relationship could be determined with certainty. Zeno may have passed over this problem in his short *Republic*, but certainly his followers would have been attacked on this ground, probably by the Peripatetics and the skeptical New Academy. When Chrysippus laid out his massive defense of Zeno's ideals in the later third century, he met this objection head on and argued that in the circumstances of the ideal city there would be nothing wrong with occasional cases of unintentional incest.

There was another context in which the subject of incest might arise: the Cynic/Stoic attack on superstition. It will be recalled that the Cynic mock tragedy *Oedipus* seems to have argued that no religious defilement could be incurred by a case of accidental incest, using examples drawn from animal and barbarian behavior. Zeno wrote on the same theme. Sextus has preserved a quotation, perhaps from *On Listening to Poetry*, in which Zeno defends the relationship between Oedipus and Jocasta: he says there was nothing wrong with his rubbing her private parts, any more than in rubbing any other part of her body (*Outlines* 3.205, 246; *Against Prof.* 11.191). The language recalls Diogenes' refusal to see any difference between rubbing his belly and his private parts. Both statements suggest an effort to demystify sexuality and strip it of religious taboos. Zeno was making the same point as the Cynic *Oedipus*: there can be no such thing as religious pollution unconnected with intention. This reinterpretation of the Oedipus legend seems to have played a prominent part in the Cynic/Stoic critique of superstition.

The antisuperstition dossier was older than the Stoic theory of sexual communism, but incest was a problem to both, and arguments inspired by the first issue could easily be applied to the second. That seems to be what Chrysippus did in his *Exhortation to Philosophy* (T), where incest is linked to other religious taboos. He mentions the commonest Greek prohibitions connected with sacrifice: participants were expected to refrain from various foods, and not to go a temple directly from a childbed or deathbed. Like the Cynic *Oedipus*, he argued that incest could not be against nature because it is practiced by animals and Persians. This had been a traditional argument for cultural relativism since the time of Herodotus. In the third century it had even greater credibility because Greeks knew more about the East, where incestuous marriage was in fact customary in some areas; and now there were even Greek examples in the brother-sister unions of the Ptolemaic dynasty. A fundamental taboo such as incest posed an important problem for those interested in developing a wholly rational approach to religion and morality. In the *Laws* (838) Plato mentioned the unwritten law against incest, with reference to the Oedipus legend, as an example of the unanimous and unthinking obedience to custom that he would like to strengthen in his ideal world. The Stoics appear to have seen it as an example of what they would like to abolish.

The Stoic defense of incest shows that they took the principle of community of women most seriously. Therefore the Stoic utopia was not just a metaphor for the life of the wise man under present conditions. No one has ever explained how "community of women" could have fitted into such a life anyway. Stoic utopia was in some fashion a plan for the reformation of society.

Did the Stoics Teach Cannibalism?

The charge of incest was often linked to that of cannibalism. It is clear there was something in the *Republic* of "Diogenes" that was thought to advocate cannibalism. Philodemus, in his sixth chapter (M), says that the *Republic* contained the same teachings as Diogenes' tragedies *Philiscus*, *Atreus*, and *Oedipus*. We do not know what the *Philiscus* was about, but the *Atreus* must be the *Thyestes*, and he must mean that the *Republic* contained similar arguments against taboos concerning incest and cannibalism. In his seventh chapter (N), describing the ideal states of Diogenes and Zeno, there is a fragmentary sentence which stated, according to the reconstruction of Dorandi, that men were to kill their dying parents and eat them. Then Chrysippus commented on the problem of cannibalism, with specific reference to the Diogenic *Republic*, in two of his ethical works—but not, apparently, in his *Republic*. In *On Justice* he occupied nearly an entire book with the argument that there was nothing wrong with eating corpses and amputated limbs (C, I, M, with my comments).

In *On Proper Functions* he wrote that we should dispose of our dead parents by the simplest means possible, and might even eat them (I). Clearly Chrysippus discussed cannibalism in connection with a critique of conventional burial customs, and his purpose was not to advocate cannibalism but to recommend indifference to funeral rites. We know that he collected information about the funeral customs of various nations (Cic., *Tusc. Disp.* 1.45.108); these will have included the corpse-eating Indians of Herodotus and Onesicritus' Bactrians who gave their dying to the dogs to eat. Contempt for conventional funerals was a Cynic/Stoic commonplace. Chrysippus was saying what they all said: we should not care what happens to our bodies after death; the question of whether they are to be buried or burned or even eaten as the Indians do should be a matter of complete indifference to us.[40] The doxographer's statement "The wise man will eat human flesh under certain circumstances" (Diog. Laert. 7.121) most likely meant, to Chrysippus, that this would be appropriate if one lived among Indians or some other society where this was customary.

What role did cannibalism play in the *Republic* of "Diogenes"? Perhaps the author attributed to his utopians some such practice as that of Iambulus' Sun People, who dispose of their dead by burying corpses in the sand of the seashore at low tide. This method would be particularly appropriate to an island, where Iambulus' novel is set, but it is probable that all the Stoic utopias proposed some simple procedure for disposing of bodies without ceremony or memorial. The author of the Diogenic *Republic*, trying to live up to Diogenes' reputation for *anaideia*, probably had them eat the bodies in Hindu fashion.[41]

Conclusion: The Community of the Wise

The evidence suggests that when Stoics responded to Plato's political theories they considered the *Republic* and the *Laws* as aspects of the same system. Aristotle also regarded them as closely similar. If we look at these dialogues in that way it becomes obvious that they contain political goals on two different levels, the one being an application of the other. The two levels are discernable even in the *Republic*, where Plato seems never quite to decide between the practical goal of the rule of the guards and the theoretical goal of the rule of the wise. I suggest that the key to Stoic utopianism is that the Stoics decided to dispense altogether with the rule of the guards. What interested Zeno was the *higher* utopian mode of Plato's *Republic*: a method for articulating an ideal of moral perfection by showing the environment in which virtue can flourish optimally. His criticism of Plato was mostly intended to eliminate the lower utopianism, the desire for power and the mechanisms for rule, which Plato allowed to compromise his ideals. Zeno began by asserting that the Platonic education, which was largely for military purposes, cannot produce the rule of the wise; justice does not exist except in the Stoic wise person; the only just city would be one inhabited solely by such types; and then he proceeded to show how such a society could eliminate practically all the existing institutional structure of the city-state, which Plato had retained in various forms in both the *Republic* and the *Laws*.

The most obviously Cynic element in Zeno's *Republic* was its sexual morality.

His philosopher-rulers behave like a group of Cynicizing Stoics, not like a group of Platonists. This was the main reason why they said it was written on the Dog's tail. We notice, though, that the positive role Zeno assigned to Eros was as un-Cynic as it was un-Platonic. Both Plato and Diogenes had relegated sexual desire to the level of animal instinct, an itch to be satisfied, differing only in their conclusions: the one thought it should not be satisfied, the other that it should be. There seems to have been no precedent for Zeno's decision to endow Eros, in every sense of the word, with philosophical and political purpose.

I have left to the end the most puzzling fragment of all. At the beginning of the *Republic* Zeno said that it set forth what was fitting (*prosphoron*) for his own time and place (J). He also revealed at the beginning that his proposals would be far more utopian than Plato's; yet somehow this would not deprive them of relevance to contemporary society. In addition to the relationship among the wise, which was the main theme of the *Republic*, a relationship between the wise and the unwise was assumed. The purpose of the Stoic utopian literature was to show how those who wished to imitate the wise should live in the here and now. But we have no clear statement about this relationship, except perhaps for Zeno's injunction about marriage (D), and even there we are not told what the connection was between this commonplace advice and the communal sexuality described elsewhere in the same book. I will offer some suggestions, based on our knowledge of early Stoic moral teaching, as to how the relationship may have worked.

The Stoics and Society

Community of Goods in Practice: All Things Belong to the Wise

The doxography of Diogenes Laertius includes the following definition of friendship: "They [the Stoics] say that friendship is for the virtuous alone, because of their likeness; they call it a certain community [*koinonia*] affecting everything in life, treating our friends as ourselves" (7.124). A few lines later (7.125) occurs the following statement about property:

> And all things belong to the wise; the law has given them complete authority. Some things are said to belong to the inferior, in the way that we say that unlawful possessions belong in one sense to the city, and in another sense to those who are making use of them.

This seems to be an elaboration of the Cynic formula about property, which contributed the basic principle, "All things belong to the wise." But the Cynic interpretation of this maxim was concerned with the relationship between the wise person and the gods, and the point was to show the godlike self-sufficiency of the wise. The Stoic version is concerned with the community of friendship that exists among the wise, and also with the relationship between the wise and unwise. It seems to be a summary of an argument that analyzed the meaning of ownership. The ordinary Greek legal vocabulary did not go much beyond the verb "to have." But the Stoics wished to show that the question of who "has" something can be considered on different levels.

(1) At the highest level, in a condition where the law of reason and nature is followed, there would be no property rights at all; people would need few goods and share them as among friends. This is the *koinonia*, based upon the love of the wise for one another, that the Stoic utopian works depicted. (2) But since nearly all are morally inadequate, property rights must exist by the law of the city; therefore we speak of inferior people as owning things. (3) It is also possible to hold property without any right at all, as in the case of a thief. The thief has a *de facto* possession, but the *de iure* possessor is the polis. (The example seems to assume a situation where the real owner cannot be found.)

The third level, which corresponds to what the Roman law called *possessio*, is introduced to draw an analogy, clarifying the relationship between levels one and two: the law of the city is to the law of nature what theft is to the law of the city. In the eyes of reason, *all* claims to exclusive ownership in civil law represent only a *de facto* possession, just as theft represents only a *de facto* possession in the eyes of civil law. Now this doctrine, on first consideration, seems to deprive the second level of all legitimacy whatever. The Stoics, anticipating Proudhon, seem to declare private property the equivalent of theft. But of course that is not what they meant. This is a typical Stoic paradox.

Paradoxa, "things contrary to common opinion," was a Stoic technical term for the apparently nonsensical statements Stoics were forever making about the perfections of the wise man. Zeno said the wise man is rich even if he is a beggar (Cic., *On Ends* 5.28.84). Stoics commonly claimed the wise man was the only king, politician, priest, head of a household, manager of property. These statements were attempts to express the implications for ordinary life and language of the central Stoic tenet that only virtue has value; riddles about the relationship between the two levels of moral consciousness. They use bald and uncompromising language to shock their audiences into a realization of the meaning of the *telos*. They do not say the wise man is *like* a rich man or the only one fit to be a rich man; he *is* the only rich man. The paradoxes do not imply that the wise man rejects everything on the lower level, only that he sees everything differently from those on the lower level. In his eyes all property is "theft," as all subordination is "slavery." But the rare wise or would-be-wise individual who tried to live on the first level had at the same time to recognize the "values" of the second level, which Stoics always admitted were endowed by nature with a certain degree of preferability. The *Republic* of Zeno may perhaps be described as an extended *paradoxon*, intended to show what life on the highest level of moral consciousness would be like were it left free to fulfill itself.

Community of Goods in Practice: The Theater Topos

There is a second important passage setting forth a Stoic theory of property:

> . . . and because the nature of man [Chrysippus said] is such that between each of us and the rest of the human race there lies something like a civil law, he who keeps this law will be just and he who departs from it will be unjust. But the theater is a common possession, and yet it can legitimately be said that each has a right to the place that he has occupied; and likewise in the common city and the common world the law does not prevent any person from having his own possessions. Cicero, *On Ends* 3.20.67

The theater was not the only symbol of public property used by Stoics. The Roman Stoic writers also use the simile of a place at the banquet, an image of Cynic origin.[42] In addition, the Roman legal vocabulary provided them with a number of analogies not available to Greeks that clarified the notion that a thing might belong to more than one person at the same time. Seneca compared the ultimate ownership exercised by the wise over all things to the *dominium* that the master of the household exercises over all the goods of the household, and private property he compared to the conditional leases or shares held by the master's tenants, children, or slaves.[43]

Only the first part of this passage is explicitly attributed to Chrysippus by Cicero. Did the theater *topos* also come from Chrysippus? There is room for doubt because we notice that here and in other passages (especially Sen., *On Benefits* 7.12; and Epict., *Disc.* 2.4) the theater *topos* is introduced in order to qualify the doctrine that all things belong to the wise. The point that the Roman Stoics often concentrate upon is that individual properties, though temporary and conditional shares in something larger, are nevertheless legitimate shares; and often with the implication that shares will be unequal, like seats in the theater and at the banquet. The social implications of the theater *topos* are usually conservative, as those of the doctrine of universal ownership by the wise are radical. This raises the possibility that the theater *topos* was of Neostoic origin.

But several considerations incline me to think that the theater *topos* goes back to the early Stoa. Its implications are not entirely conservative even for the Roman Stoics. The *topos* has at least three interpretations, and different writers emphasize one or another of these. It may demonstrate the temporary nature of property; it may demonstrate the legitimate and unequal nature of property; or it may demonstrate the communal nature of property and encourage liberality. We find all three interpretations in Seneca and Epictetus. Is there any reason to suppose that all three could not have been found in the early Stoa? Not really. The scanty surviving evidence for the practical moral teaching of Zeno and Chrysippus on property shows that they took private property for granted—how could they not, if they were to have a practical moral teaching at all?—and dispensed much the same common-sense advice concerning the use of it that we find elsewhere in the Greek moral traditon.[44] Those who think the theater *topos* was introduced later to justify private property must think it replaced some more egalitarian symbol of communal property found in the original utopia of Zeno, such as the agora. But a Greek agora was also divided into temporary shares, especially on market days. There is no kind of communal property that does not involve individual shares. And the seats in a Greek theater were all more or less equal.[45] (This was definitely not the case in Roman theaters, where separate tiers of seats were reserved for the senatorial and equestrian orders. This point was emphasized by Seneca. It imparted a much more conservative tone to the theater *topos* in the hands of Roman Stoics.) There may well have been a theater even in Zeno's city, for theaters are conspicuously absent from the list of public buildings he excluded. We conclude that the theater *topos* probably goes back to Chrysippus, and would not have been incompatible with the theories of Zeno. The theater would have been a convenient symbol of the Stoic ideal of the use of property because it was perhaps the most striking example known to the Greeks of a public building shared equally by all the citizens. The theater image provided a link between the law of reason and the law of the city. On the second level, it meant that all private property must be used like a seat in the public theater or at the public banquet. The wise, and all who wanted to become wise, were to remember at all times that the theater of this world is a common possession, our occupancy of parts of it being temporary and subject to the common good.

There is some evidence that the popular moral teaching of the early Stoics was more egalitarian than the common Greek tradition. They do not seem to have shared the contempt for manual labor so evident in Plato and Aristotle. It was said that Zeno made Cleanthes earn his living as a drawer of water (Diog. Laert. 7.168–71). Chrysippus' *On Ways of Living* discussed the popular topic of how a philosopher ought to support himself and apparently concluded that any way at all was allowable—in contrast to Plato and Aristotle, who assumed the philosopher should be a landowning gentleman. The anti-Stoic excerpt inserted at Diogenes Laertius 7.189 (quoted in part at C) includes the following quotation from *On Ways of Living*, which was probably thought objectionable because of its Cynic overtones:[46]

> The modes of earning a living are absurd: if one lives off a king one must submit to him; if off one's friends, friendship is bought and sold; if off one's wisdom, it is for hire.

Something of this attitude survived even among the Roman Stoics. Epictetus and Dio took a favorable view of the occupations of the poor and refused to consider poverty a barrier to philosophy; which were unusual attitudes at that period, even among Stoics.[47] Arius Didymus said that Stoics counted "moderate property" among the natural preferences, suggesting that their ideal was to equalize property as far as possible (Stob. 2.80.22 = SVF 3.136). And in speaking both of ideal cities and real cities the early Stoics seem to have favored the word "inhabitants" rather than "citizens," suggesting an attempt to blur the distinction between citizen and noncitizen.[48]

Community of Women in Practice

The early Stoics thought that in a world where all were wise there would be only partnerships based on free choice, no exclusive households, no kinship ties. But they also expected that in this imperfect world the wise man would become head of a household. Even in the *Republic* Zeno said the wise man would marry and have children (D), and he must have meant conventional marriage.[49] Chrysippus also said the wise man would marry, and there were treatises *On Marriage* by Zeno's disciples Cleanthes and Perseus.

What was the connection between the two levels? It is harder to find than in the case of property, because the silence of later Stoicism about sexual communism is nearly total. They remembered that with respect to property the theater-banquet *topos* had both a negative meaning: a warning against theft, and a positive meaning: an inducement to liberality. Only Epictetus (*Disc.* 2.4; *Manual* 15) mentions the *topos* in connection with family life, and he interprets it only in a negative sense, a warning against adultery. But to the early Stoics sexual communism must have had a positive meaning as well. I suggest that its main point was to emphasize the importance of *eros* and *philia* in familial and sexual relations.

The basic Stoic teaching on love never changed. They always taught that *eros* is in itself a morally indifferent thing, which becomes a proper function only when directed toward friendship. By *philia*, they meant mutual respect among the wise. The wise person loves other wise people because he or she perceives in them sparks of the same universal reason realized in the self and loves the inferior only insofar as they are teachable. The definition of the good *eros*, that controlled by reason, was "an effort to make friends through the appearance of beauty" (Stob. 2.115.1 = SVF 3.650; Diog. Laert. 7.129–30). Among his other perfections the wise man was the only fit *erotikos*. There were more early Stoic treatises on love than on marriage; five of Zeno's disciples wrote such works. Probably all emphasized the value of the physical attraction felt by the wise toward those who were youthful, unwise, and teachable. Probably all emphasized *paiderastia*. There was an early tradition—from the biographer Antigonus of Carystus, fl. 240 B.C.—that Zeno had been exclusively attracted to boys, never to girls, a rare thing for Greeks to notice (Ath. 13.563e). The Athenian decree granting Zeno a public funeral noted how he had led the youth of the city toward virtue by his teaching and example (Diog. Laert. 7.10).

On the other hand, the doxography on love at Diogenes Laertius 7.129–30, based on Zeno, Chrysippus, and Apollodorus, makes it clear that this *eros* was to apply to both genders. One of these used the example of Thrasonides, a character in Menander's lost comedy *Misumenos*, who had his mistress in his power but abstained from her because she disliked him, to show that *eros* must be based on *philia*. (The example, by the way, proves that Stoic *eros*, so long as it was based on *philia*, did not rule out physical satisfaction. The Greeks did not know of a nonsexual relationship with a mistress.)[50]

There was also a bad sort of *eros*, not associated with rational friendship, which Stoics classed among the *pathe*, the irrational movements of the soul. Hence we find Zeno and Cleanthes reproving effeminacy and infatuation for boys in Cynic terms (Diog. Laert. 7.17, 18, 23, 166, 174). And we may assume that the early Stoics, like the later, condemned adultery. But like the Cynics, they regarded sexual desires untouched by these vices as indifferent so long as they were kept under control. Antigonus of Carystus passed on the following anecdote, perhaps from the *Sympotic Memoirs* of Perseus: Zeno's disciple Perseus purchased the services of a flute girl at a symposium but hesitated to bring her into his house because Zeno was staying there; whereupon Zeno pulled her inside and shut her up with Perseus (Diog. Laert. 7.13; Ath. 13.607 ef). Zeno was himself above such indulgences but made no objection to them in others, even Stoic philosophers. The anti-Stoic polemic summarized by Sextus criticized the (early) Stoics because they did not disapprove of sexual relations between males, nor of prostitution (*Outlines* 3.200–201). Elsewhere Sextus quotes a bit of dialogue from one of Zeno's works, perhaps the *Diatribes* again, which in his day was thought shocking, and was probably thought to exhibit a Cynic frankness even in Zeno's day: a man discusses with a friend his unsuccessful attempt to have intercourse (*diamerizein*) with his boyfriend (*Against Prof.* 11.190).

Much about early Stoic sexual ethics remains mysterious. What kind of *paiderastia* did they approve? Conventional *paiderastia* was a hierarchical relationship between man and boy, strictly divided into active/passive roles. Plato had elevated it into a reciprocal exchange of affection, in which physical pleasure was replaced by moral and intellectual fulfillment.[51] Stoic *paiderastia*, we may assume, was also a reciprocal moral/intellectual relationship; but since they apparently admitted physical relations, did they so far defy Greek convention as to admit a *physical* reciprocity? If they did, then what did Zeno mean when he reproved effeminacy? One imagines that the more daring Stoic propositions, like the possibility of reciprocal sexual relations with boys (and girls!) of citizen status, were confined to the utopian area. Otherwise it is difficult to believe the Athenians would have congratulated him for setting a model for youth. In the dialogue cited by Sextus at *Against Prof.* 11.190, we do not know that the boyfriend in question is a citizen.

On the whole the evidence suggests that the popular moral teaching of the early Stoics on love and marriage was in accordance with Greek conventions of behavior, though it tested the limits of Greek conventions of language. It was much less ascetic than the position of Plato, but so were the views of most Greeks. Stoics taught that to marry and have children for the good of the city, to honor kinsmen, to love boys and women for the sake of teaching them virtue, were preeminently proper functions and in accord with nature; but only if done for those motives. The wise and would-be-wise were supposed to remember the model of the ideal city, where there are no distinctions of birth or wealth, where no households or kinship ties exist, and where all relationships are based on friendship and the true *eros*. In this world it went without saying that the wise man would be part of an *oikos* and lead a normal social life; but he would try to base all his relationships on *philia*, whether with wife, children, kin, friends, or lovers.

Sexual communism seems the most egalitarian aspect of Stoic social thought. They assumed women would ideally be treated the same as men, and this equality went far beyond what Plato had proposed. To argue that "Virtue is the same for men and women" (the title of a work by Cleanthes)[52] did not necessarily imply men and women were equal. The egalitarian quality of the

Stoic theory was the assumption that relations with wives and even mistresses should be based on friendship. Their ideal of friendship was egalitarian because it was heavily influenced by *paiderastia*, the principal cultural model for free relationships between citizens. The conventional type of *paiderastia* was not an equal relationship, but its hierarchy was based on age, not class. Plato had turned it into a reciprocal relationship between equals, but avoided making use of it in his ideal states. The Stoics appear to have made it a universal social ideal. How far they carried this in practice we do not know. As we will see, the tradition of sexual equality was not entirely dead even among the Roman Stoics.

The Drowning Men

In the preceding pages I have attempted a somewhat hypothetical description of what early Stoic practical morality may have been like. This, I suggest, is what Zeno meant when he said the proposals in his *Republic* were suitable for his own time and place. But for whom were they suitable? Who was supposed to practice them? The radical Stoic precepts are meant only for *wise* people, an entirely theoretical category. Therefore many have assumed that the utopian teachings could have had no relevance to ordinary morality in the real world. That seems to me most improbable.

The Stoic insistence on an absolute moral standard did not mean they denied the value of progress toward virtue. It is true they always emphasized the gulf separating the wise from the unwise and insisted all the unwise were equally unwise: all "progressors" (*prokoptontes*) remained unwise until the moment of enlightenment, just as a man one cubit under water and a man five hundred fathoms down are equally drowning; or as a blind man about to recover his sight is still as sightless as a man blind for life (Plut., *Common Conceptions* 1063a; Cic., *On Ends* 3.14.48). But the examples themselves show that such a thing as progress in virtue existed, could be recognized, and was of great value. The two drowning men may be in the same condition at the moment, but we can see that the first will probably be rescued and the second will surely drown. Zeno himself compared Plato to the tyrant Dionysius to show that some of the unwise could progress much closer to wisdom than others (Cic., *On Ends* 4.20.56). He obviously meant the difference was significant. (We notice, by the way, that Zeno's judgment of Plato was not always critical. The point of this comment appears to be the great gulf that separates some progressors from others, and perhaps the fallacy of Plato's attempts to directly apply his ideals to political life.) I suggest that Stoic ethical teaching was very much concerned with the *prokoptontes* from the start. Its real object was not the invisible wise one but the would-be-wise, those drowning who have reason to hope for salvation. Zeno, Cleanthes, Chrysippus, Sphaerus all wrote treatises *On Proper Functions*. The quotation from Chrysippus in I, in which he encourages his audience to ignore traditional funeral customs, has nothing to do with ordinary morality. But it is probable that these works also treated at length the proper functions of a progressor (cf. Plut. 1045e, 1047f), and tried to establish a moral code for those who wished to live as much as possible like the wise in the real world; for people like themselves.

For the early Stoics, though they thought constantly in terms of two levels of moral behavior, did not mean by this that there were two different moral codes, one for (imaginary) wise people and one for real people. They thought that a wise person, should one appear, would perform exactly the same proper functions as everybody else. He would, however, perform them all for the right reasons. *Kathekonta*, proper functions, when performed by the wise became *katorthomata*, acts of perfect rectitude. But every *katorthomaton* was also a *kathekon*. The two levels meant different levels of moral consciousness, not different codes of behavior.

There is one area where we can see the relationship between the two levels clearly. In the sphere of religion, the Stoics never quite forgot the utopian doctrine. (For reasons to be examined later, the idea of abolishing temples was much less unsettling than the idea of abolishing households.) They taught that in an ideal world the traditional cults of the gods would be entirely replaced by a philosophical cult of reason. But in practice Stoics always participated regularly in cults, considering them metaphorical approaches to true religion. One of the Stoic paradoxes was that only a wise person is fit to be a priest, because only he knows how to worship the gods rightly; and by this they meant specifically a knowledge of cultic practice and ritual (SVF 3.544, 604ff.). The bridge between the two was the Stoic theology, a systematic effort to turn the traditional myths into cosmological or moral allegory. It was said that its basic principles were established by Zeno, and developed by Cleanthes and Chrysippus (Cic., *On the Nature of the Gods* 2.24.63). Honoring the gods was a proper function for everyone; but only the progressor knew how to do it rightly, for only he understood what the gods were. If the progressor became wise he would do the same things, and then they would be acts of perfect rectitude.

Here alone are we told how the system worked. But I suggest that similar connections were made in other areas of life. Only the wise person knew how to conduct the rites because only he understood that they were not necessary. Only the wise have natural affection for children (Diog. Laert. 7.120) because only they understand that ideally this would be bestowed on all children and not just on their biological offspring. Only the wise man is fit to be an *oikonomos*, head of a household (SVF 1.216), because only he understands that in an ideal world there would be no *oikoi* and no slaves, and therefore has the disposition needed to command a household and own slaves.

If the wise or almost-wise person acts exactly like everybody else, why does the distinction between wise and unwise matter so much? The philosophical opponents of the Stoics constantly attacked them on this point, arguing that the distinction is a meaningless form of words, the Stoic wise man not really different from the ideal wise man of Plato or Aristotle (an argument best summarized in the fourth book of Cicero's *On Ends*). Among the later Stoics the distinction does seem a meaningless form of words, but that is because they had forgotten the utopian vision. It was important to the early Stoics to contemplate a world where all people were virtuous because only then could they realize that a world governed by the law of *katorthomata* would indeed be different. Those who have suggested that these utopias were meant to shock are partly correct, for one of the main purposes of the utopian method was to shock its audience into an awareness of new possibilities in human nature and society.

The Stoics and Politics

The Impediments to Political Duty

Communism had a direct moral relevance to the Stoics, but was it also intended to be a constitutional model? The question is difficult because the Stoic doxographical tradition is so confused and obscure about political matters as to suggest the presence of deep conflicts.

Only Cleanthes made politics a separate branch of philosophy,[53] the other Stoics treating it as part of ethics; but they considered it an important part, to judge from the number of their political writings, some of which dealt with such practical matters as councils, law courts, and oratory. Some interest in ethnography is also discernable.[54] Furthermore, the extant fragments indicate a positive attitude toward political life. Zeno and Chrysippus taught that participation in politics is a basic duty for the wise, provided that nothing "impede" them (*koluein, impedire*); meaning that they were required to participte in politics if they saw a reasonable chance to promote virtue thereby.[55]

But the politics of the great Stoics are shrouded in ambiguity. In later centuries both Stoic apologists and their opponents commented on the odd fact that the founders of the Stoa thought politics a primary proper function and yet avoided such activity themselves.[56] Zeno, Cleanthes, and Chrysippus all left their cities; it was said that the first two remained metics at Athens from choice, refusing Athenian citizenship; Chrysippus eventually became an Athenian citizen but apparently he may as well not have for all the imprint this left on the city. Both Zeno and Cleanthes refused places at court offered them by the most powerful kings of the age; Chrysippus' reputation for independence was such that no king seems to have made the offer.[57] Chrysippus left several maxims that reveal a high estimate of the dangers of "impediment" in politics. Asked if one should enter politics, he replied that if one does evil in politics he will displease the gods; and if good, men.[58] In *On Ways of Living* he called politics a fundamental duty, but also said the wise man should be *apragmon*, one who minds his own business (a term that usually implied an avoidance of political life); and in the same work condemned the life of study as equivalent to a life of pleasure, which does not seem to leave much room for anyone who wanted to be *apragmon.*[59] Plutarch thought all this amounted to a glaring contradiction. Certainly it seems evidence of a deep tension.

How did the Stoics decide whether or not virtue would be impeded in a given political situation? There are some excerpts that imply the existence of a Stoic constitutional theory. The epitome compiled by Arius Didymus in the Augustan age says that they thought the wise person would go into politics especially in those constitutions that show "progress" toward the perfect constitutions, *teleias politeias* (Stob. 2.94.7 = SVF 3.611). This seems to imply some sort of theory about a lower utopia. But there is no clue in the doxographies as to what this was, except for one statement in Diogenes Laertius: "The best constitution is the one mixed of democracy, monarchy, and aristocracy" (7.131). We have already seen the variety of theories that might be covered by the phrase "mixed constitution" in the fourth century and we have no notion what it meant in the third.[60] For all that we know, both these excerpts are of Neostoic origin.

Some have thought that the early Stoics favored monarchy, even that they were largely responsible for the development of a theory of Greek kingship. There were many treatises *On Kingship* in the third century, some of them by Stoics, but it was the Peripatetics who seem to have specialized in the genre, and no specifically Stoic contributions to it can be isolated. As we have seen, Stoic cosmological and ethical discourse was filled with political metaphors: they often described the world order as a political structure, a city of gods and humans with gods as rulers and humans as subjects; they often described the ideal wise person in terms of kingship and other political functions. But these metaphors had no more obvious connection with real kingship than had the "kingly art" of Socrates. The elitism of Stoic ethics does not necessarily imply an affinity with monarchy or aristocracy, because Stoics were not elitists in Plato's sense. Their wise people were too few to count, and they insisted all fools were equally foolish.

Zeno is supposed to have been a friend of King Antigonus Gonatas of Macedon, but it is possible (as suggested by Erskine, *Hellenistic Stoa*) that his connection with Antigonus was exaggerated by his disciple Perseus, a courtier of Antigonus whose memoirs were probably an important source for the biographers of Zeno. One of these biographers, Apollonius of Tyre, probably a Neostoic, preserved for us a probably spurious correspondence (Diog. Laert. 7.6–9) in which the king sets forth a philosophical justification for monarchy. But even if the letters are based upon an authentic document, as was sometimes the case in spurious epistolography, the monarchist sentiments come from the king and not from Zeno. Zeno's memoirs of Crates preserved the story of Crates and the shoemaker, the point of which is to ridicule the school of Aristotle for running after kings. The anecdote about the confrontation between Cleanthes and Antigonus in Diogenes Laertius 7.169 implies that Cleanthes preferred to be a drawer of water than to accept royal patronage. Chrysippus' *Ways of Living* included the courtier's life as one of the possible occupations open to a philosopher, but he made it clear that from the wise person's point of view this was just as foolish as the other possible occupations; and he thought any king would do, not necessarily one progressing in virtue, as Antigonus may have claimed to be for Zeno's benefit. Presumably the Stoics did not write off the possibility that a wise person might do good by advising a king who is progressing in virtue, but there is no sign they recommended this course, and

Chrysippus seems to have satirized the notion. The early Stoa had no special affinity with kingship. It was most at home in the old Greek cities, not in the new monarchies. The fact that kings occasionally tried to recruit them is merely evidence for the growing prestige of the school.

The evidence of Cicero, to which we will turn shortly, suggests there was nothing at all in early Stoic political thought useful to an oligarch. We might think it more likely, in view of the evidence discussed earlier in this chapter, that it would have been useful to democrats. But we have no evidence that early Stoics particularly favored democratic constitutions.[61]

The political context of the early Stoa may help to explain why their political views are so mysterious. Zeno lived at Athens as a metic or resident alien for about fifty years (ca. 312–ca. 261). During that time there were seven constitutional changes, several of them brought about by the intervention of kings; three unsuccessful revolts; and four sieges, in two of which the city was taken. The formative years of Stoicism were particularly unsettling. When Zeno arrived from Cyprus, Athens was under the dictatorship of Demetrius of Phalerum, pupil of Aristotle and puppet of Macedon, who had forced an oligarchical constitution on the city and ruled it with a Macedonian garrison. In 307 he was driven out by Demetrius Poliorcetes and the democracy restored. One of its first acts was to require philosophical schools to be licensed by the assembly. This measure was explicitly directed against the schools of Plato and Aristotle, which were thought to be seedbeds of oligarchical and pro-Macedonian sentiment. The great orator Demochares, Demosthenes' nephew, made a speech in favor of this law, of which fragments survive. His speech contained a mocking allusion to Plato's doctrine of communism in goods and women: the orator said this doctrine had been put into practice by Chaeron of Pellene, said to be an Academic; when the Macedonians made him tyrant of Pellene in Achaea he took away the wives and property of the citizens and distributed them to slaves.[62] It is interesting to see that in 306 theoretical communism was well enough known to figure in a demagogic speech, and that it was assumed to be an antidemocratic theory. The law was defeated and could not have affected Cynics anyway, nor the new group that within a few years began to form around Zeno in the Painted Stoa, for it was directed against formal organizations like the Academy and Lyceum. But the young Zeno had seen what might happen when philosophy became too closely identified with kings and factions.

In the years that followed the Athenian constitution shifted back and forth between democracy and oligarchy. The citizens were divided between oligarchs who looked to Macedon and democrats who looked to Egypt. Zeno appears to have become a figure of considerable public importance. We are told (Aelian, *Var. Hist.* 7.14) that he frequently negotiated with Antigonus on behalf of the Athenians, but we are not told what about. We are told that the orator Demochares asked him to use his influence with Antigonus and was rebuffed (Diog. Laert. 7.14). We are told the king of Egypt made overtures to him (7.24). That he retained the general favor of the Athenians is attested by the crown they bestowed on him during his lifetime and the statue they erected in the Ceramicus after his death. Later a statue of Chrysippus was placed beside it.[63] Cleanthes is said to have been applauded in the theater (7.173). But information about their political views is conspicuously absent. Zeno died about the time the city was besieged and taken by Antigonus in the spring of 261. Antigonus established another oligarchical constitution, and thereafter Athens was firmly in the Macedonian orbit; nor was democracy ever again restored for any long period. In the next generation the political affiliations of the leading Stoics (whatever these meant) ran in several directions. Perseus looked to Macedon, Cleanthes and Sphaerus apparently to Egypt, Chrysippus apparently nowhere.

Given this environment, it is easy to understand that the Stoics may have seen a great many impediments to political life, and may have found it difficult to convince themselves that any constitution was making much progress toward the perfect constitution. What they did say has been thoroughly obscured by later polemicists. Their political views are an enigma to us. Can we determine anything about the content of all those political writings?

The Stoic High Utopia

The philosophical works of Cicero contain several interesting generalizations about early Stoic political thought. When he approached the subject of magistracies in his *On Laws*, Cicero remarked that much had been written about this subject by Diogenes and Panaetius, leaders of the Stoa in the second century B.C.; but the older Stoics, though they had shown much brilliance as far as words went ("verbo tenus acute"), had not dealt with this or any other political subject in a way useful to cities and nations ("ad hunc usum popularem atque civilem de re publica"). Most of his material Cicero drew from the early Academy and the early Lyceum, especially the latter: Aristotle, Theophrastus, Heraclides, Dicaearchus, Demetrius of Phalerum; he particularly commends the last for his unique combination of learning and statecraft (*Laws* 3.5.14). Elsewhere he writes that Chrysippus' work on justice did not deal with realities but with quibbles about words (*On the Republic* 3.8.12). He says that the works on rhetoric by Chrysippus and Cleanthes contain nothing of use to a practical orator, being confined to themes like the perfection of the wise and comparisons between the world and the city, which might convince intellectually but could not touch the emotions of an audience; and he characterizes all the early Stoic discussion of constitutions, law, and oratory as a mass of useless nitpicking, "plucking thorns and gnawing bones" (*On Ends* 4.3.6–7). Panaetius is praised because he avoided these harsh doctrines (*acerbitas sententiarum*) and quibbling discussions (*disserendi spinas*) and returned to the early Platonists and Aristotelians (*On Ends* 4.27.79).

This is another turn on the *topos*, by now familiar to us, which compared men of words to men of action. Little survives of the early Aristotelians whom Cicero admired, but we know they continued Aristotle's interest in the comparative study of actual constitutions. Cicero seems especially influenced by Dicaearchus, a political thinker very influential in antiquity and very obscure to us; ca. 300 B.C. Dicaearchus had written a work called the *Tripoliticus* developing a new theory of the mixed constitution based on Sparta, which may have been the basis for the mixed-constitution theories found in Polybius and Cicero. What Cicero admired, in other words, was the low-utopian tradition in Greek political thought, and especially low utopias useful to an oligarchical and aristocratic constitution like the Roman. He tried to continue this tradition himself in his *On the Republic* and *On Laws*, which are ostensibly modeled on the *Republic* and *Laws* of Plato but actually describe a reformed version of the Roman constitution. And he thought of the older Stoa as the opposite pole: the most theoretical and impractical of all political thought, as Demetrius of Phalerum was the most successful example of the philosopher in action.

We do not know how much Stoic political literature Cicero had actually read, but it is difficult to discount altogether his testimony. It is supported by what we know about the content of the Stoic utopian writings, and by the few surviving early Stoic fragments that treat of real cities rather than ideal ones.[64] The writings of Zeno, Cleanthes, and Chrysippus were probably directed primarily toward "social" reform, not "political" reform. The political theory of Plato had included a high-utopian level, a model for a perfect society which was intended to encourage reform of a very deep and long-range nature; and a low-utopian level, which was a mechanism of rule. For the sake of the low-utopian theme, the ideal societies of Plato and Aristotle, and probably Dicaearchus, were always restricted to a single city. When the Stoics abandoned the kind of utopia that is restricted to a single city, that probably entailed the rejection of lower utopias. All the evidence leaves us with the impression that the Stoic utopia was a very high utopia, containing nothing but the rule of the wise. It set out principles, and in other works the Stoics showed how these principles might be applied to existing societies. But if it is true that the Stoic founders never discussed magistracies, then they never wrote a genuine low utopia. When Zeno decided to construct an ideal constitution that abolished separate cities and wars, he gave up at the same time the Platonic/Aristotelian program of directly influencing the state, and the political intrigues that accompanied it. What he kept was the broader aim of influencing society by a Fabian strategy of long-range permeation.

This approach would have been suggested to the Stoics by their Cynic connections. I have suggested several ways in which Zeno's *Republic* was written "at the tail of the Dog." Those who said this meant that the implicit model for his society of wise people was the Cynic fellowship, and that he adopted their individualistic and egalitarian social values. I suggest he also carried on the Cynic principle that the wise person must abjure politics. Cynics carried to extremes the individualistic side of the Socratic tradition, as Plato carried to extremes its authoritarian side. In the Stoic utopia the two came together again. Stoics retained the moral authoritarianism of Plato but eschewed his political authoritarianism, preferring the Cynic ideal of a sage who stands outside society in order to influence society.

Also this approach suited the world in which they found themselves. By ca. 300 B.C. many must have perceived that the time for the utopias of direct political action had passed, along with the world of small autonomous city-states that had given birth to that genre. The cities were still the primary focus of loyalty, and they were not in "decline" except in certain senses, but it was no longer realistic to think of them as laboratories for political experiment by Lycurgan lawgivers. The newer Greek world was a pluralistic society that included many different cultures and institutions, and the new Greek cities that the kings scattered across it were obviously the creation of external forces. The type of low utopia that envisioned radical reform, especially in property arrangements, was dead. Those that were still written probably resembled Cicero more than Aristotle. So Stoics lost interest in the ancient dream of founding a new colony, at the moment when this had become once again a common opportunity, and lost interest in the possibility of state-controlled education, at the moment when some degree of state intervention in education was becoming common in the Hellenistic cities. They may also have perceived that this larger and more complex world provided more opportunities for the social applications of utopian thought than the political.

The Stoic Low Utopia

Nevertheless, there is considerable evidence that some third-century Stoics entertained theories about lower forms of utopia. We should not rely too heavily on Cicero's knowledge of early Stoic literature, nor place too much trust in his judgment of it. When he dismisses it as useless, he may mean largely that it was not useful to the kinds of constitution that he favored. He uses the stereotyped terms in which late Hellenistic and Roman writers tended to refer to all utopian theories. The *topos* contrasting men of words and men of action mentions only the *Republic* of Plato, not the *Laws*; or if it mentions the *Laws*, treats that work as though it were as impractical as the *Republic*.[65] If there were a Stoic low utopia, it might easily have been forgotten. We have no evidence of such interests on the part of Zeno, Cleanthes, and Chrysippus; but in some of their disciples we can glimpse a different pattern of life and thought.

We know little about Perseus of Citium but the titles of his works, but these suggest he may have been a pivotal figure in the development of Stoic political thought. He was said to be Zeno's own freedman and secretary, sent by Zeno to the court of Antigonus Gonatas, whom he served loyally if not very effectively as a general; he was remembered as a rather untypical Stoic, something of a sybarite, and the butt of Cynic jokes, but remembered also for his fidelity to Zeno.[66] He was the first Stoic whose life and work showed signs of interest in "progressor" states. He was the first to hold high political office. Unless Cleanthes preceded him, he was the first to write *On Kingship*. As the author of a *Constitution of the Lacedaemonians*, he was the first Stoic to show an interest in Sparta, which had heretofore been a Peripatetic speciality.[67] He wrote a reply to the *Laws* of Plato in not less than seven books; we know nothing about its contents, but it is difficult to see how, in a work of such length, he could have avoided applying Zeno's principles on a more practical level. He may have been exploring certain new directions: the possibilities latent in the egalitarian institutions of Sparta, the possibilities in virtuous kingship, possibly a Stoic version of the mixed constitution to rival the theory of Dicaearchus. This range of interests was prophetic. For just when Perseus died (ca. 243 B.C.), Sparta suddenly began to transform herself into a new kind of political model under the leadership of reforming kings, and established a new connection with Stoicism.

The Spartan "revolution" was a series of increasingly violent attempts to carry out massive land redistribution, which spread to many other states and convulsed the entire Peloponnesus for about sixty years (ca. 243–ca. 180 B.C.). This phenomenon, whether or not we call it a "revolution," was probably the most serious social conflict in the history of the ancient Greeks, and the fact that it had a mysterious but undeniable connection with Stoicism has given it an almost modern ideological aspect in the eyes of some historians. Our knowledge of the earlier stages of the movement comes almost entirely from Plutarch's *Lives* of Agis and Cleomenes, based upon the pro-Spartan historian Phylarchus who wrote at Athens in the late third century. I furnish here a brief outline.[68]

By the middle of the third century the land of Lacedaemon had become concentrated in the hands of a small group of *oikoi*. Because most *oikoi* could no longer pay for their shares in the *syssitia*, the citizen body was reduced to some seven hundred men, of whom the hundred wealthiest virtually controlled Sparta. The Spartan army was a negligeable force; the Spartan state, even in Peloponnesian affairs, was dominated by the Achaean League; the Spartan territory was filled with thousands of déclassée households whose ancestors had been full Spartiates a generation or two back. Circa 243 the young king Agis IV proposed a program of land redistribution and debt cancellation for the purpose of increasing the citizen body from seven hundred to four thousand and five hundred; at the same time the lands of the *perioikoi* (Lacedaemonians of the noncitizen class), where the same economic factors had been at work, were to be redistributed into fifteen thousand lots; there may have been attempts to equalize movable property as well; and the *agoge* and *syssitia*, which it was said had become empty forms, were to be fully restored so as to ensure the social and economic equality of all citizens. The new citizens were to be recruited from ex-citizens who had lost their land, from *perioikoi*, and from foreigners. This program met with strong opposition from the wealthy, who controlled the *gerousia* and the ephorate, and they secured the execution of Agis in 241.

But in 227 the reform program was revived by Cleomenes III. By then it was obvious that ruthless measures would be needed. Cleomenes engineered a coup, exiled his opponents, abolished the ephorate and the other royal house, perhaps more. Then the reforms were carried out, the land redistributed, and four thousand new citizens created. The *agoge* and the *syssitia* were restored and a Stoic philosopher, Sphaerus of Borysthenes, was called in to organize these institutions according to the ancient forms.

Sphaerus was probably the most distinguished Stoic alive after Chrysippus. He had been the pupil of both Zeno and Cleanthes, and was the author of more than thirty works covering every branch of philosophy. Nowhere is it suggested that any Stoics regarded him as heterodox. He may have been known already as an authority on the Spartan constitution: his writings included an *On Kingship*, an *On the Lacedaemonian Constitution*, and an *On Lycurgus and Socrates* in three books; the last was perhaps a Socratic dialogue in which Socrates discussed the Spartan constitution.[69]

By the time Sphaerus came to Sparta the Spartan upheaval was spreading over Greece. The social tensions already obvious in the time of Plato had been building up for more than a century. Alexander's expansion of the Greek world widened further the gap between rich and poor in the old Greek cities and multiplied demands for land reform and debt relief. Cleomenes probably never intended to extend his reforms outside Lacedaemon, but his triumph there caused agitation for comparable reforms to flare up throughout the Peloponnesus, and he exploited this situation to restore Sparta to a position of military leadership in southern Greece. It required the intervention of Macedon to defeat him at Sellasia in 222.

Thereafter we lose the aid of Plutarch/Phylarchus, and the subsequent history of Sparta is obscure. There was endless turmoil, and in 206 the reform movement again seized power in the person of the king or tyrant Nabis. He enforced reform more ruthlessly even than Cleomenes, confiscating and redistributing the estates of his opponents; he made active efforts to spread revolution abroad, and was regarded as a terrible threat by all Greek oligarchs, who called in the Romans to crush him in 192. The last tremor of the revolution at Sparta died ca. 180.

It was once common for historians to speak of this crisis as a "socialist" or "communist" movement. It was certainly an attempt at massive social reorganization, but imposed from the top. It was a campaign by the Spartan monarchy to restore Spartan military power by the traditional method of expanding the citizen body; its avowed aim was the traditional slogan of restoring an ancient constitution; its constitutional implement was an aggrandized Spartan kingship, which it sought to raise to the same level as the great Macedonian monarchies; it assumed the existence of a privileged class of citizens, as did every other Greek political movement, and did not intend to affect the helot majority of the population, for the freeing of helots in the later stages of the reform is best interpreted as a desperate military measure. If we must seek modern parallels, some aspects of the crisis are reminiscent of the conflicts between eighteenth-century enlightened despots and their aristocracies, and others of twentieth-century fascist movements. But it is best to call it a traditional Greek reform program given a consistent ideological focus by the peculiar traditions of Sparta. The most revolutionary aspect, redistribution of land, meant something different at Sparta: there it was not a revolution of the poor, but an effort by the elite to return to the semimythical ancestral constitution of Lycurgus. And yet the fact remains that the democratic and egalitarian side of the Spartan tradition, always latent, now came to the fore. Lycurgus was now cast as a utopian revolutionary who had established complete social and economic equality among the citizens; the reformers emphasized and perhaps invented the tradition that the original Lycurgan distribution of the land had meant equal allotments; the ideology could not have been transplanted elsewhere, and it is doubtful that any of the reformers intended to do so, but their actions inspired revolts by the poor in other cities and they sometimes took advantage of this. Despite themselves, they had turned Sparta from a model of stable oligarchy to a model of sweeping land reform. We cannot separate the conservative elements in this movement from the self-consciously revolutionary. Revolutionary change in a traditional society tends to pose as a return to an idealized past, and nowhere was this so easy to do as at Sparta. We cannot even be sure what the Lycurgan tradition was like before the Great Reforms, for the version of it that we receive from Plutarch must be heavily influenced by the propaganda of Cleomenes and Sphaerus.

Those historians who saw parallels between the Spartan reforms and modern socialism naturally tended to cast Stoicism in the role of Marxism. The whole movement, it was thought, must have been inspired by Stoic communist ideology. Some thought, for no good reason, that Sphaerus must have been present even during the first phase of the reform under Agis.[70] There has been a reaction against all this, and some writers give the impression that Stoicism had nothing to do with the reform at all. We are told that Stoics had no interest in practical social and economic questions, that their utopian writings were purely theoretical, and that Sphaerus was only interested in the educational aspects of the refom, for Plutarch mentions him only in connection with the revival of the *agoge*.[71]

But of course Sphaerus was interested in the *agoge*. That does not mean he was a mere schoolteacher hired to instruct children in moral commonplaces. The *agoge* was central to everything at Sparta, and never more so than during the Great Reforms. It was the supreme ideological symbol and main institutional implement of total citizen equality, both economic and social. The most obvious explanation of Sphaerus is that his interest in the Spartan constitution was inspired not by antiquarianism but by a theory about Sparta as a political model or low utopia; and that his activities at Sparta were connected with this theory. We have already seen that the Greek low-utopian tradition and the Spartan model were practically the same thing. (Besides, *any* treatise about the Spartan constitution would surely have to say something about magistracies, which is sufficient to show that we ought not to take too literally Cicero's comments on the utter impracticality of third-century Stoic political thought.)

It seems doubtful that the Spartan reform owed anything to Stocism originally. It was based on native Lycurgan traditions. But it produced a movement unlike anything ever seen in Greece, and some Stoics saw in this the low utopia toward which they had been groping. The movement had something for everyone: monarchy, democracy, land redistribution, reaffirmation of the independent polis, the mixed constitution again. What appealed to Sphaerus was probably its unprecedented efforts to achieve social and economic equality. The only political saying attributed to him expresses contempt for the despotic Ptolemaic brand of kingship (Diog. Laert. 7.177). We have seen that some Cynics had cultivated an idealized version of the Spartan constitution that emphasized its egalitarian features, and the coming of the Great Reforms inspired hopes that this dream might become a reality.[72] Sphaerus probably believed in some such idealized and egalitarian version of the Spartan model and saw the Reforms as an opportunity to put into practice the collectivist principles of Zeno's *Republic*. So in the 220s Stoicism was imported and grafted onto the Spartan movement. Zeno had denied that any *agoge* could produce a wise person, but Sphaerus apparently convinced himself that this *agoge* might produce individuals and cities progressing toward wisdom. He created an alliance between Greek aspirations for socio-political reform and one wing of the Stoa, which would last more than a century. Such Stoics were willing to go much further than Plato and Aristotle, whose utopian theories about equalization of land were never put into practice because the authors were never willing to recommend interference with the existing organization of property.

The Place of Utopia in Stoic History and Cosmology

Stoics believed evil to be a necessary part of the universe and of nature's plan. Chrysippus said "Vice cannot be removed completely, nor is it right that it should be removed" (Plut., *Stoic Self-Contra.* 1051b, trans. Long/Sedley). Evil would be altogether eliminated only at the final conflagration at the close of the world cycle, when the cosmos would return to its original purity; then the cycle would be precisely repeated. Therefore no Stoic could ever have imagined that the perfect society would ever be realized. The only realization of moral perfection possible was that harmony with nature which the wise were capable of realizing in all their actions, and this harmony was in itself perfectly adequate for human happiness. The astonishing Stoic cosmology, with its endless sequence of precisely repeated world cycles, seems deliberately designed to preclude any hope of realizing a perfect society, so that nothing could distract the followers of Stoicism from the supreme importance of the present moment, and the perfect adequacy of achieving virtue in the present moment. Like Plato, they proposed the perfect society as a timeless ideal whose unrealizability was a matter of no importance, since striving for the ideal was everything.

Nevertheless, Stoics seem to have thought that the amount of evil in society was subject to sharp increases and decreases, and this has led some to think that their theory of a perfect society might have fitted into some sort of historical plan. Chrysippus' *Introduction to the Subject of Good and Evil* argued that society had been better in the past, using as evidence the curious statement that prostitutes at one time more masks and were not allowed inside cities; but he also seems to have thought that at other times in the past morals were worse than at present, for he believed that eunuch prostitutes had once been common in Greece.[73] He also praised the simple habits of the Homeric heroes, appealing to the common belief that the heroic age had been a time of superior virtue (Ath. 1.18b). No doubt some Stoics went back further than that and made use of the Hesiodic myth of Cronus' time, as Cynics had done before them.

Some have attributed to Stoics—and also to Cynics, as we have seen—a complete historical and anthropological theory focused on the theme of a decline from a primitive golden age. This does not seem implausible, since there was already in circulation at Athens a rationalized and euhemerized version of the Hesiodic myth. Aristotle's pupil Dicaearchus, famous as an authority on the mixed constitution, wrote a compendium of universal history in which he identified the time of Cronus with a primitive stage of society in which all property was held in common (Porphyry, *On Abstinence* 4.1.2). Whether Dicaearchus also found community of women in the primitive age we do not know, but we know this was assumed by another Peripatetic, Clearchus of Soli. Clearchus wrote that Cecrops, mythical founder of Athens, had introduced monogamy; before him there was only *koinogamia*, common marriage, in which all coupled like animals and none knew their own fathers.[74] Contemporary historians and geographers found both community of goods and community of women among various distant barbarians, like the Scythians described by Ephorus.[75] This belief in communism as a real and historical stage of society, which still existed in some parts of the world, must have been influenced by the philosophical theories about utopian communism, and in turn provided empirical support for these theories. As we have seen, Chrysippus defended sexual communism by reference to these communistic barbarians, and no doubt Stoics appealed also to the alleged communism of primitives.

Therefore it has sometimes been assumed that Zeno's ideal city was supposed to have existed at some point in the remote past and was identified with the unspoiled golden age of Dicaearchus (e.g., Pohlenz, *Die Stoa* 1.137). That seems unlikely. Sextus Empiricus says that "the younger Stoics" thought early humans were more intelligent (*Against Prof.* 9.28); surely a reference to the anthropological theories of Posidonius, which are known to us from Seneca's *Ep.* 90. We will see that the Neostoics placed great emphasis on this theory of primitive communism, but that is because they intended it to replace the theory of utopian communism. The early Stoics probably collected information about primitive peoples for the purpose of finding parallels with the practices described in Zeno's *Republic*, and it is likely that they used the primitive communistic age as an example of a period when the gap between human society and natural virtue had been relatively narrow; but they could not have thought the primitive age *was* the ideal city. The ideal city had never been and never would be realized on earth.

And yet, if there had been approximations of it in the past, other approximations were possible in the future. Such an approximation Sphaerus tried to achieve at Sparta, and later Blossius at Rome and Pergamum. But we suspect the commoner Stoic view was that of Chrysippus, who saw few signs of political progress anywhere, and could only hope that the *teleia politeia* described in his *Republic* would exercise a more gradual influence on society.

We do not know, of course, how much difference it ever made. Stoicism never affected anybody but a small minority of the small upper class of the Greek world. At least, the Stoic utopian ideal was one of the most striking manifestations of that climate of self-confident rationalism that made the third century B.C. "the nearest approach to an 'open society' that the world had yet seen, and nearer than any that would be seen again until very modern times".[76] It would be unfair to evaluate the Stoic utopian theory in terms of its results even if we had some means of measuring these. It was a long-range strategy to bring about social change, and its promise was unfulfilled, because in the second century B.C. the Stoics began to turn away from the goals described in this chapter.

Comments

Comment on A: "Tail of the dog" (*kynos ouras*) may have been a pun on Cynosura, "Dog's Tail," the name of more than one promontory near Athens. Several interpretations of the joke have been offered. They may have meant "holding on to the Dog's tail," i.e., that Zeno was then at the end of his Cynic period, or that he was no more than a marginal Cynic. Or they may have meant that the work exhibited the most obscene aspects of Cynicism. In any case the point is that the work showed strong Cynic influence. The joke is hostile, and like some other passages in the biography of Zeno shows the influence of the Neostoicism of Panaetius, which rejected the Cynic traditions of the Stoa. Philodemus tells us that their usual strategy was to dismiss the *Republic* as unworthy of Zeno because it was a youthful work or an unsavory one or both; the joke about the Dog's tail might have carried both meanings.

Comment on B: It is generally thought that the doxographical matter in Diogenes Laertius comes from collections of excerpts, of which he had two sorts: collections of opinions (*doxai*) ascribed to Stoics in general, and collections of *doxai* ascribed to individual Stoics. The excerpt quoted above seems to come from a collection of the latter type, but Diogenes Laertius does not include it in his Stoic doxography, which begins at 7.38; instead he inserts it as a sort of doxographical appendix to his biography of Zeno. The excerpt is assigned this anomalous position because it deals with the *athetoumena*, the rejected writings of Zeno, not generally considered a part of Stoic doctrine but a subject of some interest for Zeno's biography.

The excerpt comes from a work by the otherwise unknown Cassius the Skeptic, who must have written sometime between the revival of Skepticism (first century B.C.) and the time of Diogenes Laertius (second or third century A.D.). Cassius summarized part of an earlier work by Isidore of Pergamum, who probably wrote in the first century B.C., because we know that the scandal at the Pergamene library occurred ca. 80 B.C.

This excerpt belonged to a Skeptical critique of Stoicism. It was intended to point out contradictions and disagreements within the Stoa, and to show that Stoic doctrines contradicted general views about morality. According to Cassius, the *Republic* contradicted common morality in the following ways: (1) it opened by declaring the whole educational curriculum to be useless; (2) it established an absolute gulf between the wise and unwise (here we are reminded that this is a universal Stoic doctrine) and applied this teaching to the city and the household; (3) there follows a list of scandalous doctrines found in the *Republic*, in no discernable order, mostly connected with communism in goods and women, mostly resembling points in the *Republic* of Plato; but the ban on certain types of public building, on which Cassius seems to place considerable emphasis, is not immediately intelligible. This moralistic critique had originated among the Stoics themselves, and Cassius made much of their internal disputes. Some Stoics had denied that the *Republic* was the work of Zeno, and Cassius refuted this by pointing out that Chrysippus had considered it authentically Zenonian. The robust editorial methods favored by Athenodorus of Pergamum seem to have been intended not to eject the entire *Republic* from the Zenonian canon, but rather to excise certain objectionable passages, probably those dealing with sexual morals, from the *Republic*, the *Art of Love*, and the *Diatribes*. These Stoic critics of the *Republic* were clearly the Neostoics who followed Panaetius, and their opponents represented the Cynicizing Stoic tradition.

Comment on C: This is a doxographical appendix to the biography of Chrysippus. As Mansfeld pointed out, it must come from the same source as B, the doxographical appendix about Zeno. It exhibits the same curious habit of emphasizing that certain points were made "at the beginning" of a work, or "in 1,000 lines." This was an indictment of Cynicizing Stoicism by a Skeptical writer, probably all derived ultimately from Cassius the Skeptic, which Diogenes Laertius has cut up and inserted at two appropriate points. The criticisms of Chrysippus, like those of Zeno, have largely to do with sexual morality. The subject of incest certainly came up in a work about the ideal state, and the subject of cannibalism may have had some connection with ideal states. (It is not obvious why anybody thought the quotation from *On Ways of Living* so objectionable, but as it probably had nothing to do with ideal states, I reserve discussion of it till later.)

Comment on D: This occurs in the general Stoic doxography (7.38–160) which Diogenes Laertius attached to his biography of Zeno. The doxography mixes opinions that are attributed to Stoics in general (usually introduced by "they say") with opinions attributed to individual Stoics. The sentence immediately preceding D combines the two, as Diogenes Laertius does often: "They say the wise man will enter politics . . . as Chrysippus says in *On Ways of Living*." It is probable that we are to read D in the same way. It means "The Stoics say that the wise man will marry, as Zeno says in his *Republic*." By "marriage" (*gamos*) are we to understand sexual communism as described in B, C, and F? The word *gamos* could be used loosely, but it would be odd to find such ambiguity in doxographers writing about such a matter as this, and we do not find it elsewhere in Diogenes Laertius.[77] The passage probably refers to the conventional duties of marriage, as the sentence preceding it defines the conventional duties of politics. Therefore the author of this excerpt believed Zeno was recommending conventional marriage in his *Republic*.

Comment on E: Here again we find that the sentence immediately preceding E has "they say" followed by a cluster of *doxai* attributed to individual Stoics; and again there seems no doubt that we are to understand E, and the discussion of Stoic love which follows E, as general Stoic doctrine. The likeliest source of E is the last named, the *Ethics* of Apollodorus, whose importance for the Cynic/Stoic doxographies in Diogenes Laertius we have already noted.

Comment on F: The usual format, a general opinion followed by corroborating opinions from individual Stoics. But we know that most Roman Stoics could not have believed F, and we will have doubts about E. Both excerpts (and probably D as well) represent the Cynicizing tradition of Apollodorus. They present the Stoic utopian tradition in a favorable light: we do not hear about the matters mentioned in A–C; rather D–F associate Zeno's *Republic* with marriage, with an edifying type of *paiderastia*, with an elevated version of sexual communism which is said to be identical with Plato's theory. The last is a plain misrepresentation, because the permissive kind of communism described here has no resemblance to Plato's.

Diogenes Laertius' sources of information, fortunately for us, were often seriously out of date. He speaks as though D–F represented general Stoic teaching in his own day (ca. 200 A.D.), but there can be little doubt that we are dealing here with a tradition of the Hellenistic Stoa.

Comment on G–I: Chrysippus was said (F) to teach the same permissive doctrine of sexual communism as Zeno and Diogenes, but Sextus (and C) associated his name with a more specific teaching on incest, which was developed in his *Republic*. Surely this was the same work that Diogenes Laertius calls *On the Republic* (B, C, F).

There are two versions of I. In *Outlines of Pyrrhonism* 3.247 (quoted above) the teaching on cannibalism is attributed to Chrysippus' *Republic*. This attribution is accepted in Long and Sedley, *Hellenistic Philosophers* 1.430, perhaps because the passage seems more plausible in a description of an ideal state. But in the second version, *Against the Professors* 11.192, Sextus assigns the same quotation to Chrysippus' *On Justice*. There can be little doubt that the second version is correct, for this teaching is also attributed to *On Justice* by Diogenes Laertius (C) and Philodemus (M). Therefore we remain uncertain whether these bizarre statements about cannibalism had any connection with Chrysippus' theory of the ideal state.

Comment on J–N: We saw in B that some Neostoics had tried to deny the authenticity of Zeno's *Republic*, and that others, not long before Philodemus wrote, had tried to bowdlerize it. These attempts had failed, and the Neostoics known to Philodemus have three other strategies: (1) To pretend that there was nothing wrong with the *Republic* except its sexual morals. *Diamerizein* often had a homosexual connotation but might refer to heterosexual intercourse as well. How some Stoics tried to sanitize all this we may see from D, E, and F. (2) To dismiss the whole *Republic* as an early and insignificant work. (3) Most radical of all, to minimize the significance of Zeno himself. Philodemus replies simply that you cannot separate the Stoa from Zeno, nor Zeno from his *Republic*.

Comment on O: This comes from the first of two orations entitled *On the Fortune of Alexander* or *On the Virtue of Alexander*, generally considered to be epideictic display pieces by the youthful Plutarch.[78] The passage sounds panegyrical, but actually it is a rhetorical *topos* that recurs several times in Plutarch's writings. The purpose is to compare *logos* with *ergon*, the men of words with the men of deeds, the useless dreamings of the utopian writers with the achievements of practical statesmen. In Plutarch's *Against Colotes* 1126, the utopian works produced by Plato's Academy are compared to their disadvantage with the practical political activities of some members of the Academy (see above, p. 108 n. 43). The real subject of the passage quoted above is Alexander the Great, and Plutarch's purpose is to show that Alexander was a greater philosopher than either Plato or Zeno because he actually created the new world that the utopists could only imagine.

Some of Plutarch's comparisons are farfetched in the extreme, as when Alexander's success in spreading Greek culture to foreign nations is contrasted with the meager records of the Academy and the Stoa in converting barbarians: the former could boast only of Clitomachus of Carthage, the latter only of Diogenes of Babylon. But Plutarch's attempts to force the *Republics* of Plato and Zeno into this rhetorical framework produce interesting results. The single imaginary *politeia* of Plato, which was so harsh (*austeros*) that he could find no one to follow it, is contrasted with the seventy real cities Alexander founded; the *Laws* of Plato, which nobody ever followed, are contrasted with the influential legislation of Alexander; then the imaginary *kosmos* (which may mean "world" or "order," and here probably means both) of Zeno is contrasted with the real world empire, uniting Greeks and barbarians, that Alexander founded. The latter may also be meant to suggest Plutarch's own ideal of a Hellenistic world culture united under Roman rule. We are told that Zeno abolished both *demoi* and *poleis*. *Demos* could mean "people," but here it makes better sense as "deme," local unit of government.

This passage actually takes a very negative view of the classical utopists, nor does Plutarch, though himself a Platonist, treat the utopias of Plato more favorably than those of the Stoics. Plutarch does seem to suggest that their *ideals* were admirable, but he has to assume that for rhetorical purposes. When he says, a little earlier (328c), that Alexander introduced monogamy to certain barbarous nations, he may mean to assure his readers that Alexander shared none of the utopians' notorious fantasies about community of women, thereby making Alexander a more virtuous philosopher, as well as a more effective one, than Plato or Zeno.[79] The notion that Zeno's pupil Eratosthenes was the source of this passage was long ago abandoned. We can only say that Plutarch is using some excerpt of Stoic origin that described Zeno's *Republic* in these glowing terms.

Comment on P: This is a later version of the anti-utopian *topos* we met in O. Once again we have a contrast between a practical statesman and the utopian visionaries Plato and Zeno, with Diogenes thrown in for good measure. Again we begin with a statement about the leading principle (*kephalaion*) of one of these people, then proceed to a comparison between the men of words (*logoi*) and the men of deeds (*erga*), and to the conclusion that only *ergon* leaves anything behind. In this case the deed comes before the word, because Lycurgus lived before any of these writers, who must therefore be described as trying to imitate him; in the case of Alexander the process of imitation had to be the other way around; but the conclusion is the same.

We will meet this topic again in Athenaeus. There was also a Christian version of it, which adds nothing to our knowledge of Stoic texts. John

Chrysostom compared the absurd *Republics* of Plato and Zeno, which taught such things as community of women and nude exercises for women, to the true philosophy of the Gospel, which was preached by unlettered men and yet conquered the earth (*Hom.* 1 *in Matt.* 4 = SVF 1.262).

Comment on Q: In his serious treatises Plutarch drops rhetorical artifice and never refers to Stoic utopian works except in unfavorable terms. They are mentioned several times in his *On Stoic Self-Contradictions,* always to show that some point or another in the utopian theory constituted a contradiction in Stoic doctrine. Plutarch probably relied upon his own excerpts from Stoic writings and from the works of their Academic critics, assembled during his studies at the Academy. See Harold Cherniss' introduction to his Loeb Classical Library edition of *De stoicis repugnantibus, Moralia* 13.2 (Cambridge, Mass. 1976).

In the passage quoted above, Plutarch claims that Zeno declared contradictions to be pointless (perhaps a criticism of the "antilogical" type of sophistical exercise); but Zeno was inconsistent about this, for he himself tried to refute many sophisms, wrote a refutation of Plato's *Republic*, and encouraged his disciples to study dialectic so that they could do likewise. Plutarch is certainly referring to the *Republic* of Zeno; and we notice that when he thinks of Zeno's controversial writings this strikes him as the most prominent example.

Comment on R: The contradiction that Plutarch wants to point out is that Stoics approve of the doctrine cited here and yet they participate in sacrifices, mysteries, and other cult activities. Here we are told the reason for the prohibition on temples mentioned in B. The meaning of this syllogism is not self-evident, but other Zenonian fragments leave no doubt that Zeno intended the superstitions of the cults to be replaced in the ideal society by a pure worship of the cosmic reason.

This excerpt was much used by Christians. Clement of Alexandria introduces it as follows: "Zeno, founder of the Stoic school, said in his book *The Republic* that neither shrines nor images [of the gods] ought to be built" (*Misc.* 5.12.76 = SVF 1.264). Origen, Epiphanius, and Theodoret repeat the passage in almost the same terms (SVF 1.264–65).

Comment on S: Here we learn that Chrysippus' *Republic* espoused sexual ethics of a Cynic sort, and laid down extremely austere regulations for the imaginary citizens: a sparse diet, bans on ornamental plants and animals, and probably on paintings. (One wonders if it was in the Painted Stoa that Chrysippus said "We are almost at the point of painting pictures on the walls of our latrines.") Plutarch's comments seem unusually petty and obtuse because he does not understand the Cynic sexual ethic and so does not see how Diogenes' public masturbation could be compatible with asceticism.

Comment on T: Plutarch does not associate this passage with any doctrine of an ideal state; I include it here because it provides a context for the teaching on incest, which we know from C, G, H and I played a part in Chrysippus' *Republic*. What interests Plutarch is that here Chrysippus uses animal behavior as a standard, a notion that seems to be contradicted by much that Chrysippus said elsewhere.

Comment on U: This is not from a polemical work, but it is convenient to consider it with the preceding excerpts. The speaker in this dialogue is a physician who is making the point that useful discussions about sexual matters are suitable for a symposium, or for a literary dialogue set in a symposium, such as the *Convivial Questions*. To qualify as useful the discussion should take into account health factors: e.g., what is the healthiest time of day to have sexual relations? By the standards of Plutarch's circle, what Zeno had to say about sex in his *Republic* would have been unobjectionable had he said it in a *Symposium*. This throws a new light on those *diamerizein* passages in the *Republic* which so troubled the later Stoics.

Comment on V: The characters in Athenaeus' dialogue are wealthy men who meet for dinner at Rome. Some of them we know were historical figures, and it is generally assumed others were, though we know nothing about some of them, including this philosopher Pontianus of Nicomedia. Athenaeus gives him several speeches, which leave the impression that he is a sort of Stoic and a particular opponent of Platonists. In one of these (6.233a–c) he attacks Plato and Lycurgus for banning silver and gold from their ideal states, and praises Zeno for admitting that money could have a useful purpose. This shows us how little to rely on Athenaeus' knowledge of philosophy: he has heared that Plato banned currency from his ideal states, and he has heard that Zeno permitted it in real life; but he does not know that Zeno banned currency even more strictly in *his* ideal state, and it does not occur to him that Plato also would have permitted it in real life. At 11.508 Pontianus delivers another long attack on Plato, another version of the anti-utopian *topos* we met several times in Plutarch. The *Republic* and *Laws* of Plato are compared to their disadvantage with practical lawgivers such as Lycurgus, Draco, and Solon; we are told, in terms that recall a phrase used by Philodemus (J), that Plato did not write for people who really exist, but for figments of his imagination. Plato is also criticized here (508d) for his improper treatment of love, meaning the praises of *paiderastia* found in the *Symposium* and the *Phaedrus*. Pontianus may be Athenaeus' idea of a Stoic, but what he has to say about Stoicism or any other philosophy will reflect nothing but Athenaeus' woolgatherings.

Passage V occurs in a long dialogue about love, a classic subject for such a symposium as this. The first speaker parades some quotations from the poets in praise of the god Eros. Then we have the speech of Pontianus in praise of Eros (561c–562a). He opens with this quote from Zeno's *Republic*, then explains that Zeno was not the only early philosopher who held this elevated view of Eros; this is why Eros is worshipped in gymnasia alongside Hermes and Heracles; he was so worshipped at the Academy; he was celebrated at the Erotidia festival in Boeotia; he is honored at all public sacrifices; Spartans and Cretans sacrificed to him before battle; he was associated with the Sacred Band of Thebes, the army of lovers; the Samians worship him at the festival called Eleutheria (Freedom); he liberated Athens through Harmodius and Aristogeiton.

Pontianus' selection of authorities is very different from those cited by Plutarch in his dialogue on love (*Amatorius*), though such familiar examples as the Sacred Band and the tyrannicides Harmodius and Aristogeiton appear in both. Plutarch draws heavily on the dialogues of Plato; Pontianus conspicuously avoids mention of them, having condemned them for immorality in an earlier speech. The keystone of Pontianus' speech is the quotation from Zeno's *Republic*, and the other examples are meant to support it by emphasizing the political and military value of boylove, especially its contributions to "freedom." The importance of *paiderastia* as a source of civic virtue is indeed mentioned in the earlier dialogues on this theme by Plato, Xenophon, and Plutarch, but it is not emphasized to this extent. The spiritual nature of Stoic *paiderastia* is also emphasized: when he says Zeno's Eros produces "nothing else," Pontianus means that Eros does not stand for those activities which he had condemned in Plato. It is obvious this is his meaning. A little later another speaker, Myrtilus, attacks the hypocrisies of Stoic *paiderastia*, which he claims to be nothing but a front for carnality; the attack is said to be directed against Stoics in the company, who must include Pontianus.[80]

Pontianus' speech on Eros is probably based upon on excerpt of Stoic origin, picked up by Athenaeus from some anthology and inserted here because Pontianus is supposed to represent the viewpoint of a philosopher and a Stoic on the question of love. It resembles D–F in attempting to portray the sexual morality of Zeno's *Republic* in a highly respectable guise, even in throwing in inaccurate comparisons with Plato's *Republic*; and it probably emanated from the same Cynicizing Stoic tradition.

Notes

1. Mansfeld, in "Diogenes Laertius on Stoic Philosophy," thought the Cynicizing tradition a "revisionist" interpretation of Stoicism, designed to turn Cynicism into a dignified ethic. Then what was the original Cynic/Stoic ethic? We cannot tell, except that it had some connection with anarchistic doctrines about communism, incest, cannibalism, and the like. But Mansfeld admits that the Cynicized Stoic doxography of Diogenes Laertius at one point accepts the doctrine of sexual communism (343), which makes one wonder how much this "revisionism" could have differed from the original Cynicized Stoicism. It seems to me simpler to assume a unitary ethical tradition that extended from Zeno to Apollodorus, undisturbed by serious revisionism until Panaetius.

2. *Suda* s.v. Socrates (Giannantoni, fr. 1.7). The doxographer Hippobotus said Zeno was a pupil of Diodorus the Logician, leader of the dialecticians (Diog. Laert. 7.16, 25; see Mansfeld, "Diogenes Laertius," 325ff.).

3. Diog. Laert. 7.3, 17; Apuleius, *Florida* 14. The biographer Antigonus of Carystus attributed to Zeno the remark that all who heard his words without understanding would be dirty and slavelike, which could have been directed against Cynicizing Stoics, and was so interpreted later (Ath. 13.565d); but another version of the saying, attributed to Aristo of Chios, does not suggest this interpretation (Cic., *On the Nature of the Gods*, 3.31.77).

4. Diog. Laert. 7.26. There are a number of drinking anecdotes about Zeno, all probably from the *Sympotic Memoirs* of his disciple Perseus, but these generally

emphasize Zeno's abstinence, including the one explicit citation from Perseus' work, which tells us that Zeno rarely accepted dinner invitations (7.1).

5. Erskine, *Hellenistic Stoa*, 9–15, points out the tendentious nature of the statements that Zeno's *Republic* was an early work.

6. Menedemus of Eretria, sometimes called a Cynic, was so indifferent to his school that no order could be seen there, nor benches arranged in a circle, but only the teacher and his disciples sitting or walking about as they pleased (Diog. Laert. 2.130). Cf. Bernard Frischer, *The Sculpted Word: Epicureanism and Philosophical Recruitment in Ancient Greece* (Berkeley 1982), 46ff.

7. Precise references do not seem necessary for this brief sketch of Stoic teaching. The fragments of the early Stoics have been collected by A. C. Pearson, *The Fragments of Zeno and Cleanthes* (1889, reprinted New York 1973); J. von Arnim, *Stoicorum Veterum Fragmenta*, 4 vols. (Leipzig 1905), including all Stoics before Panaetius; N. Festa and R. Anastasi, *I frammenti degli Stoici antichi*, 2 vols. (Bari 1932–62), an Italian translation, extending to Chrysippus but including only his ethical fragments; A. A. Long and D. N. Sedley, *The Hellenistic Philosophers*, 2 vols. (Cambridge 1987), a selection of passages with English translations and detailed commentary, which should be the starting point for anyone wishing to explore further any aspect of Stoicism. A survey of recent scholarship will be found in J. M. Rist, "Stoicism: Some Reflections on the State of the Art," in *Spindel Conference 1984: Recovering the Stoics*, ed. R. H. Epp, *Southern Journal of Philosophy* 23 Supplement (1985), 1–11. See also Jenny Parrott, "Hellenistic Political Thought and Institutions: An Introductory Bibliography," *Polis* 2.2 (1979), 27–56; R. Müller, "Zur Staatsauffassung der frühen Stoa," in *Proceedings of the 7th Congress of the International Federation of Societies of Classical Studies*, ed. Janos Harmatta (Budapest 1984), 1.303–11; and Erskine, *Hellenistic Stoa*. Since many passages relevant to this inquiry are scattered through different sections of Arnim's collection, and for most readers may be more easily located elsewhere, I include references to Arnim (SVF) only for texts not readily available in libraries.

8. See J. M. Rist, "Zeno and Stoic Consistency," *Phronesis* 22 (1977), 161–74; and the other literature summarized by M. E. Reesor, *The Nature of Man in Early Stoic Philosophy* (New York 1989), 103–17. Zeno coined the terms *proegmena* (Stobaeus 2.84.18 = SVF 3.128) and *kathekon* (Diog. Laert. 7.25, 108), and defined the *telos* as "living in agreement" (Stob. 2.75.11 = SVF 1.179) or "living in agreement with nature" (Diog. Laert. 7.87). The first definition of the *telos* sounds more Cynic, for it may imply that only inner harmony is needed; the second implies that we must be in harmony *with* something. But even if Zeno himself did not use the word "nature," his use of jargon like *kathekon* seems to imply an un-Cynic interest in dialectic.

9. The debt of Stoicism to Platonic/Aristotelian philosophy is so obvious and so generalized that it is difficult to identify its precise sources. We know Zeno studied at the Academy, especially with Polemo; if we knew more about Polemo and other members of the post-Platonic Academy this information would be more illuminating. Whether early Stoicism was influenced by Aristotle has been disputed. I avoid these questions, taking to heart the warning of F. H. Sandbach: "We ought constantly to remind ourselves how much is not known about the intellectual life immediately preceding and contemporary with the rise of Stoicism" (*Aristotle and the Stoics*, Cambridge Philological Society, Supplement 10, 1985, 56).

10. *L'ascèse cynique*, 22, 159ff. Goulet-Cazé finds close parallels to Diog. Laert. 6.70ff. in the diatribe *On Exercise* by Musonius Rufus. Cf. Diog. Laert. 7.123: "The wise man will accept training [*askesis*] for the sake of endurance of body."

11. "The wise man will live the Cynic life, for Cynicism is the short road to virtue, as Apollodorus says in his *Ethics*" (Diog. Laert. 7.121). Goulet-Cazé attributes to the *Ethics* of Apollodorus also the following passage in Stobaeus (2.114.24–25): "They [the Stoics] say that the wise man will live as a Cynic, which amounts to saying that he will persevere in Cynicism; however, one who is [already] wise will not start living as a Cynic."

This appears to mean that anyone who attains wisdom by means of the Cynic life will continue living as a Cynic, but one who attains wisdom by other means—the longer road of study—need not bother with the Cynic life. If Apollodorus said this, he said it at a time when influential Stoics wished to get rid of the Cynicizing tradition in the Stoa altogether. The formulation implies that Cynicism is not strictly necessary yet assigns it a definite priority; the non-Cynic alternative is mentioned by way of qualification; and we are told that a Cynic will remain a Cynic even after enlightenment as though to assure us that it is no temporary phase. This is easier to understand if we assume that the "Cynicism" to which the Apollodoran tradition gave such priority was in reality a Cynicized Stocism.

12. Demetius of Magnesia (first century B.C.) relayed the tradition that Zeno's father, a Cypriot merchant, brought back Socratic books from Athens, which led Zeno to become Crates' pupil (Diog. Laert. 7.31). Another account had Zeno on his first visit to Athens read Xenophon in a bookseller's shop and ask the bookseller where men like Socrates were to be found; whereupon the bookseller pointed out Crates (7.2). Zeno is supposed to have admired the writings of Antisthenes (7.19). These anecdotes about Zeno's interest in Socratic dialogues were not produced entirely by the anti-Cynic tradition; they glorify the Cynic/Stoic connection, but it is Cynicism seen from a certain perspective. See A. A. Long, "Socrates in Hellenistic Philosophy," *Classicial Quarterly* 38 (1988), 150–71.

13. There is no space here to deal with this important and elusive figure. See A. M. Ioppolo, *Aristone di Chio e lo Stoicismo Antico* (Naples 1980); and Malcolm Schofield, "Ariston of Chios and the Unity of Virtue," *Ancient Philosophy* 4 (1984), 83–95. The most Cynic elements in Aristo were his belief in a purely ethical approach, doing away with logic and physics, and his apparent return to an intuitive Cynic concept of virtue, rejecting the possibility of "natural" moral precepts. He believed in *askesis* (Clement, *Misc.* 2.20 = SVF 1. Arist. 370), but of what sort we do not know.

14. Dudley, *History of Cynicism*, 82, 102–3.

15. Chrysippus did not think that he or any of his teachers or disciples were wise (Plut., *On Stoic Self-Contradictions* 1048e). Some said there had never been any wise men (Sextus, *Against the Professors* 9.133; Plut., *On Common Conceptions* 1076bc). Some would not say whether there had been any or not (Cic., *Acad.* 2.47.145). Some thought they were like phoenixes, appearing once in several centuries (Sen., *Ep.* 42.1; Alexander of Aphrodisias, *On Fate* 199.15 = SVF 3.658).

16. Nicola Festa, *Stoici* 1. *Zenone* (Bari 1932), 9–25, assembled thirty-one fragments. H. C. Baldry, "Zeno's Ideal State," *Journal of Hellenic Studies* 79 (1959), 3–14, apparently unaware of Festa's edition, adopted a minimalist approach and included only fragments specifically attributed to the *Republic* by ancient authors, emerging with only twelve, the more important of which are translated here. I add the seventh chapter of Philodemus' *On the Stoics*, agreeing with its recent editor, Dorandi, that it is about as useful a piece of evidence as anything.

17. The phrase *kata* ... *stichous* could mean either "at line 200" or "in 200 lines." The former translation is adopted by Long and Sedley *Hellenistic Philosophers* 1.430; but Mansfeld, "Diogenes Laertius," 345–46, points out that the latter makes more sense here, and also in C. There is no obvious reason for exact textual references, of a sort

that ancient scholars rarely bothered with, at these points; but there is reason for the author to show that these were lengthy discussions, not *obiter dicta*.

18. Diogenes Laertius does not reveal its contents, but we know from Christian writers that it was a typically Stoic bit of cosmological allegory in which the marriage of Zeus and Hera was made to symbolize the union of cosmic reason with matter. It was the candor of Chrysippus' language about divine sexuality that was thought offensive. See SVF 2.1071–75; Pepin, *Mythe et allégorie*, 454.

19. Baldry, *Unity of Mankind*, 211 n. 36.

20. Later Platonists remembered that Zeno had indulged in "shameless" attacks on Plato: Eusebius, *Evangelical Preparation* 14.6, quoting Numenius, a Platonist of the second century A.D.

21. Baldry, "Zeno's Ideal State," 6, pointed out that the citations from Zeno's *Republic*, including those that appear to be direct quotations (B, R), take the form of statements about what ought to happen.

22. Philodemus (c. 8, col. 21) says that the Stoics (or Cynics?) would transport us to the lands of the Taurians and other barbarous peoples, or back to the time of the earth-born (the Giants and Cyclopes of mythology). Sextus (*Outlines* 3.249, *Against Prof.* 11.195) says that the teachings of Chrysippus on incest and cannibalism could only be practiced among the Cyclopes and Laestrygonians.

23. That the Stoics portrayed an ideal "world" and not a city has been generally accepted. Perhaps the most distinguished skeptic was W. W. Tarn, who thought that Zeno must have written about *two* ideal states—the little one that Plutarch (P) compares to Sparta, and the big one that Plutarch (O) compares to Alexander's empire. But these are versions of the same rhetorical *topos* and neither comparison is to be taken literally.

24. For the typical Cynic attitude to the "general education," see Diogenes Laertius 6.27–28, 73, 103–104; and Goulet-Caźe, *L'ascèse cynique*, 152ff. There are anecdotes where Diogenes praises *paideia* (6.47, 68), but in this context *paideia* probably means the Cynic discipline. In Dio Chrysostom 4.29–33, the Cynic training is called *andreia* and the general education is called *paideia* ("education for men" vs. "education for boys"). Perhaps we should not take this rhetoric too literally, for even Cynics must have generally thought it useful to learn how to read and write, and we know that some were willing to contemplate a reformed and cynicized version of general education on the secondary level. There was a Cynic educational treatise by a certain Eubulus called *Sale of Diogenes* which described a Cynic educational program consisting of memorization of literature (including the writings of Diogenes), music, and athletics (Diog. Laert. 6.30–31).

25. H. I. Marrou, *History of Education in Antiquity*, trans. George Lamb (New York 1956), 244.

26. The later Stoics made a distinction between "knowledge" (*episteme*), by which they meant Stoic philosophical studies, and the "useful arts" (*epitedeumata*), consisting of the general education (SVF 3.294). They considered the useful arts an essential propaedeutic to philosophy. Chrysippus wrote much on education, including the early childhood years, and his advice extended to the prescription of nurses' lullabies (Quintilian 1.1.4, 1.1.16, 1.3.13, 1.10.32, 1.11.17). He seems to have envisioned a totally Stoicized version of the general education. The titles of Zeno's works suggest the same. Quintilian also tells us that "the leading Stoics thought that some wise men would devote some study to music" (1.10.15), implying that even the most advanced Stoics might have time for the cultivation of nonphilosophical arts.

27. Zeller believed the Stoic ideal world was a completely egalitarian society, and he has been generally followed; see especially the discussions of this point by Baldry.

But a number of scholars have held the opposite view: Pöhlmann, *Sozialismus* 2.273 n. 2; Tarn, *Alexander* 2.417–26; Ferguson, *Utopias*, 111ff.; Yvon Garland, *Slavery in Ancient Greece*, trans. Janet Lloyd, 2nd ed. (Ithaca 1988), 129.

28. In addition to the passage quoted below, see Stob. 2.99.3 (SVF 1.216, 3.567) and the other passages from Stobaeus collected in SVF 3.611ff.

29. Argued by Ferguson, *Utopias of the Classical World*, 114.

30. I am indebted here to a valuable discussion of this neglected passage by Erskine, *Hellenistic Stoa*, 43–63. He suggests that *hypotaxis*, an uncommon word, was a Stoic technical term used to describe all hierarchical relationships.

31. Stob. 2.7.96, 102.4, 102.11 = SVF 3.613–615.

32. *Stoics, Epicureans, and Skeptics*, 322.

33. *Laws* 759, 771, 778–79, 804. Temples will be built around the central agora and around the perimeter of the cirty; law courts will be built beside them; gymnasia, with state schools attached, will be built on three sites around the agora, and there will be three military training grounds in the suburbs; there is also a reference to theaters, whose place in the Stoic city we will consider in the following section. See Dyroff, *Ethik d. alten Stoa*, 210.

34. Attributed to Lycurgus (Plut., *Lycurgus* 19) and Agesilaus (*Laconian Apophthegms* 210ef, a collection of allegedly Spartan maxims probably compiled in the Hellenistic age and later included in the *Moralia* of Plutarch).

35. Baldry thought Zeno meant there were to be no artisans in the ideal city ("Zeno's Ideal State," 10–11). But that seems impossible, for it had to contain buildings. The syllogism at R is surely directed against superstition, not against artisans. To say that idols are made of base materials unworthy of divinity was a commonplace in philosophical critiques of the cults in Hellenistic and Roman times. See Ramsay MacMullen, *Paganism in the Roman Empire* (New Haven 1981), 76. The parallel between St. Paul's speech on the Areopagus and Zeno's *Republic* was noted by Clement of Alexandria (see my comment on R).

36. Cynics ridiculed athletes, but the point was always to compare a false *askesis* to the true Cynic *askesis:* Diog. Laert. 6.27, 30, 49, 70; Ioppolo, *Aristone di Chio*, 112 n. 48. The Cynic educational program of Eubulus includes the palaestra, but not a full athletic program (see n. 24). Both "Diogenes" and Zeno could have included, along with attacks on conventional athletic/military training, references to some kind of palaestrae or gymnasia, which would explain Philodemus' allusion in N. Both Philodemus (N) and Diogenes Laertius (B) suggest there were references to men and women exercising nude together, and there would have to be some place to exercise.

37. The Utopians of Thomas More use gold and silver for chamberpots, an image which may be of Stoic origin. Plutarch says Stoics compared riches to chamberpots, tassels, and oil flasks, and thought that to congratulate rich men and kings on their wealth was like praising them for using those items (*Stoic Self-Contra.* 1048b; *Common Concept.* 1069c).

38. Diog. Laert. 6.72: "He [Diogenes] said women should be common, and recognized no marriage except where a man who persuades lies with a woman who consents."

39. Chrysippus certainly mentioned this anecdote to make such a point in his *Republic* (S), and it is likely Zeno did too, for Sextus says Zeno approved of masturbation (*Outlines* 3.206).

40. On Cynic criticism of funerals: Diog. Laert. 6.52, 79; Teles, fr. 3 (Hense 29–32, containing a reference to Egyptian burial customs); *Ep. of Diogenes* 25; Cic., *Tusc. Disp.* 1.43.104; Kindstrand, *Bion*, 285. The *topos* went back to Socrates, who said that the

casual way people discard their hair and nails and amputate diseased limbs shows that the body is valueless without mind, and for this was accused of impious views about funerals (Xen., *Mem.*, 1.2.51–55). Seneca (*Ep.* 92.34–35) writes that the wise will care no more for their bodies after death than for their hair or nail clippings, and will be indifferent as to whether their bodies are buried, cremated, or eaten by animals. This sounds like a bowdlerized version of what Chrysippus said in *On Proper Functions*, with animals substituted for people.

41. If Dorandi's reconstruction of a fragmentary sentence in Philodemus, c. 7, is correct, then "Diogenes" also wrote that dying parents should be killed, presumably as a form of euthanasia. In support of this interpretation Dorandi cites the Christian apologist Theophilus, according to whom Diogenes taught that children should sacrifice their parents, and the Stoics added the corollary that parents should be eaten as well (*To Autolycus* 3.5; cf. Epiphanius, *Against Heresies* 3.39; SVF 3.746, 750). But perhaps this bizarre doxography can also be explained as a conflation of some garbled reference to the Cynic tragedy *Thyestes* with the charges of ritual murder that were brought against Christians in Theophilus' time. Theophilus was capable of writing that not only Stoics, but Epicureans, filled libraries with books advocating homosexuality and incest.

42. The banquet image was used by Bion to symbolize the transience of all gifts of fortune, and the imperturbability of the wise, who depart life as easily as banqueters leave their seats (Kindstrand, fr. 68 = Teles fr. 2, Hense 15–16). It was not particularly connected with property, but to Roman Stoics it often symbolized the division of the world's goods: Epict., *Disc.* 2.4 (the banquet and theater similes are paired), *Manual* 15; Dio, *Or.* 30; Sen., *Ep.* 73.8. Seneca equates banquets with free distributions of grain or meat, showing that the term "banquet" in this context meant a public feast such as those that followed sacrifices. In the pseudo-Lucianic *Cynic* (6–7), the Cynic is said to take anything available at the banquet, but without grabbing from the other diners. A more "rigorist," and probably less authentic, interpretation of Cynicism is found in Epictetus (*Manual* 15): the Cynic will not participate in the banquet at all.

43. Sen., *Ep.* 73.7–8, 88.12; *On Constancy* 5.5; *To Marcia* 10.1–2, 21.1–2; *On Tranquility* 11; *On Benefits* 2.35, 6.3, 7.4–12. Seneca distinguishes the same three levels of property as Cicero: indivisible public goods like peace and justice, divisible public goods like the banquet and the dole, and individual *proprietates*. He repeatedly makes the point that the last is an illusion, a temporary share in a larger whole. The distinction between private and public is compared to that between *dominium* and *usus*, or that between *dominium* and *precarium* (property held by one's son or one's slave, over which one retains ownership). He also points out that all individual properties are ultimately owned by the state.

44. Chrysippus counted mad those who counted wealth and health as nothing (Plut., *Stoic Self-Contra.* 1047e). In his *On Rhetoric* he said the wise person will speak in public *as if* he thought wealth, reputation, etc. were goods (Plut. 1034b). He said there is nothing wrong with trying to get what we want in life, so long as we do not take what belongs to others, just as upon entering a race we try to win without tripping the other contestants (Cic., *On Duties* 3.10.42). He was the author of many maxims against luxury and avarice (Ath. 4.158b; Plut. 1043e, 1044b–f), but they imply only a traditional degree of moderation. I have already referred to Athenaeus' summary of Zeno's teaching on wealth (6.233b–c): he was supposed to have said wealth is morally indifferent, but the correct use of it virtuous, and that the wise person will know how to use both superfluity and simplicity correctly.

45. To see the implications of this metaphor it is useful to look at photographs of some of the better preserved Greek theaters. *The Cambridge Ancient History*, plates to

vol. 7.1 ed. Roger Ling (Cambridge 1984), plates 196–97, shows the ruins of the Theater of Dionysus at Athens, which was rebuilt in the late fourth century B.C. This was essentially the theater that Chrysippus knew. Notice the very prominent front seats reserved for Athenian magistrates and priests who had *proedria*, the privilege of the front seat. This was such an important symbol of office that to mention theaters in this context was to remind Greeks that some individuals were more privileged than others. On the other hand, we notice that apart from the few seats of honor all seats are equal, which was true of all Greek theaters. Chrysippus' metaphor may have implied the existence of special honors, but not social inequalities.

Most commentators seem to have assumed that the theater *topos* was incompatible with equality. Tarn (*Alexander* 2.412 n. 5) thought that this proved Stoics did not believe in equality even in utopia. M. T. Griffin, *Seneca: A Philosopher in Politics* (Oxford 1976), 204, thought that Chrysippus must have been the first Stoic to admit the legitimacy of private property, since the theater *topos* is attributed to him and not to Zeno. Erskine, *Hellenistic Stoa*, 105–10, argues that the whole *topos* was of Neostoic origin because Seneca (*Ben* 7.12) emphasizes the unequal seating arrangements of the Roman theater.

46. It is also possible that the source of this excerpt thought Chrysippus' statement objectionable because it contradicted some of Chrysippus' other teachings. Plutarch (*Stoic Self-Contra.* 1043aff.) objected to *On Ways of Living* on these grounds. See below, p. 195.

47. See P. A. Brunt, "Aspects of the Social Thought of Dio Chrysostom and the Stoics," *Proceedings of the Cambridge Philological Society* n.s. 19 (1973), 9–34. But according to Arius Didymus, ap. Stob. 2.109.10–110.4 (SVF 3.686), Stoics (by the first century B.C.) held that the preferable ways of earning money were to become a courtier, to hold political office and receive support from wealthy friends, and to collect fees for teaching. Chrysippus had ridiculed all these alternatives.

48. Zeno, in the fragment quoted on p. 179 above, refers to the "inhabitants" (*oikountes*) of cities, not to *politai* as Plato and Aristotle usually did. Dio Chrysostom (36.20) says the Stoics defined a city as a crowed (*plethos*) of humans living together. I owe this observation to Erskine, *Hellenistic Stoa*, 51.

49. Baldry doubted that a work as short as the *Republic* could have discussed the wise person's role in ordinary life. But since its declared purpose was to present models relevant "to our time and place," Zeno had to discuss questions like this somewhere. For Chrysippus on marriage, see Jerome, *Against Jov.* 2.48 (SVF 3.727).

50. A point worth making because even some recent scholars have thought Stoic eros a metaphor for a purely nonphysical relationship: e.g., Daniel Babut, "Les stoïciens et l'amour," *Revue des études grecques* 76 (1963), 55–63.

51. See David Halperin, "Platonic Eros and What Men Call Love," *Ancient Philosophy* 5 (1985), 161–204.

52. See Lactantius, *Institutes* 3.25 (SVF 3.253); Clement, *Misc.* 4.8 (SVF 3.254).

53. Diog. Laert. 7.41. The usual Stoic division was threefold: logic, physics, and ethics. Cleanthes' classification does not mean he endowed politics with special importance, because he also subdivided the other areas.

54. In addition to the *Republic* Zeno wrote *On Law* (Diog. Laert. 7.4). Cleanthes wrote *The Statesman*, *On Laws*, *On Kingship*, *On Councils*, *On Judgments* (or perhaps *On Law-courts*)—Diog. Laert. 7.175. The catalog of Chrysippus' political works is lost, but we have the word of Plutarch (1033b) that his output on politics, as on everything else, was voluminous. We have mentioned his *Republic*. Plutarch mentions also an *On Judgments* (1045d), an *On Orators* (1034b), and an *On Law* (1037f), which is perhaps the

same work known to Philodemus (M) as *On the City and the Law*. He also compiled a collection of barbarian funeral customs (Cic., *Tusc. Disp.* 1.45.108). Herillus wrote *The Lawmaker* (Diog. Laert. 7.166); Dionysius, *On Ancient Kings* and *On Barbarian Customs* (7.167). I will reserve mention of the political works of Perseus and Sphaerus until the next section.

55. Dio 47.2: Zeno, Cleanthes, and Chrysippus all said the wise will honor their country and that public life is in accordance with nature. Seneca, *On Leisure* 3.2: Zeno said the wise will enter public life, if nothing hinder them; likewise Chrysippus (Diog. Laert. 7.121). Cf. Diog. Laert, 7.108, 123; Cic., *On Ends* 3.20.68; Plut., *Stoic Self-Contra.* 1033de, 1034b.

56. Dio 47.2; Sen., *On Tranquility* 1.10; Plut., *Stoic Self-Contra.* 1033b–1034a.

57. Antigonus Gonatas of Macedon often invited Zeno to court, and Zeno eventually sent him his disciples Perseus and Philonides (Diog. Laert. 7.6–9,13–15). It was said that Ptolemy invited Cleanthes to Alexandria; both Cleanthes and Chrysippus refused to go, but Cleanthes sent Sphaerus (7.177, 185). But the doxographer has gotten his Ptolemies mixed up, so there were probably two separate invitations, the second one to Sphaerus. It was thought a sign of Chrysippus' arrogance that he dedicated not one of his many works to any king, such dedications being customary by the late third century.

58. Stob 4.192.10–13 = SVF 3.694. Seneca gives the impression that Chrysippus' advice on political participation was carefully hedged: *On Leisure* 8.1, *Ep.* 68.2.

59. Plut., *Stoic Self-Contra.* 1033b–e, 1043a–1044b, 1047f; *Common Concept.* 1061d. Plutarch thinks it a contradiction that Chrysippus' *On Ways of Living* advises the wise man to become a king or a courtier—with any king at all, not necessarily a "progressor"—and yet recommends withdrawal from politics. (We know that it also ridiculed the life of a courtier, and all other ways by which a philosopher might earn a living; see p. 190 above.) Plutarch mentions here another contradictory statement found in Chrysippus' *On Proper Functions*: Chrysippus said the wise man would turn three somersaults if he could get a talent for it. Plutarch seems oblivious to the irony in these passages.

60. I would not assume, with Reesor, *Political Theory*, 20, that the mixed constitution theory goes back to the old Stoa merely because the organization of Diogenes Laertius' doxography seems to suggest this. His methods were too unsystematic. Nor would I assume, with F. E. Devine "Stoicism on the Best Regime," *Journal of the History of Ideas* 31 (1970), 323–336, that the old Stoa could not have had a constitutional theory because it was exclusively concerned with ideal cities. Nor would I assume with Erskine, *Hellenistic Stoa*, 73, that the old Stoa could not have had a mixed-constitutional theory because this would institutionalize social divisions, which would be incompatible with the Stoic principle of harmony. I am assuming that the levels of discourse among Greek philosophers allowed far more flexible approaches to the problem of an ideal society than the last two interpretations recognize.

61. There have been a number of attempts to identify the political sympathies of the early Stoics. The evidence seems to me inadequate to support any of these. W. S. Ferguson, *Hellenistic Athens* (London 1911), 232, 261, and Tarn, *Antigonus Gonatas* (Oxford 1913), 331, thought the Stoa developed from monarchism under Zeno to republicanism under Chrysippus. Heinrich and M. Simon, *Die alte Stoa und ihr Naturbegriff* (Berlin 1956), 7, 15, 26ff., suggest Zeno moved in the opposite direction, from democracy to monarchy. All place too much importance on Zeno's alleged ties with Antigonus Gonatas. Erskine, *Hellenistic Stoa*, 75–102, after a full discussion of the evidence, concludes that the early Stoics favored democracy. Some of the evidence he adduces is novel and important, especially his argument that the words "friendship"

and "harmony," key terms in Stoic political thought, were becoming popular political slogans with an anti-Macedonian ring in the third century. And it is possible there was a political allusion in Zeno's comparison of the old Athenian tetradrachms to his own concise style, and of the ornate Macedonian coinage to the speeches of sophists (Diog. Laert. 7.18). I have already suggested that the social values of Stoicism, and also Cynicism, had affinities with Greek democracy. But I have also suggested that in dealing with ancient utopian philosophy we ought not to assume that its values were immediately translated into practical political programs.

62. Ath. 11.508d–509c. See Düring, *Herodicus*, 149–51.

63. Diog. Laert. 7.10–12,182; Cic., *On Ends* 1.11.39; Pausanias 1.29.15.

64. We cannot deduce much from these excerpts taken out of context, but they do suggest Stoics were concerned with definitions of social and political values on a general and abstract level. The most famous is the definition of law from Chrysippus' *On Law* (Marcian 1 = SVF 3.314, trans. Long/Sedley), which ended up in the *Institutes* of Justinian: "Law is king of all things human and divine. Law must preside over what is honorable and base, as ruler and as guide, and thus be the standard of right and wrong, prescribing to animals whose nature is political what they should do, and prohibiting them from what they should not do."

The following syllogism from Cleanthes (Stob. 2.103.14–17 = SVF 1.587, trans. Long/Sedley), perhaps from his *On Law*, appears to be a summary of an argument designed to prove that the polis is *asteion*, civilized or refined, because it serves the social function of dispensing justice: "If a city is a habitable structure, in which people who take refuge have access to the dispensation of justice, a city is surely something civilized; but a city is this sort of habitation; therefore a city is something civilized."

For a similar passage attributed to Diogenes the Dog at Diog. Laert. 6.72, see Goulet-Cazé, "Un syllogisme stoïcien."

65. Polybius is the earliest representative of this attitude toward utopianism. He says that he will not bring Plato's *Republic* into a discussion of the best constitution because that would be like comparing statues with living people (6.47). When he praises the Roman constitution for deliberately cultivating superstition, he admits that this would not be necessary were it possible to construct a state composed entirely of the wise (6.56; cf. 12.28). The latter comment sounds like an allusion to the Stoic utopia and not the Platonic, but the two are so often conflated by later writers that we cannot tell. Polybius borrows the metaphor of the statue from Plato, but he ignores the fact that Plato had made a sustained effort to make the statue step from its pedestal. As we have seen, this rhetorical habit of lumping all utopian writers together and dismissing them as impractical and useless became common in Roman times.

66. Epiphanius, *Against Heresies* 3.38 (SVF 1.447): "Perseus taught the same things as Zeno."

67. According to Plutarch (*Stoic Self-Contra.* 1033f) and Cicero (*Acad.* 2.44.136), Stoics used Lycurgus and Solon as examples of the false law codes recognized by the inferior, as opposed to the true law of reason. As usual we cannot be sure which group of Stoics they mean; but it sounds as though Plutarch and Cicero did not think that Stoics in general attached any particular importance or value to the Spartan constitution.

68. The most recent general treatment is Paul Cartledge and Antony Spawforth, *Hellenistic and Roman Sparta: A Tale of Two Cities* (London 1989), 38ff. For older literature the reader is referred again to the notes in Tigerstedt.

69. All that we know about Sphaerus at Sparta comes from Plutarch's *Cleomenes* 2.2–3, 11. The *Life of Sphaerus* by Diogenes Laertius associates him with the Ptolemaic

court, where he seems to have fled after the defeat of Cleomenes, and does not even mention his stay at Sparta; which shows that his reputation did not depend upon his relationship with Cleomenes. The fact that the only surviving excerpts from Perseus' and Sphaerus' works on the Spartan constitution (SVF 1.454, 455, 630) concern details of the *syssitia* tells us nothing, for they were all preserved by Athenaeus, whose interests were largely culinary; our only fragment of Dicaearchus' *Tripoliticus* is also preserved by Athenaeus and also concerns the *syssitia*.

70. Pöhlmann, *Sozialismus*, 1.369ff.; Ollier, *Le mirage Spartiate*, 2.103ff.; Pohlenz, *Die Stoa* 1.26, 170; Tarn in the *Cambridge Ancient History*, 7 (1928), 742, said Agis was taught "Stoic Communism" by Sphaerus and "may perhaps have dreamt of himself as Plato's philosopher king in action." But see his later opinion in *Hellenistic Civilization*, 3rd ed. (New York 1952), 332. Max Cary, *A History of the Greek World from 323 to 146 B.C.* (London 1932), 156, wrote that Sphaerus "expounded theoretical communism" to Cleomenes.

71. See especially Michael Rostovtzeff, *Social and Economic History of the Hellenistic World* (Oxford 1941) 2.1129ff.; and T. W. Africa, *Phylarchus and the Spartan Revolution* (Berkeley 1961), 16–22. Africa thought the reforms had Cynic overtones but had nothing to do with Stoicism. I think he exaggerated the difference between Cynic and Stoic moral teaching. The connection between Stoicism and Sparta is also minimized by Tigerstedt, *Legend of Sparta* 2.69ff., and Rawson, *Spartan Tradition*, 91–92. Ephraim David, *Sparta Between Empire and Revolution (404–243 B.C.)* (Salem 1981), 162–169, is guarded in his conclusions but doubts that Stoicism could have been a decisive influence on the reform. I would agree, but I am here more interested in the influence of the reform on Stoicism. An argument for a powerful Stoic influence on the reformers is made by Erskine, *Hellenistic Stoa*, 123–49.

72. Circa 240 B.C., Teles of Megara in his diatribe *On Exile* (see p. 142 above) described the Spartan system as open to talent. The obvious connection with the reforms of Agis IV was pointed out by Fuks, "Non-Phylarchean Tradition of the Programme of Agis IV," *Classical Quarterly* 12 (1962), 118–21 (*Social Crisis* 256–59). It has been questioned by Doron Mendels, "Sparta in Teles' *Peri Phyges*," *Eranos* 77 (1979), 111–15, who points out that Teles does not refer specifically to Agis' reforms but to an older Spartan custom of granting citizenship to foreigners or helots who had passed the *agoge*; and that Teles is unlikely to speak in these terms of a reform that had already failed. But the fact remains that Teles believed in a tradition that the Spartan system had once been far more democratic, and the *agoge* open to everyone; and he could not have failed to see in the reforms of Agis a revival of this ideal. It does not matter that Agis had failed. We know that his ideals still lived.

73. Origen, *Against Celsus* 4.63–64. The statement about masked prostitutes is certainly from Chrysippus, that about eunuchs probably is. Chrysippus had some interest in collecting data about barbarian customs (see n. 54 above) and such a collection is the probable source of this bizarre passage.

74. Ath. 13.555d; Justin 2.6; Aug., *City of God* 18.9; and various scholiasts, some of them translated in Tyrell, *Amazons*, 28–31. See also Pembroke, "Women in Charge"; and H. J. Rose, *Handbook of Greek Mythology*, 6th ed. (New York 1959), 261–62. This story is unlikely to have been known in the classical period. Neither Herodotus nor anyone else made any mention of it in connection with community of women among the barbarians.

75. Strabo 7.3.9: Ephorus, abandoning Herodotus' cautious approach to the subject, wrote in his influential universal history (late fourth century B.C.) that all Scythians practiced philosophical communism in property and sex. His contemporary Theopompus

claimed that the Etruscans shared their wives and could not recognize their own children (Ath. 12.517d–f).

76. E. R. Dodds, *The Greeks and the Irrational* (Berkeley 1951)

77. Erskine, *Hellenistic Stoa*, 26, points out that *gamos* might be used for any type of heterosexual union; e.g. at Plato's *Rep.*, 459a it refers to the breeding of animals. But when Diogenes Laertius applies the word *gamos* to sexual communism he is careful to qualify it (6.72: Diogenes the Dog knew no *gamos* except for the *gamos* that exists between a man who persuades and a woman who consents).

78. See J. R. Hamilton, *Plutarch, Alexander: A Commentary* (Oxford 1969), xxiii–xxxiii; Daniel Babut, *Plutarque et la stoicïsme* (Paris 1969), 84–85.

79. Plutarch says Alexander brought marriage to the Hyrcanians, agriculture to the Arachosians; taught the Sogdians not to kill their parents, the Persians not to marry their mothers, and the Scythians not to eat their dead. All this is derived from the legend of Alexander as culture hero who brought civilization to the barbarians and put an end to all those interesting practices described in my first chapter. Ironically, this legend seems to have been started in Alexander's own lifetime by Onesicritus the Cynic, who said that Alexander cured the Bactrians of their barbarous funeral customs, which required dying people to be eaten by dogs (Strabo 11.11.3).

80. Also there is similar language in Diogenes Laertius' definition of Stoic *eros*, probably from Apollodorus *Ethics*, which has already been quoted in part (E): "They say love is an attempt to make friends through the appearance of beauty; and it is not for intercourse, but for friendship" (7.130).

5

The End of Utopia

> Nor is it right to bring Plato's *Republic* into discussion [of the best constitution] ... any attempt to judge it against the Spartan or Roman or Carthaginian constitution would be like putting forth some statue and comparing it with living and breathing men.
>
> POLYBIUS 6.47, trans. Mortimer Chambers

The Decline of the Stoic Utopian Tradition

Panaetius and the Wise Men

By the first century B.C. utopianism had dropped out of the mainstream of Stoic teaching. The Stoic doxographical summaries of Roman times do not mention an ideal city of the wise in any way that would lead us to think this a living doctrine, and the Stoic moralists of Roman times seem virtually ignorant of it. It is only from non-Stoic sources that we know the earlier Stoics had taught such things. Furthermore, we hear of a sharp controversy within the Stoa early in the first century B.C. over the canonical status of certain of Zeno's writings, particularly the *Republic*. This controversy must have been the final stage in a major break with the old Stoic tradition.

Panaetius of Rhodes (ca. 180–ca. 110 B.C.) is generally thought responsible for this break.[1] He made significant changes in several branches of Stoic philosophy; there is reason to think that his impact on Stoic social and political thought was particularly decisive; and though our sources nowhere specifically say this, it was in all probability Panaetius who buried the utopian ideal. For several crucial decades in the later second century, when the Roman establishment was taking shape in the Hellenistic world, Panaetius was a dominant figure in the Stoa; and his disciples, obscure but numerous, dominated it after him. There is no questioning the importance of his innovations, but their exact nature has long been disputed, and so has their relationship to Panaetius' political activities. In this chapter we will consider both these questions, and a third that is less often asked: to what extent did the old Stoic ethical/political tradition survive the Panaetian reforms and linger into Roman times?

The first problem is to decide exactly what it was that Panaetius did to Stoic ethical teaching. Many have thought that he rejected its central doctrine, the self-sufficiency of virtue.[2] We are told that he redefined the Stoic concept of the good so as to deny that virtue could suffice for happiness without the acquisition of certain external things, such as health and wealth (Diog. Laert. 7.128; cf. 7.103). Also we know that Panaetius reformulated the Stoic definition of the end of action: not "living according to nature," but "living according to the starting points given us by nature" (Clement, *Misc.* 2.21.129). The new language suggests a new interest in practical everyday morality, and a shift of focus away from the wise to those who are "progressing" toward wisdom. This is also suggested by Cicero's *On Duties* (*De officiis*), which we know was based upon the *Peri kathekontos* of Panaetius. All of which would seem to make it obvious why Panaetius had no use for utopias; for he could have had no use for their inhabitants, the self-sufficient wise.

Nevertheless, there are serious problems with this interpretation. If Panaetius really rejected the self-sufficiency of virtue, then he would have become something other than a Stoic, by any definition of a Stoic known to antiquity. Yet no one ever doubted that he had been a leading Stoic. Nor do we know of any Stoics after Panaetius who held the view that has been attributed to him. The Roman Stoics all upheld the founders' sacred principle that no natural advantages could be confused with virtue, which consisted solely in a right attitude of mind. This view was attributed to Panaetius himself, and also to his disciples Posidonius and Hecaton.[3] It seems unlikely that Panaetius introduced any change in this fundamental point of doctrine.

More likely is the solution adumbrated in the previous chapter: that Stoicism always had two philosophies, one for the wise and one for ordinary people. The latter department was described as the realm of *kathekonta*, "proper functions." Panaetius was far from the first Stoic to write a treatise *On Proper Functions.* Zeno, Cleanthes, Chrysippus, and Sphaerus had all produced such works. But we know the contents only of Panaetius' treatise, owing to the use made of it by Cicero. We cannot know how much of it was original. The general characteristics of the moral system of Cicero's *On Duties* may have been entirely typical of Stoic moral teaching on the second-best level. Even Cicero admits that what he is discussing in *On Duties* is not true virtue but a *simulacra virtutis*, a semblance of virtue on a level suitable for progressors (*On Duties* 1.15.46, 3.4.17).

Furthermore, it is not clear that Panaetius' redefinition of the end contradicted earlier Stoic thought. When he said we should live according to the starting points (*aphormai*) of nature, he meant that we must follow our individual propensities. Cicero understood this to mean that we must remain true to the universal nature that is in us, but at the same time follow our own particular natures, so long as these are not vicious. Even though we may recognize that other particular natures are nobler, we have a positive obligation to follow our own propensities:

> For we must so act that we do nothing in opposition to human nature in general, and yet, while keeping that secure, follow our own nature. Thus, even if a different course would be more dignified and superior, we should still

> regulate our own pursuits by the rule of our own nature. For it is pointless to resist one's own nature and to pursue something to which one cannot attain. ... *On Duties*, 1.31.110, trans. Long/Sedley

Obviously this ideal is not intended to deny or devalue the ideal of the wise person. It means that some of us will have "starting points" that lead us to become wise, and some of us will not.

Nor was Panaetius the first second-century Stoic to meddle with Zeno's definition of the end. Panaetius' reinterpretation was the culmination of a long process of refining the classical definition so as to take account of the criticisms of Carneades, head of the skeptical Academy in the mid-second century. Carneades accused Stoics of inconsistency in positing two separate ends, the good and the natural advantages, and argued that the things according to nature ought to be included in the good. Panaetius' predecessors Diogenes of Babylon (d. ca. 152) and Antipater of Tarsus (d. ca. 129) tried to deal with this objection by clarifying the relationship between the good and the natural advantages. These reformulations had the effect of placing more emphasis on the natural advantages, but their intent was to preserve the uniqueness of virtue. Against Carneades, they held that virtue could not be identified with the external objects of virtue; rather virtue was the art of obtaining those objects. Panaetius added nothing to this formula except to emphasize that this art must be conditioned by our individual natures. All these were clarifications of basic Stoic doctrine, not new directions, and none were intended to deny that virtue is sufficient for happiness.[4]

These considerations persuade us of Panaetius' basic orthodoxy. Nevertheless he must have done *something* radical. It is difficult to dismiss altogether the evidence of Diogenes Laertius 7.128: "Panaetius and Posidonius say virtue is not self-sufficient but has need of health, resources, and strength."[5] Perhaps Panaetius only meant to direct more attention to ethics for ordinary people, but he said this in such a way as to leave the impression on our doxographer that he thought this the only standard worth considering.

Perhaps his real innovation was to actively *discourage* progressors from following the wise person. That was certainly the intention of Cicero, who in the passage quoted above advised his readers not to aim at the unattainable ("nec quicquam sequi, quod assequi non queas"). A little later (1.31.114ff.) Cicero gives a new twist to the ancient dramatic simile by recommending that we imitate the good actor who avoids unsuitable parts. In Cynic/Stoic usage the dramatic simile was used to recommend a readiness to take *any* role in life, but Cicero reverses the moral. He particularly wishes to dissuade his audience from taking heroic roles. He says that few of us are called upon to choose between vice and virtue like Heracles; most of us simply follow the model of our parents or public opinion; a wise man like Socrates may flaunt established custom, but we are not to imitate him, and the Cynics are censured for attempting this (1.35.128, 1.41.148). All this represents a radical departure from the moral teaching of the early Stoics, who regarded Heracles and Socrates as their great models, and concentrated on the supreme importance of the choice between virtue and vice made independently of all opinion and custom.

One is inclined to think Cicero is following Panaetius closely here. Why, after all, should Panaetius have introduced the term *aphormai* into the central tenet of Stoicism? There is little point in advising one to follow one's own *aphormai* unless this implies one is not to follow other people's *aphormai*. We have one quotation from Panaetius about the wise man, and it confirms this interpretation:

> I think that Panaetius gave a charming answer to the youth who asked whether the wise man would fall in love. "As to the wise man, we shall see. What concerns you and me, who are still a great distance from the wise man, is to ensure that we do not fall into a state of affairs which is disturbed, powerless, subservient to another and worthless to oneself." Seneca, *Ep.* 116.5, trans. Long/Sedley[6]

It is difficult to believe that the early Stoics used such terms as these. Their emphasis on the ideal would have had no point if they had not assumed for it a universal relevance. When they talked about Diogenes' public masturbation, they probably made it clear that their audience was not supposed to imitate him literally, nor to practice community of women, nor anything else that might happen in an imaginary society of perfect rectitude. But there was *something* about that society worthy of imitation by all progressors. The moral relationship between the ideal wise man and the real world pervaded all early Stoic moral teaching. When that relationship was forgotten, the wise man became irrelevant.

If this interpretation is correct, it may explain how Panaetius and his disciples managed to bring about a revolution in Stoic ethics while professing complete loyalty to the old Stoic tradition. Panaetius' ethics probably represented the second-best morality of old Stoicism, consisting of precepts for ordinary life. This morality had always been there, but with Panaetius it lost its connection to the ideal morality. For despite the vague promise made in the passage quoted by Seneca, we doubt that Panaetius ever got around to seriously discussing the wise man at all. Cicero considered his great merit to lie in his avoidance of the harsh doctrines and thorny logical problems of the older Stoics (*On Ends* 4.28.79), suggesting that the traditional paradoxes about the wise man played no part in Panaetius' teaching. If Panaetius thought the wise man irrelevant even for such an advanced progressor as himself, then what could the wise man mean to anybody? If so, then Panaetius' ethical system is correctly represented by Cicero's *On Duties*,[7] and what is represented there is best described as a truncated version of Stoicism, not an expansion of it.

This leads one to question the widely accepted view that Panaetius "humanized," "democratized," or "Hellenized" Stoicism by making it relevant to the mass of humanity.[8] It appears that his main innovation was to divert attention from the original Stoic ideal of a rational and universal ethic that is equally valid for all human beings. This innovation must have had important social effects, but hardly of a democratizing sort. The notion that we are all bound by our individual *aphormai* and *personae* implies that some *aphormai* and *personae* are better than others. Women, for example, must be bound by the *aphormai* of gender; and in a moment we shall consider the effects of this teaching on the Stoic ideal of sexual equality. Also Cicero's contemptuous attitude toward the occupations of poor people probably reflects Panaetius' views.[9] The belief that vulgar crafts and trades are morally degrading, and the life of a landed gentleman morally ennobling, is one of the most class-bound notions in ancient philosophy, and in Cicero's *On Duties* we meet it in an extreme form, a feature which helped to make the *On Duties* the great moral handbook of the aristocracy in early modern Europe. It is hard to believe this did not constitute a departure from the old Stoic moral tradition. Earlier Stoics might have shared these prejudices, but they could not easily surrender to them so long as they had before them the image of a wise man totally indifferent to poverty, riches, and the ways of making a living. The levelling influence in Stoicism was the ideal of moral aristocracy; the loss of the ideal meant the unqualified acceptance of social aristocracies.

This loss of interest in the wise man and the ideal society meant the loss of all that was most distinctive in Stoic ethics. This development explains the view, widespread in antiquity, that Panaetius had remade the Stoa along the lines of Platonism and Aristotelianism.[10] He began that process of rapprochement which would eventually almost merge the great Socratic schools into one eclectic upper-class philosophy. Panaetius' interest in the history of philosophy suggests that this may have been his conscious aim: he may have perceived the schools of Plato, Aristotle, and Zeno as a single tradition emanating from Socrates, and emphasized the common ground among them, which entailed the dismissal of much that was uniquely Stoic and all that was genuinely Cynic.

Since Panaetius and Posidonius could not get rid of the wise man altogether, what did they do with him? Perhaps they spoke of him in much the same way as Seneca, the only later Stoic who has left us much commentary on the relationship between the two levels of morality. When Seneca wishes to console his friend Lucilius, he avoids the *Stoica lingua* which speaks always of the wise man's imperturbability in the face of misfortune. This lofty language (true though it is, by the gods!) does not console.[11] Instead, he will speak *hac submissiore*, in the milder style: the sort of plain, reassuring, useful moralizing that Cicero had admired in Panaetius; the dominant tone of Roman Stoicism. Seneca would never use such language to wise men, but a wise man comes only once in five hundred years, and his audience is composed of "good men" of the second-best sort, for whom the milder style is suited (*Ep.* 42.1). In a recurrent metaphor, he describes the wise man as a voyager who has made land, and the progressor as a voyager who is within the harbor and has land in sight. The wise man is perfectly stable, while the progressor is still in motion on the waves. But much worse off are the truly unwise, because they do not know what harbor they seek, and no wind can be right for them ("ignoranti, quem portum petat, nullus suus ventus est.")[12]

For all practical purposes, Seneca's *sapiens* and *proficiens* do not seem very far apart. The implications of his metaphor are very different from the similar metaphor used by the older Stoics. The old Stoics spoke of the wise man as standing on the shore, while the progressor is still underwater and drowning;

but Seneca puts the progressor safely in a boat and already in the harbor. The important distinction is that between the progressor and the totally unwise who toss aimlessly on the open sea without a navigator. The wise man of Seneca is merely a somewhat idealized version of the progressor. The morality of the two does not differ, or if it does Seneca is not interested in the difference. Seneca never speculates on the doings of those rare creatures, the wise. He agreed with Panaetius that on the subject of love, and probably much else, it was dangerous to do so.

The Neostoics and the Golden Age

Panaetius, Posidonius, and their successors did not merely ignore utopia. They provided a replacement for it. They pushed communism into the distant past and turned it into an historical and anthropological theory about the origins of civilization, whose implications for current social and political conditions were deeply conservative.

We have seen that Hellenistic Greeks were familiar with the theory, perhaps of Peripatetic origin, that the primitive condition of humanity had been a state of innocence in which property was held in common and the family did not exist; familiar also with writers of imaginative geography or outright science fiction who claimed that vestiges of primitive communism survived among remote barbarians. There are hints that early Stoics made some use of primitive communism as a sort of prefiguration of the ideal city of the wise. Building on these hints, the later Stoics made primitive communism one of the foundation stones of their ethical and political thought, but changed its meaning so that it ceased to represent an ideal standard of any kind. Given the absence of any genuine utopian element in late Stoic political philosophy, primitive communism could be nothing but an aetiological theory, like the legend of Cronus' time from which it had sprung. This was a pessimistic and conservative explanation for the authoritarian and exploitative way that most complex human societies are organized. It might provide material for escapist fantasy or a limited degree of social criticism, but it could not offer any alternative to existing institutions because its real purpose was to justify them and urge submission to them. Once again Panaetius seems responsible for the change.

Panaetius' *On Proper Functions* contained an account of the origins of civilization, preserved by Cicero, which clearly played an important role in Panaetius' political thought.[13] He taught that all property was originally common and is still common by nature (*privata nulla natura*); but the earth has now been divided up among states by occupation, conquest, and agreement, and within each state the land has been allotted among individuals.

Here again it is difficult to be sure how much of this was original with Panaetius, owing to our ignorance of his predecessors. But the theory presented by Cicero has two aspects that seem to have no parallels in earlier discussions of Cronus' time, and these are so closely integrated with Panaetius' ethical and political system that one is inclined to think them Panaetius' innovations.

Firstly, there is no sign that Panaetius idealized the time of Cronus at all.

He described the rise of civilization as a good and "natural" thing, dwelling at length on the origins of arts, crafts, and city life as evidence for humanity's innate capacity for cooperation and mutual helpfulness. He especially thought the establishment of law codes and the security of property rights one of the primary achievements in the progress of human society (Cic., *On Duties* 2.3.12–2.5.16). There is no trace of that nostalgia for primitive innocence which we find in Cynic references to the time of Cronus, and which was probably typical of the earlier Stoics.

Secondly, the institution of private property assumed a central place in Panaetius' scheme. He said the main reason for establishing cities and states was to safeguard property rights, and that the main function of government then and now was to guarantee the property rights of individuals. The original communism was according to nature, but the acquisition of property by individuals was equally according to nature, and so was the coercive government set up to protect the rights of these individuals. Panaetius seems interested in primitive communism solely because it provided an explanation for the rise of private property. He also added a new twist to the theory which made it an extremely conservative justification for grossly unequal distribution of wealth. He taught that the distribution of property established by the early kings and lawgivers is sacrosanct; it cannot be changed later except through established legal processes of sale, donation, and inheritance; all laws for the redistribution of land and the cancellation of debts are therefore against nature, as they violate the original compact and destroy the foundations of human society.

This theory has been described as "possessive individualism." It encourages economic individualism, but not for purposes of capitalist acquisition; rather to defend the position of landed aristocracy in preindustrial society. Through the medium of Cicero this theory would have a tremendous influence on Western conservative thought until very recent times, and if Panaetius was really responsible for it he deserves more attention from historians of political thought that he has been given.[14]

The possessive social compact was not the only conclusion Panaetius' school drew from primitive communism. His most famous disciple Posidonius left one or more detailed descriptions of the primitive state of society, which he apparently wished to place in an historical framework. He was the most polymathic Stoic, and the only Stoic historian, known to us. His account of the "golden age," as the Roman poets called it, is fully reported in the *Epistle* 90 of Seneca. It seems that Posidonius described the time of Cronus, which he considered a real stage of social evolution and not a myth, as a period of premoral innocence, in which all property was held in common and all people accepted willingly the leadership of the wisest among them, without any need for laws or coercive government. This golden age was ended by the rise of avarice, and humanity then fell under the rule of tyrants; but again was rescued by wise men, who established laws to secure justice and proceeded to invent agriculture and other useful arts and crafts.

There is no mention here of the social compact theory of Panaetius/Cicero, but neither is it contradicted. Posidonius seems interested in the origins of society from a different angle: not in the foundations of property and government, but in the role of the philosopher in history. Some idealization of the primitive is discernable, but again the dominant tone seems to be faith in progress. The role of the wise man is not confined to the primitive; he intervenes repeatedly in history as legislator and inventor. The attribution of technological progress to the wise man was probably peculiar to Posidonius, for that is the only point on which Seneca disagreed with him; but the notion of the wise man as primitive lawgiver is accepted by Seneca as though it were common Stoic doctrine.[15]

There was also a widespread belief that the golden age had been a period of pure philosophical religion. We know this chiefly from St. Augustine's summary of the encyclopedia of Roman antiquities by Varro, who is generally assumed to have been following Panaetius or Posidonius or both. Varro wrote that the early Romans worshipped god without need of images or myths for the first hundred and seventy years of Rome's history, i.e., until the introduction of Greek temples to Rome in the sixth century B.C. Varro thought this primitive philosophical religion was to some extent continued by the Jews, but otherwise it had been supplanted by a tripartite theology, with one interpretation of deity suitable for philosophers, one for poets, and one for the city. This theology made room for the rationalizations of the schools, the myths of Homer and Hesiod, and the cults of everyday life, treating them all as complementary, though reserving priority for the philosophers. Clearly Varro was applying to Roman history a general theory about the rise of religion, which fits neatly into the general Stoic theory of the rise of civilization described above.[16] Again we notice that the primitive age, though idealized, is not used as a standard by which to judge the present. The rise of the civic religion is considered a necessary development, and there is no suggestion that the primitive philosophical interpretation of the gods should be revived for anybody but philosophers.

Cicero, Varro, and Seneca have left us different versions of what would appear to be the same basic theory about the rise of civilization, and this theory seems to be of Neostoic origin. It made use of an older anthropological theory, popularized by Dicaearchus, about an historical golden age of primitive communism, but did not use this golden age as a symbol of perfection. The golden age represented only the good order that could be found in any well-organized community. The communism of the golden age survived as a principle of justice and fellowship, but in modern society this means that only those things that have *not* become anyone's private property are to be used for the common benefit. Panaetius recommended helpfulness and generosity, but what he had in mind, if adequately represented by Cicero, were cautious virtues indeed: giving should always be within our means and appropriate to the worth of the recipient, the ideal recipient being someone bound to us by social ties who has helped us in the past. He recommended, in short, the traditional upper-class patronage system. This was presented as a diluted version of the primitive communistic system, but the dilution was natural, inevitable, and in some ways represented progress. There was no great gulf between the primitive state of nature and the state of civilized society. There had been no fall of man, only a natural development out of a state of innocence, and the developed state of society was still in harmony with nature or capable of being brought into harmony with it.

The new emphasis on *primitive* communism was the other side of the decision to ignore *utopian* communism. All the potentially subversive aspects of the utopian ideal—egalitarianism, the perfectionism of the wise, the opposition to popular superstition—could be defused by pushing them into the remote past and making them mere starting points for the development of civilization. The wise man they turned into a primitive lawgiver, and thus they brought him to earth. Utopia was brought into history, and for the most part it would remain safely locked up there until the Renaissance.

On the basis of Cicero's *On Duties*, sweeping claims have been made for Panaetius' originality as a political thinker: that he was the first Stoic to recognize the legitimacy of existing states; that he was the first to recognize the unity of all humanity, including both wise and unwise.[17] I have already argued that the first view must be incorrect: the early Stoic interest in an ideal society never implied existing states were illegitimate, and the originality of Panaetius had to do with the origins of property, not the state. As to the second point, it is true that Cicero and the later Stoics frequently refer to humanity as a single world community:

> Let us take hold of the fact that there are two communities—the one, which is great and truly common, embracing gods and men, in which we look neither to this corner nor to that, but measure the boundaries of our state by the sun; the other, the one to which we have been assigned by the accident of our birth.
>
> Seneca, *On Leisure* 4.1, trans. Long/Sedley

And it is true they mean something different from what early Stoics meant by a world order. The early Stoa meant the utopian ideal, of which real people were members only potentially. Their successors do not mean anything much; their world community is a rhetorical expression for the present state of things, implying acceptance of existing society with all its inequalities. There remains a notion of shared humanity, but it may have conveyed nothing more than the shared interests of like-minded friends. Neither perhaps has much in common with later ideas of universal brotherhood, but the cosmopolitanism of the old Stoa was at least a high moral standard that challenged many conventions; and the later Stoic cosmopolitanism was not so much a broadening of the ideal as a dilution of it, implying mostly acceptance of the status quo.

Was there community of women, as well as community of goods, in the golden age of the late Stoa? The evidence is conflicting. We know that community of women dropped out of the picture at some point. During Augustan and Julio-Claudian times the theme of a revival of the golden age was officially encouraged, and was popularized by poets and rhetoricians, who proclaimed that under the benevolent rule of an Augustus or a Nero avarice would be banished and universal peace and prosperity reign. They spoke freely of reviving the primitive community of goods—by now an empty rhetorical formula expressing merely a pious hope that luxury and greed might be curbed—but they said nothing at all about a primitive community of women.[18] This Roman literary cult of the golden age owed much to the later Stoics, and the Stoics had already turned it into a thoroughly conservative ideology or it could not have been so easily adapted to the purposes of imperial public relations. So perhaps it was Panaetius or Posidonius who jettisoned the idea of primitive sexual communism.

On the other hand, we know that some Stoics and other philosophers continued to believe that primitive peoples had been sexually communistic. One of the lectures of Epictetus at Nicopolis was attended by a certain scholar (*philologus*) who had been caught committing adultery in the city, and Epictetus attacked him thus:

> What, are not women common by nature? I agree that they are; just as a pig is the common property of the guests at a feast.... But is not the theater the common property of the citizens? Yes, and when they are all seated try coming in and taking someone's seat. In that way are women common property by nature. Once the lawgiver, like the giver of the feast, has portioned them out, will you not take the portion that belongs to you, instead of grabbing the portion that belongs to another and gobbling it? "But I am a scholar and understand Archedemus." So understand Archedemus, be an adulterer and a faithless man, a wolf or an ape instead of a man. *Discourses* 2.4.8–11

Since responses to imaginary questions are a basic technique of the diatribe, we cannot assume that this unfortunate Stoic whose discomfiture has been recorded by Arrian really said "women are common property by nature" or referred to the great Stoic authority Archedemus of Tarsus (second century B.C.) in defense of his conduct; but Epictetus assumed these were arguments an adulterer might likely use. In refutation, Epictetus asserts that all that Stoic communism implies is that property and women are common like places at a banquet or in a theater; he uses the old *topos* exclusively for its negative and conservative implications, turning it into a warning against adultery and theft. He thinks that the saying "women are common by nature" means they were common in some primitive state before lawgivers introduced private property. He seems ignorant of the theory of the *utopian* communist state. In another diatribe, when he asks himself if a Cynic can marry, he allows that this might happen in a city of wise men, for there either all would be Cynics or none would be (3.22.68). He seems unaware that his heroes Diogenes and Zeno had written about such cities of the wise.

Then there is a curious interpretation of Plato's communism by Clement of Alexandria, whom we will discuss in further detail below. Clement implies that by "communism" Plato meant a primitive stage of society: civilization has divided up property and women just as seats are occupied in theaters. There is, of course, nothing in the works of Plato that could suggest such a notion. This is the Neostoic theory about the origins of property that we encountered in Cicero. Clement is conflating Platonic and Stoic communism, pushing both of them back into the primitive past, and interpreting the theater *topos* as a symbol of the replacement of primitive communism by private property. The mistake could not have arisen had there not been a widespread assumption that primitive societies were communistic both in property and sexual relationships.

We do not know just what Panaetius and Posidonius did with sexual communism. In later centuries some Stoics believed in it and others did not. If Panaetius and Posidonius referred to it at all, we can assume they treated it like communism in property, relegating it to a primitive condition of society and keeping it there.

The Triumph of the Household Codes

Panaetius or his followers were probably responsible for a new sexual morality which borrowed from Plato's *Laws* the limitation of sex "according to nature" to procreation. This is not specifically attributed to Panaetius, but the idea is common among the Roman Stoics, and we have seen that Panaetius was highly suspicious of the doctrine of the wise man as *erotikos*. This gave a new meaning to the Stoic goal of "following nature" and was impossible to reconcile with much that Stoics found in the works of Zeno and Chrysippus. Criticisms of the Stoic utopias in Roman times are largely concerned with their erotic aspects.

We know that Panaetius condemned the Cynics, and with them those Stoics who were "almost Cynic" (*paene cynici*), on the grounds that they were opposed to modesty (Cic., *On Duties* 1.35.128, 1.41.148), by which he meant that they continued the old traditions of philosophical love and candor about sexual matters. The Roman Stoics taught that sex should be confined to procreation; they disapproved of extramarital relations with male or female, slave or free, both for wife and husband. The new standard was justified by a new interpretation of "nature." The old Stoics had counted both marriage and love among the things according to nature, but their Roman disciples often speak of all "unnecessary" (nonprocreative) sex as *contra naturam* on the grounds that it is a luxury, and all luxuries are against nature. This category included, of course, all homosexual acts. This theory seems to be derived from the argument for "natural" sex in Plato's *Laws*, which condemned all nonprocreative sex because it goes beyond the degree of sexual pleasure that nature finds adequate. In the first two centuries of the Roman Empire this seems a common view among Stoics, Platonists, and adherents of other schools.[19]

The difference between the old morality and the new can easily be exaggerated. Traditional Greek morality had always upheld a "puritanism of virility" (as Veyne has called it) that placed extraordinary importance on continence and self-control, and Cynics and Stoics had carried it to extremes. The new philosophical morality only extended this standard. The new morality appealed only to a tiny minority, and even for them it was an ideal standard: only in a utopian context had Plato discussed the possibility of applying this standard to society in general; we find Epictetus at one point admitting that he does not really expect his audience to remain chaste before marriage (*Manual* 33.8). Their condemnation of "unnatural" sex was not so severe as it may sound to us, for they could describe any form of luxury as *contra naturam*, and the harshest terms were still reserved for the traditionally execrated vices of adultery and homosexual passivity in citizen males.[20] Nevertheless there had clearly been a great watershed in Stoic sexual morality, and since it involved a fusion of Stoic and Platonic ideas one is inclined to attribute this change also to the circle of Panaetius.

At the same time Panaetius' teaching that universal moral norms had to be conditioned by individual circumstances robbed the old Stoic principle of sexual equality of much of its force. Later Stoics continued to teach that women were the equals of men, but in practice this theoretical equality was limited by individual characteristics, among which gender was particularly obvious and inescapable. Musonius Rufus has often been praised for his enlightened attitudes toward women, and he did write more about this theme than other Roman Stoics: his diatribes include one arguing that women should study philosophy, another proposing that daughters should receive the same education as sons, and three on marriage, all portraying the ideal marriage as an equal partnership between husband and wife. But he does not contemplate any change in the social position of women. We are told that women should study philosophy in ways appropriate to a woman, i.e., for the purpose of making them better wives. The example of Hipparchia is mentioned to be dismissed: if she helped Crates to lead the philosophical life even without a household, then how much more philosophical would marriage be with the advantage of an *oikos* and a staff of slaves?[21] Hipparchia is praised for being a philosopher, but it is implied she would have been a better philosopher had she been a conventional wife.

As a result of these new attitudes, the morality of Roman Stoicism was increasingly centered on the household. There was nothing new in this, for the practical moral teaching of Greek philosophers had always emphasized the household and the relationships among members of the household as the basis of an orderly society. A main source of this *topos* was probably Aristotle's *Politics*, which assumes that any discussion of the polis must begin with a discussion of *oikonomia*, the art of household management, and that *oikonomia* means the manner in which the master of the household should rule his wife, children, and slaves. There are indications that this scheme had a place in the practical ethics of the early Stoa, but there it must have been subsidiary to the utopian ideal. Among the later Stoics, morality is practically reduced to this "household code."[22]

It is true that the notion of a higher morality is not forgotten. Epictetus distinguishes two levels of human personality that together define "proper function": there is the universal, rational human nature in which one participates, and there is what he calls one's "title," or role in society:

> How is it possible to discover proper functions from titles? Consider who you are: in the first place a human being, that is, someone who has nothing more authoritative than a moral purpose. ... Furthermore you are a citizen of the world and a part of it, not one of the underlings but one of the foremost constituents. ... Next keep in mind that you are a son ... next know that you are also a brother ... next if you are a town councillor, remember that you are a councillor; if young, that you are young; if old, that you are old; if a father, that you are a father. For each of these titles, when rationally considered,

always suggests the actions appropriate to it. *Discourses* 2.10.1–12, trans. Long/Sedley

We are told that the lower titles, mostly connected with the household or the city, are never to be preferred to the good, but we are never told how one's role as citizen of the world can be separated from one's role as a father, son, councillor, etc. As with Panaetius' distinctions among *personae* (of which this seems a simplified version), we receive the impression that the higher role has been blandly merged into the lower.

We have already noticed the same attitude in Seneca. Seneca is contemptuous of Stoics who constantly quote Zeno and Cleanthes; he thinks philosophers should make new discoveries, not look to the past (*Ep.* 33.11). But what he means by this is that "the ancients" (who include Socrates and Plato as well as the older Stoics) have already discovered all the remedies for the soul, and the work of contemporary philosophers is to find the application of these remedies to particular cases (*Ep.* 64.7–10). He means that the active and living branch of philosophy is that which furnishes precepts for individual cases; and the first example of a precept that occurs to him has to do with the patriarchal management of a household—how a master should treat his wife, children, and slaves (*Ep.* 94.1). Like Epictetus, he insists that precepts will not do without principles; but like Epictetus, he does not explain this relationship very clearly. He says that in human relationships, the basic principle is to remember that we should hold everything in common, for we are all born the same. ("Habeamus in commune; nati sumus." *Ep.* 95.53.) And the precepts to be derived from this principle presumably have to do with the way a master should treat his wife, children, and slaves. The principle, which retains only the rhetoric of old Stoic communism, seems a generalization from the precepts of the household code, not a challenge to them. The Roman Stoics often do this sort of thing very well, but they do not really believe any more in a universal moral code that is separable from the codes of convention, any more than they believe in a wise man separable from the progressor, or in a utopian social ideal separable from historical societies.

In the realm of family, marriage, and sexuality, the most important change in the Greek philosophical tradition took place in the late Hellenistic period. Some have thought this change came later, during the early Roman Empire; but that is probably an illusion created by the survival of larger numbers of philosophical writings from the first two centuries of the Empire.[23] The evidence suggests that the philosophers of the Empire were merely continuing a trend established in the generation of Panaetius, which eventually succeeded in imposing upon the varied traditions of Greek ethical thought a single orthodoxy representing the most conservative strain that could be found in the earlier traditions.

The Roman Conquest of Philosophy

I have mentioned several ways in which the reformed Stoicism of Panaetius' circle affected social and political thought. While making little or no formal change in Stoic doctrine, they in practice concentrated entirely on the second-level morality, which differed little from the teaching of the other major schools; and in the process so much of the egalitarianism of the old Stoa was dropped as to leave only obeisances toward traditional Stoic principles concerning women and the occupations of the poor. They introduced or gave a new importance to the theory of communism as a primitive state of society: an innocuous replacement for utopia, which was supposed to provide not an ideal standard but a justification for existing property arrangements. They may have been responsible for a new sexual morality the puritanism of which equaled Plato at his most austere. Now let us turn to the political background of these changes, and particularly to the growing ties between Stoicism and the Roman upper class.

The Roman conquest of the Greek world in the second century was the decisive event in the long struggle of Greek democracy against the propertied classes. The Roman oligarchs permanently tipped the balance in favor of oligarchy in the Greek cities, accelerating and making irreversible a trend begun by the Hellenistic monarchies. When Rome became a power in the Greek East at the beginning of the century, democracy was still vigorous in some cities and in others the demands for land reform and debt relief were more vociferous than ever. Both faded as the Roman domination became ever more complete, and the silent partnership between the Roman senatorial class and its counterparts in the Greek cities ever more overt. The last effort at Greek independence, the war of the Achaean League against Rome in 146 B.C., was largely supported by the Achaean lower classes, and in the eyes of Polybius it constituted an especially clear example of the link between democracy and anti-Roman feeling. After the defeat of Achaea, the Romans attempted to suppress democracy in all the cities and everywhere were free to express their oligarchic preferences unhindered.[24]

About this time Greek philosophy inaugurated its Roman mission in the person of Panaetius of Rhodes, who was living at Rome in the household of the most powerful man in the Senate, Scipio Aemilianus, and enjoying his patronage and friendship, by the year 140 B.C., when he accompanied the great Roman on an extensive tour of the East. He was the first of many household philosophers the Roman nobility would keep. We cannot say whether he was anything more than that in Scipio's eyes, nor do we know that Panaetius was conscious of having a Roman mission. Scholars used to speak of a "Scipionic circle" at Rome headed by Panaetius and Polybius, but this notion is based mostly on Cicero's description of Scipio discussing political questions with the two Greeks (*On the Republic* 1.21.34), and even that may be a figment of Cicero's imagination, a projection backward from a time when the Roman aristocracy had become much more Hellenized than it was in the 140s. All we know is that Panaetius had half a dozen friends among the Roman aristocracy, all of them with political or family connection to Scipio Aemilianus. It would be a mistake to imagine him tailoring his philosophy extensively to Roman tastes or serving as Scipio's mouthpiece. At least one of his innovations, his doubts about divination, could not have pleased the Romans at all. It would be equally mistaken to imagine these highborn Romans as his disciples. None of them is called a Stoic, and probably none would have appreciated the name, for few Romans in those days studied in Greek-speaking regions, and Greek philosophy enjoyed little of its later prestige. Nor did Panaetius establish Greek philosophy at Rome. His influence was uniquely personal; in the next generation we can find hardly any prominent Stoics who spent much time at Rome.[25]

Nevertheless the impression that Panaetius made a significant step toward the fusion of the two cultures is surely correct. He was the first leading philosopher to accept Roman patronage, and he created a special link between Rome and Stoicism that endured for centuries. His Roman concerns, like his Roman circle, have been exaggerated. Some have tried to make him the source of the entire political thought of Polybius and of Cicero: the first to see Rome as the true mixed constitution; the architect of a philosophical defense of Roman imperialism that is supposed to be reflected in Cicero's *On the Republic* (3.22.33–29.41).[26] We do not have to assume any of this to believe that Panaetius and his Roman hosts found a great deal in common. What they mostly had in common was an oligarchic bias, at a time when Rome was becoming the protector of Greek oligarchies and when oligarchic principles were under attack even at Rome; and Panaetius was the first Greek philosopher to show Romans that Greek philosophy could be useful.

The fusion of the two cultures that Panaetius helped to inaugurate is correctly described as a symbiosis, but it served only certain elements in the two societies, and there was never any doubt as to which was the dominant partner. Stoics were Romanized more thoroughly than Romans were ever Stoicized. As Ronald Syme said, what Romans understood by Stoicism was "nothing more than a corroboration and theoretical defense of certain traditional virtues of the governing class in an aristocratic and republican state."[27] Stoics and other philosophers who accepted Roman patronage made their teachings compatible with the *mos maiorum*, the ancestral traditions of the great Roman households, or they did not keep Roman patronage.

The main advantage that the Greek partner derived from this symbiosis was support for oligarchic values. This motive is clear enough in Polybius, the first Greek we know who thoroughly esconced himself among the Roman senators. Polybius detests democracy and land reform, and dismisses all utopian thinking as useless. His political ideal is the "mixed constitution," by now a common oligarchic slogan and a mask for antidemocratic sentiments. He thinks the Spartan constitution had once realized this ideal, but it had been ruined by the radical reforms that convulsed the Peloponnese about the time Polybius was born, and in his eyes Rome has replaced Sparta as the ideal mixed constitution.[28] Polybius' pro-Roman convictions did not spring from mere opportunism. He saw in Rome a genuine hope of political salvation for the troubled Greek world, and many conservatives must have shared this hope.

One of these, his younger contemporary Panaetius, was not so obviously identified with Roman interests, but his Roman connections were deep and supported his own political outlook. He came from the oligarchic state of Rhodes, one of the most successful examples of stable and effective oligarchic government in the Greek world, and was probably a member of its ruling class, as that connection would do much to explain his adoption by Scipio.[29] His *On Proper Functions* was written in part for a Roman readership; it was extravagantly praised by Rutilius Rufus, a member of the "Scipionic circle" (Cic., *On Duties* 3.2.10). Panaetius and his disciple Hecaton both dedicated works (the latter another *On Proper Functions*) to Aelius Tubero, Scipio's nephew, who seems to have been the most seriously interested in Stoicism of Panaetius' Roman "hearers."[30] Panaetius wrote a work called *On the Republic* or some such title, which Cicero thought one of the first useful treatises on politics written by a Stoic (*On Laws* 3.5.13ff.). It is pointless to speculate about its contents, but it seems safe to assume it shared the oligarchic values of his *On Proper Functions*. I have suggested that his main contribution to political thought was the abandonment of utopian methods and their replacement by a theory of primitive communism that amounted to a defense of private property and an argument against land reform. It was perhaps the most impressive achievement of conservative Greek political thought, and it was probably what won Panaetius a reputation at Rome.[31]

This oligarchic Greco-Roman connection was strengthened by the great upheaval of the Gracchan reforms after 133. This polarized opinion within the Roman aristocracy and also among its Greek clients, and must have split the Stoa in two. It has often been noticed that both the reformers and the conservatives in the Gracchan crisis were to some degree inspired by Stoicism. Blossius of Cumae, an Italian who had studied at Athens under Antipater, was remembered as a leading advisor of Tiberius Gracchus. His role may have been exaggerated by Roman conservatives who wanted to stress the Hellenistic connections of the Gracchan movement, but that only reminds us that the associations were obvious. The Gracchan reform attempted to duplicate the common Greek reform goals of land redistribution and debt cancellation in a Roman context. It bore an especially strong resemblance to the great Spartan reform because it aimed to use land redistribution to restore the military power of the state. These resemblances could not have been unnoticed by the reformers themselves; it is entirely plausible that such Hellenized senators as the Gracchi would have taken an interest in philosophical justifications for such reform programs, such as some Stoics had advanced in the preceding century; and so the parallel drawn by Plutarch between the role of Sphaerus at Sparta and the role of Blossius at Rome was surely based on fact, though we need not exaggerate the role of either philosopher. Blossius later joined and died for the revolt of the Attalid pretender Aristonicus in Asia Minor (ca. 130), the most violent of the anti-Roman social revolts in the Hellenistic world.[32] The mere existence of a figure like Blossius is sufficient evidence for the persistence of a strong Stoic tradition of radical social and political reform through the time of Panaetius.

The existence of this radical Stoicism has been questioned on the grounds that it is hard to "find any political beliefs common to Panaetius and to Blossius which may fairly be ascribed to Stoicism."[33] There are none, in fact. This situation is intelligible only if we assume that a serious rift in the Stoic political tradition took place in the time of Panaetius and Blossius. The early tradition, which was always closely tied to Stoic utopian ideals and was in some cases capable of linking them to practical programs, was at that time replaced by the reformed Stoicism of Panaetius, which eliminated utopianism altogether from Stoic political thought.

The Roman *optimates* did not need their convictions strengthened by a Rhodian to oppose the Gracchi. To the extent they needed an ideological justification, they probably used the one common to ancient oligarchies and familiar to us from Cicero (e.g., *Pro Sestio* 48.103): the rich are the main defenders of the state and to take away their long-held possessions is to weaken the state, as well as creating discord. But some of them were sophisticated enough to take an interest in what philosophers said about these matters, and the results were more serious for the schools than for the Senate. The failure of the great revolutions of ca. 130 gave the future of Stoicism to its conservative wing, which we may also describe as its Romanized wing, not because the Roman connections of Panaetius formed his ideas, but because they assured his triumph. Panaetius assumed the leadership of the school of Athens about 129, and within half a century his followers came to dominate the Stoa.

It is probable that Roman connections had some effect on the new Stoic sexual morality, as well as on the new Stoic political thought. The Neostoic interpretation of the "life according to nature," which identified nature with procreative sex, fitted well the traditional Roman moral code, which was centered on the *patria potestas*, the uniquely authoritarian Roman patriarchal household.

Romans believed their disciplined social order was the secret of their success, and they convinced many Greeks of this. The clearest example of this alliance between Rome and conservative Greek thought on sexual matters is to be found in the *Roman Antiquities* of Dionysius of Halicarnassus, who wrote in the time of Augustus with the avowed intention of reconciling his fellow Greeks to Roman rule by showing the superiority of Roman institutions. Dionysius is unimpressed by the efforts of Greek lawgivers to regulate the household and "relations with women." Some Greeks had been so mad as to propose "common intercourse" like animals and barbarians. Others, like Lycurgus, had recognized the importance of the monogamous household but left no means of enforcing it. Only the Romans had solved this problem by giving absolute power to the master of the household; and the stability of this system explained the greatness of Rome (2.24–27).

Dionysius was simply reflecting the common opinion of the Roman upper class, who thought that the relative freedom of Greek sexual customs, especially *paiderastia*, was one of the reasons for the decline of Greece and the superiority of Rome. Plutarch tells us they held the gymnasia responsible for the effeminacy and enslavement of the Greeks, for this institution had turned Greece from war to athletics and encouraged idleness and boylove (*Roman Questions* 274d). There were Greeks who shared this view as early as the second century B.C. Polybius diagnosed moral decline at Rome as a major threat to Roman institutions, and compared Scipio Aemilianus favorably to his loose-living contemporaries because of Scipio's fidelity to the old Roman mores (31.25).

This was not a difference between Roman and Greek. We cannot find a time when there did not exist at Rome a fashionable circle attracted to Hellenistic customs and a circle of traditionalists who resisted them; but both circles were Hellenized, for as early as Scipio's time the traditionalists found support in Greek philosophy.

In the minds of these conservatives, there existed a link between democracy and sexual freedom, both obvious manifestations of Greek indiscipline and weakness. Cicero was one of those who thought the gymnasia responsible for the ruin of Greece (*Tusc. Disp.* 4.33.70–34.73), but he could ascribe the same effect to the popular assemblies (*Pro Flacco* 16–17). The philosophical life became associated with sexual repression as well as with aristocratic/oligarchic social values. It is likely that the assimilation of philosophy and especially of Stoicism by the Roman nobility did much to popularize these views.

The reforms of Panaetius did not win out overnight. The internal history of the Stoa after he died or retired ca. 109 B.C. is obscure. Two of his disciples, Mnesarchus and Dardanus, may have shared the leadership of the school of Athens. His greatest disciple, Posidonius, set up his own school at Rhodes. We know that Posidonius' *Histories*, which continued Polybius, shared the political views of Panaetius and Polybius; and he got along well with Romans, though he avoided Roman patronage.[34] His long career (till ca. 50 B.C.) and his great influence might have made him a key figure in the propagation of Panaetius' political and ethical ideas, but this is conjecture. We know the names of half a dozen other Greek disciples of Panaetius, and little else about them.

The sack of Athens by Sulla in 86 B.C. put an end to the Athenian school and may have caused the division within the Stoa to come to the surface. It was probably not long after the fall of Athens that Athenodorus of Tarsus, called Cordylion, head of the library at Pergamum, prepared his notorious bowdlerized edition of the works of Zeno and created a scandal that delighted opponents of Stoicism. He was detected, the texts were restored, and we are told Athenodorus found it expedient to leave Pergamum. Around 70 he was invited to Rome by Cato the Younger, the first full-fledged Stoic produced by the Roman aristocracy.[35] Athenodorus thus became one of many Greek intellectuals who flooded Rome during the upheavals of the Mithradatic Wars, and who completed the conservative Greco-Roman philosophical synthesis begun by Panaetius.

Another philosopher carried to Rome by that flood, who also found a great Rome patron, was Philodemus of Gadara. It is through this Epicurean that we know some Stoics at this time were trying to dismiss Zeno's *Republic* as a youthful and Cynic work, and reviving the earlier doubts about the authenticity of the *Republic* of Diogenes. The effort to expunge utopianism from the canon failed, but the effort to deny its significance succeeded; how well, we may see from the Stoic handbook on which Cicero drew ca. 45 B.C. for the summary of Stoic ethics he put into the mouth of Cato the Younger in *On Ends*. "Cato" admits there are two camps within the Stoa with respect to Cynicism (3.20.67–68), and it is clear that the one popular at Rome is the Panaetian wing that rejected Cynicism completely. "Cato" says all things are common by nature, and uses the theater as a symbol of this natural communism, paraphrasing Chrysippus; but he does not mention the ideal city, and the theater loses its function as a link between the ideal city and the real one. It is not only a real theater, but a Roman theater, that Cicero has in mind. Social inequality was built into the Roman theater, where whole galleries were reserved for the senatorial and equestrian orders.

It is clear that in the first century B.C. a dominant and Romanized wing of Stoicism decided to shelve the utopian tradition. Yet attacks on Stoic utopianism continued for centuries, as we have seen; it is only through the efforts of these hostile critics that we can attempt to reconstruct the outlines of the utopian theory. Since contemporary Stoics seem virtually ignorant of the theory, why did their opponents go on attacking it? Ancient writers on philosophy frequently discuss long-dead theories as though they were still current, but the critics of Stoic utopia sometimes give us the impression they are attacking a living thing. In his anti-Stoic tracts Plutarch specifically says that the Stoics of his own day still praised Zeno's *Republic* for abolishing temples and discusses the monastic austerity of Chrysippus' urban planning as though that too were common Stoic teaching.

In a sense, these works *were* still part of Stoicism. A remark by Clement of Alexandria gives us the clue: he says that Stoics have certain works by Zeno which they are reluctant to give their pupils, until they had proven themselves to be true philosophers (*Misc.* 5.9.58.2 = SVF 1.43). Utopianism had become an esoteric tradition of the Stoa. The popular Stoic teaching based on handbooks and compendia knew little about it; the teachers' grasp of these matters was as uncertain as Epictetus', or their silence as deafening as Seneca's. Within the schools these works were still studied, but probably to be reinterpreted and excerpted. The difficulty of looking up references in ancient books and libraries forced everyone to rely heavily on collections of excerpts (the Stoic fragments translated in the preceding chapter probably all come from such collections), and this habit made it easy to quote excerpts out of context. Some of these excerpts continued to circulate in popular Stoic teaching. Zeno's abolition of temples was still useful to Stoics, for there had been no change in Stoic views of religion; the excerpt would also prove useful to Christians. The early Stoic disapproval of grandiose public buildings was repeated.[36] But these were topics easily taken out of context, and most of the Stoic moralists who quoted these sayings may have thought they referred to the primitive golden age.

The more radical aspects of the Stoic ethic had, of course, been shelved along with the utopian vision. Traces of them survive among the Roman Stoics: Musonius on women's equality, Musonius and Dio on the occupations of the poor. Sometimes their teachings on property show a more radical strain than we can find in Panaetius/Cicero. Seneca, in some of his moods, can urge indiscriminate giving without thought of return, which is different from the calculated Rhodian patronage recommended by Panaetius; he can advice his audience to reduce their possessions to the minimum (happily undefined) or at least to try living like a poor person (also undefined) for a few days. But he can also admit that riches, after all, have greater scope for the exercise of virtue than poverty.[37]

In any case radical sentiments of this sort were quite safe in the first century of the principate, because of the general disappearance of democracy and land reform, and the relegation of citizen equality to the world of revered and dead ideals.

Stoicism had lost its utopian element, and eventually its intellectual core, because it had adapted itself to the needs of the Roman governing class and its upper-class Greek clients. Stoic ethics was superficially unchanged, but it had lost its objective reference point. Stoics continued to speak of two levels of morality but did not in fact envision any ethic higher than the ordinary code, or different from the teachings of the other major schools, which were making similar adaptations.

Interpretations of Plato's Communism[38]

Much the same fate befell the *Republic* of Plato in the Roman Empire. It was not forgotten in the way the Stoic utopias were forgotten. Stoics apparently did not read the *Republic* of Zeno, but Platonists and others still read the *Republic* of Plato, doubtless because of its literary merit, but also because its social and political principles were more acceptable to the aristocratic society of the Empire. One could ignore the utopian sections entirely and still find much that was useful in it, such as the discussion of practical constitutions in the eighth and ninth books. (See, for example, the treatise *On Monarchy, Democracy, and Oligarchy* attributed to Plutarch.) And anyone could lift catchwords out of context, as in the inevitable comparisons between Marcus Aurelius and the philosopher-king.[39]

But when they do refer to Plato's ideal city they use the stereotyped formulas comparing men of words and men of deeds that we have often encountered. The cities of words are usually spoken of with respect, but a respectful dismissal, as irrelevant to the real problems of constitutions:

> [Plato] wanted and created a city to wish for rather than a city to hope for, as small as he could make it, not that it might be possible, but that it might be possible to observe in it the principles of political life. But I, if I am able to complete this task, shall use the same principles that Plato discerned, only not in a shadow or picture of a city, but in a very powerful state. . . . Cic., *On the Republic* 2.30.52, cf. 2.1.3

When Marcus Aurelius admonishes himself not to expect perfection, he says one should not look for Plato's *Republic* (*Med.* 9.29). The remark reveals a low opinion of the utility of utopian thinking in general, and also that when an example of the genre is needed he thinks of the *Republic* of Plato, not Zeno. Dio Chrysostom knew of no just city in the past and did not think it worthwhile to conceive of any that might exist in the future, except the *koinonia* of the gods (36.22). When he attempted to design a model society in his *Euboean Oration* he explicitly disavowed any intention of speculating on the best possible state like Plato—again we notice that in the second century A.D. Plato's *Republic* is better known than Zeno's, even to Stoics—and instead drew a picture of an idyllic but real rural community living in a backward and peaceful district of the Empire (7.125). When Musonius Rufus devoted a diatribe to the old Stoic theme that virtue is the same for men and women, he assured his readers that he did not intend to argue that women should exercise nude like men (fr. 4). In this case we are uncertain whether he was thinking of the Platonic or the Stoic utopia. Often the two seem conflated.

Plato's sexual communism was, in fact, a considerable embarrasment to Platonists in the first and second centuries A.D.[40] It might attract the wrong kind of interest, like the women in Rome reproved by Epictetus, who studied Plato's *Republic* because it enacted community of women.[41] We suppose these were aristocratic ladies interested in Plato's arguments for female equality. Epictetus tells them the communistic system described there has no direct social relevance.

Commentators generally understood that the utopian program of Plato was not meant to be literally enacted, and I have argued that they understood it correctly. But they are so concerned to sever all connection between utopia and reality that they have no way to make sense of it. A comment by Dio (7.130–31) suggests that some scholars found the description of the ideal city unintelligible: if it is only a model for the individual soul, then is not the model very overextended and filled with useless material? We have seen that in modern times those who have tried to interpret Plato's ideal city as a purely educational model without political relevance have fallen into the same trap. But by one means or another it was possible for the aristocratic culture of the early Empire to tame and assimilate Plato's utopianism. They could not do that with the Stoics.

The Survival of the Old Stoic and Cynic Traditions

The Radical Stoics

We know from the writings of Cicero (*On Ends* 3.20.68; *On Duties* 1.35.128, 1.41.148) that in the first century B.C. Stoicism split into two camps: the reformed and Romanized Stoicism of Panaetius and Posidonius, which found Cynicism obnoxious because of its sexual frankness and its flaunting of all other social conventions; and the Stoics described as "near Cynics" (*paene cynicos*), who may have referred to themselves as the "manlier" (*androdestate*) Stoa (Diog. Laert. 6.14). Acceptance or rejection of the Cynic life was the most important symbol of the difference between the old and the new Stoicism, for the Cynic wise person was a vivid reminder of the old Stoic belief that behavior cannot be determined by the household code or by any other "titles."

We may assume that the Cynicizing Stoics continued the old Stoic tradition of philosophical *eros*, usually meaning *paiderastia*. Neostoics distrusted it, but it was so much a part of Stoicism that their allusions to it reveal some ambivalence. Some said love was permitted to the wise man if purely non-physical.[42] But that was a dangerous line to draw, and Seneca preferred to get rid of the whole thing, calling it a false Stoicism (*sub specie Stoicae sectae*) and a concession to Greek custom (*Ep.* 123.15–16). Probably it remained common among Greek Stoics. In this age they emphasized the nonphysical aspects of philosophical love, but satirists considered this merely a front for homosexual indulgence, and doubtless the satirists were often correct.[43]

The teaching of these Cynicizing Stoic radicals—actually traditionalists—is known to us only from hostile allusions by their opponents. Their influence, however, was perhaps wider than it appears, for many of these Stoics must have been indistinguishable from Cynics, and they accounted for much of the revived Cynicism that is such a striking feature of the civilization of the Roman Empire.

The Revival of Cynicism

Our sources leave the impression that the Cynic tradition practically disappeared after the third century B.C., then resurfaced just as mysteriously in the first century A.D. For the next two hundred years Cynicism was a familiar feature of the society of the Empire. The Cynic crops up frequently in Greek and Latin literature, and never needs an introduction. In the seventies A.D. Dio Chrysostom describes the Cynics of Alexandria, "no small crowd," conducting their preaching and begging throughout the city, in alleys and squares and temple porticoes, addressing slaves and sailors and such people with jokes and chatter and cheap repartee. In another city, perhaps Rome, he tells his audience that they outnumber the shoemakers and every other occupation.[44] A century later Lucian (*Runaways* 16) writes that every city is filled with them. As with many other things about ancient culture, this impression of a major revival of Cynicism is partly an illusion, caused by the relative richness of literary sources in the early Empire. Cynicism had never disappeared completely.[45] Yet the impression that it revived in popularity around the time of Augustus is probably correct, and several explanations can be suggested: the growing prosperity and stability of the Greek world, which was recovering from the devastation of the last century B.C.; the decline of democratic traditions, which left Cynicism one of the few outlets for *parrhesia*; and perhaps most of all, the revolution in Stoicism. The sudden decline of Cynicism after ca. 250 B.C., which cannot be entirely an illusion created by the sources, was surely related to the fact that Stoicism had stolen much of its thunder; and likewise the Cynic revival two centuries later must be related to the great division that had appeared within the Stoa. Once the official Romanized branch had taken over most of the school and absorbed its sources of patronage, the radicals would have been driven into the Cynic life, because it was the natural inclination of many of them and because they had no place else to go. One result, of course, was to swell and invigorate the ranks of the Cynics.

It was often difficult to say who was a Cynic and who was not. Sometimes the popular street philosophers who followed the traditional Cynic dress and lifestyle are called "philosophers," with the understanding that Cynics are only the most important branch of them. Any philosopher who adopted ascetic habits and preached to the people might be called a Cynic. Many of the people called Cynics were certainly Cynicizing Stoics. We hear of some "Cynics" who were touched by the mystical doctrines of Pythagoreanism.[46] Nevertheless, there was still an identifiable Cynic tradition in the Roman Empire, which continued the teachings of classical Cynicism: the rejection of logical and physical studies, the acceptance of all pleasures that come easily, the allusions to the myths of Heracles and the time of Cronus. Its clearest expressions are to be found in the Epistles of the Cynics and the pseudo-Lucianic dialogue *The Cynic*.

But we know this tradition mostly from its enemies. The philosophers, rhetoricians, and satirists of the first two centuries A.D. have left us a large dossier of anti-Cynic polemic, from which there emerges a fairly consistent hostile stereotype of the Cynic. Its main features are the following:[47]

Cynics are misanthropes who abuse and revile everyone; busybodies (*polypragmones, periergoi*: Epictetus 3.22.82, 97) who meddle in everyone's affairs. Sometimes their abusiveness is presented as a form of extortion, forcing people to give alms to them in the hope of escaping their verbal assaults.

When they are not abusing their audience, they are flattering it, telling it only what it wants to hear rather than what will improve it.

They are vulgar exhibitionists who make a great public display of virtue with their "Socratic" slovenliness.

They are antisocial: their rejection of civilized attire and manners, their avoidance of marriage, children, useful work, and political life make them parasites; most people think them mad and ridicule them, which brings philosophy into disrepute.

They are uneducated men of the lowest classes who know nothing about philosophy. Lucian's *Runaways* expresses the mock fear that all artisans and laborers will soon join the Cynics, thereby ruining the economy of the Empire. Also their audience is the wrong audience for philosophy.

They are greedy gluttons, and their asceticism is just a facade for their rapacious begging.

They are insubordinate to authority; they revile everyone, but particularly the rich and wellborn. Establishment philosophers take pains to defend themselves from the impression that philosophers are subversive.[48]

They are sexual libertines, seducers of women and boys, connoisseurs of erotic literature. Libertinism is associated with Cynics, as philosophical *paiderastia* is associated with radical Stoics.

This battery of accusations, of course, reflects upper-class prejudice. When Seneca fears that Cynic uncouthness will repel people from philosophy (*Ep.* 5), what he means is that it will repel people who matter. Street preaching requires mendicancy ("greed") because this was normally the only means of livelihood open to a popular philosopher; and both required exhibitionism, because, in spite of what Seneca says, we may suspect that common people doubted the credentials of a philosopher who did not look and act radically unlike most people. "Abusiveness" is the Cynic diatribe style. "Flattery" is a charge always brought against demagogues or anyone else who tried to appeal to the common people. That the audience of the Cynics seemed to like this style would merely demonstrate the unfitness of that audience for philosophy. (It cannot, of course, be true that Cynics were generally unpopular, or they would not have been so numerous.) The charge of libertinism probably means that they continued the tradition of Diogenes, as radical Stoics continued the tradition of Zeno: they considered sexual appetites a matter of indifference if properly controlled, and they made at least some place for women in the Cynic life.

The real Cynics struck back against these accusers. The large collection of letters attributed to Diogenes and Crates, written at various times and by various hands between the first century B.C. and the second century A.D., is largely devoted to a defense of classical Cynicism and a rebuttal of the charges listed above. The defense of mendicancy is a recurrent theme: we are told that the Cynic only begs from those who can afford to give, and only from "friends," meaning people who will benefit from the Cynic message; he is not greedy; he only asks what is his due, for the owns everything, being a friend of the gods like the people of Cronus' time. His poverty is intended to set a model for people to imitate. His preaching is intended to make people better, not to flatter them. The old Cynic sexual morality and the equality of women in the Cynic life are defended pugnaciously by some of these authors.[49]

The Respectable Cynic

But this is not the only kind of Cynic that appears in our sources. Roman Stoics and other philosophers tried to market an ideal Cynic who would be entirely free of the suspect qualities described above. They did this to disinfect the memory of Diogenes, who was still a universal sage revered by most of the schools, and perhaps to divert some of the energy of popular Cynicism into more appropriate channels.[50] Their ideal Cynic would be a cultivated ascetic, Spartan in his manner of living but not ostentatiously so. He would reject excess property, yet he would never be seen begging. They did not ask how he would live—they assumed he would have independent means or be supported in the household of a gentleman. He would never preach in the streets; he would neither flatter nor revile his audience. He would play his part in politics and social life when necessary. He would be an educated man, though despising philosophical speculation that did not result in action.

Seneca and many others saw this ideal Cynicism realized in the philosopher Demetrius, a hero to the "philosophic opposition" in the Senate under the Julio-Claudians and Flavians. Epictetus devoted a long diatribe to the ideal Cynic, in response to a disciple who was considering the Cynic life. In the next century Lucian found the ideal realized in the Athenian philosopher Demonax and commemorated him in a biography which deliberately presents Demonax as the exact reverse of the stereotyped popular Cynic. The Stoic orator Dio Chrysostom, who dressed in traditional Cynic garb for a part of his career, was fond of comparing himself to the real Cynics of his day, with the implication that he upheld the right kind of *parrhesia* and the true tradition of Diogenes, which the popular Cynics had perverted through ignorance and greed.

They admit that this ideal Cynicism has nothing to do with the real Cynicism of their day. The latter is explained as a degenerate offshoot of the Cynic tradition, the result of a drastic decline in standards that has taken place in the Cynic life since the time of Diogenes. This explanation was not very satisfactory, for unfortunately the legend of Diogenes was well remembered and it presented a Diogenes who was very much like the Cynics of the Empire. Diogenes is a major figure in several of Dio's orations, and the Diogenes he describes is reasonably faithful to Cynic tradition. Dio's Diogenes is in fact a rather extreme "rigorist" version of Diogenes—masturbating and defecating in public, defending incest, abusing everyone viciously—because that is the Diogenes audiences wanted to hear about. When Stoics tried to explain just how Diogenes differed from the Cynics of their own day, they could only say that Diogenes was wise and his successors were not, or that Diogenes reviled everyone for the right reasons and the moderns for wrong reasons (Epict. 3.22.80; Dio 72.11).

Did the ideal Cynic ever exist outside the imaginations of these writers? There is ample room for doubt. We are not sure that the few individuals who were identified as ideal Cynics thought of themselves as Cynics at all. Lucian's Demonax certainly did not; he was an eclectic who refused to identify himself with any school, and whom Lucian thought closest to Socrates, though he admits Demonax resembled Diogenes in appearance (*Demonax* 5). Dio Chrysostom did not call himself a Cynic, though he admits many people would think him one because of his dress (34.2–3). Musonius Rufus, Dio's teacher, recommended the Cynic dress to his disciples (fr. 19–20), but he did not call it that, and as we have seen he had no use at all for the Cynic life. Demetrius is called a Cynic by Seneca, but we do not know that Demetrius called himself one.[51] An early representative of this pseudo-Cynic type was the Roman praetor Marcus Favonius, the disciple (probably the only serious one) of Cato the Younger, who according to Plutarch was labelled a "Cynic" by some of his fellow Roman aristocrats because of his outspokenness (*Brutus* 34.4). Epictetus' discourse on Cynicism names no living examples of the ideal Cynic; his point, in fact, is that an ideal Cynic must *not* resemble any of those called Cynics in modern times.

The ideal Cynic, in short, was a myth. This was an attempt by Stoics and other respectable philosophers to imitate and capture some of the most popular elements in the Cynic tradition, especially *parrhesia*. Dio's pseudo-Cynicism is a pose designed to distinguish himself from well-bred sophists who avoid the crowds and confine themselves to rhetorical flatteries in lecture rooms; Dio, by contrast, claims to represent *eleutheria* and *parrhesia*, the outspoken integrity of Socrates and Diogenes.[52] It is true that Dio did not confine himself to lecture rooms, but that is because he was a famous orator invited to address large public assemblies throughout the eastern provinces. There remained a vast gulf between Dio and the itinerant street preachers, and the pseudo-Cynic pose had to be carefully calculated so as to avoid identification with them. Many shades of meaning were possible on this spectrum. Musonius Rufus dressed like a Cynic and was justly famous for *parrhesia*, though it was not expressed in the streets; but he found the *kynogamia* of Crates and Hipparchia scarcely comprehensible, and he mentions it only to draw the odd conclusion that a philosopher must have a respectable marriage. His contemporary Epictetus went a bit deeper into the Cynic tradition: he was willing to use the word "Cynic," and to take the legend of Crates and Hipparchia at face value; but when he says a Cynic will avoid marriage he seems to imply avoidance of sex, for there is nothing authentically Cynic about his sexual morals.

This debate between the respectable Cynicism and the real found its way into spurious epistolography, that favorite instrument of ancient polemic. To counter the epistles of "Diogenes" and "Crates" defending traditional Cynicism, some author went back further and produced letters of "Socrates" in which begging is condemned and philosophers are advised to become residents in great households or otherwise accept the patronage of wealthy "friends."[53] It is more unexpected to find reflections of this debate among early Christians; but Malherbe has shown that the first letter of Paul to the Thessalonians, the earliest datable Christian document, contains unmistakable parallels to Dio Chrysostom's oration to the Alexandrians, delivered some thirty years later.[54] In effect, Paul and Dio both present themselves as "respectable Cynics," exponents of a genuine *parrhesia* that expresses truth and not flattery; but they also handle the audience gently, without any abuse or "busybodyness," and seek neither money nor reputation. Clearly this was a *topos* so common in oratory that it was familiar at all levels of urban society, and came as naturally to a poor Hellenized-Jewish rabbi as to a cultivated Greek rhetorician. The common denominator was that both Paul and Dio wanted to avoid identification with the real Cynics (and in Paul's case, perhaps, with certain mendicant Christian apostles who resembled Cynics). Cynic and anti-Cynic propaganda were pervasive in the Greek-speaking provinces of the Empire.

The Last Utopians

We have seen that the Old Stoic and Old Cynic traditions were very much alive in the first two centuries A.D. and that some of their defenders were people of some education and literary ability. Among them there may have survived vestiges of the old utopian tradition, which by this time was considered as much Cynic as Stoic, and indeed a theory of Cynic origin, since the authenticity of the Diogenic *Republic* was widely accepted. It was believed by the respectable that libertines commonly referred to the doctrine of sexual communism as an excuse for their behavior. Epictetus thought an adulterous scholar might well defend himself with a vague reference to an obsolete Stoic teaching about community of women, which Epictetus barely understood. Lucian thought that Cynics commonly shared their women and claimed to carrying out a tenet of Plato's *Republic* when they did so (*Runaways* 18). Lucian correctly points out that this was a misinterpretation of Plato; but we suspect that it was really the *Republic* of Diogenes they had in mind, if they had anything much in mind.

Lucian is an uncertain witness because he knew even less than Epictetus about the Cynic/Stoic utopian tradition. His *True Story*—a parody of imaginative Hellenistic geographers, among whom he specifically mentions Iambulus—contains an account of a voyage to the Island of the Blessed, where the departed heroes and philosophers of the past live a joyous existence on the Elysian fields. Among other pleasures they enjoy sex openly and without shame with both genders; boys give themselves to anyone who wants them; and all women are held in common without jealousy, which makes them *Platonikotatoi*, the ultimate Platonists. This word implies "more Platonist than Plato," for Plato lives apart from them in his own polis, under the *politeia* and *nomoi* that he had written himself (2.17–19). Lucian did not associate this promiscuous sexual communism with Plato. But he did not associate it with Stoics or Cynics either. (Both have their places in his satire: Diogenes has changed his ways and participates in the joys of the Elysian fields all too fully, a crack at Cynic hypocrisy; the Stoics are not even there because they are still climbing the steep hill of virtue, a comment on the glum puritanism of Stoic ethics.) The notion of free sexual communism Lucian probably took from Iambulus' novel, and knew no more about Iambulus' philosophical sources than we do. He took it to be a wild caricature of Plato's *Republic*. If contemporary Cynics really claimed to believe in community of women, they may have understood the doctrine no better than this. To most it may have been a garbled recollection that mingled familiar mythology with the fantasies of Hellenistic travel literature and echoes of forgotten political philosophy; and perhaps it was true that it was usually just an excuse for libertinism.

On the other hand, some Cynics may have understood much more about the matter. We know of one Cynic in the Empire who apparently wrote about these things on a theoretical level. Oenomaus of Gadara, who probably flourished in the time of Hadrian, came from a Greek town in Palestine that had produced more than one famous Cynic. Among other works, he was said to have written a *Republic* (according to the *Suda*); some tragedies in imitation of the burlesque tragedies attributed to Diogenes; and an *Against the Oracles*, part of which survives in the *Evangelical Preparation* of Eusebius (5.18–36, 6.6–7). Two hundred years after his death the emperor Julian treated him as a leading authority among Cynics (6.187c, 199a, 7.209a–212a). Julian calls him shameless, and a scorner of all laws human and divine. His tragedies Julian thought more scandalous than those of Diogenes, which it will be recalled were thought to sanction incest and cannibalism. He offended Julian's Neoplatonist piety by his vigorous attacks on the cults of the gods, which we know from Eusebius' citations continued the old Cynic war on superstition. Julian says also that he subverted the customs that require us to respect the property of others, and that this teaching was continued by the Cynics of the fourth century A.D., who went about everywhere confounding the common laws (*ta koina nomima syncheontes*) like so many bandits. Not much to go on, but perhaps the most plausible interpretation of it is that the *Republic* of Oenomaus was modeled on the *Republic* of Diogenes, and taught communism. If so, its five-hundred-year history as a philosophical theory ended with him.[55]

One may offer some final generalizations about the death of utopia. By the first century B.C. a clear division had appeared between the philosophies of the educated classes and the philosophies of the people, a division that was to endure to the end of paganism. The established schools patronized by the upper classes held an eclectic and conservative ethical and political teaching that varied little from school to school; it skirted theoretical questions and emphasized practical instruction in conduct centered on the patriarchal household. Its only real rival was Cynicism, a permanent philosophical underclass, the continuing Taoist counterpoint to the dominant Confucianist theme of Greco-Roman thought. All ideas excluded from official philosophy, such as utopian communism, filtered down into this underclass and may have continued to live a sort of intellectual half-life there for centuries.

This divorce between polite and impolite philosophy helped to kill creative social and political thought. In the early Hellenistic age, Stoicism and Cynicism had to some extent fertilized one another. Cynicism had for all its anti-intellectualism carried on a sort of dialogue with the more formal schools, had its upper-class auditors, and acquired from those contacts a greater sense of social responsibility. Stoicism had kept from its many Cynic contacts a sort of bridge to the world of the ordinary citizen. With the coming of Rome the bridge was broken and all contact ceased between the nervous oligarchical ideology of the rich and the inchoate demagoguery of the streets. Everything smacking of social and political radicalism, even of popular appeal, was confined to the latter.

The utopian ideal was a casualty of a gradual and profound change in society, whose principal cause was the domination of the Greek cities by Rome. Communism came to be thought an unacceptable idea, out of a complex of fears that cannot be disentangled: the terror of social revolution in Greece, which perhaps climaxed in the second century B.C.; the need of the Roman ruling class to justify and stabilize its rule and the need of its Greek clients to cater to its interests; a new sexual puritanism, which seems obscurely linked to the preservation of the existing distribution of property and privilege. All these things contributed to a defensive attitude toward the social order and an unwillingness to contemplate any serious alternatives to it. The great reaction of the late Hellenistic age gave a conservative orientation to ethical and political philosophy which would never be reversed for as long as this civilization lasted.

Notes

1. The pivotal significance of Panaetius was first recognized by Schmeckel (1892), who coined the phrase "Middle Stoicism" and considered Panaetius its founder. He divided the history of Stoicism into three periods: the Old Stoicism of the founders (ca. 300–130 B.C.), the Middle Stoicism of Panaetius and Posidonius (ca. 130–1 B.C.), and

the Roman Stoicism of Seneca, Epictetus, and Marcus Aurelius. I prefer not to use the category "Middle Stoicism." It seems to me more useful, at least in treating ethical and political doctrine, to recognize only one major break, not two, in the Stoic tradition, and to distinguish only two major periods, the early Stoicism that began with Zeno and the Neostoicism (a term suggested by Long) that began with Panaetius. The fragments of Panaetius have been collected by Modestus Van Straaten, *Panétius, sa vie, ses écrits, et sa doctrine* (Amsterdam 1946); and idem, *Panaetii Rhodii Fragmenta*, 3rd ed. (Leiden 1962); those of Posidonius, by Ludwig Edelstein and I. G. Kidd, *Posidonius* (Cambridge 1988).

2. E.g., Van Straaten, *Panétius*; Reesor, *Political Theory*; Pohlenz, *Die Stoa*; Marie Laffranque, *Poseidonios d'Apamée* (Paris 1964).

3. Attributed to Panaetius by Cicero (*On Duties* 1.20.66–67; 3.3.12); to Hecaton by Diogenes Laertius (7.128); to Posidonius by Cicero (*Tusc. Disp.* 2.25.61), Seneca (*Ep.* 87.31–40), and Galen (*On Hippocrates and Plato* 5.6.10). No one remembered Panaetius as the founder of a heterodox sect, as the later Stoics remembered Aristo of Chios. There is a solitary allusion (Ath. 5.186a) to a group of philosophers called "Panaetians" (*Panaitistai*), but as the speaker also mentions "Diogenists" and "Antipatrists" these terms must refer to minor doctrinal differences among Stoics.

4. I follow here the interpretations of Kidd, "Stoic Intermediates and the End for Man," in A. A. Long, ed., *Problems in Stoicism* (London 1971); Long, "Carneades and the Stoic telos," *Phronesis* 12 (1967), 59–90; and Long and Sedley, *Hellenistic Philosophers* 1.401–10.

5. J. M. Rist, *Stoic Philosophy* (London 1969), 7–10, tried to save the evidence of Diogenes Laertius by supposing Panaetius to have changed the relationship between virtue and the external objects: the old Stoics said externals were the material of virtue, while Panaetius perhaps called them the *necessary* material. But I cannot see how this would have differed significantly from the views of Chrysippus, if these are correctly described by Cicero (*On Ends* 4.25.68).

6. Another version of this argument will be found in Cicero, *Tusc. Disp.* 4.33.70–4.34.72.

7. Cicero tells us that the first two books of his *On Duties* were based upon the *Peri kathekontos* of Panaetius (*Letters to Atticus* 16.11.4). He also used a summary of one of Posidonius' works. In the third book Hecaton is cited (3.15.63, 3.23.89).

8. As suggested by Van Straaten, *Panétius*, 201; Pohlenz, *Die Stoa* 1.207; Ludwig Edelstein, *The Meaning of Stoicism* (Cambridge, Mass. 1966), 54; Baldry, *Unity of Mankind*, 82. Panaetius may indeed have made significant contributions to the Stoic theory of ordinary morality. Cicero's *On Duties* presents a subtle theory of proper function as an amalgam of four "roles" (*personae*): the role of universal rationality; the role assigned by individual mental and physical endowments; the roles created by circumstances, such as wealth and office; and the roles that we choose. We know of no earlier parallel to this theory, so it is possible Panaetius lent a new realism to Stoic ordinary morality, as has been suggested by Long, "Greek Ethics after McIntyre and the Stoic Community of Reason," *Ancient Philosophy* 3 (1983), 184–199; and Long and Sedley, *Hellenistic Philosophers* 1.427–28. Still, there is no explanation as to how the other roles are supposed to conform to the universal moral standard of the first role. Cicero seems to have received from Panaetius the impression that the first role could be effectively kicked upstairs—also the impression we receive from the Stoic moralists of the principate.

9. *On Duties* 1.42.150. Elsewhere Cicero tells us that through the time of Diogenes

of Babylon (d. ca. 152 B.C.) the Stoics did not count reputation among the things desirable for their own sake, and that Diogenes' successors reversed this position (*On Ends* 3.17.57).

10. Panaetius wrote a work *On the Sects* and was considered an authority on the history of philosophy. Cicero, who thought Stoicism merely an offshoot of Platonism (*correctio veteris Academiae*), congratulated Panaetius for returning to the original sources—Plato and Aristotle. Therefore Panaetius may have been the first Stoic to claim descent from Plato, and the author of the theory that Stoicism was a reformed version of Platonism, as suggested by Glucker, *Antiochus*, 28–30.

11. *Ep.* 13.4: "omittamus haec magna verba, sed, di boni, vera."

12. *Ep.* 71.3; cf. 35.4, 72.9–11. In *Ep.* 75 Seneca admits that a progressor is still among the unwise, but nevertheless clearly distinct from the mass of the unwise, and makes significant distinctions among progressors. In *Ep.* 72.6 the wise man and the progressor are compared to a healthy man and a convalescent, implying that the mass of the unwise must be diagnosed as critically ill. For another Stoic's treatment of the ship metaphor see Dio 68.7.

13. *On Duties* 1.7.21, 1.16.50–52; 2.12.41–42, 2.21.73, 2.22.78–23.84; 3.5.21–23.

14. Cicero is often called the first political thinker to affirm that the basic function of the state is the protection of private property: e.g., de Ste. Croix, *Class Struggle*, 286; Neal Wood, *Cicero's Social and Political Thought* (Berkeley 1988), 132. So he may have been. But the passages in question are among the parts of *On Duties* generally assumed to represent the thought of Panaetius, and private property is so central to the social theory laid out in the first two books that it is difficult to regard it as an interpolation by Cicero. The phrase "possessive individualism" was coined by C. B. Macpherson, *The Political Theory of Possessive Individualism* (Oxford 1962), with reference to the political thought of early modern Europe, and its relevance to Cicero was pointed out by Wood, op. cit.

15. But see Kidd's note on fr. 284 in the Edelstein/Kidd edition of Posidonius. He suggests that Seneca may be conflating various passages in the works of Posidonius for rhetorical purposes, and that Posidonius, in these comments on the origins of technology, may not have intended an historical picture of the primitive state.

16. Aug., *City of God* 3.4; 4.27, 31–32; 6.5–6; 7.5–6. On the origins of this "tripartite theology" there has been much discussion, summarized by Godo Lieberg, "Die 'theologia tripartita' in Forschung und Bezeugung," *Aufstieg und Niedergang der Römischen Welt* 1.4 (Berlin 1973), 63–115, who concludes Panaetius was probably its founder, though Posidonius may have been the first to put it in an historical framework.

17. Eleuterio Elorduy, *Die Sozialphilosophie der Stoa* (Leipzig 1936), 212; Van Straaten, *Pañetius*, 203ff.; Baldry, *Unity*, 151–66.

18. Ovid, *Metamorphoses* 1.76–215; Vergil, *Eclogue* 4, *Georgics* 121ff., *Aeneid* 8.321–27; Horace, *Epode* 16; Sen., *On Clemency* 2.1–2; Justin, 1.1–3, 43.1.3; Tacitus, *Annals* 3.26; etc. See A. Wallace-Hadrill, "The Golden Age and Sin in Augustan Ideology," *Past and Present* 95 (1982), 19–36.

19. It is unnecessary to list the numerous warnings against sexual relations with either women or boys found in the writings of the Roman Stoics. The clearest statement of the new morality is perhaps the *On Sexual Matters* of Musonius Rufus. He says sex is only for procreation, condemns relations with slaves and prostitutes, and especially condemns adultery and homosexuality. Cf. Sen., *On Consolation to Helvia* 13.3; and Lucan, *Pharsalia* 2.387–88, on the example set by Cato the Younger. On Roman sexual morality see Jasper Griffin, "Augustan Poetry and the Life of Luxury," *Journal of Roman Studies* 66 (1976), 87–105; B.C. Verstraete, "Slavery and the Social Dynamics

of Male Homosexual Relations in Ancient Rome," *Journal of Homosexuality* 5 (1980), 227–236; Ramsay MacMullen, "Roman Attitudes to Greek Love," *Historia* 31 (1982), 484–502; and Paul Veyne, "The Roman Empire," in *A History of Private Life* 1, ed. Veyne (Cambridge, Mass., 1987).

20. Stoic comments on homosexuality often refer to effeminacy, which had been a favorite symbol of luxury and vice among the older Stoics and Cynics: e.g., Sen., *On Providence* 3.13; *On Wrath* 1.21.3; *On Tranquility* 17.4; *Natural Questions* 1.16; *Ep.* 47.7, 94.21; Epict., *Disc.* 4.2.9. In Seneca's *Ep.* 122 effeminacy is said to be against nature, but so are luxurious houses, heavy meals, and staying up all night. On the other hand, Epictetus (*Disc.* 2.10.17) says the active homosexual loses his manhood along with the passive; and Dio (7.133–52) says that only procreative sex is according to nature but thinks homosexual acts a particularly serious violation of nature. "Effeminacy" could have a broader meaning: the *kinaidos* or effeminate sometimes symbolizes sexual vice and moral weakness in general. In Dio's Fourth Oration, put into the mouth of Diogenes the Cynic, effeminacy implies both homosexual and heterosexual indulgence, male passivity being only the lowest manifestation of it (101–15).

21. Musonius (trans. Cora Lutz, *Musonius Rufus*, New Haven 1947), fr. 3, 4, 11, 13–14, especially fr. 3, "That Women Should Study Philosophy", and fr. 14, "Is Marriage a Hindrance to Philosophy?". See C. E. Manning, "Seneca and the Stoics on the Equality of the Sexes," *Mnemosyne* 4.26 (1973), 170–77; and idem, "Stoicism and Slavery in the Roman Empire," *Aufstieg und Niedergang der Römischen Welt* 2.36.3 (Berlin 1989), 1518–43.

22. The phrase "household code" (*Haustafeln*) was coined by German scholars to describe the household-based moral codes scattered through the New Testament and the Apostolic Fathers: see below, chapter 6, note 22. These Christian codes, which are more schematic than their pagan counterparts, show how common it was in circles far below the social level of most philosophers to think of ethics in terms of a scheme of relationships among members of a household.

23. Some have discerned a growing climate of sexual puritanism during the first two centuries A.D.: see Paul Veyne, "La famille et l'amour sous le Haut-Empire romaine," *Annales: Économies, Sociétés, Civilisations* 33 (1978), 35–63; idem, "Roman Empire." For a corrective, see Robin Lane Fox, *Pagans and Christians* (New York 1987), 349–50. I incline to think that the more decisive turning point in the intellectual climate came in the late second and early first centuries B.C.

24. According to Livy, the Romans were always allies of the "best people" in the Greek cities in the second century B.C. (35.33–34, 42.30). Political realities were more complicated than that, especially during the early stages of Roman intervention before 146, when Roman interests sometimes coincided with those of democratic factions: see Rostovtzeff, *Hellenistic World* 2.610–13, 3.1460; E. S. Gruen, *The Hellenistic World and the Coming of Rome* (Berkeley 1984), 326, 525. But Gruen admits "Circumstances were very different when the erratic conqueror became a settled administrator" (351). There is no doubt that the long-range effect of Roman hegemony was to suppress democracy: see A. H. M. Jones, *The Greek City from Alexander to Justinian* (Oxford 1940), 170ff.; John Briscoe, "Rome and the Class Struggle in the Greek States, 200–146 B.C.," *Past and Present* 36 (1967), 1–20; de Ste. Croix, *Class Struggle*, 300–26, 518–37; and Fuks, *Social Conflict*, especially "The *Bellum Achaium* and its Social Aspect," and "Social Revolution in Greece in the Hellenistic Age," where he writes "The *multitudo, plebs, demos, okhlos* was always and everywhere anti-Roman and reposed its hopes of a change in the social and economic situation in all who manifested opposition to Rome" (48).

25. The early history of Greek philosophy at Rome is the subject of a valuable study by Elizabeth Rawson, *Intellectual Life in the Late Roman Republic* (Baltimore 1985), who is perhaps unduly skeptical about the possibility of Roman influences on thinkers like Panaetius. Among his Greek disciples the only significant figure to visit Rome was Posidonius, whose two visits seem to have left little impression. Cicero's *On the Nature of the Gods*, a dialogue set in the seventies, mentions several Romans as friends of Posidonius, but not exactly as disciples.

26. Attempts to assign theories of Polybius and Cicero to Panaetius have been cogently questioned by Hermann Strassburger, "Posidonios on Problems of the Roman Empire," *Journal of Roman Studies* 55 (1965), 40–53: "no correspondence can be securely proved between concrete issues of Roman policy and ascertained 'stoic' doctrines" (45 n. 52). I think, however, that we can discern correspondences between the fundamental political viewpoints of Greek and Roman conservatives. What they have in common is mostly common to conservative thought in antiquity.

27. *The Roman Revolution* (Oxford 1939), 57. Cf. D. C. Earl, "Terence and Roman Politics," *Historia* 11 (1962), 469–85.

28. On Polybius' dislike of democracy, 6.4–10, 43–44, 57; 20.6. His disdain for utopian thought, 6.47, 56. His negative judgment on the Spartan reforms, 4.81.12–14.

29. On his background, see the appendix "Panaetius" in Erskine, *Hellenistic Stoa.*

30. Tubero was cast as a friend of Panaetius by Cicero (*Rep.* 1.9.14ff.). Panaetius wrote Tubero a letter on endurance of pain which made no use of Stoic terms (*On Ends* 4.9.23) and recommended to him a work by the Platonist Crantor (*Acad.* 2.44.135). Panaetius knew Latin well enough to criticize poetry for Tubero's benefit (*Tusc. Disp.* 4.2.4). Hecaton dedicated his *On Duties* to Tubero (Cic., *On Duties* 3.15.63).

31. There is evidence that this conservative reaction in Stoicism began in the generation before Panaetius. We know from Cicero (*On Duties* 3.12.51–3.13.57) that there was a debate among the Athenian Stoics around the middle of the century over the competing claims of private property and the public interest. Diogenes of Babylon, head of the school, allowed remarkable liberties to property owners: he thought a seller of a villa was not obliged to reveal it was of unsound timber, nor a wineseller to tell his customers that his wine was spoiling. Also Cicero considered this Diogenes the first Stoic to have written something "useful" on politics. Diogenes might have invented the theory of possessive individualism. But his innovations, whatever they were, do not seem to have effected any decisive break with the old tradition. Cicero reports that his successor Antipater took precisely the opposite view on private property; we have seen Antipater referring to the *Republics* of Diogenes and Zeno in terms that do not seem unfavorable; and Antipater taught Blossius as well as Panaetius.

32. The role of Blossius in the Gracchan reforms has sometimes been exaggerated, but see the summation by Ernst Badian, "Tiberius Gracchus and the Roman Revolution," *Aufstieg und Niedergang der Römischen Welt* 1.1 (1972), 668–731. Attempts to deny altogether the connections between the Gracchan movement and its Hellenistic counterparts seem to me perverse.

The little-known revolt of Aristonicus included mass emancipation of slaves and expansion of citizen bodies. We are also told his followers were called *Heliopolitai*, "citizens of the sun" (Strabo 14.1.38). All this has inspired speculation that Aristonicus' revolt, uniquely among Greek reform movements, tried to appeal to slaves, and may have tried to put into practice the utopian communism of Iambulus' novel. I have nothing to add to the voluminous discussion of this question, of which there are useful synopses by Vladimir Vavrinek, "Aristonicus of Pergamum," *Eirene* 13 (1975), 109–29; and Gruen, *Hellenistic World*, 596ff. I find persuasive the arguments of J.-C. Dumont,

"A propos d'Aristonicus," *Eirene* 5 (1966), 189–96: Aristonicus' emancipation of slaves could have been a traditional war measure; his Heliopolis could have been a new city he meant to found for his freedmen, also in the tradition of Hellenistic monarchy, and the name may have signified nothing but the protection of the sun god. This is not to deny that there was an atmosphere of extreme radicalism about this movement. See the comments of Cl. Mossé, "Les utopies egalitaires à l'époque hellenistique," *Révue historique* 241 (1969), 297–308.

33. D. R. Dudley, "Blossius of Cumae," *Journal of Roman Studies* 31 (1941), 94–99, doubted there was any connection between Blossius' political activities and his Stoicism: he pointed out that Blossius' family belonged to the democratic anti-Roman faction in Campania; he argued that Stoicism was uninterested in constitutional questions and unsympathetic to democracy. The first point seems not to recognize the fact that all but the most unworldly philosophers may have political interests, as all but the stupidest politicians may have philosophical interests. And I have already argued against Dudley's view of Stoicism.

34. Posidonius condemned the democratic revolt at Athens which Sulla crushed in 86 B.C. (Ath. 5.211d–215b = Edelstein/Kidd fr. 253, with commentary). He praised the antique Roman simplicity and thought Rome had been ruined by success (Ath. 6.273ab, 274a = Edelstein/Kidd fr. 265, 266). If, as has been generally thought, the later books of Diodorus Siculus (dealing with events after 146 B.C.) are based upon the *Histories* of Posidonius, then Posidonius seems to have taken a highly unfavorable view of the Gracchan reforms (Diodorus 34/35. 7.2, 25.1).

35. Diog. Laert 7.34; Plut., *Cato* 10, 16; Strabo 14.5.14.

36. Condemnation of ornate public buildings: Cic., *On Duties* 2.17.60; Musonius, fr. 19–20; Dio 7.117–18.

37. Sen., *On Benefits* 4.3ff.; *On Clemency* 2.6.2; *On Tranquility* 8; *On Consolation to Helvia* 10; *Ep.* 19, 119; and for a more favorable view of wealth, *On the Happy Life* 16.3ff., 22.1–5.

38. A detailed study of commentary on Plato's *Republic* would be useful. In the meantime we have the material collected by Novotný, *Posthumous Life of Plato.*

39. M. Aurelius as philosopher-king: Ausonius 14.17; *Augustan History*, Capitolinus, M. Anton. 27.7.

40. Aulus Gellius (*Attic Nights* 18.2) reports a debate at Athens on the question of how Plato could have permitted community of women, and allowed warriors to kiss boys and women as a reward for bravery. Lucian (*Philosophies for Sale* 17) implies those two points were major embarrassments for Platonists of the Antonine age.

41. Epictetus, fr. 15, from the *Memorabilia* (Stob. 3.301.1–9): "In Rome women make a study of Plato's *Republic*, because he enacts community of wives; for they only attend to the man's words and not to his spirit, not noticing that he does not first enact the marriage of one man and one woman and then wish wives to be common, but removes the first kind of marriage and introduces another kind in its place. And in general men are fond of finding justifications for their own faults. . . ." Trans. Matheson in *The Stoic and Epicurean Philosophers*, ed. W. J. Oates (New York 1940).

42. Cicero (*On Ends* 3.20.68) attributes to Cato the Younger the view that the wise man is permitted *amores sanctos* outside marriage. Plutarch (*Common Conceptions* 1072f–1073c) seems to imply that when Stoics of his day spoke of the wise man as *erotikos* they meant a completely nonphysical kind of love. Cicero is probably thinking of Stoics when he expresses mistrust of those philosophers who claim their homosexuality is "pure" (*amorem negant stupri esse*, *Tusc. Disp.* 4.33.70–34.72).

43. Juvenal (Satire 2) and Athenaeus (13.563de, 565d–f) present much the same comic portrait of the radical Stoic: he resembles a Cynic in dress and manners, abuses effeminate males, pretends to practice a pure philosophical love of young men, but in fact indulges freely in homosexual pleasures, even those of a passive sort.

44. Dio 32.9, 72.2–4; and for the dates and circumstances of these oration, see C. P. Jones, *The Roman World of Dio Chrysostom* (Cambridge, Mass. 1978).

45. Zeller, *Socrates*, thought that Cynicism died out after the third century B.C. and reappeared in the first century A.D. as an offshoot of Stoicism. Samuel Dill, *Roman Society from Nero to Marcus Aurelius* (London 1905), 395: "Thus it was that, in the first century after Christ, Cynicism emerged from its long obscurity to take up the part of a rather one-sided popular Stoicism." Dudley, *Cynicism*, argued that Cynicism never disappeared completely, but he could point to very little evidence that it was a living tradition in the later Hellenistic age. See Margrethe Billerbeck, "La réception du cynisme à Rome," *L'antiquité classique* 51 (1982), 151–73; and M.-O. Goulet-Cazé, "Le cynisme à l'époque impériale," *ANRW* 2.36.4 (1990), 2720–2833.

46. The best-known Cynic of the second century A.D., that Peregrinus Proteus of whom Lucian left a hostile biography, seems to have been influenced by both Pythagoreanism and Christianity; see H. M. Hornsby, "The Cynicism of Peregrinus Proteus," *Hermathena* 48 (1953), 65–84. Still, the great Pythagorean hero Apollonius of Tyana was said to have criticized the Cynics sharply, saying they had nothing in common with the followers of Pythagoras except their ascetic life (Philostratus, *Life of Apollonius* 6.11).

47. Various combinations of these charges against Cynics, sometimes directed at radical Stoics as well, will be found in the following authors: Seneca, *Ep.* 5, 29.1; *On the Happy Life* 18.3; Martial 4.53; Epictetus, *Disc.* 3.22, 4.8; Dio Chrysostom, *Or.* 32–34, 72; Lucian, *Demonax* 5–10, 48; *Runaways* 12–21; *Symposium*; *Philosophies for Sale* 7–11; *Fisherman* 44–48; *True History* 2.18; *Passing of Peregrinus*; Marcus Aurelius, *Med.* 1.7 (a criticism of showy virtue, probably aimed at Cynicizing Stoics); Dio Cassius 65.13; Athenaeus 3.96f–97c; 4.156e–157a, 162b; 13.563de, 565d–f, 611b–d; for Aelius Aristides see below, n. 55.

48. Dio's orations 32 (Alexandria) and 34 (Tarsus) may imply that Cynics had been stirring up riots: see Jones, *Roman World*, 36–44, 71–82. Seneca, in his *Epistle* 73.1, tries to correct the impression that philosophers despise monarchs and magistrates. Epictetus records the dislike some notables felt for even his own innocuous brand of philosophy (*Disc.* 2.12, 3.8).

49. For the Cynic Epistles see Malherbe, *Cynic Epistles*; On the defense of begging, see *Epistles of Diogenes* 10, 11, 38; and *Epistles of Crates* 2, 17, 19, 22, 26, 27, 36. On women's equality with men, *Diogenes* 32,43; *Crates* 28, 29. And note the baroque expression of Cynic sexual morality in *Diogenes* 44, where it is claimed Cynics practice *no* sex except masturbation.

50. Neostoics continued to revere Diogenes. The *Chreiai* of Hecaton, Panaetius' disciple, contained anecdotes about Antisthenes, Diogenes, and Metrocles as well as Zeno and Cleanthes (Diog. Laert. 6.4, 32, 95). Neostoics often made a sharp distinction between Diogenes and the corrupt modern Cynics; this is clearest in the writings of Epictetus and Dio. But Seneca criticizes even Diogenes for his attempt to reach the masses (*Ep.* 29.1). Lucian is ambivalent: sometimes Diogenes is a great philosopher whom modern Cynics have betrayed (*Fisherman*, *Runaways*); sometimes, where it happens to suit Lucian's satirical purposes, Diogenes is a symbol of corrupt modern Cynicism (*Sale of Philosophies*, *True History*).

51. *On Benefits* 7.1.3; *On the Happy Life* 18.3. But it is also possible, as suggested by Goulet-Cazé, "Le cynisme," that Demetrius was a real Cynic or "near-Cynic" whom

Seneca tried to paint as a Neostoic. See also Kindstrand, "Demetrius the Cynic," *Philologus* 124 (1980), 83–98.

52. Especially in *Or.* 32.5–11, where Dio presents himself to the Alexandrians as one of the few who demonstrate the correct *parrhesia* and *eleutheria*, contrasting himself explicitly with the mob of Cynics who infest the city. Lucian (*Demonax* 3) says the main goals of Demonax were *parrhesia* and *eleutheria,* but the description that follows is intended to show how remote from real Cynicism was Demonax's understanding of those principles: Demonax was learned in philosophy and rhetoric, played his part in political life, admonished and encouraged his hearers gently and without abuse, led the same life as everyone else (of his class), and addressed the common people only for the purpose of quieting excited mobs.

53. The *Epistles of Socrates* are printed in Malherbe and other editions of the Cynic Epistles; see especially *Ep.* 1 and 6.

54. See A. J. Malherbe, "Gentle as a Nurse: the Cynic Background to 1 Thess. 2," *Novum Testamentum* 12 (1970), 203–17. The relevant passages are Dio 32.5–11 and 1 Thess. 2.1–8. Also note that whoever wrote 2 Thessalonians condemned Christians who live in idleness as "busybodies" (*periergazomenoi*), 3.11.

55. On the other hand, the charge that Cynics did not respect the laws of property might refer simply to the traditional Cynic teaching that "All things belong to the wise." I have argued in an earlier chapter that this slogan was a justification for mendicancy, not a utopian doctrine. Not long after Oenomaus wrote the great orator Aelius Aristides delivered the following attack on Cynics: "When they steal, they say that they 'share,' They call their envy 'philosophy' and their mendicity 'disdain of worldly goods.' They frequent the doorways, talking more often to the doorkeepers than the masters, making up for their lowly condition by using impudence. They deceive like flatterers, handle insults like superior men, combining the two most opposite and repugnant vices: vileness and insolence." See *Oration* 46.2.394ff., trans. Stephen Benko in *Pagan Rome and the Early Christians* (Bloomington 1984).

The only reasons to think Oenomaus may have gone beyond these traditional Cynic teachings are his use of the title *Republic* and his interest in imitating the works attributed to Diogenes the Dog. See Jürgan Hammerstaedt, "Der Kyniker Oenomans von Gadara," *ANRW* 2.36.4 (Berlin 1990), 2834–65.

6

The Ghosts of Utopia

We have everything in common except our wives.
TERTULLIAN, *Apology* 39

Primitive Christianity

The Mission Charge

The history of philosophical utopianism in the ancient world ends at this point, but its curious afterlife in the Christian church deserves attention because this was the channel through which the communistic ideals of antiquity were passed on to medieval Europe.

Several passages in the New Testament suggest, or were later believed to suggest, community of property. The most influential of these is the description of the primitive church in the Acts of the Apostles; but let us begin with two enigmatic passages in the Synoptic Gospels which were often associated with it.

The Gospels contain many "wisdom sayings" of a traditional Jewish sort advising detachment from wealth, and many traditionally Jewish injunctions to give alms (especially Mt. 5.42; Lk. 6.30). They preserve also traces of a more radical view of property. There was a clear tradition that Jesus' inner circle of disciples, especially the Twelve, left all their property and families. All the Synoptics say that Jesus renounced his family and replaced the bond of kinship with that of discipleship (Mt. 12.46–50; Mk. 3.31–35; Lk. 8.19–21); that the disciples left everything at their call (Lk. 5.11, 5.28, etc.); that the disciples were required to renounce their families (Mt. 10.34–38; Mk. 13.12; Lk. 12.51–53, 14.25–33). It was also remembered that Jesus advised against marriage (Mt. 19.12) and, in one of the most un-Judaic passages in the Gospels, refused to allow a disciple to turn back even to bury his father (Mt. 8.19–22; Lk. 9.57–62).

The purpose of this renunciation is not clear in the Gospels. But it was clearly remembered that Jesus called an inner circle to him and that the Twelve were of special importance, even if there was not complete agreement about their identity and no very clear notion of their function. In our Gospel texts they act mostly as "extras." Their original function was probably eschatological, for it was remembered they were to lead the twelve tribes of Israel in the coming kingdom of God—a tradition so out of place in the later Christian church as to assure us of its authenticity. The renunciation of family could have been based on Jewish eschatological tradition, which predicted the destruction of family ties in the Day of the Lord (Mic. 7.6; Zech. 13.3).

The one tradition that prescribes a specific role for the disciples probably had an eschatological background also. This is the mission charge (Mt. 10.5–15; Mk. 6.7–13; Lk. 9.1–6, 10.1–12), in which Jesus sends the disciples out to preach and heal, with instructions to take nothing for the journey:

> Provide no gold, silver, or copper to fill your purse, no pack for the road, no second coat, no shoes, no stick; the worker earns his keep. Mt. 10.10–11, New English Bible

Many commentators have thought the original setting of this instruction was an eschatological mission to proclaim the kingdom of God. The absence of any role for Jesus in this proclamation is taken as evidence of its authenticity. The apocalyptic nature of the mission implies that it was a unique event, and the disciples may be told to take nothing with them simply for the sake of speed, not ascetic discipline. Therefore it is not clear that this charge was originally meant to prescribe a regular way of life for anyone. Nevertheless, we know that the church soon interpreted the charge in this way. The saying that the laborer deserves his food (or his wages, Lk. 10.7) has the look of a later insertion, which turns the mission charge into a regulation for the support of Christian teachers by the Christian communities. That is how St. Paul understood it: he reminds his Corinthian converts, as something well known to them, that "the Lord gave instructions that those who preach the Gospel should earn their living by the Gospel" (1 Cor. 9.14). The early manual of church discipline called the *Didache* refers to the mission charge without quoting it, as a well-known teaching of the Lord which requires Christians to support their teachers.[1]

The mission charge, like so much else in the Gospels, is probably a composite, in which an original element, having to do with a unique eschatological proclamation (perhaps the original function of the Twelve) has been fused with the mission experience of the Christian movement between ca. 30 and ca. 70 A.D. The final product is a rule for the organization of Christian mission work: disciples are expected to renounce property and family so as to devote themselves entirely to their missions, and their followers are expected to support them.

But it is also clear that the ascetic elements in the mission charge were dropping out of Christian practice by the time our Gospels were written down. This change was already in progress by the time of the Pauline mission (ca. 40–50 A.D.). Paul made much of the claim that he did not take full advantage of his right to live by the Gospel, preferring to support himself by his own labor so as not to burden his converts, and he commanded his converts to do the same (1 Thess. 2.9, 4.11–12; 2 Thess. 3.6–12; 1 Cor. 4.11–12, 9.1–18; 2 Cor. 11.7–15, 12.13–18). The change is complete in the Gospel of Luke, which has Jesus withdraw the mission charge just before his death (Lk. 22.36). Then Luke proceeds to represent Paul as *always* supporting himself by his own labor (Acts 20.33–35), which is contradicted by the Pauline Epistles. Luke seems to regard the mission charge, and the apostolic renunciation of property and family that preceded it, as a special discipline that was practiced only by selected disciples and only during Jesus' earthly ministry. The *Didache* cites the Gospel precept to give alms as a basic Christian duty, and requires itinerant "apostles" to be supported, but is equally careful to regulate almsgiving and to cut off support for "false prophets."[2] In the Pastoral Epistles, written probably in the early second century, the mission charge is cited to justify regular salaries for church officials and no longer has anything to do with itinerant apostles (1 Tim. 5.17–18).

The tradition that the apostles renounced everything must have an historical foundation, for the church would not have invented a tradition that proved so embarassing to it. But the model of the itinerant mendicant preacher, despite its strong foundation in Gospel tradition, was becoming suspect in Christian communities within the first generation, and by the second it seems dead. We have seen that the reaction against it paralleled the pagan reaction against Cynicism and sometimes borrowed pagan rhetoric.

The Call to Sell All

Most traditions about the poverty of Jesus and his disciples refer only to the leadership of the movement. But one tradition, found in all the Synoptics, seems evidence for a more general and radical attitude toward property:

> (17) As he was starting out on a journey, a stranger ran up, and,kneeling before him, asked, "Good master, what must I do to win eternal life?" (18) Jesus said to him, "Why do you call me good? No one is good except God alone. (19) You know the commandments: 'Do not murder; do not commit adultery; do not steal; do not give false evidence; do not defraud; honor your father and mother.'" (20) "But Master," he replied, "I have kept all these since I was a boy." (21) Jesus looked straight at him; his heart warmed to him, and he said, "One thing you lack: go, sell everything you have, and give to the poor, and you will have riches in heaven; and come, follow me." (22) At these words his face fell and he went away with a heavy heart; for he was a man of great wealth. (23) Jesus looked round at his disciples and said to them, "How hard it will be for the wealthy to enter the kingdom of God!" (24) They were amazed that he should say this, but Jesus insisted, "Children, how hard it is to enter the kingdom of God! (25) It is easier for a camel to pass through the eye of a needle than for a rich man to enter the kingdom of God." (26) They were more astonished than ever, and said to one another, "Then who can be saved?" (27) Jesus looked them in the face and said, "For men it is impossible, but not for God; to God everything is possible." (28) At this Peter spoke, "We here," he said, "have left everything to become your followers." (29) Jesus said, "I tell you this: there is no one who has given up home, brothers or sisters, mother, father, or children, or land, for my sake and for the Gospel, (30) who will not receive in this age a hundred times as much—houses, brothers and sisters, mothers and children, and land—and persecutions besides; and in the age to come eternal life. (31) But many who are first will be last and the last first." Mk. 10.17–31 (cf. Lk. 18.18–30; Mt. 19.16–26)

This is what Bultmann called a "conflict saying," an apophthegm occasioned by a question put to Jesus. It may be a composite, consisting of an original ancedote about the rich man's question to which other sayings about riches have been attached, but it is in the form we have it a coherent and polished literary unit. Renunciation of property usually figures in anecdotes about the calling of a disciple. What makes this passage exceptional are the sayings in vv. 23–27, which broaden the issue so that it no longer concerns the conditions for entry into discipleship, but rather the conditions for salvation for all believers. The redactor's emphasis on the astonishment of the apostles leaves no doubt about this: the apostles understand Jesus to be saying that the call to sell all applies to all who hope to gain entry into the kingdom, and not just to a special group of disciples, for the apostles are already accustomed to that requirement. The exchange in vv. 26–27 seems intended to blunt the force of the call, but it presents no clear solution. (Matthew's version has a more obvious attempt at mitigation, inserting the qualification "If you want to be perfect" before the call.) The final promise contains a further ambiguity. To whom is it addressed? If to the apostles alone, it might mean they can rely on the support of the community as commanded in the mission charge. But if it is addressed to all Christians, as the context seems to imply, what could it mean to say that they will receive manifold compensation "in this age" as opposed to "the age to come" (according to Mark and Luke, though omitted by Matthew) for the property and families they have renounced?

It is possible this strange passage contains the memory of some early Christian communistic experiment or hope. The final promise may refer to a communal arrangement like that of the contemporary Essenes, the Jewish sect that lived in monastic settlements around the Dead Sea, practicing total community of property. Essenes are not mentioned in the New Testament. They resembled the Jesus movement in being an eschatological Jewish sect; they differed from it in being exclusive and withdrawn from the world. But we know so little about Palestinian Christianity between the death of Jesus and the destruction of Jerusalem that we cannot discount the possibility that some Christians envisioned the establishment of an Essene-like community of the saved.[3]

Whatever its origins, this tradition remained a troubling element which could never be entirely reconciled with the rest of the Gospel teaching. One day it would become the foundation of a new Christian social order based on the ideal of common property. But for that to happen, the call to sell all had to be merged with another tradition, the description of the primitive church in Acts.

The Jerusalem Community

We turn now to the best-known and most influential texts about communism in ancient literature:

> All whose faith had drawn them together held everything in common: they would sell their property and possessions and make a general distribution as

> the need of each required. With one mind they kept up their daily attendance at the temple, and, breaking bread in private houses, shared their meals with unaffected joy, as they praised God and enjoyed the favour of the whole people. And day by day the Lord added to their number those whom he was saving. Acts 2.44–47

> The whole body of believers was united in heart and soul. Not a man of them claimed any of his possessions as his own, but everything was held in common, while the apostles bore witness with great power to the resurrection of the Lord Jesus. They were all held in high esteem; for they had never a needy person among them, because all who had property in land or houses sold it, brought the proceeds of the sale, and laid the money at the feet of the apostles; it was then distributed to any who stood in need. Acts 4.32–35

These passages do not imply what they have often been taken to imply. The early chapters of Acts consist of a handful of anecdotes which Luke, or whoever compiled this account toward the end of the first century A.D., must have received from Christian tradition: the Pentecost miracle (2.1–41), Peter's healing of the cripple (3.1–4.31), the conversion of Barnabas (4.36–37), the conversion of Ananias (5.1–11), etc. These anecdotes are connected by short summaries in which Luke generalizes about the life of the community and the spread of the faith. Two of these summaries are quoted above. None of the summaries contain anything that could not be derived from the anecdotes themselves, or from the experience of Christian churches in Luke's own time, so there is no reason to assume Luke had any independent sources for these passages, or that he even knew much about the first Christian community apart from a few stories about the apostles' activities.[4] His traditions included the stories of Barnabas and Ananias, who sold landed property when they joined the believers—an act which must have been exceptional or it would not have been remembered. Luke juxtaposed these examples to contrast the honest gift of Barnabas with the fraud of Ananias; prefaced them with a summary describing the life of the community, in which such renunciations of property are described as a common practice (4.32–35); then repeated the summary at 2.44–47, where another stopgap was needed to separate two important speeches by Peter.

The language of these summaries reflects the Old Testament tradition of generous almsgiving. The Christian community is presented as a fulfillment of the promise of Deuteronomy 15.4 that "there will be no poor among you." The phrase "with all your heart and soul" was a common way of expressing commitment (Deut. 6.5, 10.12). And generous almsgiving was all that Luke envisioned. At 4.34 the renunciation is restricted to those who own lands (*choria*) and houses (*oikoi*), as in the examples of Barnabas and Ananias which follow. The bequest of Ananias is specifically said to be voluntary (5.4). In both summaries the proceeds are distributed not to everbody but only to needy members of the community. In both, the imperfect tense implies a periodic sale of properties as occasion arose, not an immediate and general divestment. (A point obscured by many translations, but clear in the New English Bible version of 2.45 quoted above.) In the sixth chapter it becomes clear that Luke envisioned this community operating an organized system of poor relief for the needy members, especially widows, like the Jewish synagogues and Christian churches of Luke's day. It is assumed that these Christians have their own *oikoi*, where common meals and worship take place (2.46, 8.3, 12.12). In short, Luke imagined the first Christians supporting themselves by their usual occupations, with the well-to-do occasionally selling landed property to provide a fund for the needy. He imagined them living just like the more exemplary Christian congregations of his own time. He never imagined them practicing literal communism, and he thought the age of apostolic mendicancy had already ended.

Nevertheless, Luke saw fit to describe these customary Judeo-Christian practices of organized charity in terms derived from Greek philosophy. He says the believers had all in common (*panta koina*), and that no one said anything was his own (*auto elegen idion einai*). In Greek philosophy such terms suggested abolition of private households and private property. Luke was probably not the first Christian to use these terms. There is an early catechism called by modern scholars the "Two Ways" document, different versions of which turn up in Christian writings ca. 100 A.D. As it is based on the Decalogue and is generally Jewish in tone, it is believed to stem from an earlier Hellenistic-Jewish manual of moral instruction for proselytes. The catechism instructs converts to give alms to the needy, using terms with many parallels in Jewish tradition and in the Gospels, but adds the sentence "You shall share everything (*koinoneseis in pasin*) with your brother [or neighbor] and shall not say it is your own (*ouk ereis idia einai*)." The phrasing resembles that found in the pagan biographies of Pythagoras. Probably this language was already embedded in the Jewish catechism that these Christians adapted, for there are other Hellenistic-Jewish parallels. They suggest a milieu in which a vocabulary of Greek philosophical origin had penetrated Jewish moral teaching at a very basic level.[5]

Therefore Luke may have been unaware of the pagan origins of these terms, and unaware of their communistic implications. To him this was simply a stereotyped and rhetorical way to describe Judeo-Christian charity, borrowed from the catechism mentioned above or from other Hellenistic-Jewish literature. Among these Jews and Christians the language of communism was a rhetorical *topos*, as it often was among their pagan contemporaries. Not until the middle of the third century, when the Hellenistic-Jewish background of Acts had been altogether forgotten, did it occur to any Christian to interpret its early chapters as a description of literal communism, or to think that the first believers had been required to renounce all private property.

But in the meantime philosophical doctrines of communism had entered Christianity by other routes, and within a generation or so after Luke wrote there appeared a serious Christian communism, totally unconnected with Acts and the circles for which it was written.

Gnostic Christianity

The Communism of the Carpocratians

Toward the end of the second century A.D. there appeared a series of systematic polemics by Christian writers directed against those Christians whom the bishops defined as "heretical." Often these heretics were accused of immoral behavior, including the practice of obscene rites; they were said to be responsible for the charges of incest and other crimes that pagans made against all Christians; and the heretical sect most notorious for these practices was said to be a group in Egypt called Carpocratians. They deserve attention here because they were the only Christian circle known to us during the first two centuries that was clearly influenced by philosophical communism, and because if there is any truth to the reports about them they tried to put this doctrine into practice in a fashion without parallel in the ancient world.

Let us summarize what we know about the Carpocratian Christians. The only useful information about their theology comes from the earliest of these antiheretical polemics, the treatise *Against Heresies* written ca. 180 by Irenaeus, bishop of Lyons.[6] According to him they were dualists who believed the visible world had been created not by God but by inferior angels. They believed in the preexistence of souls and in reincarnation; souls were of divine origin, but the angels who created this world had imprisoned them in bodies. Jesus had succeeded in liberating his soul from his body by recalling his preexistence, and it is possible for others to do this by imitating Jesus. We are told they also believed a soul could not be liberated from the cycle of rebirth until it had passed through every sort of experience, a doctrine which seems to contradict the doctrine of immediate salvation through Jesus. Perhaps the Carporatians, like certain orthodox fathers of the church, believed in an ultimate universal salvation after almost endless rebirths, but promised immediate salvation to those who accepted Christ.

Irenaeus considers Carpocrates the source of all the libertine heresies, whose adherents practiced promiscuous sex and plural marriage and ate meat that had been sacrificed to pagan idols (offenses of comparable heinousness in the eyes of many bishops) on the grounds that God does not greatly care about such things.[7] But at another point he attributes to the Carpocratians a somewhat different view, that the saved could do anything whatever, and the following teaching, which may or may not be an authentic quotation: "By faith and love are we saved; everything else is indifferent (*adiaphora*), for in the opinion of men some things are thought good and others evil, but nothing is evil by nature" (1.25.5 Migne ed.). Irenaeus relates this antinomianism to the doctrine of reincarnation: since Carpocratians thought a soul must experience everything to escape from the cycle of rebirth, they assumed a soul might accelerate the process by cramming every kind of experience into a single lifetime, hence their dedication to immoral practices. This interpretation seems to contradict the doctrine of indifferent things put forward in the above quotation, for there we were told that a Christian can do everything because he has been saved, not that be can be saved because he has done everything.

Irenaeus tells us that the teaching described here was believed by Carpocratians to be a secret teaching of Jesus, which Jesus had transmitted to his apostles, and which the apostles had passed on only to those whom they thought worthy, one of whom was Carpocrates. Another of their leaders was a woman named Marcellina who had brought their doctrine to Rome when Anicetus was bishop there (ca. 154–ca. 165). We know from Celsus, a pagan writer contemporary with Irenaeus, that some distinguished two sects, the Carpocratians and the Marcellinians (Origen, *Against Celsus* 5.61–62). Irenaeus says that others called them "gnostics." He believes them particularly addicted to the practice of magic, and says they kept in their shrines images of Jesus, Pythagoras, Plato, Aristotle, and other philosophers, which they worshipped in pagan fashion.

Clement of Alexandria, in whose backyard the sect flourished, provided much more information in his *Miscellanies* (ca. 190).[8] We learn they were founded by an Alexandrian named Carpocrates. His son, Epiphanius, also a leader of the sect, was educated in Platonism. When he died at the age of seventeen, his parents built a temple and a "museum" (shrine to the Muses) in his honor on the island of Cephallenia, his mother's birthplace, and there his annual festival is celebrated by the populace with sacrifices and libations. Like Irenaeus, Clement wishes to stress the pagan connections of the Carpocratians, and may exaggerate them, but there is no reason to question the extraordinary facts he relates about the history of the sect. To honor the illustrious dead with a cult was an accepted pagan practice but no common one. Carpocrates of Alexandria must have belonged to a very wealthy pagan Greek family.

To Clement, the most noteworthy thing about the Carpocratians was their doctrine that women should be common property—here and now, not in some remote past or utopian ideal. In support of this charge, he provides a long extract from a treatise by Epiphanius entitled *On Justice* or *On Righteousness* (*Peri Dikaiosyne*):

> The righteousness of God is a kind of universal fairness and equality. There is equality in the heaven which is stretched out in all directions and contains the entire earth in its circle. The night reveals equally all the stars. The light of the sun, which is the cause of the daytime and the father of light, God pours out from above upon the earth in equal measure on all who have power to see. For all see alike. There is no distinction between rich and poor, people and governor, stupid and clever, female and male, free men and slaves. Even the irrational animals are not accorded any different treatment; but in just the same way God pours out from above sunlight equally upon all the animals. He establishes his righteousness to both good and bad by seeing that none is able to get more than his share and to deprive his neighbour, so that he has twice the light his neighbour has. The sun causes food to grow for all living beings alike; the universal righteousness is given to all equally. In this respect there is no difference between the entire species of oxen and any individual oxen, between the species of pigs and particular pigs, between the species of sheep and particular sheep, and so on with all the rest. In them the universality

> of God's fairness is manifest. Furthermore all plants of whatever sort are sown equally in the earth. Common nourishment grows for all beasts which feed on the earth's produce; to all it is alike. It is regulated by no law, but rather is harmoniously available to all through the gift of him who gives it and makes it to grow.
>
> And for birth there is no written law (for otherwise it would have been transcribed). All beings beget and give birth alike, having received by God's righteousness an innate equality. The Creator and Father of all with his own righteousness appointed this, just as he gave equally the eye to all to enable them to see. He did not make a distinction between female and male, rational and irrational, nor between anything and anything else at all; rather he shared out sight equally and universally. It was given to all by a single command. As the laws . . . could not punish men who were ignorant of them, they taught men that they were transgressors. But the laws, by presupposing the existence of private property, cut up and destroyed the universal equality decreed by the divine law. . . . For God has made vines for all to use in common, since they are not protected against sparrows and a thief; and similarly corn and the other fruits. But the abolition, contrary to divine law, of community of use and equality begat the thief of domestic animals and fruits. *Miscellanies* 3.2.6–7, trans. Chadwick/Oulton

So far this sounds like the theory of primitive communism taught by many contemporary philosophers. The use of air and sunlight to symbolize the original community of property was a philosophical cliché (e.g., Sen., *On Benefits* 1.1.11, 4.25). Clement thinks this comes from Plato, and refutes it with what he considers the correct interpretation of Plato: property is common by nature only in the sense in which seats in a theater are common (3.2.10). Neither version comes from Plato, of course. It was an anthropological theory widely taught in the schools of the Roman Empire and its sources were more Neostoic than anything else. What is original about this passage is the way Epiphanius has conflated this familiar anthropology with St. Paul's teaching on the relationship between law and grace as developed in the Epistlè to the Romans. Paul implied that the Law was given so that man might become aware of sin, to prepare the way for Christ. This idea seems to have been emphasized by the Carpocratians, in whose theology it made better sense, because they assumed the author of the Decalogue to be not God at all but an inferior angel.

Nevertheless, we notice that the material world was not considered evil by the Carpocratians. They may have thought it the work of lower angels, but not of devils, and the angels must have been following a divine paradigm, for certain principles discernable in the construction of the world, such as justice and equality, reveal its divine origin. Christ and his "gnostic" imitators could grasp these principles with sufficient clarity to reject the institutions of private property set up by the Jewish Law and other human laws, and return to the original state of communism. Irenaeus says they accomplished this through recollection of their preexistence, but Epiphanius shows the process was helped by rational reflection on such matters as the spontaneous urges of human nature and the example of animals.

What follows is more novel still, for Epiphanius goes on to apply this theory to sex and marriage—definitely not a conventional part of this *topos* as it was taught in the respectable philosophical schools of his time, and not what St. Paul had in mind either:

> God made all things for man to be common property. He brought female to be with male and in the same way united all animals. He thus showed righteousness to be a universal fairness and equality. But those who have been born in this way have denied the universality which is the corollary of their birth and say "Let him who has taken one woman keep her," whereas all alike can have her, just as the other animals do. ... With a view to the permanence of the race, he has implanted in males a strong and ardent desire which neither law nor custom nor any other restraint is able to destroy. For it is God's decree.
>
> ... Consequently one must understand the saying "Thou shalt not covet" as if the lawgiver was making a jest, to which he added the even more comic words "Thy neighbour's goods." For he himself who gave the desire to sustain the race orders that it is to be suppressed, though he removes it from no other animals. And by the words "thy neighbour's wife" he says something even more ludicrous, since he forces what should be common property to be treated as a private possession. 3.2.8–9

The extract implies that the original state of communism had been or could be restored among the Christian gnostics, but Epiphanius does not explain how. Clement tells us—from hearsay, *not* from writings of the sect—that they practiced communism in two ways. Firstly, they practiced sexual promiscuity in daily life, for any man could approach any woman of the sect and command her to obey the Gospel precept, "give to anyone who asks" (Mt. 5.42; Lk. 6.30). This shows that Carpocratian communism was justified not only with arguments drawn from pagan philosophy, but also by the Gospel precepts about sharing. And though Clement does not say so, it may be taken for granted that members of the sect were expected to share property as well as women. Secondly, Carpocratians and some unspecified groups like them are said to practice an orgiastic ritual in which lights were extinguished at a certain point in the ceremony and totally promiscuous sex took place (*Misc.* 3.2.10, 3.6.54–56). Finally, Morton Smith has discovered and published a letter attributed to Clement in which Carpocratians are said to possess a secret Gospel of St. Mark.[9] If this is authentic it proves that Irenaeus was correct in attributing to them a purported secret teaching of Jesus.

It is clear that the Greek philosophical tradition of utopian communism had ended up in strange hands in Antonine Egypt, and that we deal here with a unique synthesis of pagan and Christian beliefs which, if it can be unraveled, may throw light on the relationship between paganism and Christianity at a crucial time.

The Problem of Libertine Gnosticism

The Carpocratians were perhaps the most extreme, but far from the only, Christian sect of which strange and shocking sexual practices were believed in the second century. All the groups accused of this seem to belong to the movement or trend we call "Gnosticism." But there were two kinds of Gnostics: an ascetic branch that exceeded the orthodox in hostility to the body and sexuality, and a so-called "libertine" branch that produced the kind of behavior attributed to the Carpocratians. It has always seemed puzzling that the same set of beliefs could have produced such contrary ethics, and puzzling that *any* interpretation of the basic texts and traditions of Christianity could have ended in libertinism. Therefore many scholars have suspected that the libertine Gnostics never existed outside the prurient imaginations of some orthodox heresiologists and apologists. This view was strengthened by the discovery of the Gnostic library of Nag Hammadi in 1945, for in these documents the ascetic strain is very pronounced and anything resembling sexual liberalism, let alone libertinism, totally absent.[10] But the text quoted by Clement, unless we are prepared to believe it a complete forgery, is proof that there was something behind the rumors of libertinism: there were people calling themselves Christians in the second century with beliefs about sexual morality unrecognizably different from those of what became orthodox Christianity. The problem is to explain how such a group could have arisen.

First, what do we mean when we speak of "Gnosticism"? It is a term coined by modern scholars to distinguish a large group of philosophies or theosophies that arose within Christianity in the second century. Practically all the "heresies" that were excluded from the churches by the growing authority of the episcopate in the second century were of this type. Originally they were not sects or separate organizations, but intellectualized interpretations of Christian doctrine developed by people of some education. Their principal common features were the following.

1. Rejection of the Old Testament, which was often considered not the work of God but of a lower angel or demiurge. If not rejected outright, it was allegorized out of existence. To outsiders this seemed the cardinal issue. Celsus, the first pagan to study Christianity systematically, concluded that Christians in the time of Marcus Aurelius were divided into two groups: the "great church" which worshipped the same god as the Jews, and a group of smaller sects whose God was different from the God of the Jews (Origen, *Against Celsus* 5.61–62).

2. Various forms of dualistic cosmology or mythology. Often the natural world was conceived as evil, opposed to God and uncreated by God. Their myths delighted in hierarchies, sometimes fantastically elaborate, of intermediate spiritual beings or divine emanations; often attributed the creation of the material world to one of these, against the will of God or in ignorance of it; often assumed that material and spiritual elements were mixed in human nature, and that humans could attain salvation by recognizing the divine spark within themselves, which enables them to sever their ties to matter and return to God.

3. The existence of an elite of enlightened people, the "spirituals" or "perfects," who have attained "knowledge" (*gnosis*) of the secrets of the universe. *Gnosis* was a term commonly used for the knowledge of God both in Judaism and in Christianity. The "Gnostic" interpretation of *gnosis* placed great emphasis on private revelations. Organizationally their followers were marked

off from the "great church," which was increasingly falling under the control of the monarchical episcopate, by the leadership of these charismatic "gnostic" teachers.

This system appeared with variations in one sect after another. It seems to have originated early in the second century, probably at Alexandria, out of a mixture of Platonic/Pythagorean philosophy and heterodox Judaism whose origins and nature are still the subject of intense controversy. Sects might share these features in varying degrees. The system of Marcion, the best-organized and most successful of the Gnostic sects, seems also the most Christian; it rejected the Old Testament but was not noticeably influenced by the other doctrines mentioned above. The Carpocratians, who must have originated in Egypt in the early second century and therefore were one of the earliest Gnostic groups, exhibited these characteristics only to a limited extent; they were dualists but clearly did not regard the material world and the body as altogether evil, and they showed no trace of the elaborate cosmologies produced by later sects such as the Valentinians. Can the doctrines and practices attributed to the Carpocratians be explained in terms of these beliefs? There are several possibilities.

Was Libertine Christianity Connected to Reincarnation?

Several Gnostic sects believed in the transmigration of souls, a doctrine borrowed from the Platonist and Pythagorean schools along with the rest of their dualistic cosmology. Irenaeus tried to explain the libertinism of the Carpocratians as a consequence of this doctrine, but there is a *prima facie* implausibility about this idea. Irenaeus' other comments would lead us to think that Carpocratians shared the general ancient view of reincarnation: they hoped to achieve release from the cycle of rebirth through a sudden experience of enlightenment, not through accumulation of wordly experiences. The majority might have to rely on the latter method to attain ultimate salvation, but Irenaeus attributes libertine ethics to the elite and not to the majority. If somehow they did believe that salvation could be assisted by experiencing everything in a single reincarnation, it is not obvious how this process could be facilitated by a sexual orgy, where the available experiences are limited and repetitious. Irenaeus himself found it a contradiction that the heretics thought it necessary to experience everything and yet in practice were interested only in experiencing sex (2.32.2). We notice that Clement made no connection between the sexual morals of the Carpocratians and their belief in reincarnation, nor did he even mention the latter. This is probably because Clement did not see anything heretical or even odd about the doctrine of reincarnation. Speculations about reincarnation and universal salvation were common in Alexandrian Christianity, and Clement himself entertained such. The bizarre doctrine of reincarnation that Irenaeus attributes to the Carpocratians seems best explained as a misunderstanding by Irenaeus based on a garbled version of Carpocrates' teaching. Probably a good deal went on in the church of Alexandria that would not have been easily understood in Gaul.

Was Libertine Christianity Dualist?

Another possibility is that the dualistic theology of the Gnostics led them into libertinism because it produced the conclusion that anything done by the body was of no importance. Contempt for the body, we are told, can result either in asceticism or in libertinism.

Whether this is psychologically plausible I cannot judge. It is true that the generally ascetic cults of India have produced some highly erotic offshoots. But the philosophical framework within which Gnosticism developed does not seem very likely to produce such a thing. The pagan philosophies to which the mature Gnostic systems are most akin are Platonism and Neo-Pythagoreanism, both identified with ascetic sexual ethics. It is true that Irenaeus attributed to certain Valentinian perfects the precept, "fleshly things must be allowed to those who are fleshly, spiritual things to those who are spiritual."[11] But this is practically the only evidence for a connection between dualism and libertinism, and all other sources agree that the Valentinians, one of the most common and best-known Gnostic groups, were extreme ascetics. The most notorious libertines, the Carpocratians, were only moderate dualists, and it seems evident from the treatise quoted by Clement that their libertinism was not based on contempt for the body at all, but rather on the assumption that the sex drive is good and natural. On the whole it seems very improbable that Gnostic dualism could have engendered a loose sexual ethic.

Was Libertine Christianity Antinomian?

The commonest explanation the orthodox writers offer for this scandalous behavior is an explanation of Christian origins: the Gnostics think themselves free from all moral restraints because they have been saved in Christ. Clement says there were two types of heretic, an ascetic type that rejected even marriage, and an antinomian type that held right and wrong to be matters of indifference (*Misc.* 3.5.40). He believed the latter group commonly justified their behavior by quoting sayings of St. Paul such as Romans 6.14: "sin shall no longer be your master, because you are no longer under law, but under the grace of God" (*Misc.* 8.61–62). The only example he gives of a Gnostic sect using this argument comes from an obscure group founded by a certain Prodicus, who perverted the Gospel saying that man is lord of the Sabbath to excuse adultery (3.4.30). But clearly Clement thought the Carpocratians, whom he considered the worst of all the libertines, held this antinomian doctrine. In the letter published by Morton Smith Clement says that the Carpocratians talk constantly about their "freedom." Several of the sects attacked by Irenaeus seem to fit this pattern. According to him, the Simonians thought they could do whatever they pleased because they were saved by grace and not by righteous acts, nor did they think anything righteous by nature but only by accident (*Against Heresies* 1.23.3). We have seen that he attributed a very similar doctrine to the Carpocratians (1.25.5).

All this sounds as though they exaggerated the Pauline doctrine of spiritual freedom so as to claim that the saved in Christ were free to do anything that they were moved to do. This seems plausible because the Carpocratian tract quoted by Clement relies heavily on the Pauline dichotomy between law and grace. They could not have quoted Paul's letters in the form we know them, because as Clement points out the letters are filled with warnings against precisely such an antinomian interpretation of "freedom." But they must have had a Pauline tradition of their own, just as they had their own Gospels.

Nevertheless, there is ample room for skepticism. At various periods in Christian history there has arisen a Pauline cult of freedom in the spirit which has never failed to attract accusations of anarchism and antinomianism. In late medieval Europe the mystics of the "Free Spirit" taught a doctrine of union with God in language that brought on them charges of sexual libertinism and vigorous persecution, yet there is no evidence that any Free Spirits ever held any beliefs that could be called genuinely antinomian.[12] Within living memory there were Roman Catholic apologists who made Martin Luther sound like an antinomian. Confusion is easy because nothing could sound more antinomian than certain passages in the Pauline Epistles taken out of context. One notices the absence of any clear-cut statements of antinomianism from Gnostic writings; the suspicious fact that the orthodox, while claiming the Gnostics are antinomian in everything, in practice talk about virtually nothing but their sexual morals; that Clement, who can assert so confidently that all libertine heretics are antinomians who pervert Paul's teaching, turns out to be very confused as to what the heretics actually believe.[13] All that we can make of this is that these Gnostics talked a lot in Pauline terms about their spiritual freedom. I suggest the real reason for the charge of antinomianism was that they held a moral code somewhat different from that of the great church, especially in the area of sexual morality.

Were the Libertines Christian Cynics?

Even in the first century, Christian leaders were having difficulty with their Gentile converts over the observance of the Jewish Law. When Christianity began to spread among the pagan Greeks there was an attempt to impose on new converts a residuum of the Jewish dietary code, prohibiting meat that had been sacrificed to idols, and sometimes meat containing blood as well; and a more serious effort to impose the Jewish sexual code, which banned prostitution, homosexuality, and marriages within certain degrees of kinship.[14] The First Epistle to the Corinthians is evidence of the dislike these taboos could arouse in recent Greek converts; and we note that the Corinthians' resentment arose from the fact that Paul had assured them they would be free of the Jewish Law, which could not apply to the saved in Christ. In 1 Corinthians Paul stuck to a strict interpretation of *porneia* (in the Septuagint and the New Testament, a general term for sexual sin, including all the offenses mentioned above) but capitulated on the question of dietary taboos.

Later the lines hardened. By the end of the century the ban on idol meat had become as general as the ban on *porneia.*[15] At about the same time we hear of "heretic" Christians in the cities of Asia Minor who eat idol meat and practice *porneia.*[16] There is no reason to associate any of these Christians with Gnosticism or proto-Gnosticism. There is a simpler explanation for them. They are Greek converts to Christianity who did not want to accept any part of the Torah in dietary and sexual matters on the grounds that Christians were free of the law.

By the middle of the second century, when the Gnostic systems were spreading, we find the Gnostics accused of precisely the same things. Irenaeus says that the Valentinian perfects ate meat from pagan sacrifices and took part in pagan festivals, even watching gladiatorial combats (1.6.3); that the Basilidians ate idol meat, went to festivals, and indulged all appetites (*universae libidines*, 1.24.5); that the Nicolaitans ate idol meat and considered adultery a matter of indifference (1.26.3); that eating idol meat and sexual promiscuity were typical offenses of all those heretics whose teaching stemmed from Carpocrates (1.28.2). We notice that these charges are associated with a general participation in pagan social life and custom. The sacrificial banquet was a key social institution in a Greek city; meat that had been sacrificed to idols was the only meat that most citizens ever ate; the decision whether to participate in these customs determined much about the relationship between Christians and their neighbors. It was also said that heretics discouraged martyrdom,[17] which suggests they often saw nothing wrong with participation in pagan worship.

One suspects that the accusations of sexual/dietary heresy were originally directed at Christians who merely followed the norms of most Greeks in these matters, or more so than was acceptable to most bishops by ca. 100 A.D. And then the intellectual heresies of Gnosticism appeared. The large literary output, passion for speculation, and tolerance of pagan custom that characterized most Gnostics suggest that they were better educated and more in touch with pagan culture than their rivals the bishops, with whom for a time they contested the leadership of the churches. There was an obvious affinity between social heresy and intellectual heresy, and many kinds of Gnosticism may have been touched by sexual "libertinism." But it did not find a permanent home in most Gnostic sects, because the pagan philosophy that most attracted them was the antisexual Platonic/Pythagorean tradition, and they generally ended up more ascetic than the bishops. The widespread "libertinism" attributed to Gnostics is difficult to explain unless we assume there was also a Stoic/Cynic strain in Gnosticism.

Irenaeus thought that those heretics who believed all their external actions were morally indifferent had been influenced by Cynicism.[18] This comment occurs in a passage where Irenaeus is straining to explain every aspect of Christian heresy as a borrowing from paganism. But he was, after all, correct to think that much of what was called heresy was the result of pagan influence. Several of the statements attributed to heretics have a Stoic or Cynic ring. As early as ca. 50 A.D. Paul's Corinthian converts had defended their easygoing attitude toward *porneia* and meats by claiming, "Food is for the belly and the belly for food" (1 Cor. 6.13), a slogan they thought compatible with strict celibacy. This has often been taken as evidence of proto-Gnostic tendencies, but the slogan does not necessarily imply dualism. More likely it reflects Cynic teaching about the unimportance of bodily desires, which might be picked up from any street preacher. Those Valentinian perfects whom Irenaeus quoted as saying that they repaid to the flesh what belonged to the flesh may have meant no more than this. The same may be true of those Simonians who said, according to Hippolytus of Rome (*Refutation* 6.14), "All earth is earth and it makes no difference where a man sows." When Cynics and Stoics of the old school said such things they meant that the satisfaction of bodily desires is morally indifferent so long as it does not harm the wise person's self-sufficiency; that conventional moral precepts are useless because nothing matters except virtue, and the virtuous will automatically choose the right course of action. Some heretical Christians took the same attitude and merged the Pauline teaching of freedom with the Greek philosophical vocabulary that most resembled it. To the orthodox, increasingly unwilling to recognize such a thing as a morally indifferent category of sexual acts, this sounded like antinomianism.

There is no difficulty in the assumption that early Christianity was in some quarters open to Cynic influences. The resemblance between Christian street preacher and Cynic street preacher was noticed by more than one pagan, and so was the similarity in their attitudes to property. The famous Cynic teacher Peregrinus Proteus (ca. 110–165) was a Christian for a time, though eventually ejected from the church for a violation of dietary taboos. According to the hostile biography by Lucian he gave away all his property and adopted the Cynic mendicant life while he was still a Christian. Lucian seems to associate renunciation of property equally with Cynicism and with Christianity. He describes the Christians as a sect who "consider all things to be common" (*Peregrinus* 13), implying that a belief like this makes them easy marks for a Cynic mountebank like Peregrinus. Peregrinus' teaching seems to have been thoroughly eclectic, with touches of Pythagoreanism as well, but for that very reason he was typical of the teachers who created the bizarre synthesis of Christian and pagan traditions that we encounter in the Carpocratians.

This synthesis was one of several that emerged in the early second century, when educated Christians were beginning to meet pagan culture on its own ground and to relate Christianity to various pagan philosophical schools. Those who captured the Christian mainstream and the future chose to stress the continuity between Christianity and its Judaic heritage; like the Hellenistic Jews before them, they emphasized the antiquity of Jewish wisdom and claimed that the Greek philosophers stole their ideas from the Old Testament. Others chose to exaggerate the newness of Christianity and to make a clean break with the Jewish past, remaking Christianity on the model of a pagan school. The main influence on the latter group came from the otherworldly Platonic/Pythagorean tradition, for which Christians felt a natural affinity, as Jews had before them. But a secondary influence came from the Cynic/Stoic tradition. The two could be mixed in odd ways. In Carpocratianism we seem to find a mixture of Platonic/ Pythagorean cosmology and Cynic/Stoic ethics.

To judge from the treatise of Epiphanius these Gnostics had notions about communism which were probably very similar to those held by contemporary Cynics and Cynicizing Stoics. They thought there had been a primitive period when communism in property and sex had been universal, and that this order of things was according to nature; it had been ruined by the rise of civilization and law, but it was still possible to approximate it. Cynics claimed to do this by living the mendicant life. How did the Carpocratians claim to do it? That depends on how much we are to believe of what the orthodox writers tell us about their sexual practices.

The Obscene Rites[19]

The intriguing aspect of this charge is that pagans at that time widely suspected *all* Christians of orgiastic ceremonies. In Antoninus Pius' reign the great orator Cornelius Fronto wrote a speech or pamphlet describing the scandalous Christian nocturnal rites, in which it was said lights were extinguished and promiscuous coupling took place. The earlier Christian apologists took these charges seriously and devoted much space to their refutation. Minucius Felix goes into great detail: Christians are said to sacrifice and eat babies, to worship the genitals of their elders, and to call each other brother and sister for the purpose of giving their promiscuity the appearance of incest (*Octavius* 8–9). These rumors seem to have flourished chiefly in the middle and later second century, for in the middle of the third Origen could write that they were no longer much believed (*Against Celsus* 6.27, 40).

Christian apologists had an explanation for the rumors. Justin hinted that the crimes pagans attributed to all Christians may actually be practiced by certain heretics (*1 Apology* 7, 26). Later apologists make this claim more confidently and specifically blame the Carpocratians. The pagan philosopher Celsus, writing ca. 170, claimed that some Christians "wander about in great darkness more iniquitous and impure than that of the revelers of Antinous in Egypt" (Origen, *Contra Celsum* 5.63, trans. Henry Chadwick, Cambridge 1953).

There is not the slightest reason to think anything but rumor lay behind the charge of cannibalism. Accusations of ritual murder for magical or oath-taking purposes were common in the ancient world, and circulated about every sort of social outcast—magicians, rebels, outlaws, barbarian cults. Christians might be suspected of being all those things. These charges antedated the rise of Gnosticism. Pliny had them in mind when he conducted his investigation into the rites of the Bithynian Christians in 113: he was careful to question them about the foods and oaths used at their secret meetings, because human sacrifice was something expected of a *superstitio prava et inmodica* (*Ep.* 10.96). The rumor may have become attached to Christians because of their association with Judaism, for human sacrifice was an anti-Semitic slur current in the early first century (cf. Josephus, *Against Apion* 2.102).

The charge of erotic rites is a different matter. This was a very specific accusation never associated with anyone but Christians. It did not appear till Antoninus Pius' time, and as soon as it appeared Christians tried to shift the blame onto heretical Christians. They were probably correct. The Carpocratian sect was probably founded at Alexandria in the reign of Hadrian. In the reign of Antoninus Marcellina brought it to Rome. The news that there was a Christian sect that preached the notorious doctrine of communism in goods and women would have been sufficient to start the rumors. Once linked to the older charge of ritual murder this became the same double accusation—incest and cannibalism—that had long been directed against Stoics and Cynics.

Could there have been something behind it? Something more than a pagan sexual morality, a stoicized communistic theory, a Pythagorean cult of the Muses practicing common meals? Clement says some heretics believed sexual activity was a mystical communion (*koinonia mystike*, 3.4.27), probably thinking of the Carpocratians; Hippolytus says Simonians attached sacramental significance to promiscuity (*Ref.* 6.14); but these may be scandalized exaggerations. There is considerable evidence from both orthodox and Gnostic sources that in the third and fourth centuries certain Gnostics practiced secret rites more extraordinary than anything attributed to the Carpocratians, including the consumption of menstrual blood and semen.[20] These may have been a degraded survival of a radical Christian movement that had once been far larger and more respectable. But their existence makes us less skeptical of the allegations that certain second-century Cynicized Gnostics practiced some form of erotic ritual. It is not difficult to believe they had some peculiar ceremony similar to the orthodox *agape* or communion feast (a parallel noticed by Clement) which struck outsiders as orgiastic.

The Carpocratians were said to copy pagan ritual in a way not generally attributed to Gnostics. Celsus had heard of some Christian rites more impure than those of Antinous, lover of Hadrian, whose cult had been established in Egypt about the time Carpocratianism appeared. It was perhaps the most spectacular example of a totally new cult in the second century, and the suggestion that Carpocrates borrowed something from it has been made before. We can only guess what it was that Celsus found so objectionable in the rites of Antinous. Philosophers tended to dislike any religious emotionalism or extravagant display and to connect such "superstitions" with immoral sexual behavior. (A convenient list of what they disliked will be found in Dionysius, *Roman Antiquities* 2.19) Secret nocturnal rites involving both sexes, particularly those associated with the cults of Isis and Dionysus, readily drew suspicions of sexual license. Clement's allusion to the "sacred nights" of Antinous (*Exhortation* 4.43) suggests a nocturnal initiation with erotic stimulations. It has been said that in the Bacchic cults such initiations probably varied "from outdoor picnics to an existential turning-point in life, from sublime symbolism to downright orgies."[21] Other superstitious practices likely to meet with philosophical disapproval were frenzied dancing, cultic drunkenness, ecstasies or ritual possession by a god, and the dramatic performances or mimed dances presented at many temples, which illustrated the beliefs of the cult or the myths of its god. Presumably some of the above went on at the temples of Antinous, whose background would have suggested an appropriate amount of eroticism.

Things like these went on daily among the thousand cults of Egypt, and doubtless some of them were imitated at the shrines of the Carpocratians.

Whatever their *koinonia* mystery was, it disappeared sometime in the third century, and the last distorted reflection of the ideal cities of Plato and Zeno went with it.

Patristic Christianity

The Household of God

By the beginning of the second century the Christian churches were coming under the control of an episcopal organizational structure committed to the formation of an orderly community life which would be acceptable to the larger society. The bishops gradually drove out all tendencies, such as those just described, that interfered with this objective; and in opposition to those influences, promulgated a moral code centered on the conventional *oikos*. The prosperous, well-managed household under the just rule of a master became the exclusive norm of a Christian community.

These Christian "household codes," which are more schematic than their pagan and Jewish prototypes, recur throughout the later books of the New Testament and other Christian literature of the late first and early second centuries, the fullest versions being found in the Pastoral Epistles.[22] The codes have a distinctively Christian framework: they assume that the entire church is a social structure modeled on the household, and vice versa. Their purpose is to show "how men ought to conduct themselves in God's household, that is, the church of the living God" (1 Tim. 3.15). The description of the church as *oikos theou*, household of God, is common (Eph. 2.19; Heb. 3.6; 1 Peter 4.17). The church officers must be good household managers with submissive children (1 Tim. 3.4–5, 12); their governance of the church is called an *oikonomia*, an art of household management (1 Cor. 9.17; Col. 1.25); God's plan of salvation for the world is called an *oikonomia* (Eph. 1.9–10, 3.9–10; 1 Tim. 1.4). The codes reflect the dominant social values of the Greco-Roman world and attempt to suppress all social tendencies that were suspect in the eyes of the dominant upper-class morality of the period, especially those that discredited Christianity. They were intended to remove the suspicion that Christianity was a threat to order in the household and the city. They combat the widespread pagan view that Christians subvert households and turn women, children, and slaves against their masters (e.g., Origen, *Against Celsus* 3.55). Apparently there was considerable worry that women and slaves might misunderstand such passages as Gal. 3.28. Submission of women and exclusion of women from preaching and teaching roles (a prominent feature of heretical sects) is strongly emphasized. This promotion of conformity served an internal function as well as a public relations function: the church officers, chosen from the good householders who are well thought of by pagans (1 Tim. 3.7), and the heads of households (especially the socially prominent ones) are to work together for the proper ordering of the community. The master is responsible for the instruction and behavior of his household. Hermas, author of the *Shepherd*, assumes that a Christian man has a primary duty to save his household (First Vision). In the late second century, when an apologist needs a metaphor to explain the doctrine of the Fall to pagans, he says that Adam led all creation astray like the master of a house, for when the master sins all sin with him (Theophilus, *To Autolycus* 2.17). Heretics are seen as a threat to the household, especially becasue of their attraction to women (2 Tim. 3.1—7; Titus 1.11).

The communistic tendencies described earlier were, of course, an embarrassment to this emerging Christian orthodoxy. In the second century, when the apologists set out to present the household of God to an educated pagan audience, they did make some use of the communistic rhetoric of pagan philosophy. Justin Martyr told his pagan readers that Christians put everything into a common fund which was shared with the needy (*1 Apology* 14). His language was meant to remind his readers of Stoic or Platonic or Pythagorean communistic traditions, but in fact Justin was only referring to the Christian practice of a Sunday collection to maintain a fund for the care of widows, orphans, and other needy persons, as he later admits himself (67). Such *topoi* did not necessarily imply literal communism to either Christian or pagan at this period. And it was easy for the apologists to present the Gospel sayings on wealth as philosophical apophthegms of a sort familiar to pagans, illustrating the congruence between Christian and pagan teachings on property.[23]

But certain other New Testament passages were perceived as more problematical, particularly the call to sell all and the description of the primitive church in the book of Acts. These passages, often considered in later centuries the foundation stones of Christian social morality, were in the second century conspicuously absent from apologetic works directed to pagan audiences, and rarely mentioned even in writings meant for other Christians.

Irenaeus mentioned the call to sell all briefly as part of his refutation of the Gnostics who rejected the Old Testament (*Against Heresies* 4.12.5). He was interested mostly in the fact that Christ instructed the rich young man to follow the Decalogue, implying that this is sufficient for salvation. The additional command to sell all possessions applies only to those who wish to be perfect like the apostles (*apostolorum partem promittens eis qui sic fecerint*). Irenaeus does not seem to think that even the apostles' renunciation of property was total, for he adds that in order to do away with covetousness it is sufficient to imitate Zacchaeus, the usual examplar of the rich Christian, who gave away only half his goods to the poor (Lk. 19). His contemporary Tertullian speaks of the call to sell all as something that might be followed by a Christian in exceptional and exacting circumstances, as when he is required to give up an occupation that involves him in idolatry, like that of schoolteacher, sculptor, or soldier (*On Idolatry* 12).

Irenaeus and Tertullian are also the first Christian writers to comment on the primitive church of Acts, by then accepted as part of the New Testament. Irenaeus draws attention to the word "one heart and one soul," which he sees as an allusion to the unity of the apostolic tradition held by the great church in opposition to the heretics: the church is scattered throughout the world, yet her unanimity is such that she occupies as it were a single *oikos* (*Against Heresies* 1.10.2). In another place he comments on the bestowal of property by the first believers to show that at this point the Mosaic Law of tithes had been superseded by the Christian practice of voluntary giving (4.18.2). He clearly assumes that the first believers parted with a good share of their property, but not all of it. Tertullian, in a tract written against those who try to run away from persecution, mentions in passing that the apostles certainly had money—for the believers laid the prices of their lands at the apostles' feet—yet did not use their money to escape persecution (*On Flight in Persecution* 12). Both Irenaeus and Tertullian think the primitive church of Acts is simply a description of the household of God as it was in their own day: for heretics an example of unity of belief, for pagans an example of organized charity, for the faithful a model for generous almsgiving (but in no way implying total divestment) and a model for the administration of church funds by the bishops, successors of the apostles. There are hints that the call to sell all might be taken literally by Christians in some exceptional circumstances, but they show no particular interest in this possibility.

Tertullian also takes up Luke's phrase *panta koina*, but with a significant qualification. His *Apology* contrasts pagan and Christian use of wealth in the fashion of earlier apologists, pointing out that in pagan households property causes divisions, but among Christians it promotes brotherhood: "We are of one mind and one soul and do not hesitate to share our worldly goods. We have everything in common except our wives" (*Apol.* 39: *Omnia indiscreta sunt apud nos praeter uxores*). There is a similar phrase in the *Epistle to Diognetus*, an undatable apologetic work produced sometime in the second century: Christians "offer a common table, not a common bed" (5.7: *trapezan koinen paratithentai, all' ou koiten*, an untranslatable play on the words *koinen* and *koiten*). These apologists were aware, as Luke was not, that the phrase "community of goods" was dangerous, because it might also imply "community of women." We have seen why they had good reason to be careful about such language. But they do not think that "community of goods" implies anything more than generous almsgiving or had ever implied more than that even in the primitive church.

At the same time Clement of Alexandria was advancing a different interpretation of the call to sell all, which stripped it even more thoroughly of subversive tendencies. In his *Miscellanies* he argues that the call referred only to generous almsgiving. This is part of his polemic against those Christian communist sects who, as we have seen, interpreted the call literally. Clement mentions some who would go to the opposite extreme and interpret the call in a completely allegorical sense, understanding "sell everything you have" to mean "everything in the soul," and resists this interpretation on the grounds that the call requires these things to be divided among the poor (*Misc.* 2.5, 3.6.54–55, 4.6). But in his sermon *Who Is The Rich Man Who Shall Be Saved?* (the first extended discussion of the call to sell all in extant literature) Clement himself adopts a thoroughgoing allegorical interpretation.

His reasons for addressing this topic at such length are interesting: he says there were rich Christians who took literally the saying about the camel and the needle's eye and despaired of salvation. Evidently the many attempts to explain away the call by confining it to a restricted group of people or a restricted amount of goods had not been entirely successful even among the orthodox, for the radical implications of the call are too obvious in the text. Clement accepts the view that the call was meant literally for the apostles, who really did renounce all their property. But for other Christians it is meant as a parable: they are being asked to renounce not property, but the "passions of the soul." What, he asks, explains the apostles' amazement at this saying? Many thought they were amazed at the notion that the call to sell all could apply literally to all Christians—which seems the obvious interpretation. But Clement's ingenuity finds another: the apostles are amazed because they understand for the first time the spiritual meaning of the call, and troubled because they realize they have not renounced their passions along with their property. Clement points out that some pagans, like Crates the Cynic, had renounced all their property and yet were not saved, while some Christians, like Zacchaeus, had failed to renounce all and yet were saved. In short he turns the call into a philosophical commonplace advocating detachment from worldly goods.

One senses a considerable reserve and suspicion about the apostolic call among the second-century apologists. If taken literally it is not taken generally, and if taken generally it is not taken literally. They are equally reserved about the communism of Acts, to which Clement never refers in his voluminous writings. He could suggest that the communal life of the early Pythagoreans was a prefiguration of the church (*Misc.* 1.15), but he did not mention the more obvious model of the Jerusalem community. The best explanation for this silence is that the communistic principles suggested by these texts were too closely associated with heretics. The possibility of a community of goods without community of women, which would appeal to many Egyptians in the following century, did not occur to Clement.

The Monastery

After the middle of the third century, when Christianity was emerging as a major religion in large parts of the Empire, the ascetic tendencies embedded in its basic documents began to reemerge. The orthodox leadership of the church began to develop a Christian social philosophy much less concerned with conformity and order than the household of god ideology of their predecessors, partly because of the Christians' growing numbers and wealth, partly because the orthodox had vanquished their Christian rivals at last and felt free to expropriate ideas heretofore identified with heresy. The New Testament precepts of renunciation began to receive a literal interpretation as counsels of perfection for a spiritual elite.

Some began to read Luke's account of the primitive church in a different light. The great Alexandrian scholar Origen referred frequently to Acts 4.32, usually with emphasis on the phrase "one heart and one soul," and for the purpose of promoting Christian unity and brotherhood, without specific reference to property.[24] Irenaeus had made similar use of the passage. But in Origen's commentary on Matthew his interpretation of the call to sell all reads like a deliberate refutation of the allegorical exegesis proposed by his predecessor Clement. He denies that the call should be allegorized, on the grounds that historical examples prove it is possible to take it literally: complete renunciation of property was practiced by pagan philosophers like Crates, and also by the first Christians described in Acts. Origen assumes therefore a very radical reading of Luke's *panta koina*, such as we do not find at all in earlier commentators, and would have greatly surprised Luke; and he connects this passage with the call to sell all, also taken in a very radical sense and assumed to have a general and continuing relevance for all Christians, which is never assumed in earlier comments. Furthermore, Origen put this ideal into practice by leading what Christians then called the "philosophical life," or one of celibacy and extreme poverty: "he felt that he must keep the gospel sayings of the Saviour urging us not to carry two coats or wear shoes and never to be worried by anxiety about the future" (Eusebius, *History of the Church* 6.3.9, trans. G.A. Williamson).

The same ideal appears frequently in the writings of Origen's contemporary Cyprian, bishop of Carthage. Several times Cyprian refers to the call to sell all as a precept that is still generally binding on all Christians, and to the primitive church of Acts as the perfect example of its observance, using these references as though they are well known to the clergy and laity he addresses. He seems to be the first orthodox writer who explicitly links the "communism" of the New Testament to the philosophical teaching that all property is common by nature, in the manner of the Carpocratians:

> For whatever is of God is common in our use; nor is anyone excluded from his benefits and gifts, so as to prevent the whole human race from enjoying equally the divine goodness and liberality. Thus the day equally enlightens, the sun gives radiance, the rain moistens, the wind blows, and the sleep is one to those that sleep, and the splendor of the stars and of the moon is common. In which example of equality he who as a possessor in the earth shares his returns and his fruits with the fraternity, while he is common and just in his gratuitous bounties, is an imitator of God the Father. Tract 8 *On Works and Alms* 25, trans. *Ante-Nicene Fathers*, ed. Roberts and Donaldson

As a primary example of this ideal of common possession of the earth he cites the origins (*primordia*) of the church described in Acts, "when the mind flourished with greater virtues than now." For Cyprian is also one of the first Christian writers to sense a great decline in virtue between the apostolic age and his own times. A radical interpretation of the "communism" of Acts almost requires such a sence of historical decline. Therefore on several occasions we find Cyprian drawing invidious comparisons between the fervor of the original Christians, with specific reference to their communism, and the lukewarmness of their modern descendants.[25] He did not mean, however, that Christians were obligated to renounce all their property. He distinguishes the call to sell all from the other almsgiving precepts because the call is meant to show how one who has already observed the law can become perfect and complete (*observata lege perfectum et consummatum*); it is not an essential moral requirement like the Decalogue, rather what would later be called a "counsel of perfection." Nor did he necessarily have in mind a total renunciation. To both Christian and pagan the language of communism, whether derived from the New Testament or from Plato, was often a rhetorical way of describing generous patronage. But Cyprian did envision the possibility that these precepts might be carried out literally by a few individuals; one such was Cyprian himself, who upon his conversion gave away the entire purchase money of his estate to the poor, with the intention of carrying out the call to sell all to the letter (Pontius, *Life of Cyprian* 2).

To Origen and Cyprian these precepts were no longer restricted to the apostles and no longer allegorized. As counsels of perfection, they were taken literally: if applied to all believers, they might imply nothing more than generous almsgiving in the traditional pattern; but there was emerging by ca. 250 a premium on asceticism, and a new spiritual elite following a "philosophical life" distinguished mainly by total or near-total renunciation of property. This ideal was supported by a novel configuration of New Testament passages, which brought the call to sell all into close connection with the primitive church, regarding the latter as the fulfillment of the former; a new way of looking at the history of the church, in which the apostolic age became a timeless ideal and a model for reformers; and a new confidence in drawing on pagan social and political thought, permitting extreme interpretations of Luke's communistic language.

Christian monasticism began when some of these individual ascetics withdrew physically from the Christian households and communities that had sheltered them, and from all normal participation in society.[26] This movement began with certain displaced Egyptian peasants in the last quarter of the third century. The most famous of them, Anthony, started out with a conversion experience that must have typical for Christian ascetics: after meditation on the way that the apostles and the first believers had renounced all their property, he entered a church at a moment when the call to sell all was being proclaimed as part of the gospel reading, and decided to follow it (Athanasius, *Life of Anthony* 2). Nor did his way of doing this exhibit anything very novel at first. He sold his patrimony, placed his sister in a community of virgins who presumably were practicing a form of household asceticism, and attached himself as a disciple to various ascetics who lived in solitude on the outskirts of villages. Then by gradual stages he withdrew further and further from the villages of the Nile, finally settling in an isolated cell deep in the desert to do battle with his demons. In the next generation thousands followed him.

The withdrawal amounted to a rejection of the household of God—the organized church. with its public worship and its community life. It was a grass-roots movement among Coptic and Syriac villagers who sought a new model of Christian achievement, unconnected with the old models of Greek urban society and patronage which had furnished the traditional leadership of orthodoxy. But it was also unconnected with Greek urban traditions of heresy and popular philosophy.

There developed early a clear-cut distinction which served to separate orthodox monasticism from every suspect form of asceticism: monks were required to work for a living and never to ask alms, following the anti-Cynic recommendations of St. Paul. Athanasius says that Anthony adopted this rule from the beginning of his ascetic career, even before the move into desert (*Life* 3). It meant a deliberate rejection of the ancient role of mendicant preacher, and made the monks independent of human settlements. This radical ritual of disassociation made it possible for the monks to separate themselves from the household of God and still remain loyal to it; the move into the desert insulated them from pagan and heretical influences and sealed their alliance with the bishops, with whom they could not compete. Rigorous measures were taken to keep monasticism uncontaminated by the older type of asceticism. The main threat came from the monks called Messalians (Syriac for "those who pray") who appeared in Iraq early in the fourth century and spread through the eastern provinces of the Empire. In order to devote themselves entirely to prayer, they abjured manual labor and lived by alms, which of course meant that they had to remain in contact with society. They were condemned, along with the Encratite and Gnostic ascetics, in the great heresy hunt of the fourth century. The orthodox ascetic had to prove his orthodoxy by the sweat of his brow.

Even though the call of Christ to his apostles was always considered the basic monastic profession, monks otherwise avoided identifying themselves with the apostles, probably because such a clain might suggest rivalry with the bishops, the true successors of the apostles. When monks sought models in the past they usually found them in the Old Testament prophets, especially Elijah and Elishah, and in John the Baptist.[27] When Pachomius established the cenobitical type of monasticism ca. 320 this communal way of life was naturally compared to the Jerusalem community described in Acts, but the comparison seems to have been little emphasized. There were few allusions to the Bible in early monastic literature. Many monks knew the Bible by heart, but it was a text for endless recitation, not for discussion. Nor was any connection made between monasticism and the pagan traditions of communism, in spite of the obvious hints in this direction afforded by the Acts of the Apostles. In the case of the monks themselves this silence is not surprising, as they rejected the whole culture that made such connections intelligible, and most were ignorant of Greek. But even educated church people in the early fourth century continued to regard the pagan tradition of communism with deep suspicion.

The similarity between the Genesis account of paradise and the descriptions of the golden age and Elysian fields in pagan poets had been noticed early. It is frequently mentioned by the apologists to illustrate one of their favorite themes, that pagans borrowed everything worthwhile in their traditions from the Scriptures. The golden age was a garbled misunderstanding of Genesis. The Latin apologists borrowed from Varro a completely euhemerized interpretation of the myth: Saturn, the Latin Cronus, was assumed to have been a real king who had reigned in prehistoric Italy, and the golden age was a poetic figure of speech describing his just rule. The two explanations are combined in the *Divine*

Institutes of Lactantius, written at the moment of Christianity's victory. Like earlier Latin apologists Lactantius accepted the golden age as a real historical period, but he was also willing to consider it as a continuation of the unfallen state of humanity, for Varro had said that in that period God was still worshipped purely and without idols. But Lactantius refuted the notion that community of property had been practiced in the golden age. He considered this merely a metaphor introduced by the poets, referring to the generous charity that had been practiced in that relatively uncorrupted state. Elsewhere Lactantius refuted Plato's teaching on communism in terms that recapitulated all the arguments that pagan philosophy had used against utopia: community of women would be against nature, would disrupt the household, and has never been followed by any society.[28]

Communism was so suspect an idea among Christians in the age of Constantine that most dismissed it as a pagan misinterpretation of Scripture; and even the learned Lactantius, who could accept the golden age as a partial continuation of the conditions described in the opening chapters of Genesis, was concerned to argue that it could not have included real communism in any sense, not even in property, and certainly not in women.

Therefore it is significant that Lactantius' contemporary Eusebius, influential adviser to Constantine and historian of the church, was willing to accept the idea of a Christian communism and to locate it in the primitive church. Eusebius read in Philo's *On the Contemplative Life* about the communistic practices of the Therapeutae, an otherwise unknown Jewish sect in Egypt who appear to have been an offshoot of the Essenes. Eusebius was much taken by the idea, apparently original with him, that these Therapeutae were really early Christians who had been converted by St. Mark, the apostle of Egypt according to widely accepted tradition. One of his proofs was that the Therapeutae, according to Philo, surrendered all property when they joined the sect. This, Eusebius points out, was the practice of the original Christians, as we know from the Acts of the Apostles. Therefore Eusebius assumed that this practice was followed not only in Jerusalem but everywhere the apostles preached (*History of the Church* 2.16–17).

For some time Christian ascetic circles had regarded the community life described in Acts 2–4 as a literal and total communism, but Eusebius' history probably did more than anything to popularize this idea. Also Eusebius was the first to visualize it as a permanent type of organization that was found everywhere in primitive Christianity. He did not comment on the fact that this primitive communism had evidently disappeared from the church at some point, but he probably thought this was to be explained by the well-known fact that there had been a great decline in fervor since apostolic times. Christian communism had become a respectable ideal, soon to be reborn in Egypt, and soon to be linked to pagan tradition without embarrasment.

The Christian Empire and the City of God

The last decades of the fourth century saw the Christianization of the Roman Empire and the development of a Christian social and political theory. This was largely the work of a succession of able bishops who were in close touch with the imperial bureaucracy and the new Christian aristocracy and at the same time vigorous patrons of the monastic movement: Basil at Caesarea, John Chrysostom at Constantinople, Ambrose at Milan, Augustine at Hippo. They inherited a Christian tradition dominated by two contrary tendencies. On the one hand, there was a long-established Christian ideal of community, best summarized by the phrase "household of God." It conceived Christianity as a church-society, based on the orderly household. This church society was politically disengaged from the larger society but shared many of the same values, indeed claimed to be superior to the larger society for what were essentially political reasons, such as its greater order and discipline. In the Christian Empire its political disengagement obviously mattered less and less yet was not entirely forgotten. And on the other hand there was a violently ascetic ideal that required the rejection of all households and all normal society. Christian leaders of the late fourth century had somehow to make sense of this paradoxical heritage. No area was more problematical than the question of the proper ownership and use of property, and their attempts to address this question, largely *ad hoc* attempts occasioned by practical pastoral concerns, established certain views which would become extremely influential in the Christian centuries to come.

Firstly, the Eusebian image of a totally communistic primitive church was universally identified with the monastery. In the Rules of St. Basil the Great, which have remained the foundation of Greek Orthodox monasticism to the present day, the primitive church of Acts is conceived as a monastery, and the monastery is conceived as its continuation. Basil thought that all early Christians had lived the cenobitic life, which was now awarded a clear historical and moral precedence over the anchoritic life. He perceived the monastery as a literal reenactment of the New Testament and described nearly everything in the monk's life as the imitation of some Scriptural example.[29] The theme of imitation of the primitive church soon became a commonplace in Greek Christian literature, and almost as quickly spread to the West, especially after a Latin translation of the Basilian rule appeared ca. 400.

The disappearance of the monastic life between the apostles and Anthony could be accounted for by the general decline in standards. Augustine explained it as a result of the spread of Christianity to the Gentiles: the Jews, being prepared by the Law, were able to adopt communism upon their conversion to Christianity, but Gentile converts were unable to emulate them because their spiritual understanding had been perverted by idol worship (*On Christian Doctrine* 3.6.10–11; *Sermon* 252.3). His contemporary John Cassian, for the benefit of his Gallic monks, elaborated this idea into a sort of historical myth which came to be generally accepted in Western Christianity. Cassian supposed that private property had been allowed by the apostles as one of the concessions to Gentile Christians made at the Apostolic Council of Acts 15.28–29. Those who continued the *ecclesia primitiva* (a phrase coined by Cassian to signify the original communistic way of life) withdrew into monasteries. The second type of monk, the anchorite, was a offshoot of the cenobitic life that developed centuries later, in time of Anthony (*Collations* 18; *Institutes* 2.5).

Secondly, the Neostoic theory of primitive communism was adopted and baptized. Christians generally accepted the notion that the primitive state of human society had been communistic—in property, but not of course in women—and identified this condition with the unfallen state of humanity in the garden of Eden. The unfallen state was considered "natural" because it was a state of perfect monogamy, complete equality, and common possession of all things; coercive government and law, private property, slavery, and all other social evils were considered to be results of the Fall.

The most complete conflation of Christian and Neostoic ideas was achieved in Ambrose's *On the Duties of Ministers* (ca. 390), an adaptation of Cicero's *On Duties* for the instruction of his clergy. Ambrose claimed, of course, that this was basically a Scriptural teaching. The Stoics had borrowed the idea of natural communism from the passage in Genesis where God gives Adam dominion over the earth. The original communism survived in the principle that all things on the earth should be used for the common benefit. But Ambrose emphasized that Christians were willing to go much further in this direction than Cicero and the Stoics: only Christians believed that *all* things should be used in common, and only Christians put this doctrine into practice in the primitive church and the monastery.[30]

The Christian doctrine of primitive communism carried many of the same conservative implications as its Neostoic predecessor. It justified inequality and counseled submission to authority, adding to the pagan theory the view that all this was a just punishment for sin. But the Judeo-Christian teaching of a paradisal state of innocence was a more powerful moral ideal than the classical imagery of the golden age, especially when associated with existing communal institutions. After all, no pagan philosopher had ever thought that communism might literally be put into practice. Christians did think of the monastery as a direct continuation of the primitive church, and of the primitive church as a return to the garden of Eden, a partial cancellation of the effects of orginal sin.

Often the monastery was conceived as a model for the whole of society. Basil insisted that the call to sell all applied to everyone, not just to monks. His ascetic writings make no sharp distinction between the perfect and ordinary Christian; complete compliance with the call was possible only in monasteries, but Christians in the world were also required to observe it through continual sharing of wealth with the needy.[31] John Chrysostom suggested that the citizens of Constantinople share their wealth with the poor precisely as in a monastery or in the first church at Jerusalem:

> The dwellers in the monasteries live just as the faithful did then; now did ever any one of these die of hunger? ... For if at that time, when there was no believer but only the three thousand and the five thousand; when all, throughout the world, were enemies, when they could nowhere look for comfort, they yet boldly entered upon this plan with such success; how much more would this be the case now, when by the grace of God there are believers everywhere throughout the world? *Commentary on the Acts of the Apostles* 11.2–3, trans. *Select Library of the Nicene and Post-Nicene Fathers*, ed. Schaff.

The Christian teaching about the garden of Eden and its revival in the primitive church was not utopianism as utopianism has been defined in this book, but it may be called a sort of utopian myth with considerable capacity to promote social reform.

This myth produced a third noteworthy development: a tendency to identify communism with property owned by a corporation. The Gospel of John mentions that Jesus and the Twelve kept a box (*glossokomon*) to contain money, which they used for their own support and to provide alms for the poor (John 12.6, 13.29). It is mentioned only in connection with Judas' betrayal. The money box was probably associated with Judas because of the tradition that Judas betrayed Jesus for money, leading to the assumption that Judas must have been a thief already; therefore Judas became keeper of the money box and the money box one of his "props." It seems to have received little attention until Augustine developed the idea that Christ's money box was Scriptural foundation of the *fiscus* of the church and the model for all church revenue (*forma eccelesiasticae pecuniae*). According to Augustine, Christ made use of money, thought he did not have to, in order to show that his church would have to use money while on its earthly pilgrimage. Augustine was interested in this idea because he wanted to refute certain North African monks of the Messalian type who refused to work and claimed a right to live from alms on the grounds that they were following literally the Gospel precepts. Augustine replied that there was no contradiction between those Gospel precepts and the corporate ownership of property by the church; rather the two were complementary. Christ kept the money box to show the manner in which the church should hold property. It was used for two purposes: to provide for the needs of Christ and his apostles, and to provide alms for the poor. Augustine imagined Christ and the apostles living from a common fund, and the apostles continuing this way of life in the primitive church at Jerusalem. In the same way the bishops are administrators of the fisc of the church, which is the repository for the gifts of the faithful; and the funds are to be used for the same purpose, to support the ministers of the church and to care for the poor. Therefore the right to live from the treasury of the church is restricted to the clergy, who ideally should live from it in common like the apostles. Laity were also encouraged to imitate the primitive church, but if they chose to renounce property they were required to support themselves by their own labor in monasteries.[32]

Thus Augustine merged the two New Testament images of the primitive church and the money box, and interpreted both as examples of corporate property. In effect he identified *common* property with *corporate* property. In pagan philosophy "common" property meant primarily things that could belong to no one, such as water and light and air. To Augustine it meant primarily property that belongs to a corporation, such as the Christian church, or a particular church or a particular monastery. We have seen evidence that the Stoics had attempted to clarify this distinction, and to use examples of public or corporate property, like the theater, to show how the ideal of common property might be put into practice. But there seems to be no precedent for the Augustinian conflation of the two. For medieval theories of property these would become very influential texts, producing much confusion and controversy, and diverse results: they could promote practical applications of Scriptural communism, and they could also serve as a facile justification of the growing corporate wealth of the church.

The themes discussed above were among the more original features of the patristic synthesis on the subject of property. Through these channels some of the ancient philosophical tradition of utopian communistic speculation would be passed on to medieval Christendom. The notion that in some fashion nature has decreed all property to be common would never die, but from now on the primary texts to which scholars turned to elucidate that doctrine would be the books of Genesis and the Acts of the Apostles, not the *Republics* of Plato and Zeno. In the greatest of all patristic works on social and political thought, the *City of God* of Augustine, the word "city" loses at last all connection with the secular utopias whose history I have attempted to chart, and the possibility of realizing on earth the heavenly Jerusalem, or even the communistic earthly Jerusalem of apostolic times, is at last relinquished.

Notes

1. For the Mission Charge and its context see D.L. Dungan, *The Sayings of Jesus in the Churches of Paul* (Philadelphia 1971); Gerd Theissen, *Sociology of Early Palestinian Christianity*, trans. John Bowden (Philadephia 1978); and Martin Hengel, *The Charismatic Leader and his Followers*, trans. James Greig (New York 1981). For the *Didache* see below, note 2. For early Christian theories of property in general, see Martin Hengel, *Property and Riches in the Early Church*, trans. John Bowden (Philadelphia 1974); R. M. Grant, *Early Christianity and Society* (New York 1977); L. W. Countryman, *The Rich Christian in the Church of the Early Empire* (New York 1980); J. L. Gonzalez, *Faith and Wealth: A History of Early Christian Ideas on the Origin, Significance, and Use of Money* (San Francisco 1990).

2. The *Didache*, or *Teaching of the Twelve Apostles*, is generally dated to the late first or early second century. It is of uncertain provenance. For almsgiving, see *Didache* 1.5–6. It quotes a saying, possibly thought to be a saying of Jesus himself, which seems to contradict flatly the precept of unreserved almsgiving that is attributed to Jesus at Mt. 5.42 and LK. 6.30: "Let your alms sweat into your hands until you know whom you are giving them to." Itinerant "apostles" are to be supported by the Christian community, but if they stay more than two days, or ask money, they are to be considered *pseudoprophetai.* Resident "prophets" and "teachers" in the community are to be supported, but the payments are precisely defined, and a prophet who asks for money or anything else when the spirit is upon him is a false prophet (11, 13). Hospitality to traveling Christians is required, but if they stay longer than two or three days they must go to work. "No idle Christian shall live among you." Idle Christians are called *Christemporoi*, sellers of Christ (12).

3. The history of the interpretation of this passage is discussed by R. W. Haskin, "The Call to Sell All" (Ph.D. diss., Columbia University, 1968). An alternative explanation is possible. Perhaps we are dealing here with a plain mistake, caused by stringing together unrelated sayings of Jesus. The camel and the needle's eye saying would not have such radical implications were it not attached to the rich man's question, and perhaps

originally it was not. If so, then we must assume a final redactor who made a not wholly successful attempt to impose sense on the anecdote, leaving us with the version we have.

4. This theory about the composition of Acts was advanced in the 1920s by Martin Dibelius, *Studies in the Acts of the Apostles*, ed. H. Greven (London 1956) and has won general acceptance. See Lake, "The Communism of Acts II and IV–VI," and Cadbury, "The Summaries in Acts," both in Kirsopp Lake et al., eds., *The Beginnings of Christianity* (London 1933); and Ernst Haenchen, *The Acts of the Apostles: A Commentary*, trans. R. M. Wilson et al. (Oxford 1971), 190–96, 230–35, 259–69.

5. This passage from the Two Ways document occurs both in *Didache* 4.8 and in *Epistle of Barnabas* 19.8. Cf. Diog. Laert., *Life of Pythagoras* 8.23: the early Pythagoreans were taught to call nothing their own. Hellenistic-Jewish writers had spread the notion that the Jewish tradition of almsgiving, which was a more effective system of poor relief than anything known to the Gentiles, fulfilled the Greek philosophical ideal of communism. A poem written by an Alexandrian Jew about the time of Jesus contains a series of injunctions to give alms, followed by the precept "Let all of life be in common" (P. W. van den Horst, ed., *The Sentences of Pseudo-Phocylides*, Leiden 1978, line 30). There is similar language in another Hellenistic-Jewish poem, the *Third Sibylline Oracle*. Behind these utterances were certain assumptions widespread among Greek-speaking Jews: that there is a universal ethic common to the Old Testament and to Greek philosophy, and that the Old Testament is the original and perfect expression of it, the Greek philosophers having borrowed their basic ideas from the Scriptures. For this background see J. J. Collins, *Between Athens and Jerusalem* (New York 1983), 137–48.

6. Migne ed., 1.25. At 1.31.2 Irenaeus attributes the same teaching on reincarnation, with the same disastrous moral consequences, to the even more obscure sect of the Cainites.

7. "Alii autem rursus a Basilide et Carpocrate occasiones accipientes, indifferentes coitus et multas nuptias induxerunt, et negligentiam ipsorum, quae sunt idolothyta, ad manducanum; non valde haec curare dicentes Deum" (1.28.2). Here Irenaeus pairs Carpocrates and Basilides as the founders of libertine heresy, but the inclusion of Basilides is probably Irenaeus' error, for Basilides was generally considered one of the ascetic Gnostics, and no one else accuses Basilidians of sexual communism.

8. The relevant parts of the *Miscellanies* are translated by Henry Chadwick and J. E. L. Oulton, *Alexandrian Christianity* (Philadelphia 1954).

9. Morton Smith, *Clement of Alexandria and a Secret Gopel of Mark* (Cambridge, Mass. 1973). In his Appendix B Smith assembles all the patristic texts dealing with Carpocratians. Sources later than Irenaeus and Clement add little but confusion.

10. See R. van den Broek, "The Present State of Gnostic Studies," *Vigiliae Christianae* 37 (1983), 41–71. The process by which the Nag Hammadi texts were selected and preserved may have left us with a false impression in this respect, for it is possible the library belonged to a fourth-century Pachomian monastery, which might have collected it for devotional as well as heresiological purposes, in which case the monks would have weeded out texts of libertine tendency.

11. "Ta sarkika tois sarkikois kai ta pneumatika tois pneumatikois apodidosthai" (1.6.3).

12. See R. E. Lerner, *The Heresy of the Free Spirit in the Later Middle Ages* (Berkeley 1972).

13. *Misc.* 3.1.3. There were certain Basilidians whom Clement classed among the libertines, though he admits most Basilidians were of the ascetic type, and he suggests two quite different explanations for their immorality: perhaps they believe they have the power to commit sin because they are perfect, or perhaps they believe they will be saved in spite of sinning because they are elected.

14. According to Acts 15.20, 15.29, 21.25, an "Apostolic Council" ca. 50 A.D. imposed on Gentile converts prohibitions on *idolothyta* (meat that had been sacrificed to idols), meat containing blood, and *porneia.* But in 1 Corinthians Paul permits idol meat to the church at Corinth and seems to know nothing of any prohibition on blood. These dietary rules were not generally enforced on Gentile Christians until about the end of the century, when the Acts of the Apostles was written; its author has read them back into apostolic times. See Haenchen, *Acts*, 468–72; J. C. Hurd, Jr., *The Origins of 1 Corinthians* (New York 1965), 246–53; C. K. Barrett, "Things Sacrificed to Idols," *New Testament Studies* 11 (1964–1965), 138–53; and on the meaning of *porneia*, F. Hauck and S. Schultz, "*porne*," in *Theological Dictionary of the New Testament* (Grand Rapids 1969); Bruce Malina, "Does *Porneia* Mean Fornication?", *Novum Testamentum* 14 (1972), 10–17; Joseph Jensen, "Does *Porneia* Mean Fornication? A Critique of Bruce Malina," *Novum Testamentum* 20 (1978), 161–84.

15. Idol meat is prohibited in Rev. 2.14, 20, and in *Didache* 6.3. Justin says that all Christians consider eating idol meat the same as idolatry (*Dialogue with Trypho* 34). By the second century it was said also that Christians would not eat meat containing blood: Tertullian, *Apology* 9; Minucius 36; Eusebius, *History of the Church* 5.1.26.

16. Rev. 2 attacks false prophets who follow the error of Balaam, who led Israel into idolatry and *porneia.* One of their leaders is a prophetess called Jezebel, another Old Testament name with unsavory associations similar to Balaam's. Jude and 2 Peter attack false prophets who follow the error of Balaam, emphasizing the sexual nature of this error (Jude 4, 7–8; 2 Peter 2.2, 14, 18–20.).

17. Irenaeus 3.18.5, 4.33.9; Tertullian, *Scorpiace* 1.

18. Irenaeus 2.14.5: "Ipsam autem eduliorum, et reliquarum operationum indifferentem sententiam, et quod putent a nemine in totum posse coinquinari propter generositatem, licet quodcunque manducent vel operentur, a Cynicis possederunt, cum sint eis eiusdem testamenti." Cf. 2.32.2. Evidence for contacts between Christianity and Cynicism has been collected by Benko, *Pagan Rome*, 30–53. R. M. Grant, *Gnosticism and Early Christianity* (New York 1959), 96, suggested that libertine sects practiced a "Cynicizing gnosis." Smith, *Clement of Alexandria*, 270, pointed out the use of Stoic terms.

19. See Albert Henrichs, "Pagan Ritual and the Alleged Crimes of the Early Christians: A Reconsideration," *Kyriakon: Festschrift Johannes Quasten*, ed. P. Granfield (Münster 1970), 1.18–35; R. M. Grant, "Charges of Immorality against Various Religious Groups in Antiquity," *Studies in Gnosticism and Hellenistic Religion*, ed. R. van den Broek et al. (Leiden 1981), 161–70; Benko, *Pagan Rome*.

20. See Stephen Benko, "The Libertine Gnostic Sect of the Phibionites according to Epiphanius," *Vigiliae Christianae* 21 (1967), 103–19; Stephen Gero, "With Walter Bauer on the Tigris: Encratite Orthodoxy and Libertine Heresy in Syro-Mesopotamian Christianity," *Nag Hammadi, Gnosticism, and Early Christianity*, ed. C. W. Hedrick et al. (Peabody 1986), 287–307.

21. Burkert, *Greek Religion*, 292. But Pausanias (8.9.7–8) implies nothing scandalous about the cult of Antinous as it was practiced in Greece.

22. The earliest versions of the *Haustafeln* are found in the Deutero-Pauline Epistles: Col. 3.18–4.1; Eph. 5.21–6.9. Other versions: Titus 1.5–9, 2.2–10; 1 Tim. 2.1–6.2; 1 Peter 2.13–3.7; *Didache* 4.9–11; *Epistle of Polycarp* 4.2–6.1; *First Epistle of Clement of Rome* 1.3, 21.6–9. See D. L. Balch, *Let Wives Be Submissive: The Domestic Code in 1 Peter* (Chico 1981); J. H. Elliott, *A Home for the Homeless: A Sociological Exegesis of 1 Peter, Its Situation and Strategy* (Philadelphia 1981); J. E. Crouch, *The Origin and Intention of the Colossian Haustafeln* (Göttingen 1982); D. C. Verner, *The Household of God: The Social World of the Pastoral Epistles* (Chico 1983); and for the social

background, Wayne Meeks, *The First Urban Christians* (New Haven 1983).

23. *Epistle to Diognetus* 5.5; Athenagoras 11; Justin, *I Apology* 15, a collection of Jesus' sayings on wealth, for which see A. J. Bellinzoni, *The Sayings of Jesus in the Writings of Justin Martyr* (Leiden 1967). Justin appears to be quoting from a series of harmonies of the Synoptic Gospels. His conflation of Mt. 5.45 and Lk. 6.36 has the effect of associating the almsgiving precept with the image of the sun rising on all alike, an association familiar in pagan philosophy.

24. Origen, *Commentary on Mathew* 15.15. Patristic references to these passages in Acts have been collected by P. C. Bori, *Chiesa Primitiva: L'immagine della communità delle origini (Atti 2. 42–47; 4.32–37) nella storia della chiesa antica* (Brescia 1974).

25. Tract 1 *On Unity* 25–26; Tract 3 *On the Lapsed* 11, 35; the quotation below is from Tract 8 *On Works and Alms* 7. Cf. Tract 4 *On the Lord's Prayer* 20; *To Quirinus* 3.2, 3, 61; *Epistle* 7.3.

26. I pass over here certain obscure Christian traditions of rural asceticism that antedated monasticism, most notably the "Encratite" communities of Asia Minor and Syria, which practiced group celibacy and apparently some form of communal property. For them, and for illuminating discussions of many other aspects of early Christian asceticism, see Peter Brown, *The Body and Society: Men, Women, and Sexual Renunciation in Early Christianity* (New York 1988).

27. See Jerome, *Ep.* 58 *To Paulinus* 4–5; idem, *Life of Paul the Hermit*, prologue; and the beginning of the *First Greek Life* of Pachomius. Allusions to the apostolic call as the monastic profession are recurrent in the *Lives* of Pachomius and other early monastic writings. The cenobium is compared to the community of Acts 4 in the *Bohairic Life* 194; the *First Sahidic Life* 11; the *First Greek Life* 131, in A. Veilleux, trans. *The Life of Saint Pachomius and his Disciples*, Pachomian Koinonia 1 (Kalamazoo 1980).

28. Lactantius, *Institutes* 1.11–14; 3.21–22; 5.5–8. Earlier Christian interpretations of the myth of Saturn: Tert., *Apol.* 10; *To the Nations* 2.12–13; Minucius 21; Cyprian, Tract 6 *On the Vanity of Idols*.

29. See especially Basil's *Long Rules* 5, 7–10, 19, 32, 34, 37, 44; *Shorter Rules* 183, 187. In the *Long Rules* 35 he suggests that all monasteries be united under the same supervisors, as the five thousand believers were united in Jerusalem.

30. Ambrose, *On the Duties of Ministers* 1.11.38; 1.28.132–33; 3.6.41. Cf. his *On the Psalms* 118.8.22, and *The Six Days* 5.15.52–5.21.72; and Gregory Nazianzen, *Oration* 14.25–26. For the later history of this theme see Doyne Dawson, "Primitive Church, Concept of," in *The Dictionary of the Middle Ages* (New York 1988). For other Stoic influences on the fathers see Marcia Colish, *The Stoic Tradition from Antiquity to the Early Middle Ages*, 2 vols. (Leiden 1985).

31. Basil, *On Mercy and Justice*; *On Renunciation of the World*; *Homily on Psalm* 14.6.

32. Aug., *On the Work of Monks*, especially 5.6.; *On the Gospel of John* 50.11, 62.5; *On the Psalms* 146.17. See M. J. Wilks, "The Problem of Private Ownership in Patristic Thought and an Augustinian Solution of the Fourteenth Century," *Studia Patristica* 6 (1962), 533–42. Monasticism, a lay institution in the East, often took a clerical form in the West. Augustine's conception of the common life was primarily clerical; he imposed the monastic life on his cathedral clergy at Hippo, promoted the same program elsewhere in Africa, and provided a rule for monastic clergy in his sermons, letters, and probably in the original redaction of the document later known as the *Rule of St. Augustine*.

Bibliography

The bibliography includes only works mentioned in the notes, excluding standard editions of classical texts.

Aalders, G. J. D. *Die theorie der gemischten Verfassung im Altertum*. Amsterdam 1968.

———. *Political Thought in Hellenistic Times*. Amsterdam 1975.

Adams, James, ed. *The Republic of Plato*. Rev. ed. D. A. Rees. Cambridge 1963.

Adkins, A. W. H. *Moral Values and Political Behaviour in Ancient Greece*. New York 1972.

Africa, T. W. *Phylarchus and the Spartan Revolution*. Berkeley 1961.

Alexander, Peter, and Roger Gill, eds. *Utopias*. La Salle 1984.

Andrewes, Antony. "Two Notes on Lysander," *Phoenix* 25 (1971), 206–26.

Andrews, Paul. "Aristotle, Politics 4.11.1296a38–40," *Classical Review* 66 n.s. 2 (1952), 141–144.

Andria, R. G. "Diogene Cinico nel papiri Ercolanesi," *Cronache Ercolanesi* 10 (1980), 129–151.

Annas, Julia. *An Introduction to Plato's Republic*. Oxford 1981.

Babut, Daniel. "Les stoïciens et l'amour," *Revue des études grecques* 76 (1963), 55–63.

———. *Plutarque et la stoïcisme*. Paris 1969.

Badian, Ernst. "Tiberius Gracchus and the Roman Revolution," *Aufstieg und Niedergang der Romischen Welt* 1.1. Berlin 1972, 668–731.

Balch, D. L. *Let Wives Be Submissive: The Domestic Code in 1 Peter*. Chico 1981.

Baldry, H. C. "Who Invented the Golden Age?," *Classical Quarterly* 46 n.s. 2 (1952), 83–92.

———. "Zeno's Ideal State," *Journal of Hellenic Studies* 79 (1959), 3–14.

———. *The Unity of Mankind in Greek Thought*. Cambridge 1965.

Bambrough, Renford, ed. *Plato, Popper, and Politics: Some Contributions to a Modern Controversy*. Cambridge 1967.

Barker, Ernest. *Political Thought of Plato and Aristotle*. London 1906.

———. *Greek Political Theory: Plato and His Predecessors*. London 1918.

Barrett, C. K. "Things Sacrificed to Idols," *New Testament Studies* 11 (1964–1965), 138–153.

Barrow, Robin. *Plato, Utilitarianism, and Education*. London 1975.

Bellinzoni, A. J. *The Sayings of Jesus in the Writings of Justin Martyr*. Leiden 1967.

Benko, Stephen. "The Libertine Gnostic Sect of the Phibionites According to Epiphanius," *Vigiliae Christianae* 21 (1967), 103–119.

———. *Pagan Rome and the Early Christians*. Bloomington 1984.

Berneri, M. L. *Journey Through Utopia*. London 1950.

Billerbeck, Margrethe. "La réception du cynisme à Rome," *L'antiquité classique* 51 (1982), 151–73.
Bloom, Alan. *The Republic of Plato*. New York 1987.
———. "Response to Hall," *Political Theory* 5 (1977), 315–30.
———. *The Closing of the American Mind*. New York 1987.
Bluestone, N. H. *Women and the Ideal Society: Plato's Republic and Modern Myths of Gender*. Amherst 1987.
Bori, P. C. *Chiesa Primitiva: L'immagine della communità delle origini (Atti 2, 42–47; 4, 32–37) nella storia della chiesa antica*. Brescia 1974.
Boring, T. A. *Literacy in Ancient Sparta*. Leiden 1979.
Boyd, T. D., and M. H. Jameson. "Urban and Rural Land Division in Ancient Greece," *Hesperia* 50 (1981), 327–342.
Briscoe, John. "Rome and the Class Struggle in the Greek States, 200–146 B.C.," *Past and Present* 36 (1967), 1–20.
Brown, Peter. *The Body and Society: Men, Women, and Sexual Renunciation in Early Christianity*. New York 1988.
Brown, T. S. *Onesicritus: A Study in Hellenistic Historiography*. Berkeley 1949.
Brunt, P. A. "Aspects of the Social Thought of Dio Chrysostom and the Stoics," *Proceedings of the Cambridge Philological Society* n.s. 19 (1973), 9–34.
Burkert, Walter. *Lore and Science in Ancient Pythagoreanism*. E. L. Minar, Jr., trans. Cambridge, Mass. 1972.
———. "Craft versus Sect: The Problem of Orphics and Pythagoreans," *Jewish and Christian Self-Definition*, E. P. Sanders et al., eds. Philadelphia 1980–1982, 3.1–22.
———. *Greek Religion*. John Raffan, trans. Cambridge, Mass., 1985.
Burnet, John. *Greek Philosophy, Part One: Thales to Plato* (London 1914).
Bury, J. B. *A History of Greece*. Rev. Russell Meiggs. London 1951.
Caizzi, F. D. *Antisthenis Fragmenta*. Milan 1966.
Calvert, Brian. "Slavery in Plato's Republic," *Classical Quarterly* n.s. 37 (1987), 367–72.
Cartledge, Paul. *Agesilaos and the Crisis of Sparta*. Baltimore 1987.
———, and Anthony Spawforth. *Hellenistic and Roman Sparta: A Tale of Two Cities*. London 1989.
Cary, Max. *A History of the Greek World from 323 to 146 B.C.* London 1932.
Chadwick, Henry, and J. E. L. Oulton. *Alexandrian Christianity*. Philadelphia 1954.
Cherniss, Harold. *Plutarch's Moralia* 13.2. Cambridge, Mass. 1976.
Chesneaux, Jean. "Egalitarian and Utopian Traditions in the East," *Diogenes* 62 (1968), 76–102.
Cole, Thomas. *Democritus and the Sources of Greek Anthropology*. Cleveland 1967.
Colish, Marcia. *The Stoic Tradition from Antiquity to the Early Middle Ages*. Leiden 1985.
Collins, J. J. *Between Athens and Jerusalem*. New York 1983.
Conley, T. M. "Dating the So-Called 'Dissoi Logoi': A Cautionary Note," *Ancient Philosophy* 5 (1985), 59–65.
Countryman, L. W. *The Rich Christian in the Church of the Early Empire*. New York 1980.
Creed, John. "Aristotle's Middle Constitution," *Polis: Newsletter of the Society for the Study of Greek Political Thought* (Swansea, U.K.) 8.2 (1989), 2–27.
Crossman, R. H. *Plato Today*. London 1959.
Crouch, J. E. *The Origin and Intention of the Colossian Haustafeln*. Göttingen 1982.
David, Ephraim. *Sparta Between Empire and Revolution, 404–243 B.C.* Salem 1981.

———. "Aristotle and Sparta," *Ancient Society* 13 (1982), 67–103.

———. *Aristophanes and Athenian Society of the Early Fourth Century B.C.* Leiden 1984.

Davis, J. C. *Utopia and the Ideal Society: A Study of English Utopian Writing, 1516–1700.* Cambridge 1981.

Dawson, Doyne. "Primitive Church, Concept of," in *The Dictionary of the Middle Ages.* New York 1988.

de Laix, R. A. "Aristotle's Conception of the Spartan Constitution," *Journal of the History of Philosophy* 12 (1974), 21–30.

de Ste. Croix, G. E. M. *The Origins of the Peloponnesian War.* Ithaca 1972.

———. *The Class Struggle in the Ancient Greek World.* Ithaca 1981.

Devine, F. E. "Stoicism on the Best Regime," *Journal of the History of Ideas* 31 (1970), 323–36.

Dibelius, Martin. *Studies in the Acts of the Apostles.* H. Greven, ed. London 1956.

Dill, Samuel. *Roman Society from Nero to Marcus Aurelius.* London 1905.

Dodds, E. R. *The Greeks and the Irrational.* Berkeley 1951.

Donzelli, G. B. "Il *Peri Haireseon* di Ippoboto e il *Kynismos*," *Rivista di Filologia e di Istruzione Classica* n.s. 37 (1959), 24–39.

Dorandi, Tiziano. "Filodemo. Gli Stoici (PHERC 155 E339)," *Cronache Ercolanesi* 12 (1982), 91–133.

Dover, K. J. *Aristophanic Comedy.* London 1972.

———. *Greek Homosexuality.* Cambridge, Mass. 1978.

Dudley, D. R. *A History of Cynicism.* Hildesheim 1937.

———. "Blossius of Cumae," *Journal of Roman Studies* 31 (1941), 94–99.

Dumont, J.-C. "A propos d'Aristonicus," *Eirene* 5 (1966), 189–96.

Dungan, D. L. *The Sayings of Jesus in the Churches of Paul.* Philadelphia 1971.

Düring, Ingemar. *Herodicus the Cratetean: A Study in Anti-Platonic Tradition.* Stockholm 1941.

Dyroff, Adolf. *Die Ethik der alten Stoa.* Berlin 1897.

Earl, D. C. "Terence and Roman Politics," *Historia* 11 (1962), 469–85.

Edelstein, Ludwig. *The Meaning of Stoicism.* Cambridge, Mass. 1966.

———, and I. G. Kidd. *Posidonius.* Cambridge 1988.

Edgerton, Franklin. "Dominant Ideas in the Formation of Indian Culture," *Journal of the American Oriental Society* 62 (1942), 151–56.

Ehrenburg, Victor. *The People of Aristophanes.* Oxford 1951.

Eliav-Feldon, Miriam. *Realistic Utopias: The Ideal Imaginary Societies of the Renaissance, 1516–1630.* Oxford 1982.

Elliott, J. H. *A Home for the Homeless: A Sociological Exegesis of 1 Peter, Its Situation and Strategy.* Philadelphia 1981.

Elorduy, Eleuterio. *Die Sozialphilosophie der Stoa.* Leipzig 1936.

Emeljanow, V. "A Note on the Cynic 'Short Cut to Happiness'," *Mnemosyne* 18 (1965), 182–84.

Erskine, Andrew. *The Hellenistic Stoa: Political Thought and Action.* Princeton 1990.

Ferguson, John. *Utopias of the Classical World.* Ithaca 1975.

Ferguson, W. S. *Hellenistic Athens.* London 1911.

Festa, N. and R. Anastasi. *I frammenti degli Stoichi antichi.* Bari 1932–1962.

Finley, M. I. ed. *Slavery in Classical Antiquity.* Cambridge 1960.

———. *The Use and Abuse of History.* New York 1971.

———. *The Ancient Economy.* Berkeley 1973.

———. *Ancient History: Evidence and Models.* New York 1986.

Freeman, Kathleen. *Ancilla to the Pre-Socratic Philosophers*. Cambridge, Mass. 1948.
Frischer, Bernard. *The Sculpted Word: Epicureanism and Philosophical Recruitment in Ancient Greece*. Berkeley 1982.
Fuks, Alexander. *Social Conflict in Ancient Greece*. Jerusalem 1984.
Fustel de Coulanges, N.D. *La cité antique*. Paris 1905.
Gallo, Italo. *Frammenti biografici da papiri. 2: La biografia dei filosofi*. Rome 1980.
Garland, Yvon. *Slavery in Ancient Greece*. Janet Lloyd, trans. Ithaca 1988.
Gerhard, G. A. *Phoinix von Kolophon*. Leipzig 1909.
———. "Zur Legende vom Kyniker Diogenes," *Archiv für Religionswissenschaft* 15 (1912), 388–408.
Gero, Stephen. "With Walter Bauer on the Tigris: Encratite Orthodoxy and Libertine Heresy in Syro-Mesopotamian Christianity," *Nag Hammadi, Gnosticism, and Early Christianity*. C. W. Hedrick et al., eds. Peabody 1986, 287–307.
Giangrande, Lawrence. *The Use of* Spoudaiogeloion *in Greek and Roman Literature*. The Hague 1972.
Giannantoni, Gabriele. *Socraticorum Reliquiae*. Naples 1983.
Glotz, Gustave. *Ancient Greece at Work*. M. R. Dobie, trans. New York 1926.
Glucker, John. *Antiochus and the Late Academy*. Göttingen 1978.
Gomperz, Theodor. *Greek Thinkers*. G. G. Berry, trans. London 1901–1912.
Gonzalez, J. L. *Faith and Wealth: A History of Early Christian Ideas on the Origin, Significance, and Use of Money*. San Francisco 1990.
Gould, John. "Law, Custom, and Myth: Aspects of the Social Position of Women in Classical Athens," *Journal of Hellenic Studies* 100 (1980), 38–59.
Gouldner, A. W. *Enter Plato: Classical Greece and the Origins of Social Theory*. New York 1965.
Goulet-Cazé, Marie-Odile. "Un syllogisme stoïcien sur la loi dans le doxographie de Diogène le Cynique. A propos de Diogène Laërce VI 72," *Rheinisches Museum für Philologie* 125 (1982), 214–40.
———. *L'ascèse cynique: Un commentaire sur Diogène Laërce VI 70–71*. Paris 1986.
———. "Le cynisme à l'époque impériale," *Aufstieg und Niedergang der Römischen Welt* 2.36.4. Berlin 1990, 2720–2833.
Graham, A. J. *Colony and Mother City in Ancient Greece*. Manchester 1964.
Grant, R. M. *Gnosticism and Early Christianity*. New York 1959.
———. *Early Christianity and Society*. New York 1977.
———. "Charges of Immorality against Various Religious Groups in Antiquity," in *Studies in Gnosticism and Hellenistic Religion*, R. van den Broek et al., eds. Leiden 1981, 161–70.
Griffin, Jasper. "Augustan Poetry and the Life of Luxury," *Journal of Roman Studies* 66 (1976), 87–105.
Griffin, M. T. *Seneca: A Philosopher in Politics*. Oxford 1976.
Griswold, C. L., Jr., ed. *Plantonic Writings, Platonic Readings*. New York 1988.
Gruen, E. S. *The Hellenistic World and the Coming of Rome*. Berkeley 1984.
Gulley, Norman. *The Philosophy of Socrates*. New York 1968.
Guthrie, K. S., et al. *The Pythagorean Sourcebook and Library*. Grand Rapids 1987.
Guthrie, W. K. C. *History of Greek Philosophy*. Cambridge 1962–1981.
Haenchen, Ernst. *The Acts of the Apostles: A Commentary*. R. M. Wilson et al., trans. Oxford 1971.
Hall, Dale. "The 'Republic' and the 'Limits of Politics'," *Political Theory* 5 (1977), 294–313.

Hall, R. W. *Plato*. London 1981.

Halperin, David. "Platonic Eros and What Men Call Love," *Ancient Philosophy* 5 (1985), 161–204.

Hamilton, J. R. *Plutarch, Alexander: A Commentary*. Oxford 1969.

Hammerstaedt, Jürgen. "Der Kyniker Oenomaus von Gadara," *Aufstieg und Niedergang der Römischen Welt* 2.36.4. Berlin 1990, 2834–65.

Hands, A. R. *Charities and Social Aid in Greece and Rome*. Ithaca 1968.

Hansot, Elisabeth. *Perfection and Progress: Two Modes of Utopian Thought*. Cambridge, Mass. 1974.

Harrison, A. R. W. *The Law of Athens: The Family and Property*. Oxford 1968.

Hartog, François. *The Mirror of Herodotus*. Janet Lloyd, trans. Berkeley 1988.

Haskin, R. W. "The Call to Sell All." Ph.D. dissertation, Columbia University, 1968.

Hauck, F., and S. Schultz. "*Porne*," in *Theological Dictionary of the New Testament*. Grand Rapids 1969.

Helm, Richard. "Kynismus," *Paulys Realenzyklopädie der klassischen Altertumswissenschaft*. Georg Wissowa et al., eds. Stuttgart 1912.

Hengel, Martin. *Property and Riches in the Early Church*. John Bowden, trans. Philadelphia 1974.

———. *The Charismatic Leader and his Followers*. James Greig, trans. New York 1981.

Henrichs, Albert. "Pagan Ritual and the Alleged Crimes of the Early Christians: A Reconsideration," in *Kyriakon: Festschrift Johannes Quasten*. P. Granfield, ed. Münster 1970, 1.18–35.

Hense, Otto. *Teletis Reliquiae*. Tübingen 1909.

Hock, R. F. "Simon the Shoemaker as an Ideal Cynic," *Greek, Roman, and Byzantine Studies* 17 (1976), 41–53.

Höistad, Ragnar. *Cynic Hero and Cynic King*. Uppsala 1948.

———. "Cynicism," *The Dictionary of the History of Ideas*. New York 1968.

Hope, Richard. *The Book of Diogenes Laertius*. New York 1930.

Hornsby, H. M. "The Cynicism of Peregrinus Proteus," *Hermathena* 48 (1953), 65–84.

Horsburgh, H. J. N. "The Relevance of the Utopian," *Ethics* 67 (1957), 127–38.

Humphreys, S. C. *Anthropology and the Greeks*. London 1978.

Hurd, J. C., Jr. *The Origins of 1 Corinthians*. New York 1965.

Inwood, Brad. "Commentary on Striker," in *Proceedings of the Boston Area Colloquium in Ancient Philosophy*. J. J. Cleary, ed. Lanham 1987, 2.95–101.

Ioppolo, A. M. *Aristone di Chio e lo Stoicismo Antico*. Naples 1980.

Irwin, T. H. *Plato's Moral Theory*. Oxford 1977.

Jaeger, Werner. *Aristotle: Fundamentals of the History of His Development*. R. Robinson, trans. Oxford 1948.

Jensen, Joseph. "Does *Porneia* Mean Fornication? A Critique of Bruce Malina," *Novum Testamentum* 20 (1978), 161–84.

Jones, A. H. M. *The Greek City from Alexander to Justinian*. Oxford 1940.

Jones, C. P. *The Roman World of Dio Chrysostom*. Cambridge, Mass. 1978.

Jones, J. W. *The Law and Legal Theory of the Greeks*. Oxford 1956.

Kaelber, W. O. "Asceticism," in *The Encyclopedia of Religion*. New York 1987.

Kagan, Donald. *The Great Dialogue: A History of Greek Political Thought*. Westport 1965.

Kautsky, Karl, el al. *Die Vorläufer des neueren Sozialismus*. Stuttgart 1895.

Keuls, Eva. *The Reign of the Phallus: Sexual Politics in Ancient Athens*. New York 1985.

Kindstrand, J. F. *Bion of Borysthenes: A Collection of the Fragments*. Uppsala 1976.
———. "Demetrius the Cynic," *Philologus* 124 (1980), 83–98.
———. *Anacharsis: The Legend and the Apophthegmata*. Uppsala 1981.
———. "Diogenes Laertius and the Chreia Tradition," *Elenchos* 7 (1986), 217–43.
Kirk, G. S., et al. *The Presocratic Philosophers*. Cambridge 1983.
Klosko, George. *The Development of Plato's Political Theory*. New York 1986.
Kraus, Richard. *Socrates and the State*. Princeton 1984.
Krentz, Peter. *The Thirty at Athens*. Ithaca 1982.
Kumar, Krishan. *Utopia and Anti-Utopia in Modern Times*. Oxford 1987.
Lacey, W. K. *The Family in Classical Greece*. Ithaca 1968.
Laffranque, Marie. *Poseidonios d'Apameé*. Paris 1964.
Lake, Kirsopp, et al., eds. *The Beginnings of Christianity*. London 1933.
Lana, Italo "L'utopia di Ippodamo di Miletos," *Rivista di Filosofia* 40 (1949), 125–51.
———. "Le teorie egualitarie di Falea di Calcedone," *Rivista critica di storia della filosofia* 5 (1950), 265–76.
———. *Protagora*. Pubblicazioni della facoltà di lettere a filosofia, Università di Torino, 2.4 Turin 1950.
Lane Fox, Robin. *Pagans and Christians*. New York 1987.
Lerner, R. E. *The Heresy of the Free Spirit in the Later Middle Ages*. Berkeley 1972.
Levinson, R. B. *In Defense of Plato*. Cambridge, Mass. 1953.
Lieberg, Godo. "Die 'theologia tripartita' in Forschung und Bezeugung," *Aufstieg und Niedergang der Römischen Welt* 1.4. Berlin 1973, 63–115.
Ling, Roger, ed. *Cambridge Ancient History*. 7.1 Plates. Cambridge 1984.
Lintott, Andrew. *Violence, Civil Strife, and Revolution in the Classical City, 750–330 B.C.* Baltimore 1981.
Littman, R. L. "Kinship in Athens," *Ancient Society* 10 (1979), 5–31.
Long, A. A. "Carneades and the Stoic telos," *Phronesis* 12 (1967), 59–90.
———. ed. *Problems in Stoicism*. London 1971.
———. "Greek Ethics after McIntyre and the Stoic Community of Reason," *Ancient Philosophy* 3 (1983), 184–99.
———, and D. N. Sedley. *The Hellenistic Philosophers*. Cambridge 1987.
———. "Socrates in Hellenistic Philosophy," *Classical Quarterly* n.s. 38 (1988), 150–71.
Lovejoy, A. O., and George Boas. *Primitivism and Related Ideas in Antiquity*. Baltimore 1935.
Lutz, Cora. *Musonius Rufus, "The Roman Socrates."* New Haven 1947.
McCredie, J. R. "Hippodamos of Miletos," in *Studies Presented to George M. A. Hanfmann*. D. G. Mitten et al., eds. Cambridge, Mass. 1971, 95–100.
McIlwain, C. H. *The Growth of Political Thought in the West*. New York 1932.
MacMullen, Ramsay. *Paganism in the Roman Empire*. New Haven 1981.
———."Roman Attitudes to Greek Love," *Historia* 31 (1982), 484–502.
Macpherson, C. B. *The Political Theory of Possessive Individualism: Hobbes to Locke*. Oxford 1962.
Malherbe, A. J. "Gentle as a Nurse: The Cynic Background to 1 Thess. 2," *Novum Testamentum* 12 (1970), 203–17.
———. "Cynics," in *The Interpreter's Dictionary of the Bible: Supplement*. Nashville, 1976.
———. *The Cynic Epistles*. Missoula 1977.
Malina, Bruce. "Does *Porneia* Mean Fornication?", *Novum Testamentum* 14 (1972), 10–17.

Malkin, Irad. *Religion and Colonization in Ancient Greece.* Leiden 1987.
Mannheim, Karl. *Ideology and Utopia: An Introduction to the Sociology of Knowledge.* Louis Wirth and Edward Shils, trans. New York 1936.
Manning, C. E. "Seneca and the Stoics on the Equality of the Sexes," *Mnemosyne* 4.26 (1973), 170–77.
———. "Stoicism and Slavery in the Roman Empire," *Aufsteig und Niedergang der Römischen Welt* 2.36.3. Berlin 1989, 1518–1543.
Mansfeld, Jaap. "Diogenes Laertius on Stóic Philosophy," *Elenchos* 7 (1986), 295–382.
Manuel, F. E., ed. *Utopias and Utopian Thought.* Boston 1966.
———, and F. P. Manuel *Utopian Thought in the Western World.* Cambridge, Mass. 1979.
Marrou, H. I. *History of Education in Antiquity.* George Lamb, trans. New York 1956.
Meeks, Wayne. *The First Urban Christians.* New Haven 1983.
Mejer, Jorgen. *Diogenes Laertius and his Hellenistic Background.* Wiesbaden 1978.
Mendels, Doron. "Sparta in Teles' *Peri Phyges,*" *Eranos* 77 (1979), 111–15.
Minar, E. L., Jr. "Pythagorean Communism," *Transactions of the American Philological Association* 75 (1944), 34–46.
Moellering, H. A. *Plutarch on Superstition.* Boston 1963.
Momigliano, Arnaldo. *The Development of Greek Biography.* Cambridge, Mass., 1972.
More, Thomas. *Utopia.* Yale Edition of the Complete Works of St. Thomas More. New Haven 1964.
Morrow, G. R. "Aristotle's Comments on Plato's *Laws,*" in *Aristotle and Plato in the Mid-Fourth Century.* Ingemar Düring et al., eds. Göteborg 1960, 145–62.
Mossé, Cl. "Les utopies egalitaires à l'époque hellenistique," *Revue historique* 241 (1969), 297–308.
Müller, R. "Zur Staatsauffassung der frühen Stoa," in *Proceedings of the Seventh Congress of the International Federation of Societies of Classical Studies.* Janos Harmatta, ed. Budapest 1984, 1.303–311.
Mumford, Lewis. *The Story of Utopias.* London 1922.
Murphy, N. R. *The Interpretation of Plato's Republic.* Oxford 1951.
Nettleship, R. L. *Lectures on the Republic of Plato.* London 1901.
Nichols, M. P. *Socrates and the Political Community.* Albany 1987.
Novotný, František. *The Posthumous Life of Plato.* The Hague 1977.
O'Brien, M. J. *The Socratic Paradoxes and the Greek Mind.* Chapel Hill 1967.
Ollier, François. *Le mirage Spartiate.* Paris 1933–1943.
Oltramare, André *Les origines de la diatribe romaine.* Geneva 1926.
O'Neill, E. N. *Teles: The Cynic Teacher.* Missoula 1977.
Pacquet, Léonce. *Les cyniques grecques: Fragments et témoignages.* Ottawa 1975.
Parente, I. M. "La politica della Stoa antica," *Sandalion* 3 (1980), 67–98.
Parke, H. W. "The Development of the Second Spartan Empire," *Journal of Hellenic Studies* 50 (1930), 37–39.
Parrott, Jenny. "Hellenistic Political Thought and Institutions: An Introductory Bibliography," *Polis: Newsletter of the Society for the Study of Greek Political Thought* (Swansea, U.K.), 2.2 (1979), 27–56.
Partridge, P. H. "Politics, Philosophy, Ideology," in *Political Philosophy.* Anthony Quinton, ed. Oxford 1967, 32–52.
Pearson, A. C. *The Fragments of Zeno and Cleanthes.* 1889, reprinted New York 1973.
Pembroke, Simon. "Women in Charge: The Function of Alternatives in Early Greek

Tradition and the Ancient Idea of Matriarchy," *Journal of the Warburg and Courtauld Institutes* 30 (1967), 1–35.
Pepin, Jean. *Mythe et allégorie*. Paris 1958.
Philip, J. A. *Pythagoras and Early Pythagoreanism*. Toronto 1966.
Pohlenz, Max. *Die Stoa: Geschichte einer geistige Bewegung*. Göttingen 1959.
Popper, Karl. *The Open Society and Its Enemies*. London 1962.
Randall, J. H. *Plato: Dramatist of the Life of Reason*. New York 1970.
Rankin, H. D. *Sophists, Socratics, and Cynics*. London 1983.
Rawson, Elizabeth. *The Spartan Tradition in European Thought*. Oxford 1969.
———. *Intellectual Life in the Late Roman Republic*. Baltimore 1985.
Reesor, M. E. *The Political Theory of the Old and Middle Stoa*. New York 1951.
———. "The 'Indifferents' in the Old and Middle Stoa," *Transactions and Proceedings of the American Philological Association* 82 (1951), 102–10.
———. *The Nature of Man in Early Stoic Philosophy*. New York 1989.
Reeves, C. D. C. *Philosopher Kings: The Argument of Plato's Republic*. Princeton 1988.
Rich, A. N. M. "The Cynic Conception of ΑΥΤΑΡΚΕΙΑ," *Mnemosyne* 4.9 (1956), 23–29.
Rist, J. M. *Stoic Philosophy*. London 1969.
———. "Zeno and Stoic Consistency," *Phronesis* 22 (1977), 161–174.
———. "Stocism: Some Refelections on the State of the Art," in *Spindel Conference 1984: Recovering the Stoics*. R. H. Epp, ed. *Southern Journal of Philosophy* 23 Supplement (1985), 1–11.
Rose, H. J. *Handbook of Greek Mythology*. New York 1959.
Rostovtzeff, Michael. *Social and Economic History of the Hellenistic World*. Oxford 1941.
Sabine, G. H. *A History of Political Theory*. Rev. T. L. Thorson. Hinsdale 1973.
Salin, Edgar. *Platon und die griechische Utopie*. Munich 1921.
Sandbach, F. H. *Aristotle and the Stoics*. Cambridge 1985.
Sayre, Ferrand. *Diogenes of Sinope: A Study of Greek Cynicism*. Baltimore 1938.
———. *The Greek Cynics*. Baltimore 1948.
Schlatter, Richard. *Private Property: The History of an Idea*. New Brunswick 1951.
Schmeckel, A. *Die Philosophie der mittleren Stoa*. Berlin 1892.
Schofield, Malcolm. "Ariston of Chios and the Unity of Virtue," *Ancient Philosophy* 4 (1984), 83–95.
Simon, Heinrich, and M. Simon. *Die alte Stoa und ihr Naturbegriff*. Berlin 1956.
Sinclair, T. A. *A History of Greek Political Thought*. London 1967.
Skinner, Quentin. *The Foundations of Modern Political Thought*. Cambridge 1978.
Smith, Morton. *Clement of Alexandria and a Secret Gospel of Mark*. Cambridge, Mass. 1973.
Sprague, R. K. *The Older Sophists*. Columbia, S. C. 1972.
Stone, I. F. *The Trial of Socrates*. Boston 1988.
Strassburger, Hermann. "Posidonios on Problems of the Roman Empire," *Journal of Roman Studies* 55 (1965), 40–53.
Strauss, Barry. *Athens after the Peloponnesian War*. Ithaca 1986.
Strauss, Leo. *The City and Man*. Chicago 1964.
Striker, Gisela. "Origins of the Concept of Natural Law," in *Proceedings of the Boston Area Colloquium in Ancient Philosophy*. J. J. Cleary, ed. Lanham 1987, 2.79–94.
Sullivan, E. D. S., ed. *The Utopian Vision*. San Diego 1983.
Syme, Ronald. *The Roman Revolution*. Oxford 1939.
Tarán, Leonardo. *Academica: Plato, Philip of Opus, and the Pseudo-Platonic Epinomis*. Philadelphia 1975.

Tarn, W. W. *Antigonus Gonatas*. Oxford 1913.
———. arts. *Cambridge Ancient History* 7. Cambridge 1928.
———. *Alexander the Great*. Cambridge 1948.
———. *Hellenistic Civilization*. New York 1952.
Taylor, A. E. *Plato: The Man and His Work*. Oxford 1952.
Theissen, Gerd. *Sociology of Early Palestinian Christianity*. John Bowden, trans. Philadelphia 1978.
Tigerstedt, E. N. *The Legend of Sparta in Classical Antiquity*. Stockholm 1965–1974.
Toynbee, Arnold. *A Study of History* 6. Oxford 1939.
Tyrell, W. B. *Amazons: A Study in Athenian Mythmaking*. Baltimore 1984.
Usher, S. "This to the Fair Critias," *Eranos* 77 (1979), 39–42.
Ussher, R. G. *Aristophanes'* Ecclesiazusae. Oxford 1973.
Van den Broek, R. "The Present State of Gnostic Studies," *Vigiliae Christianae* 37 (1983), 41–71.
Van den Horst, P. W. *The Sentences of Pseudo-Phocylides*. Leiden 1978.
Van Straaten, Modestus. *Panétius, sa vie, ses écrits, et sa doctrine*. Amsterdam 1946.
———. *Panaetii Rhodii Fragmenta*. Leiden 1962.
Vavrinek, Vladimir. "Aristonicus of Pergamum," *Eirene* 13 (1975), 109–29.
Vatai, F. L. *Intellectuals in Politics in the Greek World from Early Times to the Hellenistic Age*. London 1984.
Veilleux, Armand. *The Life of St. Pachomius and His Disciples*. Kalamazoo 1980.
Verner, D. C. *The Household of God: The Social World of the Pastoral Epistles*. Chico 1983.
Verstraete, B. C. "Slavery and the Social Dynamics of Male Homosexual Relations in Ancient Rome," *Journal of Homosexuality* 5 (1980), 227–36.
Veyne, Paul. "La famille et l'amour sous le Haut-Empire romaine," *Annales: Economies, Sociétés, Civilisations* 33 (1978), 35–63.
———. "The Roman Empire," in *A History of Private Life* 1. Paul Veyne, ed. Cambridge, Mass. 1987.
———. *Did the Greeks Believe in Their Myths*? Paula Wissing, trans. Chicago 1988.
Vidal-Naquet, Pierre. *The Black Hunter: Forms of Thought and Forms of Society in the Greek World*. Andrew Szegedy-Maszak, trans. Baltimore 1986.
Vinogradoff, Paul. *Outlines of Historical Jurisprudence* 2. Oxford 1922.
Vlastos, Gregory, ed. *The Philosophy of Socrates*. Garden City 1971.
———, ed. *Plato: A Collection of Critical Essays*. New York 1971.
———. *Platonic Studies*. Princeton 1973.
———. "Socrates' Disavowal of Knowledge," *Philosophical Quarterly* 35 (1985), 1–31.
Vogt, Joseph. *Ancient Slavery and the Ideal of Man*. Thomas Wiedemann, trans. Cambridge 1975.
Von Arnim, Johann. *Stoicorum Veterum Fragmenta*. Leipzig 1905.
Von Fritz, Kurt. *Quellenuntersuchungen zu Leben und Philosophie des Diogenes von Sinope*. Leipzig 1926.
———, and Ernst Kapp. *Aristotle's Constitution of Athens*. New York 1950.
———. "Cynicism," in *Oxford Classical Dictionary*. Oxford 1970.
Von Pöhlmann, Robert. *Geschichte der sozialen Frage und des Sozialismus in der antiken Welt*. Munich 1925.
Wallace-Hadrill, A. "The Golden Age and Sin in Augustan Ideology," *Past and Present* 95 (1982), 19–36.
Weber, Max. "Religious Rejections of the World and Their Directions," *From Max Weber*. H. H. Gerth et al., eds. New York 1958, 323–59.

West, M. L. *Hesiod: Works and Days.* Oxford 1978.

Whitehead, David. "Sparta and the Thirty Tyrants," *Ancient Society* 13 (1982), 105–30.

Wild, John. *Plato's Modern Enemies and the Theory of Natural Law.* Chicago 1953.

Wilks, M. J. "The Problem of Private Ownership in Patristic Thought and an Augustinian Solution of the Fourteenth Century," *Studia Patristica* 6 (1962), 533–42.

Wilson, J. F. *The Politics of Moderation: An Interpretation of Plato's Republic.* Lanham 1984.

Winspear, A. D. *The Genesis of Plato's Thought.* New York 1956.

Wood, E. M., and Neal Wood. *Class Ideology and Ancient Political Theory: Socrates, Plato, and Aristotle in Social Context.* Oxford 1978.

Wood, Neal. *Cicero's Social and Political Thought.* Berkeley 1988.

Zeller, Eduard. *Socrates and the Socratic Schools.* O. J. Reichel, trans. New York 1885.

———. *The Stoics, Epicureans, and Skeptics.* O. J. Reichel, trans. New York 1879.

Index

Aelius Aristides, 257n.55
Aeschines of Sphettos, 103n.9
Aeschines the orator, 103n.10
Agoge (upbringing), the Spartan system of training boys, 26–35, 74, 79, 82, 85, 142, 201–4. See also *Paideia*
Albinus, 106n.31
Alcidamas, 136
Alexis, 50n.42
Ambrose, 284–85
Amphis, 50n.42
Anaideia (shamelessness), 122, 139, 158n.53, 161, 186
Anarchism, 3–6, 111–13, 128, 143, 181–82
Ancestral constitution of Athens, 32–35, 47n.28
Anthony of the Desert, 281–82
Antigonus of Carystus, 191–92, 212n.3
Antipater of Tarsus, 147, 170, 225, 238, 251n.3, 254n.31
Antisthenes, 58–62, 138, 152n.9, 164; and Cynicism, 112, 114, 117, 121, 129–31, 135, 147, 156nn.35–36, 160, 256n.50
Apatheia (freedom from passion), 120, 127, 145, 147
Apollodorus of Seleucia, 117, 128, 131, 148, 159n.65, 160, 164, 174, 191, 207–8, 212
Apollonius of Tyana, 256n.46
Apollonius of Tyre, 160, 196
Arcesilaus, 138
Archedemus, 232
Architecture and city planning, 11n.12, 21–25, 50n.38, 71, 74, 179–80, 241. *See also* Gymnasia; Theaters
Arete (virtue, excellence), 41, 55, 95, 145, 193, 224–25; two roads to virtue, 128, 162–64
Arete, daughter of Aristippus, 135
Aristippus and the Cyrenaics, 60–62, 114, 127, 135, 138, 140, 149
Aristo, 165, 212n.3, 251n.3
Aristocracy, 33, 48n.34, 49nn.36–37, 196, 227
Aristophanes, 21, 37–40, 58, 104n.10
Aristotle: *Constitution of Athens*, 94; *Metaphysics*, 55, 130; *Nichomachean Ethics*, 55, 93, 104n.11; *Politics*, on utopianism, 6–8, 13, 21–31, 35–36, 94–99; *Protrepticus*, 50n.38; *Rhetoric*, 123. *See also* Citizenship; Mixed constitution
Aristoxenus, 15, 18, 20–21
Arius Didymus. *See* Stobaeus
Askesis (training) and asceticism: Cynic, 113–16, 120–32; Stoic, 163–65; Christian, 165, 279–84
Athanasius, 281–82
Athenaeus, 108n.43, 171–72, 174, 182–83, 211–12, 221n.69. *See also* Cronus, time of
Athenodorus, 167, 206–7, 240
Augustine, 139, 230, 283–87
Autarkeia (self-sufficiency), 60, 120–30, 139, 143–46, 163, 224–25

Barbarian customs, 18–21, 39–40, 87, 143–45, 174, 184–86, 204–5, 221n.73, 222n.79, 228. *See also* India and Indian religions
Basil, 284–85
Basilides and the Basilidians, 272, 288nn.7, 13
Bion, 114, 118–20, 123, 125, 132–34, 140–41, 153n.9, 157nn.43–44, 159n.61
Bios (way of life), 16–17, 122, 127–30, 190
Blossius, 205, 238
Books and libraries, ancient, 89, 127, 149, 241
Bryson, 155n.21

Cannibalism, 147, 151n.2, 158n.53, 168–69, 185–86, 208, 212n.1, 274–75
Carneades, 225
Carpocrates and the Carpocratians, 264–76, 280
Cassian, 284
Cassius the Skeptic, 167–68, 175–78, 206–7
Cato the Younger, 240–41, 247, 252n.19, 255n.42
Celsus, 265, 268, 274–75
Cercidas, 125, 142–43, 153n.9
Chreiai (anecdotes), 119, 133–34

Chrysippus: *Republic*, 167–71, 173, 175, 178–85, 207–8, 210; *On Ways of Living*, 167, 190, 195–96, 207, 218n.46, 219n.59; other works, 167–71, 177, 185–86, 193, 204, 208, 218n.54, 224; social and political theories, 177–78, 189–90, 195–99, 205, 215n.26
Cicero, 166, 189, 194, 197–200, 203, 220n.67, 238–43, 255n.42; *On Duties*, 224–31, 285; *On the Republic*, 4,7,198–99, 236–37, 242
Citizenship, Greek concept of, 8, 26–27, 34–35, 91
Cleanthes, 131, 147–48, 159n.62, 162, 169, 173, 190, 201, 224
Clearchus, 205
Clement of Alexandria, 46n.16, 172, 210, 216n.35, 232, 241, 265–71, 275, 278–80
Clitomachus, 209
Colonization, 6, 11n.12, 21–24, 30–31, 36; and Plato, 73–75, 82, 92; and Aristotle, 97; and the Stoics, 200
Communism, ancient. See *Koinonia*
Communism and socialism, modern, 3–5, 64–65, 110n.52
Constitutions. *See* Ancestral constitution of Athens; Aristocrăcy; Democracy; Mixed constitution; Monarchy; Oligarchy; *Politeia*; Tyranny
Crantor, 138
Crates, 112, 114, 119, 132–42, 149–50; and Zeno, 111, 140, 142, 160–61, 164, 166–67, 175, 196
Cratinus, 180
Critias, 26–35, 51n.47, 58, 74
Cronus, time of, 3, 7, 11n.12, 13–14; and Plato, 72–73, 75–77, 81, and Cynics, 131–34, 143–45, 245, 249; and Stoics, 204–5, 228–33, 236, 241; and Christians, 282–83, 285
Cyprian, 280–81

Dardanus, 240
Deisidaimonia (superstition), 144–45, 184–85, 216n.35, 274–75
Demetrius of Phalerum, 99, 102, 133, 140, 154n.14, 198–99
Demetrius the early Cynic, 159n.61
Demetrius the later Cynic, 246–47
Demochares, 108n.43, 197
Democracy, 23, 43; and Hippodamus, 25; and Sparta, 33–35, 202; and Aristophanes, 38–40; and Socratics, 58–62; and Plato, 63, 74, 91–93; and Aristotle, 94, 96, 98–99; and Cynics, 141–43; and Stoics, 197, 226, 236, 242
Demonax, 246–47, 257n.52
Despoteia (mastery), 26–27, 35, 177–78
Diatribe (discourse), 118–19
Dicaearchus, 15, 198–99, 201, 205, 221n.69, 230
Didache, 259–60, 288n.5
Dikaiosyne (justice), 55, 65–67, 80, 141–42, 173
Dio Chrysostom, 114, 116–17, 151n.2, 157nn.42, 45, 180, 241–48, 253n.20
Diodorus of Aspendus, 129
Diodorus Siculus, 44n.5, 172, 255n.34
Diodorus the Logician and the Dialecticians,127, 161
Diogenes Laertius, 115–18, 160–61, 166–68, 206–8
Diogenes of Babylon, 198, 209, 225, 251n.3, 254n.31
Diogenes of Sinope: *Republic*, 111–13, 115, 117–18, 131, 146–51, 173–75, 179, 182–86; *Tragedies*, 119, 131, 144, 147, 184–85, 217n.41
Dionysius of Halicarnassus, 239, 275
Dionysius the Renegade, 219n.54
Dissoi Logoi, 20

Echecles, 159n.61
Education. See *Agoge; Paideia*
Elenchos (refutation), 53, 59–60
Eleutheria (freedom), 35, 136, 142–43, 177, 211–12, 247, 270–73
Elysian fields. *See* Cronus, time of
Ephorus, 205
Epictetus, 117, 157n.41, 189–91, 232–35, 241, 243, 245–49, 256n.50
Epicurus and the Epicureans, 44n.3, 122, 147, 161, 169–70, 174, 217n.41
Epiphanius the Gnostic, 265–74
Epistle of Barnabas, 288n.5
Epistle to Diognetus, 278, 290n.23
Epistles of the Cynics, 116–17, 133, 155nn.22, 28, 156nn.37–38, 157nn.43, 45, 158n.52, 159n.66, 216n.40, 246–48
Eratosthenes, 137, 156n.37, 209
Eros (love), Cynic, 137–39; Stoic, 181–85, 191–93, 211–12, 233–34, 243–44. See also *Paiderastia*
Eubulus, 153n.10, 215n.24, 216n.36
Eudaimonia (happiness, blessedness), Socratic, 55; Platonic, 84; Aristotelian, 95; Cynic, 113–14, 120–21, 125, 127, 143; Stoic, 163, 224–25
Euhemerus, 144, 172
Euripides, 21, 132, 155n.30
Eusebius, 249, 283–84

Favonius, 247
Favorinus, 45n.13, 158n.55
Freedom. See *Eleutheria*
Fronto, 274

Gellius, 255n.40
Gerousia (Council of Elders at Sparta), 27, 29, 32–33, 82, 201
Golden age. *See* Cronus, time of
Gymnasia, 151n.3, 159n.59, 167, 175, 179–80, 239

Hecaton, 160–61, 251n.7, 254n.30, 256n.50
Helots and serfs, 25, 27–32, 49n.35, 97, 136, 142, 202. *See also* Slavery
Heracles, 130, 144–45, 211, 225
Heraclides, 198
Herillus, 219n.54
Hermas, 277
Hermippus, 104n.10
Herodes, Pseudo-, 47n.23
Herodotus, 18–21, 23, 39–40, 144, 185–86, 221nn.74–75
Hesiod. *See* Cronus, time of
Hipparchia, 122, 135–40, 161, 234, 248
Hippobotus, 127, 149, 212n.2
Hippodamus, 6, 21–26, 29–31, 36, 71, 73, 91
Hippolytus of Rome, 273, 275
Homer, 7, 13, 22, 58, 87, 132, 176, 204
Homonoia (concord, harmony), 21, 42, 84–87, 182–84, 220n.61
Homosexuality. See *Paiderastia*
Household. See *Oikos*

Iamblichus, 14–15, 50n.38
Iambulus, 172, 181, 186, 249
Incest, 88, 96–97, 144, 146, 167–68, 171, 181–85, 208, 217n.41, 274–75
India and Indian religions, 19, 114–16, 124, 128–29, 132, 142, 146, 150, 181, 270. *See also* Barbarian customs
Irenaeus, 264–73, 277, 280
Isidore of Pergamum, 167, 206
Isocrates, 33–34, 42, 49n.36

Jerome, 290n.27
Jesus, 258–61, 264–67
John Chrysostom, 209–10, 284–85
Josephus, 274
Julian, 117, 127–28, 158n. 55, 249
Justice. See *Dikaiosyne*
Justin Martyr, 274, 277, 290n.23
Juvenal, 256n.43

Kathekon (proper function, duty), 163, 168–69, 186, 193–95, 219n.59, 224–29, 238
Koinonia (community, association), 8, 18, 37–43, 44n.5, 73, 87–91, 132, 187–88; between Cynic and Stoic, 117–18, 136–37, 148, 151, 160–65, 199

Laconism (imitation of Sparta), 11n.12, 25–36, 40, 43, 199, 237; Socratic, 58, 61; Platonic, 74–75, 78–93, 166, 179; Aristotelian, 97–98; Cynic, 123, 141–42, 150; Stoic 200–204, 209, 215n.23. *See also* Mixed constitution; *Syssitia*
Lactantius, 282–83
Lucian, 11n.12, 117, 119, 134, 139, 141, 153n.9, 156n.33, 157n.44, 179, 244–49, 255n.40, 273
Lucian, Pseudo-, *Cynic*, 156n.31, 217n.42, 245

Marcellina, 265, 275
Marcion, 269
Marcus Aurelius, 242
Meleager, 115
Menander, 122, 135, 156n.37, 158n.57, 191
Menedemus of Eretria and the Eretrian school, 138, 141, 158n.55, 213n.6
Menedemus the Cynic, 155n.21, 159n.61
Menippus, 111, 119, 125, 134, 153n.10, 159n.61
Metagenes, 44n.1
Metrocles, 120–21, 154n.14, 156n.32
Minucius, 274
Mixed constitution, 26, 32–36, 237; Aristotelian, 94, 98–99; Stoic, 196, 201, 203
Mnesarchus, 240
Monarchy, 23, 33–34, 58; and Cynics, 140–42; and Stoics, 196–97, 200–203
Monimus, 119, 158n.57
More, Thomas, 4, 11n.12, 69, 216n.37
Musonius Rufus, 213n.10, 234, 241, 243, 252n.19

Natural law. See *Physis*
Nomos (law, custom). See *Physis*
Numenius, 215n.20

Oenomaus, 249–50
Oikist. *See* Colonization
Oikos (household), 8, 18, 28, 37, 41–43, 104n.10; and Plato, 88–89; and Aristotle, 96–97; and Cynics, 130, 134–36; and Stoics, 167, 177, 192, 233–35; and Christians, 258, 262–63, 276–78
Oligarchy, 23, 25–29, 43; and Plato, 59, 74, 82, 87, 91; and Aristotle, 94–99; and Stoics, 197, 236–40

Onesicritus, 124–25, 129, 140–42, 150, 181, 222n.79
Origen, 182, 274, 279–81

Pachomius, 282
Paideia (education), 30, 85, 97, 175–77, 183–84, 186. See also *Agoge*
Paiderastia (love of boys), 88, 96, 135, 137–38, 146–47, 191–93, 211–12, 217n.41, 233–34, 239–40, 249
Panaetius, 198, 223–43
Parrhesia (outspokenness), 139–42, 145, 247–48
Pasiphon, 158n.55
Paul, 216n.35, 248, 259, 270–72, 282
Pausanias, 289n.21
Peregrinus Proteus, 273
Perioikoi (Lacedaemonians of the non-citizen class), 34, 201
Perseus, 191–92, 196, 198, 200–201, 212n.4, 219n.57, 221n.69
Phaleas, 29–31, 36, 38, 73–74, 79, 110n.48
Pherecrates, 43n.1
Philemon, 122
Philia (friendship), 16–17, 42, 84, 100, 131–33, 167, 177–78, 183–84, 187–88, 192–93, 219n.61
Philiscus, 158n.55
Philodemus, 117, 139, 146–49, 156n.33, 157n.43, 169–70, 174, 179, 182–87, 208, 214n.16, 240
Phocylides, Pseudo-, 288n.5
Phylarchus, 201–3
Physis (nature), 56, 131, 136–37, 143–45, 162–63, 233–35
Plato: *Alcibiades I*, 59; *Apology of Socrates*, 55, 58–61; *Critias*, 86; *Crito*, 58; *Epistle 7*, 44n.8, 92; *Gorgias*, 57; *Laws*, 7, 64–65, 68, 73–77, 81, 85–94, 179–80; *Phaedrus*, 108n.39, 183, 211; *Republic*, and its relationship to *Republic* of Zeno, 3–6, 166, 171, 173, 175, 178, 183–84, 186–87, 193–94, 199; *Statesman*, 75–76, 107n.38, 144; *Symposium*, 183, 211; *Timaeus*, 86. *See also* Utopianism
Pliny the Younger, 274
Plutarch, 11n.12, 108n.43, 113n–14, 154n.16, 195, 201–3, 216n.37, 218n.54, 220n.67, 238; source for Stoic utopianism, 170–71, 174–75, 208–11
Polemo, 213n.9
Polis, definition of, 8
Politeia (constitution, regime): general definition, 8; Aristotelian definition, 94
Polybius, 33, 220n.65, 223, 236–37
Polycrates, 103nn.7, 10
Porneia (Judeo-Christian term for sexual sin), 271–72
Porphyry, 205
Posidonius, 224–25, 228–33, 240, 243, 251n.7, 254n.25
Prodicus the Gnostic, 270
Prodicus the Sophist, 144, 155n.29
Protagoras, 19–21, 23, 77–79, 86, 144–45
Pythagoras and the Pythagoreans, 11n.12, 14–18, 20, 129–30, 245, 270, 273

Quintilian, 215n.26

Rhaidion (ease), 121, 126–27, 132, 245
Roman law, 41, 188–89, 220n.64

Satyrus, 147
Seneca, 189–90, 217n.40, 219nn.55–56, 58, 226–28, 235, 241, 245–47, 252n.19, 253nn.20–21, 226
Sextus Empiricus, 45n.14, 157n.43, 168, 174, 205, 208
Slavery, 25–27, 30–31, 34, 37–38, 51n.47; and Plato, 84, 87, 90–91; and Aristotle, 97, 105n.23; and Cynics, 135–36, 142, 150; and Stoics, 177–78, 188, 255n.32; and Christians, 276
Socrates and Socratic circle, 53–62; Socratic problem, 53–54; Socrates and Plato, 63, 69, 75, 83; and Cynics, 112, 114, 121, 129–31; and Stoics, 117, 160, 164
Solon, 22, 99, 154n.17, 211, 220n.67. *See also* Ancestral constitution of Athens
Sotion, 117, 147, 149
Sparta. *See* Laconism
Sphaerus, 193, 201–4, 219n.57, 224
Spoudaiogeloios (seriocomic), 118–19, 131–34, 144, 150
Stasis (faction, factional strife), 43, 100–101, 124, 154n.17
Stilpo, 138, 158n.57, 160–61
Stobaeus, 119, 122, 166, 196
Suda, 135, 159n.62, 212n.2
Syssitia (common meals), 16–17, 28, 31–35, 37, 40, 73–74, 97, 201–2

Teles, 119–27, 131
Telos (end of action), 163, 169, 188, 224–25
Tertullian, 277–78
Theaters, 189–91, 216n.33, 241, 286
Theodorus the Atheist, 138, 159n.65
Theombrotus, 159n.61
Theophilus, 217n.41, 277
Theophrastus, 17, 44n.3, 121, 123, 145, 198

Theopompus, 221n.75
Thibron, 26, 35
Thrasymachus, 30
Thucydides, 32
Timaeus, 15–18
Timarchus, 159n.61
Timon, 162
Topos (rhetorical topic or commonplace), on men of words vs. men of deeds, 108n.43, 151n.4, 198, 200, 208–11
Tyranny, 33–34, 74, 133, 142, 154n.17, 212

Utopianism, types of, 3–8, 40, 61–62, 74–75, 166, 186, 199–200

Varro, 230
Virtue. See *Arete*

Warfare, and Laconism, 25–26, 35; and Plato, 78–86; and Cynics, 142, 149–50; and Stoics, 175, 179–80, 199
Women and feminism, 8, 37–40, 42–43, 58; and Plato, 64, 73–74, 88–89, 93; and Cynics, 135–37, 246; and Stoics, 183–84, 191–93, 226–27, 234–35, 243; and Christians, 276

Xenocrates, 121
Xenophon, 8, 28–29, 32, 57–62

Zeno: *Art of Love*, 167, 173, 207; *Diatribes*, 167, 173, 192, 207; *Memoirs of Crates*, 140, 142, 154n.14, 161, 196; *Republic*, sources and commentary, 166–74, 206–12; works on education, 176–77, 184. *See also* Plato, *Republic*; Utopianism